...itical Violence

Political violence in the form of wars, insurgencies, terrorism, and
violent rebellion constitutes a major human challenge today as it has
so often in the past. It is a challenge not only to life and limb, but also
to morality itself. In this book, C. A. J. Coady brings a philosophical
and ethical perspective to the subject. He places the problems of war
and political violence in the frame of reflective ethics. In clear and
accessible language, Coady reexamines a range of urgent problems
pertinent to political violence against the background of a contemporary approach to just war thinking. The problems examined include
the right to make war, the right way to conduct war, terrorism, revolution, humanitarianism, mercenary warriors, conscientious objection,
combatant and noncombatant status, the ideal of peace and the right
way to end war, pacifism, weapons of mass destruction, and supreme
emergency exemptions from just war prohibition. Coady attempts
to vindicate the relevance of the just war tradition to contemporary
problems without applying the tradition in a merely mechanical or
uncritical fashion.

C. A. J. Coady is an Australian philosopher with an international reputation for his research in both epistemology and political and applied
philosophy. In addition to his academic work, he is a regular contributor to public debate on topics having to do with ethical and philosophical dimensions of current affairs. A professor of philosophy at
the University of Melbourne, he has served as the founding director
of the Centre for Philosophy and Public Issues and the deputy director of the Centre for Applied Philosophy and Public Ethics and head
of its University of Melbourne division. In 2005, he gave the Uehiro
Lectures on practical ethics at Oxford University.

Morality and Political Violence

C. A. J. COADY
University of Melbourne

CAMBRIDGE
UNIVERSITY PRESS

CAMBRIDGE UNIVERSITY PRESS
Cambridge, New York, Melbourne, Madrid, Cape Town, Singapore, São Paulo, Delhi

Cambridge University Press
32 Avenue of the Americas, New York, NY 10013-2473, USA

www.cambridge.org
Information on this title: www.cambridge.org/9780521560009

First published 2008

Printed in the United States of America

A catalog record for this publication is available from the British Library.

Library of Congress Cataloging in Publication Data
Coady, C. A. J.
Morality and political violence / C. A. J. Coady.
p. cm.
Includes bibliographical references and index.
ISBN 978-0-521-56000-9 (hardback) – ISBN 978-0-521-70548-6 (pbk.)
1. Violence – Moral and ethical aspects. I. Title.
BJ1459.5.C63 2007
172′.1 – dc22 2007002277

ISBN 978-0-521-56000-9 hardback
ISBN 978-0-521-70548-6 paperback

For my parents, Phyllis and Jack, in gratitude

The air is loud with death,
The dark air spurts with fire,
The explosions ceaseless are.
    Isaac Rosenberg,
    "Dead Man's Dump"

Contents

Preface

My interest in war and related forms of political violence dates back to my early childhood, when, before conscription was instituted, my father volunteered for service in World War II. I recall being shocked when I realised that war involved people who didn't know each other and had no direct grievance against each other trying desperately to kill each other because they were on opposite "sides." My shock was of course all the greater and more personal for the realisation that my father might kill or be killed. He was not killed or physically wounded, as it happens, though he took part in one of the bloodiest battles of the Australian involvement in the Pacific war against the Japanese on the island of Tarakan off the Borneo coast. I don't know what part he played in the killing of enemy soldiers, since, like many combat soldiers, he was most reluctant to speak to his family of his war service.

Since then, my conviction that there is something affronting, even absurd, and certainly morally problematic about the resort to war has been strengthened by reading and reflection about war's reality. I have never myself experienced what Keegan once called "the face of battle," and hope never to do so. My nearest brush with military realities was when I had a commission from the British (and, sadly, still Australian) queen as a cadet lieutenant in my school cadet corps and learned the arcane skills of firing the Bren gun, the .303 rifle, and the anti-tank six-pounder. All these weapons were, even then, antiquated, and are now almost antique, so I hardly qualify as "a trained killer," but I got a whiff of the atmosphere of military training, and it did nothing to promote the romance of war for me.

I will not here elaborate my position on political violence, since what follows is an attempt to do that, but I will foreshadow my attitude. I am sympathetic to some strands in the just war tradition, but also to some central elements in the pacifist tradition. Indeed, I think that there is more convergence between the two traditions than is usually acknowledged. The third tradition often invoked in the discussion of war and political violence more

generally is the one known as realism, and again I think that there is more
affinity between central elements in realism (understood as the creation of
political theorists like Morgenthau) and the just war tradition than is usually
allowed. But to say this much is only to gesture at a position; my defence of
it is to be found in what follows.

I owe thanks to many people and many institutions. In the course of
researching and writing this book over far too many years, I have published
articles on the themes of a number of its chapters in learned journals, and I
must thank various journal publishers for allowing me to make use of rewrit-
ten versions of those articles or extracts from them. The journals are *Ethics,
Inquiry, Philosophy, The American Catholic Philosophical Quarterly, The Journal of
Applied Philosophy,* and *The Journal of Ethics.* I thank Jeff Ross for permission
to use some material in Chapter 13 that I wrote for our joint publication in
The American Catholic Philosophical Quarterly (2000), "St. Augustine and the
Ideal of Peace." I have also drawn upon work of mine that has appeared
in edited books, most notably in *The Encyclopedia of Ethics,* second edition,
ed. Laurence and Charlotte Becker (Routledge, 2001); *Terrorism and Justice:
Moral Argument in a Threatened World,* ed. C. A. J. Coady and Michael O'Keefe
(Melbourne University Press, 2002); *A Companion to Applied Ethics,* ed. R. G.
Frey and K. Wellman (Blackwell, 2003); *Ethics and Foreign Intervention,* ed.
Deen K. Chatterjee and Don Scheid (Cambridge University Press, 2003);
Terrorism: The Philosophical Issues, ed. Igor Primoratz (Palgrave, 2004); *Ethics
and Weapons of Mass Destruction,* ed. Sohail Hashmi and Steven Lee (Cam-
bridge University Press, 2004); *Ethics of Terrorism and Counter-Terrorism,* ed.
Georg Meggle (Ontos Verlag, 2005); and *Righteous Violence: The Ethics and
Politics of Military Intervention,* ed. Tony Coady and Michael O'Keefe (Melbourne University Press, 2005). My thanks to the publishers for permission
to draw upon these writings.

I have been supported in my research by the University of Melbourne
and its Philosophy Department and by the Centre for Philosophy and Public
Issues (CPPI) and later the Centre for Applied Philosophy and Public Ethics
(CAPPE) at the University of Melbourne. I also gratefully acknowledge several grants and a Senior Fellowship from the Australian Research Council,
and Fellowships at the University Center for Human Values at Princeton University (1993–94), Corpus Christi College Oxford (2005), and the United
States Institute of Peace in Washington, D.C. (1999–2000). I learned from
my participation in a variety of workshops and seminars on issues to do
with the themes of this book at the University of Melbourne, the Center for
International Security and Cooperation (CISAC) at Stanford University, the
Institute for Philosophy and Public Policy at the University of Maryland, the
Philosophy Department at the University of Arizona in Tucson, the Jean Beer
Blumenfeld Centre for Ethics at Georgia State University, Princeton Univer-
sity (both the Center for Human Values and the Philosophy Department),
Oxford University, and Leipzig, Bonn, Berlin, and Bielefeld Universities.

I have received particularly helpful comments and criticism on topics discussed in the book from too many people to mention here, but special thanks are due to Andrew Alexandra, Robert Fullinwider, Mark Johnston, Arthur Kuflik, John Langan, David Lewis, Judith Lichtenberg, David Luban, Jeff McMahan, Igor Primoratz, David Rodin, Debra Satz, Henry Shue, and Janna Thompson. My thanks also to David Coady for discussion of some issues involved in causation that are relevant to the discussion of C. D. Broad's position in Chapter 11 and of some problems concerning intention and terrorism in Chapter 8. I have also learned from many who have published on these topics, especially Anthony Coates, Robert Fullinwider, Robert Holmes, Jeff McMahan, Richard Norman, David Rodin, Henry Shue, and Jenny Teichman, to name only a few. (Others are cited in the text.) It is unlikely that anyone who writes on the central topics dealt with in this book can fail to be indebted to Michael Walzer's restatement and recasting of traditional just war thinking in his book *Just and Unjust Wars*, and I am happy to acknowledge the stimulation I received from his work. Much of this has been stimulation to disagreement, for philosophers are disagreeing, if not disagreeable, people.

I would also like to thank a number of people who helped me with research assistance over the years, especially Will Barrett, Mianna Lotz, Andrew Schaap, Jeff Ross, Toni Morton, Anna Goppel, Jessica Wolfendale, and, most helpfully, Ned Dobos, who was in at the death, so to speak, and who worked very hard to help organise the final presentation of the manuscript. He also provided invaluable help in compiling the index. My wife, Margaret, deserves more than the usual ritual of thanks to a life partner, for she has supported me through the thick and thin of my work on these themes, even though I suspect that she has never fully accepted my obsessional interest in this rather depressing topic. It is certainly very depressing at the time of this writing, though a recent report marshaling statistics to show that the number and intensity of wars has declined dramatically since 1992 offers some encouragement that the stubborn capacity of human beings to fail to learn from history may be suffering some slight erosion.

Finally, the topics addressed in this book are discussed from a philosophical point of view, but since everyone has, or should have, an interest in the bearing of morality upon political violence, I have attempted to write in a way that avoids philosophical technicalities where possible. My hope is that much of the argument will be accessible to those in disciplines beyond philosophy and to interested nonspecialists. I admire philosophy that is clear and embodies standards of rigorous argument – standards that I aim to emulate here – but on topics having to do with political violence, I have little sympathy with thought that is enclosed in houses of intellect locked and shuttered against the world.

October 20, 2006

Morality and Political Violence

1

Staring at Armageddon

...my thoughts were powerless against an unhappiness so huge. I couldn't alter European history, or order the artillery to stop firing. I could stare at the War as I stared at the sultry sky, longing for life and freedom and vaguely altruistic about my fellow-victims. But a second-lieutenant could attempt nothing – except to satisfy his superior officers; and altogether, I concluded, Armageddon was too immense for my solitary understanding.

Siegfried Sassoon[1]

Sassoon's ironic articulation of the enormity of war and its capacity to reach beyond understanding or individual control captures something that has been echoed in the thoughts and writings of many participants, observers, and theorists of warfare. Indeed, the impotence and blankness that Sassoon describes is one of the perceptions that lies behind a famous dictum propounded by the philosopher Thomas Hobbes in the seventeenth century. Always a foe of euphemism and evasion, Hobbes succinctly posed a central issue with which much of this book will be concerned: "Where there is no common power, there is no law: where no law, no injustice. Force and fraud, are in war the two cardinal virtues."[2] Amongst other things, we shall examine whether this bleak view is true and what would follow if it were. Initially, the existence of laws of war, just war theories, and codes of military ethics would seem to give the lie to Hobbes, and it is interesting that he makes virtually no reference to the extensive body of writing on such matters that existed at the time he wrote, though he must have been familiar with it. Hobbes may have thought most of this to be "mere words," and we must ask whether it is so. We must also ask whether the "force and fraud" outlook, if true, could form the basis of arguments for the total rejection of war ("pacifism") or for the removal of war altogether from the scope of morality (some forms of

[1] Siegfried Sassoon, *Memoirs of an Infantry Officer* (London: Faber and Faber, 1965), pp. 82–83.
[2] Thomas Hobbes, *Leviathan*, ed. C. B. Macpherson (Harmondsworth: Penguin, 1968), p. 188.

"realism"). Both of these options have in fact been urged by people impressed with what they see as the truth in such an outlook as Hobbes's.

Hobbes's comment, while it poses a challenge to any treatment of the ethics of war, is first of all addressed to the question of whether there are moral constraints upon *how* a war should be conducted, upon the ways and means of waging war. This question has been discussed in the just war tradition under the heading of the *jus in bello* (or as I shall hereafter refer to it, the JIB). But the question that is, in some sense, prior to this is the question of whether morality has anything to say about going to war in the first place. (In just war terminology, this is the matter of the *jus ad bellum*, or as I shall abbreviate it, the JAB). Hobbes, in fact, thought that resort to war was often morally legitimate, an exercise of natural right by the state, but he insisted that rebellion was always immoral. In keeping with his generally "tough" outlook on the power of the state and his theory of absolute sovereignty, Hobbes might be thought to give carte blanche to the sovereign state's right to go to war, but his discussions of war between states, though not fully developed, suggest otherwise. The sovereign cannot be called to account by the citizens, but has certain obligations as a ruler to preserve the peace and is bound before God to conform to the tenets of Natural Law. Consequently, many resorts to war would be ruled out on prudential and moral grounds (insofar as this distinction can be made in Hobbesian theory – and, in a complex way, I think it can). Moreover, Hobbes, at least sometimes, allows for some, admittedly minimal, restrictions on how warriors should conduct themselves in the course of a war. In *The Elements of Law*, for instance, he rejects the resort to unnecessary violence or cruelty. After mentioning with approval the idea that laws are silent about war (captured in the Latin saying that he cites, *inter arma silent leges*), Hobbes draws back from this terrifying brink by adding: "Yet thus much the law of nature commandeth in war: that men satiate not the cruelty of their present passions, whereby in their own conscience they foresee no benefit to come. For that betrayeth not a necessity but a disposition of the mind to war, which is against the law of nature."[3] He continues by noting that even in those times when "rapine was a trade of life," some restraint in killing and dispossessing victims was nonetheless exercised, both in obedience to the law of nature and as a matter of honour. He concludes "that though there be in war no law, the breach whereof is injury, yet there are those laws, the breach whereof is dishonour. In one word, therefore, the only law of actions in war is honour; and the right of war providence."[4] In this discussion, he echoes some of the views of medieval theologians about proportionality in the use of military violence and also seems to have in mind some of the military codes of honour, but he

---

3 Thomas Hobbes, *The Elements of Law: Natural and Politic*, ed. Ferdinand Tonnies (Cambridge: Cambridge University Press, 1928), Part 1, Chapter 19, section 2, p. 100.

4 Ibid.

also looks forward to the doctrine of "military necessity," which, as we shall see, can be used both to restrict certain forms of immoral activity in war and to license others.

I have begun with Hobbes and war, but the key term in the title of this book is "political violence" rather than "war," and this requires a terminological explanation, since the choice of terms raises substantial issues. My use of the expression "political violence" includes war as the primary instance of such violence, but it is also meant to cover other violent activities that some would not include under the heading of war. Such activities encompass terrorism, armed intervention (for "humanitarian" or other purposes), armed revolution, violent demonstrations or attacks by citizens aimed at less than the overthrow of their government, and the deployment of mercenary companies or individuals. It could also include other activities, which, for reasons of space, I will not discuss in great depth, such as certain forms of torture, assassination, and violent covert operations. There are common usages, especially, I think, in the United States, which would restrict the term "political violence" to the activities of nonstate agents and strongly separate ethical questions concerning such activities from those having to do with war or intervention. This form of discourse would have it that war and armed intervention by states are not uses of political violence.

I want to resist this restriction of the term on semantic, political, and ethical grounds. Since the usage I object to is often linked to a "legitimist" definition of violence, which I discuss in Chapter 2, my reasons need to be supplemented by the discussion to come in that chapter and in Chapter 6. Nonetheless, they can be briefly outlined here. Given the appalling record of states in the unjustified employment of lethal force to devastate populations, economies, and cultures over the centuries, I am unimpressed by any attempt to put a conceptual or moral gulf between the resort to such force (or, as I would prefer to say, violence) for political purposes by state agencies and its political employment by nonstate actors. The tendency to talk of the state as using "force" and of terrorists or revolutionaries as using "violence" embodies an attempt to bring initial opprobrium upon the nonstate actors (via the negative connotations of "violence") and to give an a priori mantle of respectability to the state actors. When the qualification "political" is added only to the activities of the nonstate agents and withheld from the state's operations, even where the means employed are identical or similar in kind, this can suggest that the purposes of state violence are somehow above politics and presumptively acceptable, at least when employed by "our" state. But we should not smuggle into the terms of our discussion some bias in favour of states when they employ morally contestable means. Indeed, given the power of states, their deployment of the sword is more likely to wreak morally objectionable damage, at least in terms of scale, than anything nonstate agents can achieve. These facts can be concealed by the anodyne expression "force," which is one reason why I prefer to use the term "violence"; military cum political jargon is replete with euphemisms for the state's efforts to inflict death, carnage, and damage, and a serious discussion of the ethical problems these efforts pose should be plainspoken. Talk of "force" makes it sound as if we are proposing to move things by using superior physical strength (as we might lift protesters out of the way without seriously harming them), when what is usually on the agenda is killing, maiming, and destroying.[5]

So I shall view the moral problems of international war as a central part of the wider issue of the use of violence for political purposes. It is true that there are aspects peculiar to international war that cause grave moral concern, such as the scale of actual and possible carnage and the capacity for escalation. These help to explain the tendency to concentrate upon it. It is also true that the last quarter of the twentieth century and the beginning of the twenty-first century have seen a dramatic decline in warfare understood as direct state-versus-state conflict, and a proportionate increase in other forms of warfare such as revolutionary and secessionist war; client war, such as the U.S.-Pakistani sponsorship of Mujahideen violence against the Soviet Union in Afghanistan; tribal war, such as the Hutu massacres of Tutsi in Rwanda; violent terrorist attacks like that of September 11 and the "war on terror" it provoked, and so on. These developments have induced the Archbishop of Canterbury, Rowan Williams, to declare that "we have come very near to the end of war," and others have made similar claims.[6] Of course, they don't mean that there is an end to violence on behalf of political or ideological causes. It is rather that they identify war with war between nation-states and an associated paraphernalia of formal declarations, opposing massed armies, clearly identified enemy states, and so on. What Archbishop Williams believes to be outmoded is war "conceived as sovereign states squaring up," and he thinks that this means that just war theory is similarly outmoded.[7] But I do not believe that this was ever an adequate understanding of war, and I doubt that it was essential to the operation of the just war tradition. After all, sovereign states in the way Williams seems to think of them – namely, nation-states – are held by many scholars to be products of the modern world, and the evolution of just war thinking predates them by many centuries. Civil wars, tribal wars, wars against invading "barbarians," and wars of imperial conquest have been common enough throughout the ages, and many of these have not comfortably conformed to

---

[5] Even the United Nations Charter falls victim to this linguistic habit, referring consistently to "force" rather than "violence" and avoiding the use of "war" altogether. The crucial paragraph 4 of Article 2 of the Charter says, for instance: "All members shall refrain in their international relations from the threat or use of force against the territorial integrity or political independence of any State, or in any other matter inconsistent with the Purposes of the United Nations."

[6] Rowan Williams, "Chaos Dogs the End of War" *Common Theology* 1, no. 2 (2002), p. 9.

[7] Ibid.

the conception Williams invokes. Moreover, from the other direction, the war against Iraq begun in 2003 has made it clear that the days of sovereign states "squaring up" have by no means disappeared. Yet Williams is not alone in thinking that the developments of the late twentieth and early twenty-first centuries have made just war theory out of date. My own view is that such scepticism is at least premature. It may indeed be that just war thinking needs adjusting in the light of recent developments, and this is part of what I shall examine in what follows. Nonetheless, it seems to me that other forms of war, or of violent conflict with a political orientation, share many of the problems of moral justification associated with international war, and it is plausible to seek a general framework within which the debate can be conducted. It seems at least promising to begin with the tradition of just war theorising and to see if it can be adapted to the broader discussion. As for a definition of war, we could modify slightly that provided by Clausewitz in his classic treatise *On War*. He says: "War is thus an act of violence to compel our enemy to do our will."[8] There is no reference here to states, but Clausewitz obviously has in mind, what the plural pronoun indicates, namely, groups of some sort. He has earlier declared that war is like a duel "on a larger scale," and he later makes it clear that war must have a political purpose, so we should slightly adapt his definition to read: "War is the resort by an organized group to a relatively large-scale act of violence for political purposes to compel an enemy to do the group's will."

The reference to "relatively" is to allow for small wars that are nonetheless large-scale compared, for instance, to an individual or small group sniper attack on a hated political figure. There will also be grey areas created by the definition, such as bloodless wars where one side is overwhelmed without bloodletting. These are rare enough to ignore and, in any case, probably should count as marginal forms of war just because the coercive occupation is effected by soldiers and their armaments, with palpable violence directly threatened and always available for use against resistance. Then there is the category of "violence short of war" or, as Michael Walzer calls it (or something very like it), "force-short-of-war," a description that embodies the unsatisfactory softening of issues that I have already discussed. The "short-of-war" description seems meant to cover interventions such as rocket strikes and bombing raids intended to punish, rescue, or deter, though Walzer uses it, *inter alia*, for more sustained violence such as the American

---

[8] Carl von Clausewitz, *On War*, ed. and trans. Michael Howard and Peter Paret (Princeton, NJ: Princeton University Press, 1976), Chapter 1, section 2, p. 75. I cite this English edition because it is a very good one, but the quotation in my text departs from Howard and Paret's translation of *gewalt*. The German word can mean "force" or "violence" according to context, and other translations opt for "violence." For reasons given earlier in the text (and in Chapter 2) where I comment on the difference between force and violence, I think "violence" is more appropriate here. For a translation that also prefers "violence," see that edited by Anatol Rapoport (London: Pelican, 1968), p. 1.

"no-fly zone" bombing of Iraq carried out as part of the "containment" system imposed after the Gulf War.[9] The strike authorized by President Clinton against Sudan's supposed chemical weapons factory in 1998 would presumably count as well, and it might be said that we shouldn't call this war because the United States was not at war with Sudan and because the incident was brief and self-contained. These reasons are not particularly impressive. In the conceptual and moral analysis of war, the fact that a war has not been "declared" is not overwhelmingly significant, nor should the target's incapacity to fight back absolve the attacker of the need to justify the attack by the moral standards appropriate to war. The duration of the conflict is relevant in many ways to the moral assessment of it, but short and long episodes of war are still war. Clinton's "strike" killed and maimed people for a political purpose, using the military might and technology at the disposal of the United States. It has been claimed that the factory produced half of Sudan's medicine, including drugs necessary to treat malaria and tuberculosis.[10] If this claim is true, the attack was highly damaging to Sudanese civilians. That the conflict was short-lived is as much the result of the overwhelming power and distant reach of American military capacity and the relative weakness of the enemy than anything else, nor should we ignore the contribution that such strikes have made to the way in which the United States is viewed in much of the Middle East as an aggressive war maker. As for the "no-fly zone" bombing, Walzer portrays that exercise in altogether too mild a fashion. The bombing covered 60 per cent of Iraq, and it was estimated in 2002 that the United States had averaged more than 34,000 military sorties per year since 1991. Confidential UN reports are said to put the number of civilian casualties between 1998 and 2002 at something over 300, though other estimates are higher.[11] In addition, there were many Iraqi military deaths and much property destruction, though I have been unable to find any reliable estimates of these for this nonwar. Moreover, this protracted exercise was not authorised by the UN, though its justification was couched in terms of enforcing UN Security Council resolution 688, which called on Iraq to

9 Michael Walzer, "Regime Change and Just War," *Dissent* 53 (2006), pp. 106–108. This article was taken from the new introduction to the 2006 edition of Walzer's *Just and Unjust Wars: A Moral Argument with Historical Illustrations* (New York: Basic Books).

10 Richard Becker, Sara Flounders, and John Parker, "Sudan: Diversionary Bombing," The Institute for Media Analysis Inc., May 17, 2006, at http://www.covertaction.org/content/view/105/75.

11 Jeremy Scahill, "No-Fly Zones over Iraq: Washington's Undeclared War on 'Saddam's Victims,'" at www.IraqJournal.org, claims the figure of 300 as a "UN statistic" and cites Hans von Sponeck, the coordinator of the UN Humanitarian Program in Iraq from 1998 to 2000, as claiming that in 1999 alone 120 civilians were killed. Von Sponeck is also quoted to similar effect by Susan Taylor Martin in "'No-Fly' Zone Perils Were for Iraqis, Not Allied Pilots" in *The St. Petersburg Times*, October 29, 2004. Scahill is the source for the estimate of 34,000 sorties and the 60 percent area, and he cites as his authority the Washington Institute for Near East Policy.

cease repression of its civilian population. The purported justification of the bombing was to prevent Saddam Hussein using his military capacity against the Kurds in the north or the Shi'a in the south. But critics have argued that the motivation for the bombing was much more complex than this, especially during the later stages of the campaign. This is not the place to enter into that debate or a further analysis of the "containment" policy, but it should be clear that this sustained bombardment lasting well over a decade is a poor candidate for the title of something short of war.

Michael Walzer argues that "force-short-of-war" is easier to justify than war itself.[12] My discussion of the containment bombing of Iraq suggests some caution about this, since that bombing was hardly something softer or morally less troubling than war. What is true is that some wars are going to be easier to justify than others, and it counts as some presumption in favour of a use of violence that it involves far less killing and damage than some other proposed resort to violence might. Where some nation or group of nations possesses massive military superiority over an adversary, it will be tempting to see the resort to political violence at the less spectacular end of the scale as an example not of war but of something more like forceful correcting or policing; but that is unlikely to be how it is seen on the ground by those being "forced." Such episodes can turn into "asymmetrical war," where the enemy, lacking the standard military tools, resorts to less direct and "conventional" forms of violence such as suicide bombing to deal with the attacks. Even where no such outcome eventuates, the episodes can often escalate into or prepare the ground for large-scale warfare. Walzer does allow that considerations parallel to just war principles should govern force-short-of-war, and this surely indicates that it is a phenomenon of the same kind, but he insists that the just war condition of "last resort" and perhaps other conditions are much easier to satisfy in the case of force-short-of-war than in the case of war.[13] I shall defer further discussion of this until Chapter 5, but I will foreshadow my view here by saying that conditions like last resort are equally relevant to war and to force-short-of-war (where that involves actual political violence).

As for "political purposes," I intend this phrase to cover such gross and obvious phenomena as are involved in attempts to change, overthrow entirely, defend and maintain, or simply modify in some important respect one's own or another group's political arrangements, structures, or priorities. So I exclude such phenomena as family violence and child abuse, even though in an extended sense of "politics" some might well argue that these serve certain more subtle political purposes. It is one thing to act to promote a political end; it is quite another to act for personal ends that, perhaps quite unknown to the actor, serve to promote political purposes.

[12] Walzer, "Regime Change and Just War," p. 106.
[13] Ibid.

Whether my account should cover the morality of the state's "normal" use of violence in what is usually viewed as legitimate police work or the output of the legal system is another matter. These are more obviously "political," and I shall have a little to say about them, but it will be incidental, since the subject matter of my inquiry needs some limitations, and these matters also raise broader questions in political philosophy than I can usefully tackle here.

The distinction between war and revolution, from the perspective of just war theory, is interesting. In the 1960s, and sometimes today, many people rejected war between nations but were enthusiastic about, or at least endorsed, certain forms of revolutionary activity. Others tend to champion the occasional resort to international war but reject all forms of revolutionary war. Still others think that a case can be made on somewhat similar grounds for the moral legitimacy of some wars between nations and some revolutions. If we are talking about violent revolution, rather than dramatic peaceful changes such as those brought about by the "velvet" revolutions of Eastern Europe during the dismantling of communism, then we are, in all fundamentals, discussing a form of warfare. Any definition of war that restricts it to violent conflict between states is far too narrow. It would be absurd to rule out *ab initio* a case for including the American Civil War, for example, within the scope of a discussion of the morality of war, and it certainly represents an instance of political violence. We shall later discuss the morality of revolution and of the terrorist tactics often associated with it, as well as some of the special problems facing the use of violent tactics in pursuit of political reform within a state. We shall also discuss problems raised by weapons of mass destruction, nuclear war and deterrence, and some specific issues connected with conscientious objection and mercenary soldiering.

The Moral Scandal of War

Any attempt to justify the waging of war and to give moral sanction to some or all of the so-called rules of war risks underestimating the degree to which war is morally problematic, even scandalous. It is for this reason that students and other relative innocents with respect to the theory of war are liable to be astonished, amused, or even angered by the very vocabulary of "just wars" and "rules of war" with which philosophers, lawyers, politicians, and theologians discuss this difficult subject. I recall one student saying to me when I introduced the topic in lectures: "Just war? You might as well talk of 'just rape'!" Given the close empirical association of war and rape, the challenge cannot be lightly dismissed.

Certainly what must be acknowledged from the outset is the sheer scale of the evil usually attendant upon war and its consequences. As Erasmus put it more than 400 years ago (and subsequent history has hardly made his picture irrelevant):

War, on a sudden, and at one stroke, overwhelms, extinguishes, abolishes, whatever is cheerful, whatever is happy and beautiful, and pours a foul torrent of disasters on the life of mortals – no sooner does the storm of war begin to lower, than what a deluge of miseries and misfortune seizes, inundates, and overwhelms all things within the sphere of its action! The flocks are scattered, the harvest trampled, the husbandman butchered, villas and villages burnt, – cities and states, that have been ages rising to their flourishing state, subverted by the fury of one tempest, the storm of war. So much easier is the task of *doing harm* than of *doing good*; of destroying than of building![14]

These broad destructive effects of war have hardly decreased since Erasmus's day, and we now know much more about the cultural and social psychological damage that continual warfare produces. And in addition to physical, psychological, and cultural harms, we need to take into account the moral degeneration, even madness, that often seems to afflict ordinary soldiers in warfare. A scene from Guy Chapman's excellent memoir of World War I, *A Passionate Prodigality*, illustrates the point. Chapman asked a fellow officer at the front, who seemed upset, what was wrong:

"Oh, I don't know. Nothing – at least. Look here, we took a lot of prisoners in those trenches yesterday morning. Just as we got into their line, an officer came out of a dugout. He'd got one hand above his head, and a pair of field glasses in the other. He held the glasses out to S—, you know, the ex-sailor with the Messina earthquake medal – and said, "Here you are Sergeant, I surrender". S— said, "Thank you, sir", and took the glasses with his left hand. At the same moment, he tucked the butt of his rifle under his arm, and shot the officer straight through the head. What the hell ought I do?"

"I don't see that you can do anything", I answered slowly. "What can you do? Besides, I don't see that S— is really to blame. He must have been half mad with excitement when he got into the trench. I don't suppose he even thought what he was doing. If you start a man killing, you can't turn him off again like an engine. After all, he is a good man. He was probably half off his head."[15]

These sorts of effects show the inadequacy of Michael Walzer's dramatic dictum "War kills: that is all it does." Walzer intends to show the horror of war with this aphoristic comment, but in fact it does not go nearly far enough. War kills, sure enough; but it also maims, distorts, and injures in many complex, enduring ways. It transforms people, both warriors and those caught up in the violence, and radically alters the normal conditions of their existence.

---

[14] Desiderius Erasmus, "A Tract of the Society for the Promotion of Permanent and Universal Peace," in *Extracts from the Writings of Erasmus on the Subject of War* (London: Thomas Ward & Co., 1838), p. 7.

[15] Guy Chapman, *A Passionate Prodigality* (London: MacGibbon & Kee, 1965), pp. 99–100.

As Glenn Gray observes in his moving account of the experience of combat, *The Warriors*, it turns cruelty into a commonplace and creates "a stupefaction of consciousness [that] is doubtless a function of the total environment of war."[16] Yet in spite of this, there is at present a remarkable concern with just war theorizing, and this represents a marked intellectual change, because early last century there was little sympathy for the tradition outside Roman Catholic circles. It would be interesting to explore the causes of this shift in fashion, but here I shall only offer some suggestions about beliefs and occurrences that have probably been significant in creating a more congenial reception for the two basic ideas in the just war tradition: that the waging of war may be morally justified and that there are moral limits to how it may be waged. Among these influences are: the belief that World War II was special, not only because the Allied cause seemed justified at the time, but also because the passing years have added weight to that judgement in spite of the colossal casualties, suffered by both civilian and military in that conflict; the feeling that a morally respectable case can be made for *some* revolutionary wars of "national liberation" against very oppressive regimes; the conviction, nonetheless, that some of the methods used in World War II by the Allies and in otherwise legitimate revolutionary wars have been morally suspect; the experience of many Americans of finding a specific war that their country was waging in Vietnam morally indefensible by standards that seemed, in theory at least, possible to meet; the persistence of conventional wars under the grim protection of the nuclear stalemate during the Cold War, and the feeling that at least some of the states involved in those wars were victims whose military response could be seen as a morally legitimate way to defend their rights; and finally, at least for some, the case of Israel, a state whose people have an intimate connection with the victims of Nazi violence but whose politics commit them to persistent, dramatic, and often contentious violence in defence and pursuit of what they and their numerous external sympathisers see as their rights. This provides only (a part of) the broad moral and political background. I have ignored more narrowly economic, ideological, and military factors that would certainly be important for a full sociological analysis, but the sketch is sufficient to make the revival of interest in just war theory more intelligible.

The Charges of Futility and Hypocrisy

The just war tradition and the very idea of philosophers, theologians, lawyers, political theorists and others trying to get a moral purchase on warfare – or, more broadly, on political violence – is sometimes attacked for its futility, and even for its hypocrisy. Maybe the words are not utterly empty, but they

---

[16] J. Glenn Gray, *The Warriors: Reflections on Men in Battle* (New York: Harper and Row, 1970), p. 105.

are doomed to be, and have been, without beneficial effect. What effect they have had, critics of this stamp often add, is generally harmful: either they give (and perhaps are meant to give) an aura of legitimacy to an unrestrained resort to war, or, as critics of a different character claim, they add to the strategic and political problems of war the additional complication of unrealistic moralising. The second criticism is easy to answer in a preliminary way, since "unrealistic moralising" is something we can do without in any sphere of life; the real issue, of course, is whether just war thinking *is* unrealistic moralising. As for the first criticism, partisans of particular wars have been quick to enlist just war theory as a propaganda aid with little regard for its constraining and prohibiting capacities; but, of course, partisans will enlist and distort many valuable ideas, such as democracy, loyalty, and economic efficiency, without those ideas being thereby discredited in themselves. Whether the tradition itself is implicated in the excessive legitimation of war is harder to answer in a categorical way, since the term "just war tradition" is so protean; but I would readily concede that certain forms of theorising within the complex tradition may well be vulnerable to the criticism of improper legitimation. It has been argued against St. Augustine, for instance, that his seminal contribution to the development of the theory, under the influence of his views on sin and the role of the church, gave far-too-sweeping powers to rulers to wage holy (and unholy) wars.

I am not principally concerned with history here or in what follows, so I will not pursue this and related exegetical matters in any depth, though it should be remarked that the writings of the medieval canonists, penitentialists, and theologians present an interesting dialectic in which extremely disparate elements contend with each other and produce outlooks and syntheses that are sometimes complementary but often opposed. These elements include: a revulsion from violence, a concern for the spiritual and temporal welfare of the church, an interest in the punishment of wrongdoers, a desire to restrain the avarice and cupidity of contemporary rulers, a need for a measure of realistic accommodation to the facts of contemporary life, an anxiety to be consistent both with the New Testament's predominant emphasis on nonviolence and the Old Testament's history of apparently divinely sanctioned bloody battles, a stress upon the importance of individual virtue and salvation, and an equally powerful emphasis upon obedience and political authority.[17] There is plenty of scope for tension here, and many

[17] For historical reviews of some of the complex traditions of debate about morality and war that themselves have very different emphases, see James T. Johnson, *Ideology, Reason and the Limitation of War* (Princeton, NJ: Princeton University Press, 1975), and his *Just War Tradition and the Restraint of War: A Moral and Historical Inquiry* (Princeton, NJ: Princeton University Press, 1981) and *The Quest for Peace: Three Moral Traditions in Western Cultural History* (Princeton, NJ: Princeton University Press, 1987); Ronald G. Musto, *The Catholic Peace Tradition* (Maryknoll, NY: Orbis Books, 1986); and Frederick H. Russell, *The Just War in the Middle Ages* (Cambridge: Cambridge University Press, (1975).

of these tensions remain with us in modern discussions of the morality of political violence, but there has certainly been development in the continuing debate and, I would suggest, some degree of progress in the answering of ancient questions and the posing of new ones. The detachment of just war theory from the idea of holy or religious war has clearly been one such progressive step, a step that owes much to late medieval thinkers like Vitoria, Suarez, and Grotius. Of course, critics are right to worry about the way in which holy war modes of thought can persist in secular clothing, but that is another matter. The explicit disavowal of the legitimacy of wars to eradicate infidelity or heresy is at least a theoretical and human advance.

On the matter of futility, one needs to tread warily. In some of the literature critical of just war theory, the suggestion is made that the theory's claims are futile because they do not offer sufficiently detailed prescriptions for all the contingencies of war. So we find it claimed that the test of proportionality in the conduct of war is useless because it is imprecise and open to conflicting interpretations.[18] No doubt it is important to eliminate as much vagueness as is realistically possible, but it cannot be an objection to a moral principle or condition that it is open to interpretation. This is an essential feature of all moral principles and rules, including such everyday ones as "Do not steal," "Do not cheat," and "Do not lie." A more serious charge is that, for whatever reason, the actual practitioners of war – whether rulers, generals, or common soldiers – take no notice of the JAB or the JIB. One could of course reply to this by pointing out that it is the fate of stringent moral prescriptions to be honoured more in the breach than the observance. There is a certain force to this rejoinder, and it offers a partial defence to the allegation, but it is only partial, since it would be disturbing if the moral injunctions and constraints that are claimed to be appropriate for a particular area of life were simply treated as irrelevant by all those who lived that life. Such a phenomenon would at least raise the suspicion that the moral talk was sham talk, having no real capacity to enter into people's lives, no connection with their lived experience. If the people and the activities are corrupt, then this disconnection is what we might expect; but where we are loath to make that judgement, and where the moral discourse precisely claims that the activities and people are not necessarily corrupt, then the disconnection must be disturbing.

In fact, the allegation of futility is exaggerated. The JAB and the JIB have certainly had less influence on the conduct of nations, soldiers, and insurgents than one might have hoped, but their impact has not been negligible. In the first place, there has been the impact on the rhetoric of polemics about war; it is a point often noted that denunciations of the enemy frequently have recourse to a critical vocabulary that embodies the concerns

---

[18] See, for instance, Donald A. Wells, *War Crimes and Laws of War* (Lanham, MD: University Press of America, 1984), p. 29.

and concepts of just war theory. *They* have gone to war against us without just cause, recklessly, malevolently, and *they* are prosecuting the war through massacre and atrocity, cruelly disregarding civilian populations and mistreating prisoners of war. *We*, by contrast, present ourselves as free of such faults, though the reality is that we are commonly blind to the potential application of these categories to our own belligerent behaviour. Nonetheless, our critique of the enemy gives the language and values the sort of currency that makes them employable for the criticism of anyone, including us. True, nations are skilled at deflecting the criticism and reluctant to engage in self-scrutiny, but the criticism retains its power to disturb, if not at the time then later on. One interesting example of the awareness of the categories of the JIB comes from the autobiography of the famous American test pilot and war ace General Chuck Yeager. Yeager was no shrinking violet, but he registered his disgust at certain Allied "atrocities" he knew of or was ordered to perform in World War II during the air war over Germany. He was especially "not proud" of one "dirty mission" he and the seventy-five Mustangs in his group were ordered to carry out, which required the strafing of "anything that moved" in a fifty mile square area of Germany. No one refused the mission, principally, it would seem, out of fear of court-martial, but Yeager registered his consciousness of the enormity of the orders by remarking to the pilot next to him: "If we're gonna do things like this, we sure as hell better make sure we're on the winning side."[19]

At the individual level, the concepts can be amazingly potent, as the case of the Austrian peasant Franz Jagerstatter shows very well. Jagerstatter refused to serve in Hitler's wars because he had consulted just war principles and determined that the causes were palpably unjust. This led, as he knew it would, to his execution.[20] Nor should we forget the heroic German soldier who refused to be part of an execution squad ordered to murder Dutch hostages and was then put amongst them and shot.[21] Even when looking at the behaviour of nations or revolutionary groups, it is as well to take a long view of the influence of theories like those of the just war. Vitoria's, Las Casas's, and Montesinos's opposition to the Spanish wars against South American Indians had little effect at the time, but over the centuries their moral critique was embodied in the general revulsion against colonialism.

Writings in moral theory, by themselves, will inevitably take time to influence conduct if they are to influence it at all. For more direct effect, they must be embodied in institutions, laws, or conventions. As Aristotle pointed

---

[19] General Chuck Yeager and Leo Janos, *Yeager: An Autobiography* (London: Arrow Books, 1986), pp. 89–90.

[20] See Gordon C. Zahn, *In Solitary Witness: The Life and Death of Franz Jagerstatter* (New York: Holt, Rinehart and Winston, 1965).

[21] See Michael Walzer, *Just and Unjust Wars: A Moral Argument with Historical Illustrations*, third edition (New York: Basic Books, 2000), p. 314. Walzer's telling of the story is taken from Gray, *The Warriors*, Chapter 5.

out long ago: "if discourses on ethics were sufficient in themselves to make men virtuous," then those who propounded them would "quite rightly" earn "large fees and many" for their efforts.[22] Since, by and large, they don't, we may assume that something more is generally required, even though, as Aristotle thought, some people, such as "generously minded youths" of good disposition and noble character, can be made susceptible to the influence of virtue merely by exposure to theory.[23] That "something more" was, for Aristotle, a combination of moral education and law. Here resides the importance of international law (and related institutions) dealing with warfare and armed conflict, and this has developed impressively since the pioneering efforts of such thinkers as Vitoria and Suarez, and later Grotius and Pufendorf.

Many of the most notable developments have occurred within the last hundred years or so. Beginning in the middle of the nineteenth century, at the height of the fundamentally amoral doctrine of *raison d'etat*, efforts to achieve international agreement on various moral and "humanitarian" limitations on the pursuit of war have been a significant feature of international relations, and increasingly so since the establishment of the United Nations. The International Red Cross movement, born from the sympathetic responses of Henry Dunant to the horrors of the Battle of Solferino, has been a prime mover in attempting to give effective recognition and detailed, practical implementation to moral values and principles in the context of war and, later, other forms of armed struggle. The first Geneva Convention of 1864 was followed by a number of Hague Conventions leading to the updated Geneva Conventions of 1949 and the subsequent Protocols of 1977. I shall have more to say about these developments later. For now, I merely want to suggest that they have sometimes had some effect in moderating the frequency and ferocity of war and in legitimating internal opposition and conscientious objection to wars perceived to be unjust. Noncombatant immunity, for instance, has gradually emerged from many of the ambiguities of medieval theorising as a central principle in the modern JIB, and this has been in part a response to the frequent violation of such noncombatant protections since the emergence of aerial bombardment as a crucial tactic of warfare in the twentieth century. Such has been the power accruing to the prohibition at least of direct attacks upon noncombatants that the Allied forces in the 1990–91 Gulf War, especially the U.S. forces, were adamant that attacks upon Iraqi civilian targets were no part of their strategy. The same claim was made in the NATO bombing of Serbia in 1999 and in the invasion of Iraq in 2003. On a somewhat narrow interpretation of civilian immunity, this restriction may have been honoured in those bombing policies. I shall

---

[22] Aristotle, *Nicomachean Ethics*, trans. H. A. Rackham (London: William Heinemann Ltd., 1962), Book 10, Chapter 9, p. 629.
[23] Ibid.

later argue that this interpretation is indeed too narrow, but the degree to which it was honoured represents a small but significant achievement in the implementation of just war doctrine.[24] It is not, however, the case that the soldier/civilian distinction exactly matches the combatant/noncombatant distinction as I shall be using it. Nonetheless, there is sufficient overlap for present purposes.

As for hypocrisy, most intellectuals who today write about such matters are themselves part of what John Kenneth Galbraith once referred to as "the culture of contentment."[25] They occupy comfortable jobs and are integrated into societies that they, to some degree, serve. Where the military policies of such societies promote the interests of the contented, one may be right to entertain a degree of suspicion of the motives of those intellectuals who offer moral and philosophical justifications for any form of war. Nonetheless, when all due scepticism has been exercised, it remains true that the proposed justifications must first be scrutinised in terms of what they say, what arguments they offer, and what insights they contain, rather than reductively in terms of the hidden motives of their propounders. Nor should we lose sight of the fact that a society's severest critics can come from its most favoured ranks, Galbraith himself being a case in point.

Just War Doctrine as Restrictive

A theme running through this book will be the idea that just war theory is essentially restrictive, and strongly so. We need just war theory in the way

---

[24] As more information becomes available about Allied activities during the war, the degree to which the prohibition was honoured becomes more and more disputable. A report by the U.S. General Accounting Office, for example, explicitly states that the Desert Storm air campaign of 1991 was aimed at five basic categories of targets: "...command and control, industrial production, infrastructure, population will, and fielded forces." The bombing of civilian infrastructure, including electricity, water, sanitation, and other life-sustaining essentials, was intended, according to the report, to "degrade the will of the civilian population." U.S. General Accounting Office, "Cruise Missiles: Proven Capacity Should Affect Aircraft and Force Structure Requirements", 20/04/95, GAO/INSIAD-95–116, p. 22. As a direct result of this bombing campaign against civilian life, according to another analyst, at least 25,000 men, women, and children were killed; and the Red Crescent Society of Jordan estimated a week before the end of the war that 113,000 civilians had been killed, 60 percent of whom were children. These figures are cited by Nafeez Mosaddeq Ahmed in "The 1991 Gulf Massacre: The Historical and Strategic Context of Western Terrorism in the Gulf," Media Monitors Network, February 10, 2001, at http://iraqaction.org/oldsite. It is hard to get objective information, and these figures may well be exaggerated; the respected organisation Human Rights Watch puts direct civilians deaths during the war at an upper limit of 2,500 to 3,000, though they note that a "substantially larger" number of deaths were caused by the embargo and the destruction of Iraq's electrical system. See "Needless Deaths in the Gulf War: Civilian Casualties during the Air Campaign and Violations of the Laws of War" (New York: Human Rights Watch, c. 1991), online at http://www.hrw.org/reports/1991/gulfwar.

[25] John Kenneth Galbraith, *The Culture of Contentment* (New York: Houghton Mifflin, 1992).

that we do not need just enjoyment theory, or just marriage theory, or just music theory. I do not mean that there is nothing to be said about the moral limits to enjoyment, or about the moral rights of parties to marriage, or even about the moral limitations of music (Plato certainly had a good deal to say about this). But enjoyment, music, and (with all due respect to certain critics of the family) marriage are all good things involving other good things, though they can be corrupted and distorted and, like all good things, you can have too much of them. War, by contrast, belongs to the class of things that are best avoided rather than best sought. This insight can be found in Aristotle, who has never been accused of pacifism, when he says that "no-one desires to be at war for the sake of being at war, nor deliberately takes steps to cause a war: a man would be thought an utterly bloodthirsty character if he declared war on a friendly state for the sake of causing battles and massacres."[26] People who support particular wars are likely to admit that war is an evil, but to claim that it is here a necessary evil, as is sometimes true of amputation or fasting. And, even if one did not want to claim categorically that war is an evil, it would have to be admitted that it is standardly attended by such evils that even the resort to a justified war is regrettable. Consequently, just war theory is basically there to tell us not to engage in war unless certain hard-to-satisfy conditions are met. This restrictive attitude is one that can be shared, and usually is, by theorists of a utilitarian cast of mind who may be reluctant to locate themselves within the just war tradition.

Mention of utilitarianism naturally raises the question of how the philosophical underpinnings of just war thinking are best understood. My exploration of just war theory will treat it as a non-utilitarian, indeed broadly non-consequentialist, moral theory. By this I mean that it does not determine moral issues *only* by recourse to the maximising or optimising of outcomes. As we shall see, there are moral imperatives, such as the prohibition on attacking noncombatants, that are not principally justifiable solely in terms of their beneficial outcomes. But this is not to say that consequences are of no importance in the just war tradition. A nonconsequentialist approach to morality will often be sensitive to the calculation of beneficial or damaging consequences of the various policies proposed or enacted. The approach will merely reject the idea that the whole of morality is to be treated in this fashion and will suspect that the sort of large-scale maximising calculations characteristic of utilitarianism pose illusory prospects for understanding the moral enterprise.

---

[26] Aristotle, *Nicomachean Ethics*, Book 10, Chapter 7, p. 615. An alternative translation has it that "no one chooses to be at war, or provokes war, for the sake of being at war; any one would seem absolutely murderous if he were to make enemies of his friends in order to bring about battle and slaughter." *The Basic Works of Aristotle*, ed. Richard McKeon (New York: Random House, 1941), p. 1105.

But saying that just war theory is non-consequentialist in the sense outlined leaves much unsaid. In particular, it doesn't tell us which non-consequentialist philosophical theory, and there are many of them, is best adapted to the presentation of just war theory. Historically, much just war thinking has operated within the natural law tradition, but although I am sympathetic to some of the insights of this tradition (broadly construed), I do not think that recourse to the just war framework must carry with it a commitment to natural law moral theory. This is partly because any such commitment would be entangled in the unfortunate connection between natural law theory and what seem to me to be certain confusions in contemporary Roman Catholic teachings, especially those on sexual morality. But even more importantly, it is because there may well be no exclusive non-consequentialist way to support just war principles or conclusions. On the face of it, much of the just war apparatus can be supported by Kantian theory, by intuitionism, or even by social contract theory; indeed, the most influential contemporary philosophical statement of just war theory comes from Michael Walzer, who is not obviously within the natural law tradition.[27] I think it likely that the broad resources of what has been called "commonsense morality," which offers an ecumenical home to a variety of non-consequentialist theories, provide a sufficient basis for the development of an account of just war thinking suitable for our purposes.[28] Another thing left unsaid by the comment that just war thinking is non-consequentialist is the possibility that consequentialist and non-consequentialist thinking often converge in the discussion of concrete issues of practical moral concern. This convergence is partly the outcome of a certain distance that exists between high moral theory and circumstantial moral judgement, so that people on hospital ethics committees, for example, can often come to agreement on what is morally required even though their underlying outlooks on morality differ sharply. But it is also aided by the fact that complex versions of utilitarianism are adept at accommodating themselves to commonsense morality, with the result that their verdicts on particular moral puzzles can be indistinguishable from those of non-utilitarian theories. We

---

[27] Walzer, *Just and Unjust Wars*. Walzer operates mainly within a somewhat idiosyncratic social contract framework, though he has expressed in another connection a muted sympathy for natural law. See Walzer's pamphlet "Universalism and Jewish Value," the twentieth Morgenthau Memorial Lecture on Ethics and Foreign Policy (New York: Carnegie Council on Ethics and International Affairs, 2001), pp. 34–35.

[28] For the origin of the term "commonsense morality" see Henry Sidgwick, *The Methods of Ethics* (London: Macmillan, 1962). For recent debates about it, see Derek Parfit, *Reasons and Persons* (Oxford: Clarendon Press, 1984). See also Arthur Kuflik's discussion in "A Defense of Common-Sense Morality," *Ethics* 96 (1986), pp. 784–803. My own views on the complexities of natural law and the just war tradition are more fully expounded in "Natural Law and Weapons of Mass Destruction," in Sohail H. Hashmi and Steven P. Lee (eds.), *Ethics and Weapons of Mass Destruction: Religious and Secular Perspectives* (Cambridge: Cambridge University Press, 2004).

may anticipate, therefore, a considerable degree of overlap between utilitarian thinkers and adherents of the classical just war tradition. Given the horrendous consequences and disutility of so much warfare, we may expect many utilitarians to endorse what I have been calling the restrictive attitude toward war embodied in just war thinking.

At any rate, this is how I propose to treat the theory of the just war, and I shall support this proposal not only by an appeal to common sense and moral-cum-political analysis but also by a certain interpretation of the history of the evolution of just war theory. It is of course possible – though not, I claim, desirable – to take a quite different and more permissive stance toward war, whether from within the just war tradition or from outside it. I shall call those who take this other attitude "militarists," though the term is not intended to be merely abusive. Hegel (as I read him) and de Maistre are typical advocates of an extreme version of such militarism. Hegel's contempt for Kant's aspirations after "perpetual peace" reveals the attitude nicely: "...just as the blowing of the winds preserves the sea from the foulness which would be the result of prolonged calm, so also corruption in nations would be the product of prolonged, let alone 'perpetual' peace."[29] We shall further discuss this outlook in Chapter 3. It has its own lessons to teach, but other, less extreme forms of militarism are more influential today, and they are often found amongst advocates of just wars and proponents of just war theory. What these attitudes share with the Hegelian outlook is a certain suspicion of peace, of peace makers, of peace activists, and of the place of the gentler virtues in international affairs. This cast of mind tends to use just war theory as a way of "normalizing" war, of treating it as a standard part of diplomacy, thereby losing sight of its enormity. The language such militarists use about war aids this strategy by the deployment of softening euphemism: "surgical strikes," "taking out," "teaching lessons," "neutralizing" and the like. Militarists of this type commonly favour large standing armies and huge "defence" budgets; they endorse strong theories of deterrence and defend heavy investment in spying (or, as it is now called, "intelligence") in the name of that shifting shibboleth "national security"; they see the dangers of "appeasement" as ever-present, and their slogan is "If you want peace, prepare for war." There are important insights in all of this, but it seems to me not to take seriously enough either the value of peace or the prospects and opportunities for achieving it.

This reference to peace is important. Militarists have, I believe, lost sight of the way in which the justified resort to war must be conditioned by a commitment to the ideal of peace. This commitment is built into Augustine's treatment of the just war and also in various ways into the treatment of many who later contributed to the theory. Suarez, for example, states very clearly

---

[29] Georg Wilhelm Friedrich Hegel, *The Philosophy of Right*, trans. T. M. Knox (Oxford: Clarendon Press of Oxford University Press, 1952), p. 210.

that "the chief end of war is to establish such a future peace."[30] As we shall see, there are problems with the way in which Augustine manages to give such centrality to the desire for peace, and the profession of a love for peace is no guarantee of the authenticity of a commitment to it. (The possibility of this mismatch is delightfully illustrated by the ambiguities in the slogan embraced by the U.S. Strategic Air Command: "Peace is our profession.") While there is no rubric or algorithm for implementing it, a genuine concern for peace should make us wary of the drive for military solutions to all manner of political problems. This is a drive that soldiers and politicians may often share, though my experience is that members of the military (in democracies, at least) are often far less enamoured of military solutions to political problems than are politicians and their advisors. Soldiers will often be less militaristic than civilians.

I have spoken of just war theory but also of the just war tradition, and in many ways the second expression is preferable. Talk of "theory" usefully calls attention to the fact that a great deal of hard thinking and generalizing is required in working out a plausible way to relate morality to war and other forms of large-scale political violence, but it can be misleading if it suggests that there is just one theory to which all the various thinkers have been contributing under the heading of "the just war." This suggestion would obscure the variety of interpretations of core ideas that have developed over the centuries under the mantle of the just war. Talking of a tradition does more justice to this diversity, and also respects the way in which the core ideas have continued to animate these developments even when they are divergent. One very important divergence, which helps to illustrate what I mean, is that between the idea that the permissions of just war theory apply only to the justified side (if any) in a war and the idea that such permissions apply to all sides. Some theorists hold, for instance, that (strictly speaking) only the just warriors are entitled to kill enemy soldiers; unjust warriors have no moral license to kill at all. Others hold that there is a moral equality of soldiers such that both sides are entitled to kill their opponents. The second position reflects the legal position in international law and is espoused by Michael Walzer as a moral position in his influential book *Just and Unjust Wars*. But in some respects the first position is more consonant with the origins of the tradition and with various accounts of the basis of just cause. This important disagreement will be addressed in the course of this book.

To make any headway at all, however, we need to be much clearer about the concept of violence. This concept is one that plays a part in many contemporary discussions of a variety of controversial social issues. It is clear

---

[30] Francisco Suarez, *Selections from Three Works of Francisco Suarez*, vol. 2 (Oxford: Clarendon Press of Oxford University Press, 1944), p. 839. The quotation, from *A Work on the Three Theological Virtues: Faith, Hope and Charity*, is from Chapter VII of the "Disputation on Charity," entitled "What Is the Proper Mode of Conducting War?."

from an examination of such discussions that there is a great deal of confusion about the use of the term "violence." This emerges in debates about censorship, child abuse, police behaviour, school discipline, and, of course, war and revolution. To make clear the sense in which I shall understand the term, and the advantages of thinking about violence in the way I recommend, is the purpose of the discussion in Chapter 2.

2

The Idea of Violence

And the soldiers likewise demanded of him, saying, And what shall we do? And he said unto them, Do violence to no man, neither accuse any falsely; and be content with your wages.

Luke 3:14, King James Version

Hannah Arendt once complained that the careless use in political theory of such key terms as "power," "strength," "force," "authority," and "violence" indicated not only a deplorable deafness to linguistic meanings but also a kind of blindness to significant political realities. The blame for this she traced to the obsession with reducing public affairs to "the business of dominion."[1] I share her belief that conceptual carelessness or misunderstanding about such ideas as violence has political importance, and I suspect that she may be right in her diagnosis of what lies behind a good deal of such confusion. My present concern, however, is rather different from that specifically addressed by Arendt, although the two are related. Nowadays it is not so much that theorists are, as Arendt objected, indifferent to distinctions between the key terms listed but that they offer explicit definitions of the term "violence" that exhibit both the deafness to linguistic patterns and, more significantly, the blindness to political and moral realities of which she complained. In what follows, I shall try to support this claim by examining several fashionable definitions of violence with an eye to both their conceptual adequacy and their moral and social implications. I shall also suggest an alternative definition, urge its advantages over the ones criticised, and defend it against certain difficulties.

Of course, as Arendt herself was well aware, any such definition has to cope with the untidiness, indeterminacy, and variety of purpose involved in natural languages and ordinary speech contexts. Hence any definition proposed by a theorist will involve some degree of sharpening and legislation,

---

[1] Hannah Arendt, *On Violence* (London: Allen Lane and Penguin, 1970), pp. 43–44.

with a consequent recognition of borderline cases and the dismissal or down-grading of certain kinds of existing usage. Social and political concepts of any importance have, however, an additional interest and complexity in that they may and often do embody diverse moral and political outlooks or visions, and so a theorist's definitions of such terms will reflect, and often be part of, a programme for advancing certain enterprises at once theoretical and practical. Sometimes, understanding is best served by defining a concept such as "justice" in very abstract and relatively neutral terms that allow competing theories and outlooks pertaining to the subject matter to be compared and criticised. Here it has proved useful to deploy a (relatively unanalysed) contrast between concept and conception, as Rawls does in his work on justice and as Dworkin recommends in the case of law.[2] Nonetheless, the literature on violence mostly proceeds in terms of definitions that aim to capture a conceptual territory believed to be at least implicit in ordinary discourse, and so I shall frame my discussion in terms of definition but with the background social and political issues very much in mind. Were the concept/conception strategy applicable to the present topic it would, I believe, require only a rearrangement of what I want to say and not a revision of it.

The definition of violence provides a nice illustration of the complex interplay between concept and commitment. There are roughly three types of definition to be found in the philosophical, political, and sociological literature on violence. We might label these "wide," "restricted," and "legitimate."[3] Wide definitions, of which the most influential is that of "structural violence," tend to serve the interests of the political left by including within the extension of the term "violence" a great range of social injustices and inequalities. This not only allows reformers to say that they are working to eliminate violence when they oppose, say, a government measure to redistribute income in favour of the already rich, but also allows revolutionaries to offer, in justification of their resort to violence – even when it is terrorist – the claim that they are merely meeting violence with violence. Their own direct physical violence is presented as no more than a response to and defence against the institutional or quiet violence of their society.[4] An instance of

[2] John Rawls, *A Theory of Justice* (Oxford: Oxford University Press, 1972), pp. 5–6; Ronald Dworkin, *Taking Rights Seriously* (London: Duckworth, 1978), pp. 134–136 and 266, and also in lectures at Oxford in 1982. I have some reservations about Dworkin's use of the concept/conception distinction, but this is not the place to discuss them or even to argue a case for believing (as I do) that the distinction is likely to have less fruitful application in the case of violence than in that of justice or law.

[3] There is a discussion of those types under the labels "expansive," "observational," and "narrow" in Kenneth W. Grundy and Michael A. Weinstein, *The Ideologies of Violence* (Columbus, OH: Merrill, 1974), pp. 8–13. Their discussion is useful but not entirely convincing.

[4] It is not just that they can accuse their critics of like behaviour and, crying *tu quoque*, expose their inconsistency. This is the interpretation Ted Honderich places upon this sort of use of

such a wide definition is Newton Garver's: "The institutional form of quiet violence operates when people are deprived of choices in a systematic way by the very manner in which transactions normally take place."[5] But if wide definitions are naturally more congenial to the left, we must not ignore the possibility of their use by the right, since it is possible for the right to see social structures as deforming in that they expose people to moral danger, for example, or leave them too free or not economically free enough, and so on.

Restricted definitions are typically those that concentrate upon positive interpersonal acts of force, usually involving the infliction of physical injury. There is something to be said for this being the normal or ordinary understanding of "violence," not only because it has the authority of dictionaries, most notably the *Oxford English Dictionary*, but because the proponents of the wide definitions usually take it that they are offering an extension of just such a normal or usual idea.[6] It has been argued by some that this definition has natural affinities with a reformist liberal political outlook.[7] And it may be so, though I think myself that it is the most politically neutral of the definitional types (which may just show how "liberal" it is and I am). In any case, it is the type of definition in support of which I shall later argue.

The third type of definition – that called "legitimist" – arises naturally in the context of conservative or right-wing liberal political thought, for it incorporates a reference to an illegal or illegitimate use of force. I think it probable that this style of definition has much more currency in the United States than elsewhere, but the usage to which it corresponds does exist in other communities, too. Sidney Hook is operating in this tradition when he defines violence as "the illegal employment of methods of physical coercion for personal or group ends";[8] and Herbert Marcuse is commenting upon this usage when he says, "Thanks to a kind of political linguistics, we never use the word violence to describe the actions of the police, we never use the word violence to describe the actions of the Special Forces in Vietnam. But the word is readily applied to the actions of students who defend themselves from the police, burn cars or chop down trees."[9] One can see the advantages

---

the notion of structural violence. See Ted Honderich, *Violence for Equality: Inquiries in Political Philosophy* (Harmondsworth: Penguin, 1980), pp. 96–100. But Honderich fails to observe that revolutionaries can try to justify their own violence as a form of defence against structural violence.

[5] Newton Garver, "What Violence Is," *The Nation* 209 (1968), p. 822, reprinted in James Rachels and Frank A. Tillman (eds.), *Philosophical Issues: A Contemporary Introduction* (New York: Harper Collins, 1972), pp. 223–228. The quoted passage is on p. 228.

[6] See Garver, "What Violence Is," p. 822; and Johan Galtung, "Violence, Peace and Peace Research," *The Journal of Peace Research* 6 (1969), pp. 168 and 173.

[7] Grundy and Weinstein, *The Ideologies of Violence*, pp. 10–11, where they also see it as involved in revolutionary attitudes toward totalitarian regimes.

[8] Ibid., p. 12.

[9] *New York Times Magazine*, October 27, 1968, p. 90.

of this outlook for the defenders of established orders, but once more the connection, though natural, is not inevitable. A more political definition in the legitimist tradition, but certainly not one geared to the defence of the established order, is that employed by Robert Paul Wolff. Wolff accepted this sort of definition in order to argue a kind of left-wing case by purporting to show that the concept of violence is incoherent.[10] I shall consider Wolff's view in detail as a representative legitimist definition, even though he gives it an atypical twist; but I want to begin with a wide definition. The one I shall consider is that given by the Norwegian philosopher-sociologist Johan Galtung.[11] Although Galtung was writing in the late 1960s, the idea he promoted has become a stock-in-trade for both popular and academic discussion of social and political problems to the present day, though its validity is usually merely assumed rather than argued for, and detailed criticisms or defences of the idea are rare.[12]

Before doing so, however, it is instructive to reflect on the understanding of violence that is in play in the translated quotation from St. Luke's gospel with which this chapter began. It would seem that, unless Christ is saying that the soldiers should lay down their arms completely, he must mean that they should refrain from violence in the sense that would be rendered by the restricted definition as "unjustified violence." This suggests that a legitimist idea of violence is at work, though it is not a legitimist reading in any political sense, since the implicit reference to legitimacy is more broadly moral. The fact that this special legitimist reading of "violence" is probably at work in the quotation is revealed by the different translations given elsewhere. The Catholic Confraternity version of the quotation gives "Plunder no one" instead of the rendition "Do violence to no man" in the King James version. Indeed, the Greek (and Latin) is so clear on this that the translators of the King James version must have had a legitimist understanding (perhaps with some elements of the structuralist outlook as well) firmly implanted in their heads to have given so unspecific a rendition. The Greek is clearly talking about extortion of money (*diaseisete*) and something like fraud (*suxophantesete*) rather than violence as such, and the context clearly refers to the requirements and prohibitions of a sort of professional ethic. The paradoxical idea that it is all right to be a soldier but that you must never use violence arises only because of the peculiarity of the legitimist outlook informing the translator.

---

[10] Robert Paul Wolff, "On Violence," *Journal of Philosophy* 66 (1969), pp. 601–616.

[11] Galtung, "Violence, Peace and Peace Research," pp. 168 and 173.

[12] A brief selection of recent invocations of structural violence by theorists might include Mary K. Anglin, "Feminist Perspectives on Structural Violence," *Identities* 5, no. 2 (1998), pp. 145–150; Richard E. Ashcroft, "Ethics Committees and Countries in Transition: A Figleaf for Structural Violence?," *British Medical Journal* 331 (2005), pp. 229–230; Susan Beckerleg and Gillian Lewando Hundt, "Women Heroin Users: Exploring the Limitations of the Structural Violence Approach," *International Journal of Drug Policy* 16 (2005), pp. 183–190.

As for Galtung and structural violence, he claims that there are various types of violence and that it is important to have a very broad concept of violence in order to accommodate them all. He distinguishes, for instance, between physical and psychological violence, giving as cases of the latter lies, brainwashing, indoctrination, and threats; but, more interestingly, he locates both of these within the category of personal violence, which he then contrasts with structural violence. By so doing he generates a perspective from which one can see two types of peace. On the one hand there is negative peace, which is the absence of direct or personal violence (roughly what a restricted definition determines as violence); and, on the other, positive peace, which is the absence of indirect or structural violence.[13] Structural violence is also referred to as "social injustice" and positive peace as "social justice." At this point Galtung's definition of violence should be cited, a definition that is meant to support the possibility of the two types of violence mentioned. What he says is: "Violence is present when human beings are being influenced so that their actual somatic and mental realisations are below their potential realisations."[14] Galtung confesses to some unease about this definition as soon as he formulates it, saying that it "may lead to more problems than it solves," but this avowal seems to have no more than ritual significance, since no such problems are raised in the course of the article. Galtung is, however, aware that he has framed what he calls "an extended concept of violence," and he feels obliged to try to justify the extension as "a logical extension." By talking of his definition as extending the concept of violence, Galtung seems to be acknowledging what is, indeed, surely the case, that in its usual use the term "violence" covers only what he calls personal violence, whereas he wants to hold that violence also exists where social arrangements and institutions have the effect of producing substandard "somatic and mental realisations." Indeed, if we were to invoke the authority of the *Oxford English Dictionary* we might conclude that even personal violence is too extended, since that authority gives a "restricted" definition of violence in purely physical terms as follows: "The exercise of physical force so as to inflict injury on or damage to persons or property; action or conduct characterised by this."

I shall discuss this definition later, since it faces certain difficulties and requires some clarification. First we should notice that, on this definition, there can be various metaphorical or otherwise extended uses of "violence," "violent," "violently," and suchlike words that relate in more or less direct ways to episodes of the infliction of damage by physical force: "Sir John Kerr did violence to the Australian Constitution" or "Dennis waved his arms about violently" or "The violent motions of the machine surprised him." It seems plausible to treat the use of the noun "violence" in the utterance about Sir

---

[13] Galtung, "Violence, Peace and Peace Research," p. 183.
[14] Ibid., p. 168.

John Kerr as an attempt to dramatise the awfulness of the governor-general's behaviour with respect to the Constitution, but the adjectival and adverbial uses are more interesting in being less metaphorical. Neither Dennis nor the machine was engaged in violence, yet their movements are intelligibly described as violent because of affinities between the way their limbs and parts behaved and the way in which genuine violence manifests itself. In this respect, the employment of "violent" and "violently" in such contexts is like the use of such expressions as "furious," and "furiously," since we do not suppose that the team that rows "furiously" is actually in a fury.

Once this is understood, we should be under no temptation to think that such usages somehow license the sort of extension that Galtung is promoting. (John Harris seems to think something of the kind, but we will look more closely at his view later.) Certainly it would normally be very queer to say that violence is present when (and because) a society legislates more tax concessions for big business, or refuses to remove unjust legislation such as the denial of voting rights to certain minority groups. It seems no less bizarre, however, to characterise such enactments as violent in anything like the way Dennis and the machine can be so characterised.

We should pause to eliminate some sources of possible confusion. When people speak of structural or institutional violence, they often run together three things that should be kept separate. First, there is what Galtung is principally concerned with, namely, the way in which people are injured and harmed by unjust social arrangements even though no violence in the restricted (or "personal") sense is being done to them. Second, there is the phenomenon of ordinary person-to-person violence with pronounced social or structural causes (for example, police harassment of racial minorities, race riots, and prison brutality, to name just a few plausible candidates). Third, there is the widespread readiness to resort to socially licensed violence that is implicit in much of social life. Galtung puts this into the category of "latent violence" but still appears to treat it as a type of violence, which seems wrong for the perfectly general reason that tendencies and dispositions should not be confused with their display.[15] There are, of course, plenty of displays of the State's capacity for violence, both domestically and externally, and the role of (restricted) violence in civil life is both easy to ignore and almost equally easy to exaggerate. It is easy to ignore in part because when one has a comfortable position in society it is hardly ever personally encountered (in peacetime), and in part because secondhand knowledge of the facts tends to be clouded by euphemism. The presumed legitimacy of state violence can also create the feeling that it is a quite different activity from unauthorised violence and so lead to the legitimist idea that it is not violence at all. The point about state violence is easy to exaggerate

[15] Ibid., p. 172.

from a different direction, especially if the distinctions made earlier are neglected. Some thinkers and activists speak as if nothing but violence goes on in such a state as Britain or Australia and as if political obedience rests entirely upon the fear of violent treatment by the authorities. If we are thinking of restricted violence, then both of these claims are absurd. And even if we allow reference to the state's capacity for violence in discussing the roots of political obedience, then it is surely implausible to hold that most people accept political authority because they fear the state's capacity for violence against them. More plausible is Thomas Hobbes's view that the state's power to use violence ("the right of the sword") enters into most people's thinking about obedience primarily through the reassuring thought that it provides a sanction against someone else's violent behaviour. As Hobbes argued, most people in an ordered, half-decent society get such benefits from civil life that it is clearly in their interest to accept civil authority most of the time, but this is conditional upon those who don't have such an interest (or who don't think that they have such an interest) being intimidated into conformity and upon the majority being so intimidated on those occasions (necessarily rare, so Hobbes may have believed) when conformity does not *seem* to be in their interest. There is some plausibility in this sort of picture of the role of violence in securing political obedience, but it is more complex than the picture often presented in popular polemics.

If Galtung is not merely concerned to draw attention to the social causes of much personal violence, or to the amount of latent personal violence involved in normal social life, what good reason does he have for extending the concept of violence in the way he does?

First, let us look briefly at the formulation of his definition, which has some rather curious features. It seems to follow from it that a young child is engaged in violence if its expression of its needs and desires is such that it makes its mother and/or father very tired, even if it is not in any ordinary sense "a violent child" or engaged in violent actions. Furthermore, I will be engaged in violence if, at your request, I give you a sleeping pill that will reduce your actual somatic and mental realisations well below their potential, at least for some hours. Certainly some emendation is called for, and it may be possible to produce a version of the definition that will meet these difficulties (the changing of "influenced" to "influenced against their will" might do the job, but at the cost of making it impossible to act violently toward someone at their request, and that doesn't *seem* to be impossible, just unusual). I shall not dwell on this, however, because I want rather to assess Galtung's reason for seeking to extend the concept of violence in the way he does. His statement of the justification of his definition is as follows:

However, it will soon be clear why we are rejecting the narrow concept of violence – according to which violence is *somatic* incapacitation, or deprivation of health, alone (with killing as the extreme form), at the hands of an *actor* who *intends* this to be the consequence. If this were all violence is about, and peace is seen as its negation, then too little is rejected when peace is held up as an ideal. Highly unacceptable social orders would still be compatible with peace. Hence an *extended concept of violence is indispensable* but the concept should be a logical extension, not merely a list of undesirables.[16]

So, for Galtung, the significance of his definition of violence lies in the fact that if violence is undesirable and peace desirable, then if we draw a very wide bow in defining violence we will find that the ideal of peace will commit us quite a lot. Now it seems to me that this justification of the value of his definition is either muddled or mischievous (and just possibly both). If the suggestion is that peace cannot be a *worthy* social ideal or goal of action unless it is the total ideal, then the suggestion is surely absurd. A multiplicity of compatible but noninclusive ideals seems as worthy of human pursuit as a single comprehensive goal, and, furthermore, it seems a more honest way to characterise social realities. Galtung finds it somehow shocking that highly unacceptable social orders would still be compatible with peace, but only the total ideal assumption makes this even surprising. It is surely just an example of the twin facts that since social realities are complex, social ideals and ills do not form an undifferentiated whole (at least not in the perceptions of most men and women), and that social causation is such that some ideals are achievable in relative independence from others. Prosperity, freedom, peace, and equality, for instance, are different ideals requiring different characterisations and justifications, and although it could be hoped that they are compatible in the sense that there is no absurdity in supposing that a society could exhibit a high degree of realisation of all four, concrete circumstances may well demand a trade-off amongst them – the toleration, for example, of a lesser degree of freedom in order to achieve peace, or of less general prosperity in the interests of greater equality.

On the other hand, it may be that Galtung does not mean to say that a narrower definition of violence would provide us with a notion of peace that was not sufficiently worth pursuing, but rather that since people are against violence (narrowly construed) and for peace (narrowly construed), their energies can be harnessed practically on a wide front against all sorts of social injustice. There are some indications in the text that this is what Galtung means and that he is not averse to achieving this goal through the promotion of what he himself sees to be confused thinking:

The use of the term "peace" may in itself be peace-productive, producing a common basis, a feeling of communality in purpose that may pave the ground for deeper ties later on. The use of more precise terms drawn from the vocabulary of one conflict group, and excluded from the vocabulary of the opponent group, may in

[16] Ibid., p. 168.

itself cause dissent and lead to manifest conflict precisely because the term is so clearly understood. By projecting an image of harmony of interests the term "peace" may also help bring about such a harmony. It provides opponents with a one-word language in which to express values of concern and togetherness because peace is on anybody's agenda.[17]

Nonetheless, it is not clear how seriously this is intended. The passage occurs before the attempt at definition, and it may not be charitable to take it as an indication of the true significance of Galtung's definitional strategy. If it were so taken, then it should be remarked that the strategy not only has much the same moral status as propaganda, it also shares the disadvantages of propaganda in that it is likely in the long term to defeat the ends, good or ill, that it is designed to serve. The deliberate promotion of muddle or unclarity is liable to be detected and when detected resented, because it is seen for what it is, namely, an exercise in manipulation. One is reminded of some of the Communist Party's operations with United Front (and other "front") organisations of the 1940s and 1950s, and of the subsequent damage done to numerous radical causes by the disillusionment of those who had been manipulated.

Let us suppose, however, that Galtung's strategy is not as dubious as this, and let us rather interpret him as seeking to call attention to genuine similarities between personal and structural violence in the hope that once they are seen, people who are concerned to oppose the violence of, for example, war will also work to oppose the structural violence of (as it may be) inequitable tax scales, income inequities, inadequate health services, and so on. (I am deliberately not using such instances of social injustice as racism, which usually involve the use of "restricted" violence and so can lead to some confusion, as noted earlier.) To this I think there are three replies.

(a) The similarities between personal violence and structural violence seem to be far too few and too general to offset the striking differences between them. The basic similarity that Galtung's definition enshrines in a somewhat cumbersome way is that violence and social injustice both involve the production of some sort of hurt or injury broadly construed, but the types of harm and the conditions of their production are terribly different.

In English writings in the 1970s and 1980s on moral and political philosophy, a good deal of ingenious and often impressive effort was expended on arguments that might seem to make the similarities more convincing and the differences less striking. Most of the effort has gone into an attack upon what Jonathan Glover has called the acts/omissions doctrine, and writers like Glover, Singer, Bennett, Harris, and Honderich (most of them utilitarians of one sort or another) have drawn various, though related, conclusions

[17] Ibid., p. 167.

from their critique.[18] Insofar as the discussion has served to stress the ways
in which various failures to act may be morally significant, it seems to me
to have been of great importance. But the critique has more ambitious –
if, at times, confusingly presented – intentions. So it sometimes seems that
the project is to show that there is no real conceptual distinction between
acts and omissions; at other times that there is a distinction but that it is
never of moral significance; at still other times that there is a distinction
that is sometimes morally significant but not in the special circumstances of
interest to the moral theorist (e.g., euthanasia or abortion). This is not the
place to explore this important issue further, but it is worth noting that while
Honderich concludes that the positive acts of the violent are in the relevant
respects quite unlike the omissions of the nonviolent (e.g., their failure to
aid third world countries) even though such omissions are seriously culpable, Harris claims that such omissions or, as he prefers, negative actions,
are acts of violence.[19] Some of his arguments for this conclusion are similar
to Galtung's, but others involve an attempt to undermine the "restricted
definition" by appeal to counterexamples. The latter I will consider when
I look more carefully at attempts to provide a restricted definition, but the
former can be briefly considered here.

Harris is not interested only in extending the notion of violence; more
generally, he does not want to include any reference to the *manner* in which
harm or injury is done, other than its being done knowingly. His definition
is as follows:

An act of violence occurs when injury or suffering is inflicted upon a person or
persons by an agent who knows (or ought reasonably to have known), that his actions
would result in the harm in question.[20]

He asserts that the questions of interest about violence would be trivial if
they were concerned only with injuries brought about in a certain manner.
Our concern with such questions is motivated by the desire to solve "the
problem of violence," that is, "to minimise its use or even remove it entirely
from human affairs," and in the restricted sense of the term we might do this
"and yet leave intact all the features of the problem of violence which make
a solution desirable. Death, injury and suffering might be just as common as
before, only the characteristic complex of actions by which they are inflicted
would have changed."[21] He adds that we are not so much interested in the

[18] See Jonathan Glover, *Causing Death and Saving Lives* (Harmondsworth: Penguin, 1977);
Peter Singer, *Practical Ethics* (Cambridge: Cambridge University Press, 1979); John Harris,
Violence and Responsibility (London: Routledge & Kegan Paul, 1980); and Honderich, *Violence
for Equality*.
[19] Honderich, *Violence for Equality*, pp. 96–99 and 152–154; Harris, *Violence and Responsibility*,
Chapter 2.
[20] Harris, *Violence and Responsibility*, p. 19.
[21] Ibid., p. 18.

particular methods men use to inflict injury, suffering, or death, but in the fact that they cause each other such harms.[22] As his definition indicates, Harris's primary concern, unlike Galtung's, is with personal violence, although he wants to make a dramatic extension of that category. If certain kinds of omission can count as violence, then the way to structural violence is at least clearer, since the damage done to people by the structures and institutions of their society can be seen as sustained by personal failures to act. Moreover, a successful extension of the term "violence" to cover omissions might make the further move to violence without individual agents more palatable.

Clearly, a good deal here turns upon how we determine the question of negative actions; but even if we allow that failure to give money to Oxfam (a favoured example in the literature) with the foreseeable consequence that someone in India dies is causing some person to die, it still does not follow that we do or must have the same interest in both kinds of deed. In fact, it is quite clear that most people are interested in and exercised about the one to a much greater degree than, and in a different way than, they are concerned about the other. Whether this differentiation is morally praiseworthy or defensible is another question, but the fact that they do so differentiate is indisputable. So Harris's claim that we are not really interested in the manner in which damage is caused is, as a factual claim, simply mistaken. Furthermore, such generalised differentiation is surely plausibly explained by the striking dissimilarities between what is done, on the one hand, in stabbing a beggar to death and, on the other hand, in ignoring his plea for assistance. These dissimilarities usually extend both to the manner of acting and to the way in which the outcome ensues. I say "usually" because although cases can be constructed in which death is immediately consequent upon our refusal of aid, the more common cases involve our negative action being, at most, merely a partial cause of death and injury, and hence it is usually left open that, for instance, someone else will aid the beggar.[23] This, I suspect, is one reason why most people are more impressed by, and worried about, restricted violence than about other ways in which human beings contribute to harming one another.

---

[22] A similar attitude lies behind Steven Lee's treatment of poverty as a case of structural violence. See Steven Lee, "Is Poverty Violence?," in *Institutional Violence*, ed. Deanne Curtin and Robert Litke (Amsterdam/Atlanta: Rodopi, 1999). Lee's argument is complicated by the fact that he runs a legitimist strand into his account of violence, insisting that an action can count as violence only if it conflicts with a norm. I criticise legitimist definitions later in this chapter.

[23] The dissimilarities with respect to the ways in which outcomes are tied to positive acts and to failures to act do not obtain universally, since there may be circumstances in which a positive act takes a long time to realise its outcome and allows for some high prospect of failure, but I do not think that this sort of case can yield a model for the normal case of action, and hence it does not vitiate a contrast drawn in terms of that case.

A related, and important, point is that our positive actions to cause injury are standardly intentional under some relevant description (such as killing, stabbing, or battering), whereas our omitting to do something that would have prevented injury or suffering may or may not be intentional with reference to that upshot, even if we are fully aware that failure to act will probably have just such consequences. This will not show that the act/omission distinction *always* makes a moral difference; quite the contrary, for there will be cases where someone may omit to do something precisely because his failure to act will contribute to bringing about injury, and he may even choose the negative rather than the positive action in order that the victim suffer more. Imagine a malevolent nurse who stands to gain a lot from the death of a detested patient and who decides to inflict a more painful death by omitting to give a vital medicine rather than simply hitting him over the head. Here, the course, of intentional omission seems to be more reprehensible than the positive action. Nonetheless, the difference between the ways in which positive and negative actions are generally related to the category of the intentional does show that there is a moral significance to the distinction. Just what that significance is will depend upon the role that one's moral outlook gives to intentional action. I do not claim that morality is concerned only with intentional action – the category of negligence shows that this cannot be so – but it does appear that intentional action is of distinctive importance. It is true that utilitarian moral theory either makes light of the idea or tries to stretch it so as to make all foreseen consequences of one's act intentional, thus obliterating this difference between the homicidal nurse and the man who spends all his money on his family rather than giving some of it to Oxfam, whose workers will, he believes, use it to save lives. It is, I think, fairly clear that any such conceptual manoeuvre is a departure from ordinary thinking about intention, and I am not sympathetic to the reasons usually offered for so departing; but further discussion of this issue would take us into a debate about the best structure for an adequate moral theory and hence too far afield. My aim here is only to show that there is much more to the widespread interest in sharply distinguishing positive acts of violence from harmful failures to act than such theorists as Harris allow. I conclude, then, that the objection from dissimilarity still stands.

(b) Furthermore, even certain similarities that do exist are not all that they appear. Both the existence of social injustice (i.e., "structural violence") and restricted violence within, or between, communities are matters for moral concern, but the way in which each relates to morality seems to be different. It is hard to be confident about this, if only because of the obscurity of the expression "social justice" and the different moral understandings that are implicit in its use by different people, but on the whole, the allegation that some procedure or activity is unjust is a more decisive moral condemnation than the criticism that it is violent. It seems clear that, quite apart from the debate about just wars, some acts of local violence may be morally legitimate, for example, the violent restraint or hindrance of someone who is violently attacking someone else. By contrast, the idea that social injustice may be morally legitimate is more surprising. All but fairly extreme pacifists would agree that we could be morally justified in using violence to defend ourselves against violent attack, but there is no ready parallel to this idea in the case of social injustice. There could indeed be a reason for restricting the liberty or wealth of a class of citizens or for otherwise injuring them, but such a reason would normally preclude our describing the restriction or injury as unjust. It is not that one social injustice has been rightly used to defeat another, but rather that the good reason for using some measure that rectifies a social injustice renders that measure socially just or, at least, not unjust. This is, I think, how it would be natural to describe most justified acts of social reform, even cases of positive discrimination that are usually defended as embodiments of social justice rather than violations of it. Some may prefer to say that while this is generally so, nonetheless social injustice is sometimes morally justifiable (just as restricted violence is) because, being only one ideal amongst others, it can be overridden by some other value, like maximising happiness or, more plausibly, the needs of social order. So someone might admit that slavery offends against social justice but argue that it may justifiably continue or be freshly imposed because the economy or the intellectual culture would collapse without it. Suppose such a claim were accepted as true and overriding. Would we best describe the situation by saying that slavery here is unjust but morally acceptable or by saying that slavery here is unjust and hence immoral but that it is nonetheless required or necessary here to be immoral? These are difficult issues (reminiscent of some of those addressed by Machiavelli), but I think that if we allow such an overriding (as I should, in fact, be loath to do), it is best described in the second fashion, and if so, there is still no parallel with the case of restricted violence. The first form of description will, however, preserve the similarity and so suit the theorist of structural or other forms of wide violence. The preservation is, however, purchased at a price that I suspect few such theorists would be willing to pay because it involves the admission that social injustice – usually their primary social evil – can sometimes be *morally* acceptable.

(c) Perhaps more important than either of these points is the fact that the wide definition of violence and peace is likely to have undesirable practical consequences. As remarked earlier, the realities of social causation are such that some ideals are achievable in relative or even total independence of others, and it is very plausible to suppose that such goals as the reduction of the level of armed conflict between or within nations – or even its total elimination – may be achievable independently of the achievement or even the significant advance of social justice within one or more such nations. Furthermore, as a corollary, it may well be that quite different techniques, strategies, and remedies are required to deal with the social disorder of (restricted) violence than are needed to deal with such issues as wage injustice, educational inequalities, and entrenched privilege. Use of the wide definition seems likely to encourage the cosy but ultimately stultifying belief that there is one problem, the problem of (wide) violence, and hence it must be solved as a whole with one set of techniques.

An analogy with slavery may be instructive. It would be possible to produce a Galtung-style typology of slavery that had as its subdivisions physical slavery and structural slavery; indeed, the notion of a "wage slave" is perhaps a contribution to this sort of enterprise. Yet not only is physical slavery, for the most part, very different from structural slavery, it is palpably eliminable independently of eliminating structural slavery, since in much of the world it *has* been eliminated, whilst structural slavery remains. Furthermore, some of the methods used to eliminate physical slavery may not be appropriate to the elimination of structural slavery (e.g., the use of the British fleet).

It is worth saying something under this heading about Harris's claim mentioned earlier that one might deal with the problem of violence narrowly conceived and indeed eliminate all such violence from the face of the Earth, and yet find that "death, injury and suffering might be just as common as before, only the characteristic complex of actions by which they are inflicted would have changed."[24] We should not here be seduced by the philosopher's typical and understandable concern for fantastic possibilities because *here* such a possibility will surely fail to be instructive, and the fact equally surely is that this suggested possibility is merely fantastic. Suppose, what is hard enough, that we have vastly reduced the number of wars, revolutions, assassinations, riots, military coups, violent acts by police and criminals, is it really conceivable that, other things being equal, the lot of humankind *could* remain unimproved with respect to death, injury, and suffering?[25] One can answer "No" to this question even while believing that violence may sometimes be morally permissible and while deploring other ways in which human suffering occurs. This is because the most telling justification for violence is as a defence against other violence, and because even justified violence is regrettable. In our world and in any empirically similar world, a vast reduction in the level of (restricted) violence would surely mean the elimination of a great deal of what serves to bring premature death and extensive misery. Think of the parallel with slavery. No doubt many awful indignities must remain after slavery is abolished, and the act of abolition may itself create new disabilities for the former slaves, but in

---

[24] Harris, *Violence and Responsibility*, p. 18.
[25] Actually, Harris has some special views about poisoning and other "non-forceful" positive acts of killing that are germane to his position here, but which I shall consider later.

most imaginable circumstances it is hard to believe that their lot is not an improved one. It seems to me that the matter is even clearer in the case of violence.

Insofar, then, as wide definitions like Galtung's are open to these criticisms, their underpinnings are theoretically unsound, and the practical consequences of adopting them are likely to be, at the very least, disappointing.[26]

I come now to a rather different attempt at defining violence, one belonging to the "legitimist" category and offered by Robert Paul Wolff in "On Violence."[27] We shall not here be able to engage with all of Wolff's manoeuvres in this swashbuckling piece of polemic, but we should note that his strategy is to use a legitimist definition of violence in order to show that the concepts of violence and nonviolence are "inherently confused" because they rest fundamentally upon the idea of legitimate authority, which is itself incoherent. He thus feels entitled to dismiss as meaningless (except for its role as "ideological rhetoric" aimed at helping certain political interests) all debates and discussions about the morality of violence and about the respective merits of violent and nonviolent political tactics.[28] Some of what I have to say bears upon these startling conclusions, but I shall not comment upon his basic argument against the notion of legitimate political authority except to record my conviction that it is unsuccessful.

Wolff defines violence as "the illegitimate or unauthorised use of force to effect decisions against the will or desire of others."[29] Like one interpretation of Galtung's definition, this has the consequence that one could never be violent to another if he sought to be injured. But this is surely wrong, for a bank robber's accomplice may want the robber to beat him up in order to throw the police off the scent. More significantly, perhaps, it also makes a normative political element part of the meaning of the term "violence." Wolff does allow what he calls a descriptive sense of the word too, but this is

---

[26] I do not mean to deny the value of metaphorical or extended employment of the term "violence" in appropriate contexts. Heinrich Boll's novel *The Lost Honour of Katherina Blum*, for instance, is subtitled *How Violence Develops and Where It Can Lead*, and it makes impressive play with the devastating effects of media smears and distortions upon the personality of an innocent woman caught up in a police investigation. Katherina's actual violence (she eventually murders the journalist principally responsible for the destruction of her reputation) is made to seem an almost natural, healthy reaction against the unscrupulous power of the popular press that has shattered her private world in ways analogous to a series of blows. There may well be a case for treating some of the episodes in the narrative as psychological violence, a category about which I shall have more to say later, but much of the novel's success lies in its symbolic and metaphorical deployment of the idea of violence and the ironic parallels between the effects of violence and the impact of journalistic irresponsibility and sensation seeking.

[27] Wolff, "On Violence," pp. 601–616.

[28] Ibid., p. 602.

[29] Ibid., p. 606.

not, as might be suspected, a restricted sense, since it still contains a reference to political authority but this time merely de facto instead of legitimate. A de facto authority is one "generally accepted" as legitimate in the territory. He goes on to say,

Descriptively speaking, the attack on Hitler's life during the second World War was an act of violence, but one might perfectly well deny that it was violent in the strict sense, on the grounds that Hitler's regime was illegitimate. On similar grounds, it is frequently said that police behaviour toward workers or ghetto dwellers or demonstrators is violent, even when it is clearly within the law for the authority issuing the law is illegitimate.[30]

The strange consequences of Wolff's position are here strikingly illustrated. It is tempting to think that anyone who believes that the deliberate blowing up of the conference room in the attempt to kill Hitler, thereby successfully killing and wounding others, is *not* a violent act needs sympathy. Independently of any question of legitimacy, this is, on the face of it, the sort of act that should be a test of a definition of violence. If the definition doesn't determine it as an act of violence, then it is a defective definition. The question of whether the act was illegitimate or unauthorised is simply irrelevant. It may be replied that such a reaction merely shows the strength of my own commitment to a restricted understanding of the term "violence"; but, on the contrary, it is surely rather an indication of how remote Wolff's usage is from linguistic realities, and of how difficult it is to discuss serious political issues clearly with such a definitional apparatus.

As Wolff develops his discussion, the problem becomes even more striking. He says, for instance, apropos of the student demonstrations at Columbia University in 1968, that it is "totally wrong" to say such things as "In the Columbia case violence was justified," even though, as he believes, the whole affair seems to have been a quite prudent and restrained use of force. Wolff believes this to be so in part because of his definition of violence, since the sentence comes close to saying "In the Columbia case violence as the illegitimate use of force to effect decisions against the will or desire of others was legitimate." (Actually he does not object to the sentence in quite such direct terms but argues that it implies the doctrine of legitimate government or legitimate authority, and since this is an absurdity, so is the sentence itself.) Yet if there is any absurdity here it surely resides in the implications of Wolff's definition, since on a more restrictive definition of "violence" that makes no reference to legitimate authority, we can ask reasonably clear moral and political questions about the students' use of violence and hence decide the quite separate question of whether or not it was justified. Some of the issues thus raised will be similar, if not identical,

[30] Ibid.

to, those Wolff wants to treat in the more roundabout and, I think, contrived way of employing the much looser terminology of "force."

Wolff seems at times to recognise this, and in discussing what he calls "the doctrine of non-violence" he says that if violence is understood (nonstrictly) as the use of force to interfere with somebody in a direct physical way or to injure him physically, then the doctrine of nonviolence is "merely a subjective queasiness having no moral rationale." He cites the case of a sit-in at a lunch counter that not only deprives the proprietor of profits, but also may ruin him if persisted in. Wolff says that he has been done

...a much greater injury than would be accomplished by a mere beating in a dark alley. He may deserve to be ruined, of course, but, if so, then he probably also deserves to be beaten. A penchant for such indirect coercion as a boycott or a sit-in is morally questionable, for it merely leaves the dirty work to the bank that forecloses on the mortgage or the policeman who carries out the eviction.[31]

Stirring stuff, but not, I believe, a contribution to the debate about the respective merits of violent and nonviolent forms of political action or protest. This is not the place to engage in that debate, but plainly it raises serious issues that are simply obscured by Wolff's treatment. Just to take the example of the sit-in: the normal defence of such an action would not be in terms of an intention to ruin the proprietor and bring him to destitution, but to bring sharply to his attention and the attention of apathetic or hostile citizens, *within* the framework of laws and conventions that you all to some extent share, your belief that his operations have severely harmed others and are likely to bring inconvenience and financial discomfort upon him unless he mends his ways. There are numerous considerations that may be advanced to support a preference for this way of proceeding over beating him up or maiming or killing him. It may plausibly be argued that it is tactically better from the point of view of public reaction, that it has better social consequences, that violence is prone to get out of hand, and that the victim suffers much less. When Wolff says, "He may deserve to be ruined, of course, but, if so, then he probably also deserves to be beaten," he is engaging in no more than schoolboy bravado. Even if ruin were the object of the exercise it is far from obvious that this is worse or on a par with the effects of a beating, which include possible permanent physical and psychological damage, if not death. One may very well have good reason for putting someone out of business without thereby being justified in mutilating or killing him.

On the assumption that no more needs to be said about Wolff's detailed argumentation, I want to conclude my consideration of legitimist definitions by raising a final objection to their procedures that is, I think, a very serious one. What will such definitions allow us to say about that preeminent use of

---

[31] Ibid., p. 610.

violence, warfare? In the case of Wolff's definition, for instance, the absurd consequence is immediately generated that if there are two sovereign states, both of which have politically legitimate governments, then they may not be engaged in violence even though they are bombarding each other with nuclear rockets. This will happen if both legitimate governments legally authorise the particular resort to war. This is surely not an uncommon or fantastic case. Wolff would be saved from this absurdity only by his belief that there is no such thing as political legitimacy, but others who propose legitimist definitions, such as Hook and Honderich, have no such escape route. Honderich, it is true, explicitly excludes warfare from the scope of his discussion but purports nonetheless to be discussing political violence. The restriction of political violence to internal or domestic political contexts is, I think, astonishing, and the case of warfare rightly raises difficulties for his definition, which includes reference to "a use of force prohibited by law." His full definition of political violence is: "a considerable or destroying use of force against persons or things, a use of force prohibited by law and directed to a change in the politics, personnel or system of government, and hence to changes in society."[32] As we can see from this definition, the problem posed by the example of warfare strikes at the roots of the legitimist outlook. For Honderich, even the *illegal* internal use of severe force by police, security organisations, and even by nongovernmental agencies is not political violence if it is aimed at preserving the status quo! Given Honderich's generally radical stance, this is not only a curious outcome but also exhibits starkly the tendency of legitimist theories to present the use of violence as posing a moral problem only for those who think of deploying force *against* the established or legitimate government. Yet surely even the legal employment of "destroying force" raises issues about the role and nature of political violence. Comparisons between states, for instance, can rightly raise questions about the moral standing of greater or less recourse to violence, and degrees of readiness to have such recourse, in the legitimate administrations of the different polities. Such questions not only are real but also are clearly related to the questions faced by those who contemplate the use of violence against legal authority, whether that of their own state or of another.

Let me turn all too briefly now to a clarification and defence of a restricted definition of violence. In a sense, most of this chapter has been a defence of

---

[32] Honderich, *Violence for Equality*, p. 154. Honderich's general definition of violence makes reference neither to law nor to political change but only to a use of force (etc.) "that offends against a norm" (p. 153). He could thus admit a category of illegal state violence and presumably even such legal state violence as could be construed as offending against a norm (whatever that might mean). Yet the facts remain that he (i) shows no interest in working with the broader notion of violence, (ii) gives no idea of what sort of norms he has in mind, and (iii) is, in any case, committed to seeing these exercises of violence as nonpolitical whatever their rationale.

such a definition, for it has sought to show the inadequacies of its competitors, but I think that a little more is required at least by way of clarification of possible misunderstandings.

I cited earlier the OED definition, and I want to endorse something like it, but first we must distinguish violence from *force* and from *coercion*. A good deal of confusion in the literature is generated by the failure to make these distinctions. A few examples will make clear the need to distinguish. Take the examples of what Ronald Miller has called "gentle removal" – the courteous use of force to remove unresisting but uncooperative demonstrators from a building (admittedly rare, but not impossible), or the gentle but firm restraining of someone who wants to rush into a blazing building to rescue relatives, or even, a slightly different kind of case, the use of force by a surgeon in operating to remove a piece of shrapnel from a man's leg in order to save his life.[33] For coercion, we need only consider that threats are coercive, and they need not even be threats to do violence (e.g., a threat to tell someone's wife of his disreputable behaviour). Various classical nonviolent tactics of resistance and demonstration are coercive – for example, the blocking of a road on which officials usually proceed by having large numbers of demonstrators lie down on the roadway. Violence is, of course, one way of coercing, but only one.

Ideally, at this point I should provide definitions of force and coercion, but limitations of space will have to be my excuse for dodging that difficult task here.[34] Instead I want to turn to the OED definition of violence mentioned earlier and raise some questions about it. Recall that it defines violence as: "The exercise of physical force so as to inflict injury on or damage to persons or property; action or conduct characterised by this."

The first problem with this is that it rules out the possibility of psychological violence, and there is at least a case for including it. I suspect that whether we want to allow for a nonmetaphorical use of the term "violence" in the psychological cases will depend upon whether we can realistically view some of these cases as involving the application of force. It is useful here to think of the notion of overpowering that seems as if it must figure as an element in the analysis of force. Now if we consider a case in which someone skilfully works upon another's emotions and fears with a combination of words and deeds short of physical force, but with intentionally overpowering effects, then we may well feel that this is close enough to the physical model to be a case of violence. Newton Garver gives an interesting and profoundly sad example of the Arizona parents who decided to punish their daughter's

---

33 Ronald B. Miller, "Violence, Force and Coercion," in Jerome A. Shaffer (ed.), *Violence* (New York: McKay, 1971), p. 27.

34 Ibid. For an extended treatment of coercion, see Robert Nozich, "Coercion," in Sidney Morgenbesset, Patrick Suppes, and Morton White (eds.), *Philosophy, Science, and Method* (New York: St. Martin's Press, 1969).

sexual transgression in an unusual way. The girl, Linda Ault, owned a dog, Beauty, of which she was very fond. According to a newspaper report,

the Aults' and Linda took the dog into the desert near their home. They had the girl dig a shallow grave. Then Mrs. Ault grasped the dog between her hands, and Mr. Ault gave his daughter a 22 calibre pistol and told her to shoot the dog. Instead the girl put the pistol to her right temple and shot herself.[35]

Clearly a dreadful act, and perhaps deserving of the name of violence, but if we do so treat it this will not be because of the reasons given by Garver (which have to do with deprivation of autonomy and lead pretty quickly to a version of structural violence). There is a tendency in the literature to slide from psychological violence to structural violence, but this seems to embody a confusion, since it rests on the tendency to think of psychological violence as *impalpable* and then to feel that its admission endorses the even more impalpable structural violence. However, the examples that make the category of psychological violence plausible are all very palpable indeed. In Garver's example, for instance, what strikes one is the sheer immediacy and specificity of the pressure that is brought to bear upon the unfortunate girl with such overwhelming effect. Even if she had not shot herself, we would feel that she had still been the victim of severe and damaging force. The surrounding circumstances of the outrage are tinged with physical violence, for not only was she ordered to kill with a gun, one also imagines that force was used to get her to dig the grave and even to get her to the place of punishment (though we are given no details of this). Consequently, to describe the case as one of quiet violence and hence a "halfway house" to structural violence is unconvincing.

A further category concerns those cases of great damage that do not seem to involve force though they do involve physical means. Poisoning is often given as an example, and Harris gives as well the case of the Belfast children who tie a cheese-wire between two lampposts across a street at a height of about six feet. As one of the kids says, "There's always a soldier standing on the back of the jeep; even with the search lights he can't see the wire in the dark. It's just at the right height to catch his throat."[36] Harris concludes from such examples that we can have an *act of violence* in the absence of a *violent act*. But for most of his examples we can surely appeal to the "accordion effect" beloved of philosophers of action. The planned and fully intended results of stretching the wire are properly describable as what the children did, as their act. Their violent act was not merely stretching gently a wire across a road but ripping a man's throat open. This resort is certainly available where the incorporated consequences are intended by the agent, and Harris's cases are all of this kind. Two of his examples, however, seem to raise problems for the

---

[35] Garver, "What Violence Is," pp. 225–226.
[36] Harris, *Violence and Responsibility*, p. 16.

restricted definition, even acknowledging the accordion effect. They both focus upon the interpretation of the term "force" in the definition rather than upon the idea of a positive act. One example is stabbing to death with a stiletto gently slid between the ribs. (Harris somewhat painfully jokes that this is "the thin edge of the wedge.") A second example (or class of examples) concerns poisoning or gassing. I have not produced a definition of force, but my instinct is to treat the stiletto case as a use of force, especially when the immediate, overpoweringly forceful effects upon the victim's body are taken into account (and the killer's intention certainly encompasses them.) As to poisons, if we take a case of slow poisoning (i.e., slow-acting and requiring repeated dosing) where the destructive effects are gradual and cumulative, easily mimicking a slow-acting sickness, I suspect that we should not call the poisoning a violent act – it is one that could be ordered or done by the proverbially fastidious criminal who abhors violence. By contrast, the use of poison gas in war, or similar swift-acting poisons, would be much more like dealing a blow, and fairly clearly a violent act.

The concept of force needs more attention, but I shall assume that this can be successfully negotiated and that the poisoning cases can either be dealt with in the way suggested or else treated as territory lying on an uncomfortable borderline between violence and nonviolence. It is also relevant to certain cases of poisoning that a background of violence will colour our attitudes to a particular case. Consider, for instance, a siege or a blockade that may not be violent inasmuch as troops or ships are just patrolling and waiting for starvation or despair to produce surrender. Nonetheless, the waiting part of the siege is usually a sort of interlude in a violent campaign, and the siege itself essentially involves the declared intention to use very considerable violence against anyone who attempts to leave the besieged area. Most sieges, in fact, produce a great deal of actual violence. Against such a background it would be natural to describe even a siege in which no shooting or killing occurred as an exercise in violence.

Finally, we might ask: what is the point in having a concept of violence of this kind? Without an answer to this question, the criticism of alternative definitions is incomplete. An answer must begin by noting certain very general facts about our condition. Life is hazardous in many different ways, and we may be harmed by natural disasters and accidents, or by disease, or the indifference and lack of consideration of our fellows, or by social arrangements that are to our disadvantage. We can sometimes take steps to guard against all of these – we can avoid certain areas, move from certain communities, cultivate friends, and so on. But in addition to all of the hazards mentioned, there is another that many people fear very greatly, namely, the forceful intrusion into their lives of those who are intent upon inflicting harm and injury upon their person. It is not surprising that this should be so and that a distinctive way of speaking should arise to mark the reality to which we react in this way.

Nor is it surprising that a particular type of concern should exist for this kind of intrusion into our lives. In the first place, we know that human malevolence is liable to be effective and difficult to avoid just because it is directed by intelligence; in the second place, the unjustified employment of violence damages the character and worth of the user in distinctive ways, or so many people believe – hence the point of expressions such as "bully," "sadist," and "thug"; third, the principal way of avoiding such malevolent intrusion is to resort to violence oneself or to have agents do it for you, and this in turn may be dangerous both in the short and the long term, as is so vividly dramatised in Hobbes's picture of a State of Nature;[37] fourth, it is arguable that even the justified resort to violence has damaging effects upon those who employ it even if they remain physically unharmed – this argument marks one area in which pacifist contentions are commonly introduced, but even nonpacifists can acknowledge the appeal of some such arguments; fifth, and relatedly, there is the fact that violence, particularly large-scale violence, is hard to control and that its consequences are hard to predict. The third, fourth, and fifth reasons make it plausible that resort to violence, even when morally justifiable, should commonly be regarded as a matter for regret. More generally, all of those considerations bear upon debates about the comparability of violent and nonviolent tactics, about the advantages of societies with a low level of officially sanctioned violence, and about the appeal as a social ideal of what Galtung would call negative peace.

It must of course be conceded that this ideal does not have equal weight with all who consider it. Although anyone can recognise the distinctive facts that underpin the concept of violence I have been defending, not everyone will have the same reactions to them. There will be variations in both personal and cultural terms here even amongst persons and communities who are in no obvious way corrupt or wicked. There are individuals who are much more sensitive to and worried about violence than others, just as there are whole groups, such as warrior castes, for whom violence is, to some degree, an accepted and even welcome part of their lives. Such groups may be less enthusiastic than others about projects to limit the scope of violence within and between communities, and an argument with them would involve exploring further the value of peace in comparison to other values as well as some further discussion of the negative effects of violence. This further discussion will be pursued in the next few chapters, and in Chapter 13 the ideal of peace will be directly addressed.

---

[37] The mention of Hobbes should remind us that one traditional way of viewing the legitimacy of the state is to see it as the safest form of the agency defence against the dangers of violence. Here too we may locate some of the point behind legitimist definitions of violence, because the authorised violence of the state is seen as so different from the violence against which it offers protection as not to deserve the name violence at all. Nonetheless, violence it is, and even where authorised there remain moral questions about its employment.

3

Violence and Justice

War is waged by men; not by beasts, or by gods. It is a peculiarly human activity. To call it a crime against humanity is to miss at least half its significance; it is also the punishment of a crime. That raises a moral question, the kind of problem with which the present age is disinclined to deal.

Frederick Manning[1]

We have been discussing the nature of violence, and it is time to turn more directly to its moral assessment. Thomas Hobbes argued persuasively that the problem of violence lies at the heart of civil society. Hobbes thought that violence was endemic to human life and that in pre-civil or noncivil conditions (his "state of nature") it created such miseries that reason required men to alienate, almost entirely, their natural right to self-protection in order to set up a sovereign with the sole right of the sword. In Hobbes's vision, the natural desire for self-preservation, and the peace that ensures it, will enable people to live together in security so long as they can be certain that there are workable violent sanctions to restrain and control those who break the peace or are tempted to do so. The solution to the awful problem posed by the widespread violence of the state of nature is to monopolise the potentiality for violence in the one agency.

There are many problems with Hobbes's picture of civil society and its title to legitimacy, just as there are many problems with his theory of human nature. It may be argued, in particular, that his description of nonsocial life is, at once, too atomistic and too bleak, and also that the state exists to do more than protect its citizens against violent onslaughts. I have a good deal of sympathy with these two criticisms (though there are nuances in Hobbes's

---

[1] Frederick Manning, *The Middle Parts of Fortune* (London: Granada, 1977), Author's Prefatory Note. Manning, an Australian, himself fought in World War I in the British forces. The novel was first published under the title *Her Privates We*. The reference of both titles is to Shakespeare's *Hamlet*, act 2, scene 2, lines 233–234.

theory that may blunt some of their force), but it can hardly be denied that Hobbes presents a powerful case for three things:

1. The pervasiveness and deep-rootedness of the tendency to violence in human life, and the damage it does.
2. The need for limiting the damage by placing violence under the control of agreement, convention, and law – in short, at least common reason, and preferably common morality (which Hobbes thought amounted to the same thing).
3. The legitimacy of the state viewed at least as a protection agency and hence the legitimacy of the state's use of violence in certain circumstances.

We do not need to endorse the details of Hobbes's own political philosophy to find these conclusions persuasive, and together they constitute a minimum case for the legitimacy of the state's employment of violence for internal purposes, that is, for the protection of citizens against violence and other severe violations or injuries within the state. But our concern here is with more external matters, such as violence between states or violence within the state aimed not at particular personal injuries or their prevention but at the state's overthrow or at dramatic political change. And here our ready agreement with Hobbes at least needs more discussion. Hobbes himself thought that the protection rationale extended to the state's entitlement to wage wars in order to protect its citizens from foreign attack, but that it constituted a barrier to citizens taking arms against their own state.

On the question of interstate war, the ready acceptance of (2) and to some extent (1) needs further exploration, since there are certain attitudes toward war represented amongst ordinary people and voiced by distinguished thinkers and leaders that depart from the concern to restrict and control violence embodied in (2). These are what I shall call "romantic" outlooks on war or more generally on political violence. They are clearly part of what has been called militarism by some thinkers, and would qualify as extreme militarism on my understanding of the term.[2] Romantic militarism sees war in a positive, enthusiastic light because it is in itself thought to be liberating or virtue-promoting. The romantic approach to the benefits of war is thus more intrinsic than militarism that is nourished by pessimism about the possibilities for peace and international cooperation. The latter emphasises the need for large standing armies and encourages military industries and constant weaponry innovations, because it regards major military enterprise and its institutions as indispensable to security and even peace. But the instruments themselves such militarists tend to regard as morally neutral. Not so the romantics.

---

[2] See Martin Ceadel, *Thinking about Peace and War* (Oxford: Oxford University Press, 1987), Chapter 3.

Such romantics are these days apt to be ignored, and, for my part, I could wish that there were fewer of them, but romanticism has been historically influential and far more common than we are inclined to think today. Its existence qualifies the common thought that everyone is for peace; they only differ about the means for achieving it. We earlier saw romantic militarism at work in Hegel's picture of war as a prophylactic against "foulness" and "corruption" in nations. What is essentially the same thought, plus some of the traditional sexism associated with this outlook on war, occurs in Mussolini's reflections on war:

War alone brings up to their highest tension all human energies and puts the stamp of nobility upon the peoples who have the courage to meet it. . . . War is to the man what maternity is to the woman. I do not believe in perpetual peace not only do I not believe in it but I find it depressing and a negation of all the fundamental virtues of man.[3]

This was written in 1932, but it echoes a romanticism about the fulfilling nature of violence that was common before World War I. There is an equally extreme instance in the futurist anarchist Marinetti's writings in 1909:

We want to glorify war – the sole hygiene of the world – militarism, patriotism, the destructive gesture of the anarchists, beautiful ideas that kill, and contempt for women.[4]

Georges Sorel's *Reflections on Violence*, with its enthusiasm for working-class violence, was perhaps the most interesting manifestation of it. Sorel's example suggests that the outlook was not restricted to conservative or right-wing thinkers, and indeed a striking version of it can be found in that bastion of liberal thought, the German romantic Wilhelm von Humboldt, whose writings on liberty so influenced John Stuart Mill. Speaking of the influence of war on national character, von Humboldt proclaimed that

war seems to be one of the most salutary phenomena for the culture of human nature; and it is not without regret that I see it disappearing more and more from the scene. It is the fearful extremity through which all that active courage – all that endurance and fortitude – are steeled and tested, which afterwards achieve such varied results in the ordinary conduct of life, and which alone give it that strength and diversity, without which facility is weakness, and unity is inanity.[5]

Another liberal thinker who goes part of the way with this sort of thinking is Benjamin Constant, who believed that at "certain stages in the history

[3] Quoted in Sissela Bok, *A Strategy for Peace* (New York: Pantheon, 1989), p. 174.
[4] Filippo Tommaso Marinetti, "The Futurist Manifesto," *Le Figaro*, February 20, 1909.
[5] Wilhelm von Humboldt, *The Limits of State Action*, ed. and trans. J. W. Burrow (Indianapolis: Liberty Fund, 1993), p. 41.

of mankind, war is simply in man's nature" and that, during those stages, warfare

favours the development of his finest and grandest faculties. It opens up to him a treasury of precious enjoyments. It forms in him that greatness of soul, skill, sangfroid, scorn for death, without which he could never be confident that there was any form of cowardice he might not display, and even crime he might not commit. War teaches him heroic devotion and makes him form sublime friendships.[6]

Even Kant himself, whose advocacy of perpetual peace provoked Hegel's indignation, was filled at times with an almost identical euphoria about the merits of war and an anxiety almost comically similar to Hegel's about the vices that peace might produce. Speaking of the "special reverence" for the soldier that he thought distinctive of even highly civilised societies, Kant says:

War itself, provided it is conducted with order and a sacred respect for the rights of civilians, has something sublime about it, and gives nations that carry it on in such a manner a stamp of mind only the more sublime the more numerous the dangers to which they are exposed, and which they are able to meet with fortitude. On the other hand, a prolonged peace favours the predominance of a mere commercial spirit, and with it a debasing self-interest, cowardice, and effeminacy, and tends to degrade the character of the nation.[7]

The vogue for this sort of outlook was seriously damaged by the static horror of the events of 1914–18, but the attitude persists in our day, as some of the popular reactions in Britain to the Falklands war seemed to show, and some revolutionary tracts have endorsed it in the fairly recent past, most notably Frantz Fanon's *The Wretched of the Earth*.[8] It is important to note that the attitude of romantic militarism, as revealed in these quotations, shows a surprising indifference to the question whether a war is justified in the first place. This is a matter to which we shall return.

The horrible history of warfare, especially, though not exclusively, the dramatic carnage of the twentieth century, makes it easy to dismiss romantic militarism as repellent and renders mysterious its appeal to so many illustrious intellects and to ordinary people. There are, however, some genuine realities that partially explain the appeal. The militarist euphoria about violence stems from a distrust of passivity and an enthusiasm for action, striving,

---

[6] Benjamin Constant, *Political Writings*, ed. and trans. Biancamaria Fontana (Cambridge: Cambridge University Press, 1988), p. 51. Constant argues more cautiously, however (pp. 52–55), that those days are now (in the early years of the nineteenth century) long gone, and war "has lost its charm as well as its utility. Man is no longer driven to it either by interest or by passion" (p. 55).

[7] Immanuel Kant, *The Critique of Judgement*, trans. J. C. Meredith (Oxford: Clarendon Press, 1928), Book 11, "Analytic of the Sublime B: The Dynamically Sublime in Nature," pp. 112–113.

[8] Frantz Fanon, *The Wretched of the Earth*, trans. Constance Farrington (New York: Grove Press, 1963).

and contention. Such commitments may not be beyond dispute, especially where they involve a certain glorification of competition and disdain for more reflective modes of life, yet, in appropriate contexts, they are perfectly intelligible and in part defensible. Whether they can be fully defended will not concern me here, but what must be insisted on is that the emphasis upon vigour, action, courage, healthy striving, and so on need not reach so far as to endorse violence and war. It is one thing to point to the virtues of self-discipline, energetic activity, endurance against adversity, courageous risk taking, vigorous competition, and the overcoming of obstacles. It is quite another to maintain that these virtues require, or are best realised in, maiming and killing fellow human beings, and that war is, as Sidgwick puts it (without endorsement), "an indispensable school of virtue."[9] The same point applies to those who rightly extol the values of solidarity, comradeship, and self-sacrifice that can be found in armies in time of war and that may even extend at such times to endangered civilian populations.[10] These values are important, but they can, and should, be found in other communities than armed forces, and in other contexts than war. To be fair to von Humboldt, he recognised that there were other activities that could foster the character traits he admired, but he thought that they were somehow dependent on the primary fostering power of war. They did not themselves promote the same kind of greatness and glory as war.[11] It is, I think, mysterious how war can be given this preeminence when it is admitted that other activities can equally involve risk of death and injury, solidarity with comrades, vigorous competition, and so on. The only feature distinctive of war seems to be that you get the opportunity to maim and kill and to be maimed and killed by other human beings; even if this is in a good cause, it can hardly add to the moral value of war compared to its peaceful counterparts. If the rightness of one's cause is deemed irrelevant, the case against romanticism is even stronger. And this case would be decisive even were the values of solidarity, self-sacrifice, and so on to be more intensely realised in combat than in more peaceful communal activities involving high risk, since the existence of these virtues needs to be weighed, not only against the suffering and loss of life involved in war, but also against the flourishing of vices that is characteristic of most warfare. The removal of so many normal restraints of civil life tends to foster the vices of arrogance, insularity, contempt for the enemy and anyone who can be seen to stand in the way of victory, conformism, and, of course, sexual violence against women. Those who enthuse about violence and war with a focus only on the virtues it may promote are like

---

9 Henry Sidgwick, "The Morality of Strife," in his *Practical Ethics* (London: Swann Sonnenschein and Co., 1898), p. 90.

10 In Sidgwick's words, "the unreserved devotion, the ardour of self-sacrifice for duty and the common good, which war tends to develop." See ibid., p. 90.

11 See von Humboldt, *The Limits of State Action*, pp. 41–42.

people who recognise the bonds of loyalty and honour amongst certain sorts of thieves and take this as a ground for advocating theft. But romanticism about war generally has not traditionally extended to romanticism about mere criminal violence, no matter how much risk and solidarity the latter requires.

Nonetheless, in rejecting romantic militarism, we should realise, as did William James in an important antiwar essay, the necessity of fostering what James called "moral equivalents of war," that is, activities and contexts in which the virtues and values that can be exhibited in war have a chance to be less damagingly embodied.[12] James certainly goes too far, however, in accommodating the war party's vision of these virtues, with its contempt for the feminine and its emphasis on toughness, competition, and dominance. Summarising the romantic militarist's case for war, he catches the flavour of their horror of the supposed alternative to war: "a world of clerks and teachers, of co-education and zo-ophily, of 'consumer's leagues' and 'associated charities', of industrialism unlimited, and feminism unabashed. No scorn, no hardness, no valour any more! Fie upon such a cattleyard of a planet!"[13] He proposes as a substitute for war

a conscription of the whole youthful population to form for a certain number of years a part of the army enlisted against *Nature*. . . . The military ideals of hardihood and discipline would be wrought into the growing fibre of the people; no one would remain blind as the luxurious classes now are blind, to man's relations to the globe he lives on, and to the permanently sour and hard foundations of his higher life.[14]

After working in coal mines and fishing fleets, on railroads and skyscrapers, and so on, "our gilded youths" would get "the childishness knocked out of them" and, having "paid their blood-tax, done their own part in the immemorial human warfare against nature; they would tread the earth more proudly, the women would value them more highly, they would be better fathers and teachers of the following generation."[15] James's picture of what is worth preserving of military values and virtues for nonmilitary purposes is clearly contaminated to some degree by dubious attitudes toward nature and toward the gentler aspects of life, but there is no doubt that his general strategy of providing alternative outlets for the valuable energies and laudable ideals currently harnessed to warfare is a promising one, though we may debate the value of compulsion for achieving it.

In rejecting romantic militarism, we must surely conclude that Hobbes's moral about the need to place violence under the control of agreement,

[12] William James, "The Moral Equivalent of War," in his *Essays in Religion and Morality* (Cambridge, MA: Harvard University Press, 1982).
[13] Ibid., p. 166.
[14] Ibid., p. 171.
[15] Ibid., p. 172.

convention, and law applies at least as strongly to the international sphere and its ramifications as it does to the domestic scene. The search for alternatives to war, and other forms of large-scale violence, is an important one, but in the meantime there is surely an imperative to place the resort to and conduct of war and related forms of political violence under the control of common reason and common morality.

Violence and Human Nature

As for lesson (1) drawn from Hobbes, if it is treated as an empirical fact about people over the centuries it is unlikely to be denied, though we need from time to time to be reminded of it. Under one interpretation, however, it is more disputable, for if by "deep-rooted" we mean that the tendency to violence is entirely or mostly the product of human nature rather than environment, then some social and political theorists would reject the suggestion. Some, if not all, strands of pacifist thinking would reject it, as would most anarchist thought, which stresses the basically cooperative nature of human beings and tends to attribute our violent tendencies to the effect of malign social structures and arrangements. Anarchist philosophy also rejects (3) because it sees small-scale cooperative self-governing communities as providing better ways of dealing with the problem of violence (as it conceives of it).

The debate about nature versus nurture, the innate versus the acquired, is difficult to settle wherever it arises, in part because of the obscurity of the basic terminology and in part because of the opacity of much of the evidence that is supposed to bear upon the debate. I suspect that the tendency to resort to violence to achieve one's ends is both much less "innate" than some intellectual fashions suppose and much harder to eradicate than some pacifists would have us believe. The innateness hypothesis is usually associated with a concept of aggression that is at once too individualist and too little related to the cultural and symbolic values that usually dominate resort to war to be as illuminating as theorists like Lorenz and Ardrey require.[16] Even if some notion of aggression as innate helps to explain certain observations of animal behaviour, and some human behaviour, war is a very different phenomenon from that usually invoked under the heading of aggression in such studies. Indeed, the aggressive displays of animals within their own species seldom involve killing, since they usually result in flight or submission and its acceptance. Moreover, if we are to speak of what is innate, then there is considerable psychological, historical, and indeed common-sense evidence to suggest that there is in most human beings a deep, primal

---

[16] Robert Ardrey, *The Territorial Imperative: A Personal Inquiry into the Animal Origins of Property and Nations* (New York: Atheneum, 1966); Konrad Lorenz, *On Aggression* (New York: Harcourt Brace and World, 1966).

resistance to killing other humans, a resistance that military and political leaders often need to work very hard to overcome.

This resistance is illustrated by the striking claims made in the latter part of the twentieth century about the low percentage of infantry soldiers in various wars who actually used their weapons against the enemy. Brigadier General S. L. A. Marshall's pioneering, but controversial, work purported to show that only 15 to 25 percent of U.S. riflemen in certain combat theatres during World War II actually shot at the enemy.[17] Some subsequent research has tended to confirm some of Marshall's conclusions about reluctance to kill. A British analysis of killing rates in more than 100 battles selected from the nineteenth and twentieth centuries showed that the killing potential of the weapons in the hands of soldiers with opportunity to kill was much greater than the actual number of casualties. The researchers highlighted "unwillingness to take part [in combat] as the main factor."[18] It should be noted, however, that Marshall's research has been subjected to severe criticism, one critic going so far as to describe him as "something of a charlatan."[19] Certainly, it seems that Marshall's methodology, especially with respect to his confident declaration of firing ratios, was flawed.[20] It has even been argued persuasively that he simply invented his statistics and the famed firing ratio.[21] Nonetheless, the widespread acceptance of Marshall's claims for so long in the military and elsewhere suggests that there is something in the "reluctance to kill" thesis, though no doubt the differing circumstances of various combat conditions will have something to do with how soldiers respond. David Grossman argues plausibly that the massive rates of psychological illness found among combat troops who have been under fire is attributable in large part to the stress caused by being put in a position where there is a requirement to kill other human beings, rather than solely to the effects of fear and anxiety about being killed or injured. There is clearly a case for seeing the reluctance to kill as something that deserves to be invoked as much as the drive to aggression in the context of discussions of human nature.

On the other hand, it is hard to believe that the resort to war that is so persistent a part of our history has no roots in the human make-up.

---

[17] Reported in Lieutenant Colonel Dave Grossman, *On Killing: The Psychological Cost of Learning to Kill in War and Society* (Boston: Little, Brown, 1995), p. 3.

[18] Ibid., p. 16.

[19] Andrew J. Bacevich, reviewing Russell W. Glenn, *Reading Athena's Dance Card: Men against Fire in Vietnam* (Annapolis, MD: Naval Institute Press, 2000), *Journal of Cold War Studies* 4, no. 2 (2002), pp. 135–137. This description is probably exaggerated, but the doubts about Marshall's methods are real enough.

[20] See also, Roger J. Spiller, "S. L. A. Marshall and the Ratio of Fire," *RUSI Journal* 133 (1988), pp. 63–71.

[21] Ibid., p. 68.

What roots it has may, of course, be deeply conditioned by continuing social circumstances rather than provided by genes; the nature/nurture division, or, for that matter, the genes/environment division, is too neat for most of the interesting things we need to say in explaining human behaviour. One intriguing hypothesis that has recently emerged is provided by Barbara Ehrenreich's speculations about the role of a certain sort of fear in our history. She argues that much of the impetus to war has its roots in the centuries of human conflict with animal predators during which a premium was placed on the capacity to organise killing of the feared predators. Hunter warriors became crucial, heroic figures who delivered small communities from the horror of the wild predating animals. With the development of agriculture and the decline in the availability of wild animals to be hunted for food, the valued hunter warrior needed a new role and became himself a predator on the food stocks of other human communities. So began the institutionalising of war. Ehrenreich does not believe that this development can be wholly explained in terms of genetic disposition, and there is clearly a deal of imaginative speculation in her story.[22] It also suffers from some of the defects of all "single key" explanatory theories that hope to provide the one big idea to explain a very complex phenomenon. Nonetheless, it offers one plausible account of the way in which war could have come to have the prominent significance in community life that has marked much of the history of our species, without invoking deeply problematic deterministic myths such as genes for war or aggression.

I do not here propose a final adjudication on the general problem of explaining the endurance of war. I shall merely take it that the historical record shows how prevalent and persistent the tendency to organised political violence actually has been and is, but I shall also assume that it is possible to do something about it, since there are other profound but countervailing human tendencies to which reasoned and emotional appeal may be made. That is, I shall assume that the resort to violence is part of the sphere of human agency and action, unlike the persistent phenomena of sweating and sleeping, and so comes under moral judgement and possible human control. This is as true of political as of criminal violence. We should then refuse to view warfare as a purely natural disaster like an earthquake or a flood. When people talk of the permanence, persistence, or "normalcy" of war they sometimes make it sound like that – or rather, not so much like a natural disaster as like unpleasant weather, the inevitability of war is made to seem like the inevitability of winter. Georges Santayana gets close to this when he writes: "There is eternal war in nature, a war in which every cause is ultimately lost and every nation destroyed. War is but resisted change:

[22] Barbara Ehrenreich, *Blood Rites: Origins and History of the Passions of War* (London: Virago, 1997).

and change must needs be resisted so long as the organism it would destroy retains any vitality."[23] Nonetheless, although the persistent recurrence of war points to something important, it does not annul the obvious fact that wars are fought by men *for reasons*, though no doubt very complex and sometimes secret reasons. As William James puts it concisely: "The fatalistic view of the war-function is to me nonsense, for I know that war-making is due to definite motives and subject to prudential checks and reasonable criticisms, just like any other form of enterprise."[24]

The intellectual tradition of the just war is one way of providing such checks and criticisms. There are other ways, most notably the traditions of realism and pacifism.[25] Both of these are, I think, rather closer to just war thinking than is usually supposed. I shall argue for this later in the case of realism, though I shall also reject some of its key doctrines. I shall examine pacifism in Chapter 13. At a minimum, the just war tradition allows (on one plausible construal) that just as there is, in certain circumstances, a right to defend oneself or others with violence against the violence of others, so the state has a right to use violence against outsiders that is similarly grounded in a right of protection (whether or not this is justified, as Hobbes thought, by a social contract). More expansively, the tradition has allowed that the state's right to enforce justice domestically may also extend, in certain circumstances, to the enforcement of justice in the international order. We shall examine how natural and how problematic these extensions of a "domestic analogy" can be, but, for now, let us turn to realism.

The Place of Realism

Both the persistence of war and its extreme nature have led some to conclude that war is either beyond the reach of moral judgement or that it is outright immoral. The former direction is the path of what is called "realism" and the latter of pacifism. As we shall see, these paths are a little more confusing than this simple picture suggests. Realism is an intellectual tradition much at home in schools of international relations and politics, especially in the United States. It is often cited in philosophical writings about war, usually as the view that morality has no place in the discussion of war, in which role it is then cheerfully, and effectively, criticised. But although the idea that morality has nothing to tell us about war or, more generally,

[23] Georges Santayana, *Soliloquies in England and Later Soliloquies* (Ann Arbor: University of Michigan Press, 1967), p. 104.
[24] James, "The Moral Equivalent of War," p. 170.
[25] It might be urged that utilitarianism provides another way of approaching the morality of war, and there is justice in this thought, but, at this point, I prefer to treat it (and allied forms of consequentialism) as offering a different basis for just war theory or perhaps a reconstitution of it.

international affairs is easily refuted, realism itself has more lessons to teach than such summary dismissal would indicate.

The first problem is in understanding precisely what realism is asserting. Here realists have often been their own worst enemies. Although their slogans are dramatically amoral, their arguments and occasional qualifications suggest more nuanced positions. In addition, there is considerable diversity within the realist (and neo-realist) camp. It is with much justice that Stanley Hoffmann declared of realism, "The first problem is its essential elasticity and indeterminateness."[26]

We should first distinguish realism as a theory or intellectual tradition from the brutal practices of states in the conduct of war. Michael Walzer's well-known treatment of what he calls "realism" in Chapter 1 of *Just and Unjust Wars* is somewhat misleading, since he concentrates on the brutally amoral outlook of the Athenian generals in Thucydides' account of the arguments for the vicious sacking of Melos, and links that with parts of Hobbes's outlook on war. He makes no reference there to the academic tradition that embraces the term "realism," though he has a brief discussion of it later in the book, where he makes it clear that he does not think those realists are implicated in the Thucydian realism he had discussed in Chapter 1. Perhaps they aren't, but the nature of realism is often clouded by both its critics and its adherents.

We may better succeed in understanding what is significant in realism if we treat it less as a sharply defined theory and more as a loose tradition or even an intellectual mood. In some respects it is even more like a religion, and its litany of saints is a long and venerable one, dating back at least to Thucydides and St. Augustine, and including along the way Machiavelli, Hobbes, von Clauswitz, Max Weber, E. H. Carr, Reinhold Niebuhr, Hans Morgenthau, George Kennan, Dean Acheson, and Henry Kissinger. Indeed, some realists, like some religious, have a very expansive, ecumenical sense of their saintly antecedents; one list includes as well as St. Augustine, "John Calvin, Edmund Burke, James Madison, and most other classical Western thinkers."[27]

When we survey the rich diversity of thought and attitude encompassed by even those figures on the more restricted list and scores of lesser lights, it is tempting to despair of the prospect of discovering any unity of belief and stance amongst them. But I think it is worth spelling out some strands that might bind this diverse group together, even if the strands do crisscross in the way Wittgenstein had in mind when he spoke of concepts that were

---

[26] Stanley Hoffmann, *World Disorders: Troubled Peace in the Post-Cold War Era* (Lanham, MD: Rowman & Littlefield, 1998), p. 59.

[27] Ernest W. Lefever, *Moralism and US Foreign Policy* (Washington, DC: The Brookings Institute, 1973), p. 397.

united by overlapping strands of family resemblance. Here are five such strands:

1. a certain opposition to idealism and morality in foreign affairs;
2. an opposition to moral self-inflation on the part of nations and other political groups;
3. a concern for the national interest as a focal value for foreign policy;
4. a concern for stability in the international order;
5. a concern for close attention to the realities of power.

All of these can be abundantly illustrated by examples from realist writings. So can a certain amount of confusion about what each of them means or entails. Arthur Schlesinger, Jr.'s brilliant and provocative paper "The Necessary Amorality of Foreign Affairs" is instructive here, especially about items (1) and (2).[28] (I shall have more to say about items [3], [4], and [5] later, but how they are understood and supported must hinge on our interpretation of [1] and [2].) His article is principally a stinging indictment of the Vietnam War, but it also objects to the moral stances of some opponents of the war. Schlesinger thinks that foreign relations are actually *somehow* beyond morality (hence his title), but he concedes rather nervously that morality cannot be banished entirely from the subject. Hence his strongest denunciations of the intrusion of morality are often followed by qualifications. We find him posing and answering a question about the matter as follows: "Should – as both supporters and critics of the Indochina war have asserted – overt moral principles decide issues of foreign policy? Required to give a succinct answer, I am obliged to say: as little as possible." But then he adds, "Moral values in international politics... should be decisive only in questions of last resort. One must add that questions of last resort do exist."[29]

Similar uncertainties can be culled from other notable realists. For example, E. H. Carr, one of the few non-American writers in the modern realist canon, furiously denounces various dangers of the resort to morality in foreign affairs, and characterises a basic conflict therein as that between realism and utopianism. Nonetheless, he is unequivocal in his belief that there is a place for morality and idealism in foreign policy, saying, "Utopia and reality are thus the two facets of political science. Sound political thought and sound political life will be found where both have their place."[30] Later, he states as "the realist view" that "no ethical standards are applicable to relations between states...."[31] Later still, he refers to "that uneasy compromise

---

[28] Arthur Schlesinger, Jr., "The Necessary Amorality of Foreign Affairs," *Harper's Magazine,* August 1971, pp. 72–77.

[29] Ibid., p. 72.

[30] E. H. Carr, *The Twenty Years' Crisis, 1919–1939: An Introduction to the Study of International Relations* (London: Macmillan, 1956), p. 10.

[31] Ibid., p. 153.

between power and morality which is the foundation of all political life."[32] And in spite of his intermittent taste for a fairly simple version of moral relativism, he gives a significant and positive role to the operation of an understanding of "grounds of justice" in international relations.[33] Hans Morgenthau roundly asserts that "the individual may say for himself: *"Fiat justitia, pereat mundus,"* but the state has no right to say so in the name of those who are in its care."[34] Yet Morgenthau describes as a "misconception" the idea that "international politics is so thoroughly evil that it is no use looking for moral limitations on the aspirations for power on the international scene."[35] What are we to make of all this? Is the realist position on the place of morality just a tissue of confusions?

Not just, though there are confusions. What I want to suggest is that realism is misunderstood, and sometimes misunderstands itself, as involving *total* opposition to morality or ethics in international affairs. The realist target is, or should be, not morality but certain distortions of morality, distortions that deserve the name "moralism." This is a name that they are sometimes given in realist writings, though often the word "moralism" is there used as if it were virtually synonymous with "morality." Indeed, it is the failure consistently to distinguish morality from moralism, and the associated absence of any sort of theory of moralism (or of morality), that largely explains the curious convolutions about the role of morality that we have already noticed in the authors cited.[36] But that it is moralism and not morality they attempt to exorcise is indicated by some of the specific targets that concern Schlesinger in his article. In the course of his critique, he condemns not morality but a variety of what are surely distortions of it: "moral absolutism," "moral self-aggrandizement," "superior righteousness," "fanaticism," and "excessive righteousness."[37]

Several of these are clearly vices, even if a precise account of their viciousness would need some spelling out. For instance, even the slightest sympathy with the Aristotelian theory of virtue as a mean between opposite extremes would count excessive righteousness and moral self-aggrandizement as vicious, and no person who regards him- or herself as moral would accept

32 Ibid., p. 220.
33 Ibid.
34 Hans Morgenthau, *Politics among Nations: The Struggle for Power and Peace*, fifth edition (New York: Knopf, 1973), p. 10.
35 Ibid., p. 231.
36 Kenneth W. Thompson is one of the few who makes an explicit distinction between morality and moralism and gives a brief account of what the distinction might be. Citing Morgenthau and Kennan, he defines "moralism" as "the tendency to make one moral value supreme and to apply it indiscriminately without regard to time and place." Kenneth W. Thompson, *Moralism and Morality in Politics and Diplomacy: The Credibility of Institutions, Policies and Leadership* (Lanham, MD: University Press of America, 1985), p. 5. As we shall see, this is a far too simple, and possibly misleading, account of moralism.
37 Schlesinger, "The Necessary Amorality of Foreign Affairs," pp. 73–75.

cheerfully the description "fanatic." The epithets "superior righteousness" and "moral absolutism" need a bit more discussion, but it is surely open to us to treat them as indicating ways in which morality is distorted rather than standard features of it. The same conclusion is suggested by perusal of other realist arguments. Raymond Aron, for instance, says, "The criticism of idealist illusion is not only pragmatic, it is also moral. Idealist diplomacy slips too often into fanaticism."[38] Clearly, this is a moral critique of a false use of morality. In Aron's case, he associates the distortion of morality with a certain kind of idealism.

It would, I am confident, be possible to bring in evidence vastly more citations from contemporary realist writers and classical "saints" to support my contention that it is moralism rather than morality that is most plausibly viewed as the target of realist critique. It is an important task to sketch the contours of moralism, and I have made a start on that elsewhere.[39] But here it is sufficient to note that the realist critique does not really amount to a rejection of a role for morality in foreign affairs or in war. Its demand is that morality be realistic, pay close attention to consequences and circumstances, be conscious of the difference that the responsible use of power and authority (mentioned earlier in item [5]) makes to moral judgement. The opposition to moral self-inflation (mentioned as item [2]) should be shared by anyone seriously interested in a place for moral evaluation in foreign affairs, or anywhere else for that matter. Similarly, the realist concern for international stability (item [4]) can be shared by the just war theorist and is related to the role played by an ideal of peace in the theory. In principle, all of this can be accepted by just war theorists. Indeed, it is directly pertinent to those conditions in the theory that are governed by the virtue of prudence, especially the conditions of the JAB that are concerned with last resort, prospect of success, and proportionality. In this respect, much of the opposition between realism and just war thinking is misconceived.

Yet there remain claims in realism that distance it from typical just war concerns. One of the most significant of these is mentioned in item (3), namely, the dominance of national interest. This is most prominent in thinkers like Hobbes and Machiavelli, who, in their very different ways, are at the minimalist end of moral concern in the realist spectrum as far as war or international relations is concerned. Nonetheless, it is present in virtually all who lay claim to the realist title. Sometimes, as with the antimoralist claims generally, it is presented as a descriptive thesis, claiming that morality actually plays little

---

[38] Raymond Aron, *Peace and War: A Theory of International Relations*, trans. Richard Howard and Annette Baker Fox (Garden City, NY: Doubleday, 1966), p. 307.

[39] C. A. J. Coady, "The Moral Reality in Realism," *Journal of Applied Philosophy* 22, no. 2 (2005), pp. 121–136. Other articles in this issue also explore moralism. The contents of this issue of the journal may be found in C. A. J. Coady (ed.), *What's Wrong with Moralism?* (Oxford: Blackwell, 2006).

or no part in foreign affairs. But, as such, it is at odds with the realist critique of idealism in international politics insofar as that critique claims that idealism has played a significant, and dangerous, role. In any case, the merely descriptive thesis is palpably false, since moral considerations such as rights of protection, self-defence, humanitarian assistance, patriotism, loyalty to allies, religious integrity, contractual and treaty obligations, and so on are regularly in play in the international arena. This fact is even more palpable once we concede that states are not the only players on the international stage; religious bodies, aid agencies, human rights organisations, corporate multinationals, United Nations agencies, and various other groups all play a part, and increasingly one that includes moral motivations. They are not states, but states in fact pay some attention to their moral and legal pressures. All this suggests that the interesting core of the realist thesis must be normative rather than descriptive.

But as a normative thesis, the realist retreat to national interest as the sole or primary justificatory concept in the international order is beset with problems. One concerns the implicit assumption that there is a harmonious connection between the pursuit of national interest and the other realist goal of international stability. It is far from clear that such harmony is assured; indeed, history surely teaches the contrary. This difficulty leads to the second problem concerning the interpretation to be given the notion of national interest. Some realists (such as Oppenheim) interpret it very narrowly in terms of material advantage, and here the first problem becomes acute. On a more expansive interpretation, it could be in the national interest to promote the peace, well-being, and prosperity of foreigners even at considerable cost to our own national position. On this view, it might really be in the deeper interests of nations like Australia and the United States to support international treaties on the environment (like the Kyoto Protocols) that are in conflict with their immediate, but superficially interpreted, national interest. Plainly, the notion of national interest, to have any value, must be broader than merely material interests, but it is debatable how far it can be stretched without losing all theoretical utility. Communitarian writers correctly stress the ways in which individual interests are enmeshed with group interests, but this does not mean that self-interest must always coincide with community interest. So, at the international level, space must be left for national interest to conflict with the common good of the international community. But when it does, the realist insistence that the national interest ought always to triumph is hardly persuasive. Yet its triumph is taken by most realists as simply axiomatic. This is partly because they think of the national interest as something obvious and easily ascertainable in comparison to the elusive complexities of morality. But it is no simple matter to know what is in the national interest where this is conceived of as some outcome of individual interests in huge communities; indeed, the demands of international morality will often be much clearer. This problem is frequently avoided by simply substituting the very partial interests of the governing party or individual for the national interest, but this substitution has a disastrous record. Given these interpretive problems, it is simply astonishing that realism has made such a fetish of the national interest.

It is clear that realism is deeply flawed as a complete approach to the normative assessment of war and political violence more generally, but it contains cautionary lessons that should be included in a more adequate response. We must turn, then, to the prospects of the just war tradition.

The Just War Tradition

Modern just war thinking has medieval roots, and the medieval tradition of the just war stems primarily from St. Augustine and is well presented in Barnes's chapter on "The Just War" in the *Cambridge History of Later Medieval Philosophy*.[40] As indicated in Chapter 1, it consists of two parts, the first concerned with what makes it right to go to war (the *jus ad bellum* – what justifies waging a war) and the second concerned with the right way to conduct a war (the *jus in bello* – what means are justified morally and what means are not).[41] On the *jus ad bellum* (the JAB), the medieval theory was generally more permissive than modern theory, though sometimes the differences are only terminological. The classical theory, as both Barnes and Johnson make clear, tended to allow a wider range of causes than a modern theory like Walzer's or any theory that could plausibly be extracted from the UN Charter and its declaration of rights.[42] The medieval theory is restrictive – the prince cannot wage war as he pleases nor conduct it as he likes – but the medievals envisaged legitimate causes for military intervention other than self-defence, which is what the modern idea of outlawing "aggression" comes down to. In this, the medieval picture bases itself on natural law thinking and portrays the international order as a sphere under the governance of justice, however imperfectly realised in practice. Legitimate self-defence certainly comes under the rubric of justice, but so, potentially, does much else. As even the post-medieval Hugo Grotius put it, "the sources from which wars arise are as numerous as those from which law suits spring."[43] Even so, it should also be remarked that Grotius's subsequent discussion of this

---

[40] Jonathan Barnes, "The Just War," in *The Cambridge History of Later Medieval Philosophy*, ed. Norman Kretzmann, Anthony Kenny, and Ian Pinlorg (Cambridge: Cambridge University Press, 1982), pp. 771–784. See also Robert L. Holmes, *On War and Morality* (Princeton, NJ: Princeton University Press, 1989), Chapters 4 and 5.

[41] The terminology sounds ancient but seems to have originated relatively recently, during the period of the League of Nations. Nonetheless, it serves a useful purpose and describes realities that are much older than itself.

[42] James Turner Johnson, *Ideology, Reason, and the Limitation of War: Religious and Secular Concepts 1200–1740* (Princeton, NJ: Princeton University Press, 1975).

[43] Hugo Grotius, *The Rights of War and Peace (De Jure Belli ac Pacis)*, vol. 2, trans. Francis W. Kelsey (Oxford: Clarendon Press, 1925), Book II, Chapter 1, section ii, p. 171.

point places considerable emphasis upon the centrality of self-defence and response to aggression.[44]

Barnes asks whether the medieval theory sanctioned what he calls "humanitarian wars" (what I shall call "altruistic wars"), such as one waged against a government that is injuring its own citizens.[45] He replies that the letter of the theory appears to countenance this but that the spirit is against it; and he quotes Suarez approvingly as saying, "what some assert that sovereign kings have power to punish injuries over the whole world is altogether false, and confounds all order and distinction of jurisdictions."[46] This raises both an interesting historical and an interesting substantive ethical question – one which, as the Tanzanian invasion of Amin's Uganda, the Vietnamese invasion of Pol Pot's Cambodia, and the more recent desperate scenarios in the former Yugoslavia, in Rwanda, and in Somalia show, is very much a contemporary issue. On the historical question, it is worth noting that Barnes quotes one of the very late medieval theorists, the sixteenth-century Jesuit Suarez, to make his point about the spirit of the theory. It is possible to argue, however, that by the time of the Spanish theologians Suarez and Vitoria, the spirit of the theory had begun to change quite a bit, in part under their influence. Although self-defence had always loomed large – perhaps largest – as a legitimate ground for resort to war, it is clear, for instance, that Aquinas allowed among the morally permissible causes for war various "injuries" of a religious nature, so that a war to return some heretical peoples to orthodoxy, or even, in some circumstances, to conquer heathens, was at least a candidate for a just war. Both Vitoria and Suarez and later Grotius are anxious to remove most wars of religion from the category of just wars, and so it is plausible to see them as standing at the beginning of a move toward a more restrictive attitude to the JAB.[47] Indeed, it is a

---

[44] Ibid., sections ii–xi, pp. 175–181.

[45] Barnes, "The Just War," p. 778. The term "humanitarian war" seems to have first been used in international law to refer to military interventions for the purpose of protecting one's own nationals endangered in a foreign country, though Barnes's use and my use of "altruistic war" is much wider, and somewhat differently motivated, since it includes fighting on behalf of foreign nationals endangered in their own country. See Paul W. Kahn, "From Nuremberg to the Hague: The United States Position in Nicaragua v. United States and the Development of International Law," *The Yale Journal of International Law* 12, no. 1 (1987), p. 45, n. 161.

[46] Barnes, "The Just War," p. 779.

[47] Francisco de Vitoria: *Political Writings*, ed. Anthony Pagden and Jeremy Lawrance (Cambridge: Cambridge University Press, 1991); *De Indis at de Jure Belli Reflectiones*, ed. Ernest Nys (Washington, DC: Carnegie Institute of Washington, 1917); *De Indis*, II, 10–16; *De Jure Belli*, 10; Francisco Suarez, *A Work on the Three Theological Virtues: Faith, Hope, and Charity* (*De Triplici Virtute Theologica, Fide, Spe, et Charitate*): XVIII, *On Faith*, vi; XIII, *On Charity*, v, in Suarez, *Selections from Three Works, Vol. 2* (Oxford: Oxford University Press, 1944); Griotius, *The Rights of War and Peace*, II, xx, xlviii, pp. 516–17; II, xxii, xiv, pp. 553–554. All three authors to varying degrees express opposition to waging wars of religion, especially wars to convert heathens. To give some of the flavour of the motivation for their resistance to wars of religion, it may be enough to quote part of Vitoria's spirited rejection of the claims of Spanish conquistadors to be waging war for Christ against the American Indians: "Besides,

plausible hypothesis that, with the exception of such aberrations as the holy war tradition, powerfully revived in seventeenth-century England, and the *raison d'etat* theory of the nineteenth century, the evolution of just war theory has been towards a more and more prohibitive attitude towards war. The current ban on "aggressive war" can be seen, I think, for all its obscurity, as the outcome of such a development.

The strength of this ban is also, of course, connected with the rise of the modern state and the doctrine of sovereignty that has accompanied it. Many contemporary discussions of what is called "humanitarian intervention" take it as axiomatic that the moral case against military intervention in the internal affairs of another state rests primarily upon the doctrine of sovereignty as it developed in and after the Treaty of Westphalia that put an end to the wars of religion in 1648. The quotation from Suarez above already makes it clear, however, that some moral presumption against armed intervention in the affairs of other peoples predates the Peace of Westphalia, and is based on considerations other than the apparent sanctity of sovereign rights in the modern sense. Hence any presumed breakdown in the modern conceptual framework of sovereignty, such as the development of "conditional sovereignty," may offer less in the way of a moral licence for intervention than is increasingly believed.[48] I shall examine these matters further in Chapter 4.

Admittedly, the contemporary abhorrence of "aggression" and the concern to outlaw aggressive war has other critics; moreover, the exact meaning of "aggression" is elusive and open to exploitation. To take the second point first, there can be no doubt that the concept of aggression is often used in such a loose and flexible way as to raise the question of its utility as an analytical and moral instrument and to create the suspicion that its only employment is in the interests of propaganda. A delightful, if somewhat grisly, example of such a use is George Bernard Shaw's characterisation of Belgium's neutrality prior to World War I as an act of aggression against Germany.[49] Shaw was criticising the British government's case (or part of it) for declaring war on Germany. Part of the case was claimed to be the need

war is no argument for the truth of the Christian faith. Hence the barbarians cannot be moved by war to believe, but only to pretend that they believe and accept the Christian faith; and this is monstrous and sacrilegious," *Political Writings*, p. 272.

[48] For a good critique of "absolute sovereignty," see Henry Shue, *Basic Rights: Subsistence, Affluence, and U.S. Foreign Policy*, second edition (Princeton, NJ: Princeton University Press, 1996), pp. 173–180; and his "Eroding Sovereignty: The Advance of Principle," in Robert McKim and Jeff McMahan (eds.), *The Morality of Nationalism* (New York: Oxford University Press, 1997), pp. 340–359. See also Jeff McMahan, "The Ethics of International Intervention," in Kenneth Kipnis and Diana T. Meyers (eds.), *Political Realism and International Morality: Ethics in the Nuclear Age* (Boulder, CO: Westview Press, 1987), pp. 75–101.

[49] George Bernard Shaw, *Common Sense and the War*, quoted by A. J. P. Taylor, "The Great War: the Triumph of E. D. Morel," in Peter Stansky (ed.), *The Left and War: The British Labour Party and World War I* (Oxford: Oxford University Press, 1969), p. 123.

to defend Belgium's neutrality against Germany's aggression, and Shaw, with typical perversity, was trying to tip the British pro-war case on its head by concentrating on the way that Belgium's neutrality posed problems for Germany's national interests, and mischaracterising this as aggression.

This is nonetheless a mischaracterisation, and although we can admit that the concept of aggression (like so many concepts) has fuzzy boundaries, we can be clear that a nation's established status as a neutral *cannot* constitute an act of aggression. Behind Shaw's wild claim lies the legitimate insight that some nonbelligerent acts or policies can run contrary to the interests or even the security of another country, just as Norway's neutrality in March 1940 seemed inimical to British interests – so much so, indeed, that a British invasion of part of Norway was seriously urged by Churchill though ultimately rejected by the British cabinet. The strategic and moral issues raised by such problems, however, are inevitably obscured by describing the neutral power as an aggressor.

The moral power of the idea of aggression, or rather of the idea of defence against aggression, comes from the moral significance of self-preservation and particularly self-defence. It is not a uniquely modern concept (as Anscombe, as we shall later see, seems to believe), since it may be found at virtually any time or place where questions about the legitimacy of war are raised. Suarez, for example, makes a clear distinction between aggressive and nonaggressive (defensive) wars, and feels it necessary to make a special case for the legitimacy of some aggressive wars.[50] Moreover, ancient Chinese discussions of the morality of war are specifically concerned to reject the legitimacy of aggressive war, and although the concept of aggression at work is somewhat different from that enshrined in the UN Charter, it is a recognisable relation of that idea.[51] Once again, Hobbes is also pertinent, since he made such notions as self-defence central to his accounts both of morality and of political legitimacy, but he was, at least in part, drawing here upon a long-standing tradition of moral philosophy that stressed these concepts.[52]

The right of self-defence against aggression is often supported by resort to a "domestic analogy." But there is an ambiguity in this resort that we should attend to before discussing the right of self-defence more fully. There are at least two senses of the expression "domestic analogy," or better, two types of domestic analogy. One is that which is supposed to get you from one state's admitted right of the sword "domestically" – that is, within a given society

[50] Francisco Suarez, *A Work on the Three Theological Virtues: Faith, Hope and Charity (De Triplici Virtute Theologica, Fide, Spe, et Charitate)*, XIII, *On Charity*, in Suarez, *Selections from Three Works*, pp. 803–804.

[51] See H. Tzu, H. F. Tzu, and M. Tzu, *Basic Writings of Mo Tzu, Hsun Tzu, and Han Fei Tzu*, trans. B. Watson (New York: Columbia University Press, 1967).

[52] See my discussion of the underpinnings of Hobbes's moral philosophy in C. A. J. Coady, "Hobbes and the Beautiful Axiom," *Philosophy* 65 (1990), pp. 5–17.

and its framework of laws, rules, and agreed procedures – to that state's right to wreak violence against another state. The other analogy concerns the way you get from an individual's right to use violence against other individuals to the state's right to use it within a given society. There is a complex interplay between the two employments, and two extensions. It is, however, plausible to see the second as the more fundamental. This comes out very clearly in the thought of Hobbes, where the individual, in the state of nature, is morally entitled to use violence in pursuit of self-preservation, even to the point of killing in self-defence where necessary. For Hobbes, in the civil state, the Sovereign has the same right and exercises it on behalf of the community, so that individuals no longer have need for, or title to, violence for their self-preservation, except *in extremis*. Hobbes does not think that the international order is quite the same as a state of nature, but he thinks it is close enough for the different sovereigns to be licensed to preserve their own states by resort to violence against others, using what is basically the original form of reasoning about individuals.[53] Whatever we think about Hobbes, or about the use of the right of self-defence to legitimise the state and in particular to license the internal employment of violence by state authorities, there is a certain naturalness about the direct employment of the domestic analogy to legitimate the state's resort to war. Certainly, the idea of treating the state as being like an individual facing threats from other individuals is constantly invoked in discussions of war. We find it prominent in Grotius's introduction to the discussion of the legitimate causes for war, for instance.[54] For now, I shall utilize the analogy below and discuss some of its problems in Chapter 4.

The Domestic Analogy

This basic employment of the domestic analogy may be illustrated as follows.[55] Suppose you are walking peacefully home from work one night when someone jumps out of an alleyway and attacks you with an axe. You struggle with the assailant, call for help, but to no avail. Then you remember that you have confiscated a handgun from one of the children you teach at school and still have it on you. As you struggle, your hand closes on it, and you find yourself able to point it at your attacker's chest. Surely, when all else has failed, you are entitled to shoot and even kill the assailant? Extended to

---

53 See Michael W. Doyle, *Ways of War and Peace: Realism, Liberalism and Socialism* (New York and London: Norton, 1997), pp. 116–128, for a good discussion of Hobbes's view of the international order.

54 See Grotius, *The Rights of War and Peace*, vol. 2, Book II, Chapter 1.

55 My development of this analogy is similar to that of Robert K. Fullinwider in "War and Innocence," in Charles R. Beitz, Marshall Cohen, Thomas Scanlon, and A. John Simmons (eds.), *International Ethics: A Philosophy and Public Affairs Reader* (Princeton NJ: Princeton University Press, 1985), pp. 89–98.

collective agents, this is the basic idea of legitimate violent defence against aggression that lies at the heart of modern just war theory. Moreover, in addition to throwing light upon the JAB, it also illuminates certain aspects of the JIB.

We can note several features of this simple, but persuasive, example:

a. There is a sense in which your use of violence is a last resort. If you know he has mistaken you for a tax inspector, or a CIA assassin, and you know you can easily and safely dispel his illusion with a few quick words, your use of the gun is out of order.
b. There is some reason to believe that your defence will be successful. (What if it were a needle filled with AIDS-infected blood, not a gun? The attacker is in the wrong and resort to the needle will eventually kill him, but if you can only inflict a slight wound it is not going to aid your self-defence.)
c. Your defiance of the normal moral constraints against killing another human being is based on the right to defend one's life against unjustified attack, and this seems to be an unequivocal and fundamental moral entitlement.
d. You are directing violence at the perpetrator of the wrong you are suffering in order to prevent his inflicting further grave wrongs on you, including, very possibly, death.
e. Your response is proportional to the crisis, as it wouldn't be, for example, if in the middle of a crowded city you had recourse to a small nuclear bomb in your pocket.

All of these conditions are reflected in just war theory dealing with violence between states, though there is one further condition of some importance (listed here as the first condition). So we have as conditions for the JAB:

1. War must be declared and waged by legitimate authority;
2. There must be a just cause for going to war;
3. War must be a last resort;
4. There must be reasonable prospect of success;
5. The violence used must be proportional to the wrong being resisted;
6. The war must be fought with the right intention.

There are heuristic and practical advantages in having these considerations set out as separate conditions, but clearly there are intimate connections among several of them. When a nation resorts to war without due exploration of nonviolent alternatives, not only does its response violate condition (3), it is also thereby arguably disproportional, so violating (5). Indeed, proportionality is such a broad notion that it may well be interpreted to cover other conditions such as (4).[56] Nonetheless, listing the conditions in the usual fashion has the advantage of allowing us to focus on specific tests that deliberation about going to war should address. Later, I shall examine these conditions in more detail.

The domestic analogy also helps us to see the rationale for some of the provisions of the JIB, which are sometimes called the "rules of war." These are reflected in UN and international legal codes for dealing with the regulation of war. I shall discuss the problems raised by the JIB and the utility of our analogy with respect to them in a later chapter. It is worth noting at this point merely that the JIB is crucially concerned with characterizing the sort of targets that may be legitimately attacked. This immediately raises an important issue having in part to do with the relations between the JAB and the JIB, an issue that we shall discuss more fully in Chapter 6. One reason I have preferred to speak mostly of the just war tradition, rather than of just war theory, is because of the variety to be found within the tradition, even where it is viewed as primarily non-consequentialist in outlook. Recent work on the history of the tradition has revealed an underlying tension between two approaches to the relations between the JAB and the JIB, and the relations of both, especially the JIB, to the legal regulation of war. This tension arises from different approaches to the question to whom the permissions and prohibitions of the JIB are addressed. I spoke earlier of "the sort of targets that may legitimately be attacked," but I might just as readily have said "the sort of targets that may legitimately be attacked in a just war." This qualification makes a big difference. If we take it that just war theory begins with the problem of when (if ever) it is right to go to war and promulgates restrictive conditions (the JAB) that yet allow some justified resort to war, then it is natural to see the conditions of the JIB as offering certain further restrictions and permissions that are consequent upon the satisfaction of the JAB criteria. On this understanding, there is a close connection between the JAB and the JIB, so that the rights and prohibitions (or at any rate, the rights) of the JIB are aimed only at those warriors and their leaders who are justified in fighting in the first place. Call this approach the theory of justified war. By contrast, there is a strand in the tradition, most fully developed by later theorists like the Swiss Emmerich de Vattel, that strongly separates the JAB and the JIB for certain purposes. (Actually, Vattel's own complex position unites them at one level and separates them at another, but we shall examine this in Chapter 6.) In this strand of thought, which (following Vattel) I shall call the doctrine of "regular war," the starting point tends to be the assumption that wars are an inevitable part of politics and that the problem is to regulate

---

[56] Thomas Hurka has argued for the absorption of several of the just war conditions under the heading of proportionality in "Proportionality in the Morality of War," *Philosophy and Public Affairs* 33, no. 1 (2005), pp. 34–66.

their conduct to conform to mutually acceptable norms.[57] The word "regular" is an apt description because it captures a key perspective in the theory: a perspective that seeks to regulate wars viewed as common occurrences between nations that stand in relations that approximate a state of nature, the primary task being to control their course in accord with morality, convention, and law. Hence, whatever the deliverances of the JAB, the opposing warriors are treated as equal with respect to the permissions and restraints of the JIB. Indeed, for Vattel, even where morality delivers the clear verdict that one side has a just cause and the other does not, the justice of cause should be "reputed equal between two enemies."[58] Most importantly, they have an equal, "symmetrical" right to attack and kill each other, regardless of the justice of their cause. This outlook is embodied more recently in Michael Walzer's doctrine of "the moral equality of soldiers," though his position has special flavours of its own. I think there are good reasons to be suspicious of the proposed independence of the JAB and the JIB, and of the "symmetry thesis" (as it is sometimes called) to which it gives rise. At least, it is a poor starting point for the ground-floor *moral* discussion of the JAB and the JIB, though, as I shall later argue in Chapter 6, there are insights behind the symmetry thesis that may need to be accommodated in a fully developed account of the JIB, especially with regard to political and legal considerations.

A further point of interest concerning the relation between the JAB and the JIB is that the requirement of proportionality is relevant to both: there are questions to be raised about whether the resort to war is a proportional response to some injury, and also about whether some tactic or means employed in the prosecution of an initially legitimate war is proportionate to what is being sought in using it.[59] Indeed, there is here an inevitable overlap, since going to war is itself a means to certain ends, and resort to war needs to be justified against certain alternatives. Equally, there is an issue of proportionality raised by the question of what kind of war or warlike resort to violence may be justified in response to a political crisis or act of aggression.

Consider the persistent and defiant French intrusion into what were recognised as English fishing waters in 1992, accompanied by a low level

---

57 Emmerich de Vattel, *The Law of Nations or The Principles of Natural Law*, trans. Charles Fenwick (Washington, DC: Carnegie Institution of Washington, 1916), Book 3, Chapter 12. For an excellent discussion of these strands in the just war tradition and the tensions between them, see Gregory Reichberg, "Just War and Regular War: Competing Paradigms," in David Rodin and Henry Shue (eds.), *Just and Unjust Warriors*, forthcoming, Oxford University Press.

58 Vattel, *The Law of Nations*, Book 3, Chapter 12, para. 190.

59 There is an interesting issue about whether any means employed by those whose cause is actually unjust *can* be proportional, given that we need to judge proportionality in terms of the end being sought. This point is related to the symmetry thesis mentioned earlier and will be explored when we come to discuss the JIB.

of French violence (cutting English nets and damaging English boats a little). This offence *may* have justified such violent acts as forcible British boarding of intrusive French fishing boats, forcible confiscation of fishing equipment, and retaliatory cutting of nets, but it would certainly not license the bombing of French fishing villages or mooring facilities. Compare this to a variation on our simple domestic analogy where you are not under threat from an axe-man but have been deeply insulted by a colleague: it would clearly be wrong to shoot him, but some sharp words or even a slap on the face *might* be a reasonable reaction. As we shall see more clearly in later chapters, although there is real point in distinguishing between the JAB and the JIB, total logical separation of the two sets of criteria is dubious for a number of reasons.

The realities of international relationships and of aggression itself have been thought to call for certain plausible extensions of the self-defence justification for war, and it requires only minor adjustments to see at least some of these reflected in the simple domestic model. The scenario is much as before, except that the gun has been knocked from your hand by the axe-man and is twenty yards away on the pavement. Your friend Emily happens to wander by as you are in the throes of the struggle, and not doing too well. She can easily pick up the gun, and she is a trained sharpshooter who has shot in the Olympics. She knows you well and knows that it is extremely unlikely that the axe-man is defending himself against an unprovoked attack by you. You and she have helped each other out a lot in the past in various important enterprises. You call for help. Surely she is entitled at least to threaten the axe-man with the gun, and if this is unsuccessful, to shoot him. If the attack morally licenses you to employ violence in defence of yourself, why doesn't it license Emily to support your defence with violence?

Similarly in the international case. If a nation is sometimes entitled to use violence in its own defence, then surely other nations may come to its aid as long as their objective is indeed to help repel the attack and no more. Of course, in both the domestic and international cases, what is morally permissible in the abstract is not the whole story. There may be powerful prudential reasons for not helping others to defend themselves. When the Soviet Union invaded Hungary and later Czechoslovakia the world stood by, principally because of fear of widespread nuclear war, and that fear was realistic enough at least to make a reasonable case for such agonising inaction. But such qualifications relate to the more prudential conditions of the JAB to be discussed later.

The domestic analogy may also be utilised to throw light on interesting scenarios concerning the preparation for and aftermath of an attack. You are on your way home from work again, and you know that you must pass through an area where others have been attacked before by an axe-man. Cautiously, you take a slightly indirect route home, and you see someone with a fierce demeanour sharpening an axe on a side street adjacent to the street where the attacks have taken place and through which you must shortly pass. Are you entitled to shoot before the imminent attack? Another scenario: you have repelled the axe-man with violence, but without needing to kill, and as he flees, you ask yourself what you are entitled to do to prevent any further attacks. Do you have a right to kill him as he flees, because of his attack? If not, do you have a right to punish him less severely? I pose these issues as questions because I believe that our intuitions are less secure in the domestic case here than in the earlier scenarios, and so raise further problems for the analogy. We can see this if we consider the proposed extensions:

1. Supporting allies;
2. Balancing interventions by others;
3. Preemptive strikes;
4. Punishment of the wrongdoer (aggressor).

The first two of these need little attention, except to note that there is a problem about the right to balance interventions if one allows (as we shall see that Walzer does) that some primary interventions may be legitimate. We should then more properly allow that balancing interventions can be licit only where the original intervention is immoral, and, of course, where the other prudential conditions of the JAB are satisfied. If Lucy sees Emily's supporting intervention on your behalf and realises that you are the victim of an unprovoked attack by the axe-man, she has no legitimate cause to even up the odds. Similarly, military support for allies cannot be morally justified simply by the fact of alliance, since it depends crucially upon what the support is needed for.

The problems raised by preemptive strikes and punishment I shall largely defer until a later chapter, where I consider the other conditions of the JAB listed earlier. But now it is time to turn, in Chapter 4, to examine further the idea of defence against aggression as the primary embodiment of just cause.

4

Aggression, Defence, and Just Cause

Every violation of the territorial integrity or political sovereignty of an independent state is called aggression. It is as if we were to brand as murder all attacks on a man's person, all attempts to coerce him, all invasions of his home.... All aggressive acts have one thing in common: they justify forceful resistance, and force cannot be used between nations, as it often can between persons, without putting life itself at risk.

Michael Walzer[1]

How then should we understand "aggression"? The UN General Assembly has defined "aggression" as follows: "Aggression is the use of armed force by a State against the sovereignty, territorial integrity or political independence of another State or in any other manner inconsistent with the Charter of the United Nations."[2] This is a definition that Michael Walzer makes his own, and we should turn to his discussion as he is the author who has probably given the most cogent account of how the concept of aggression may be made central to a just war theory that licences some wars of defence against aggression under the heading of the JAB.[3] As explained earlier, Walzer uses "the domestic analogy" to argue that war comes into its own, morally speaking, when a state exercises its right of self-defence against an attacking power. This right it gains, in his view, from the way legitimate political power is rooted in communal life. Even autocratic, incompetent, and distinctly unpleasant regimes can have this right if they somehow embody the social identity of the community they govern. Clearly we have here a sort of contract theory, though Walzer presents neither a detailed defence nor even a detailed characterisation of it. It is perhaps worth quoting in full what he does say:

[1] Michael Walzer, *Just and Unjust Wars: A Moral Argument with Historical Illustrations*, third edition (New York: Basic Books, 2000), p. 52.
[2] UN General Assembly Ruling 3314 (1974).
[3] Ibid., p. 52.

The rights of states rest on the consent of their members. But this is consent of a special sort. State rights are not constituted through a series of transfers from individual men and women to the sovereign or through a series of exchanges among individuals. What actually happens is harder to describe. Over a long period of time, shared experiences and cooperative activity of many different kinds shape a common life.

"Contract" is a metaphor for a process of association and mutuality. . . . 4

The contract "metaphor" is really Walzer's way of giving most (though certainly not all) states the standing of individual entities with rights of self-defence against other such individuals in the international order. Many of the criticisms of Walzer's position begin by objecting to this move. I shall begin in a different way, but then turn to this style of objection. The first difficulty I want to raise for the theory of aggression objects that the theory is too strong, the second that it is too weak, and the third that Walzer's way of giving states international status and rights of war canonises existing nation-states in a way that is, amongst other things, insensitive to human rights.

By objecting that Walzer's theory of defence against aggression as just cause is *too strong*, I am claiming that he interprets the justice of responding to aggression in too expansive a way. Other versions of the theory are not explicitly susceptible to this criticism, but the spirit in which they are applied often is. This spirit and, in certain places, the letter of Walzer's text violate the requirements of proportionality as illustrated and discussed earlier. This violation stems from the exalted moral status Walzer gives to the prerogatives of existing states. In fact, in Walzer's book the moral status of response to aggression is such as not merely to *license* violence but to *require* it.

Walzer's language echoes some of the emphasis of the UN Charter, but it is nonetheless inconsistent with the spirit and letter of just war thinking, as I understand it. This is because aggression is not the undifferentiated crime that Walzer paints it. He says,

Every violation of the territorial integrity or political sovereignty of an independent state is called aggression. It is as if we were to brand as murder all attacks on a man's person, all attempts to coerce him, all invasions of his home. This refusal of differentiation makes it difficult to mark off the relative seriousness of aggressive acts. . . . But there is a reason for the refusal. All aggressive acts have one thing in common: they justify forceful resistance. . . . Aggression is morally as well as physically coercive. . . . [it] is a singular and undifferentiated crime because in all its forms, it challenges rights that are worth dying for.5

This quotation catches the flavour of much else in Walzer's discussion of aggression, in particular the idea that *any* form of aggression somehow

4 Ibid., p. 54.
5 Ibid., pp. 52–53.

warrants violent response. Here, Walzer's vocabulary and practice fail to discriminate among various moral possibilities; in particular, the morally obligatory, the morally permissible, and the morally presumptive. He often writes as if the victim of aggression, no matter what the degree, is morally obliged to embark on war. What else could be meant by "morally coercive"? At other times, he vacillates between the morally obligatory and the merely permissive, as when he says that the theory of aggression explains when war is "permissible, perhaps even morally desirable."[6] Often he uses the language of permission, but sometimes he speaks only of the "presumption in favour of military resistance."[7] We should distinguish three Walzer positions: hard, medium, and soft, corresponding to obligation, permission, and presumption.

The hard line is surely too hard. Suppose a clear case of aggression where state A bombs outlying villages of state B, causing extensive damage and some loss of life. State A does this in the culpably mistaken belief that state B is giving aid to rebels in its territory, whereas it is state C that is responsible. Militarily, state A is more powerful than state B; moreover a military response by state B will likely produce a conflict involving states D and E, with unpredictable results except for the certain prospect of much bloodshed. It is pretty certain that A will not offer further aggression against B now that the mistake is known. Surely it is absurd to claim that state B has a moral obligation to fight, that its citizens are "morally coerced" into war. It has certainly been wronged, but it may well find other ways to redress its grievance, and even if it does not, the most respectable course may be to shrug and bear it. Or consider the responses appropriate to the aggression discussed earlier that is involved in state-sanctioned violations of territorial waters in pursuit of commercial fishing advantage.

The medium line holds paradox, too, when we recall what aggression is supposed to permit. One does not have to be a utilitarian to object to the idea that State B has a right to wage war involving high risks to itself and the certainty of considerable death and destruction. Of course, much depends on the strength of the permission. We are here in the area of moral rights, and their somewhat elusive logic. Perhaps my objection shows only that the right to violence may be overridden. If so, the medium line collapses into the soft line, and the permission becomes merely what lawyers call a rebuttable presumption. But even if there is some presumption in favour of an armed response, it may be very weak indeed, depending upon the type of aggression and the circumstances surrounding it. The presumption may reflect no more than the injured party's need for redress and the possibility that resort to violence may under certain circumstances be legitimate. To

[6] Ibid., p. 59.
[7] Ibid.

say this is to call attention to the fact that just cause is only one condition of the JAB. Just cause has a certain preeminence, since the other conditions do not come into play unless it is satisfied, but Walzer's rhetoric about aggression obscures the role of last resort, prospects for success, and proportionality. If we return to my employment of a simple domestic analogy, we can see what might have gone wrong with Walzer's thinking here. In the person-to-person case, there are many attacks that are not attacks on one's life or on other central values or rights. The axe-man is one thing, but your assailant may merely be hurting your dignity by giving you a push, or even by shouting at you in an offensive way. Neither of these scenarios would normally oblige, permit, or even create a presumption for anything like a lethal response.[8]

This review of options suggests that Walzer's approach to aggression and the morality of self-defence is wrong-headed. The concept of aggression is neither undifferentiated nor morally coercive; rather it is amorphous and at most weakly presumptive. Its current role in thinking about war is wrongly explained by treating it as the type of occurrence that positively, almost automatically, licenses a military response. The language of rights can here be misleading, as can the domestic analogy, especially in the form employed by Walzer. We shall look at this more closely later, but the important thing to note at this point is that the status that the concept of aggression now enjoys is the end point, or at least the current benchmark, of a complex process of retreat. As already remarked, the history of just war theory has shown a distinct, though not altogether uniform, tendency to limit the right to war under the pressure of increasing scepticism about the motives of statesmen, the reliability of their calculations, and the supposedly beneficial effects of war. The recent stress on the idea that only resistance to aggression can justify recourse to arms is thus a deliberate rejection of the Clausewitzian idea that war is no more than an unusual form of diplomacy, as well as a departure from the older strand in just war theory that held war to be a morally appropriate means for dealing with a variety of international evils. Rather than investing the concept of aggression with mysterious moral trappings, we do better to see its employment as part of an attempt to outlaw war except for those circumstances where war offers a defence against murderous attack. Viewed thus, the state's right of self-defence is both more pragmatic and less morally grandiose than it appears in Walzer's presentation. It is very

---

[8] More recently, even so perceptive a critic as Thomas Hurka seems to overstate what aggression may allow or demand. In his paper "Proportionality in the Morality of War," Hurka concludes that "a conventional war fought to defend a nation's sovereignty against aggression is normally proportional" (p. 66), though he had earlier more cautiously described the issue as "difficult" and claimed only to have "vindicated the common-sense view that at least sometimes, and certainly when a large, popular democracy faces total political absorption, national self-defence can justify lethal military force" (p. 57). See *Philosophy and Public Affairs* 33, no. 1 (2005).

important to emphasise this, because recent developments have shown a renewed enthusiasm both for the Clauswitzian position and, as we shall see, for the broader moral interpretation of just cause that licenses "humanitarian war."

Further Problems with Self-Defence

Others have criticised modern just war theory's emphasis upon the central, and even unique, role of self-defence as too weak. The basic line of criticism here is that restriction of just wars to *defence against aggression* (even on the extended model discussed earlier and employed by Walzer) leaves all manner of evils in the international order undealt with. One of the earliest forms of the contemporary version of this criticism is put trenchantly if rather briefly by Anscombe. As she puts it: "The present day conception of 'aggression', like so many strongly influential conceptions, is a bad one. Why *must* it be wrong to strike the first blow in a struggle? The only question is, who is in the right?."[9] As stated, this criticism would not seem to jettison the concept of aggression as dramatically as she supposes, since her argument seems to presume the existence of a struggle in which actual blows have not yet been struck, though they or something like them have been extensively prepared for. The model may be one like this: A has decoyed B into a room and locked him inside for some nefarious purpose. Later A enters the room believing B to be asleep. Surely B is entitled (if he can get away with it) to strike A in order to escape, even though A has not struck him. This seems very plausible, but it is also plausible to see this first blow as part of B's defence against A's initial and ongoing aggression and ominous plans for the future, even if it was an aggression that did not involve a blow. What this example shows is merely that there can be different forms of attack or aggression. This is why certain forms of military blockade may be regarded as acts of war.

The concept of aggression is certainly subject to a considerable amount of elasticity, and its edges are rather fuzzy, but, for well-known reasons, this need not make it unusable. We are familiar with the idea that perfectly usable nonmoral concepts like "beard" or "day" may lack a sufficiently precise definition to allow us to settle borderline questions such as whether *this* is still day rather than night. In ethics, it will often be of more importance to have some agreed way of deciding on the applicability of a vague concept, so it is necessary to think much harder about how to resolve the matter. In the case of aggression, the idea of some deliberate action of attacking another, or of depriving another of rights, seems at the heart of the notion and gives us

9 G. E. M. Anscombe, "War and Murder," in Richard A. Wasserstrom (ed.), *War and Morality* (Belmont, CA: Wadsworth, 1970), pp. 43–44.

at least a sufficient condition for aggression. But where we are dealing with nations, there is obviously room for further debate about what constitutes national rights, and even what constitutes nations. I discuss some of these issues later, but for now I will assume that the notion has enough clarity to guide us in the more obvious cases and will continue our discussion of Anscombe's argument.

I claimed that her wording might have made the argument more plausible by implying that aggression, in some form, had already occurred, as might happen if some country's economy had been put under severe strain by a military blockade. If so, the argument is not effective against any but the crudest use of the "defence against aggression" construal of "just cause." But perhaps this is not what Anscombe means to rely upon. When she talks of "the first blow in a struggle," she may really mean the blow that initiates the struggle. It is not that the other party has already done, or seriously prepared, something injurious to your nation's territory or sovereignty, but rather that he has done something you judge to be *wrong* (gravely wrong, let's say) and that needs to be dealt with. That this is what she really means is suggested strongly by an example with which she introduces the discussion. She says, "there being such a thing as the common good of mankind, and a visible criminality against it, how can we doubt the excellence of such a proceeding as that violent suppression of the man-stealing business which the British government took it into its head to engage under Palmerston?"[10] Here, she clearly has in mind justifying resort to war by the idea of suppressing some evil in the international order even where it constitutes no aggression against your state. Taken along with her remark about "the only question" being that of "who is in the right?," this marks a return to the earlier and broader understanding of just cause, and it could be extended to the idea of military intervention in another state's affairs in order to remove an awful government or to remedy some great internal evil, such as persecution of a minority group. There is a great range of cases here, but I will, for convenience, lump them together, as already indicated, under the heading of "altruistic wars." Cases can range from deposing a bad government to preventing genocide, and they are not philosopher's fantasies, as wars in Uganda, Cambodia, Granada, and the former Yugoslavia have shown, and as arguments for the intervention in Iraq on the grounds of "regime change" also highlight.

My general response to the moral legitimacy of altruistic wars is a sceptical one. Remember the starting point of just war theory: there is a presumption against the moral validity of resort to war given what we know of the history of warfare, of the vast devastation it causes (nowadays even more so) and the dubious motives that have so often fuelled it. The development of just war

[10] Ibid., p. 43.

theory has been progressively away from altruistic legitimations of war for just this reason. Our experience of wars of religion (the dreadful carnage of the Thirty Years' War in Europe, for example), of trade and imperialist wars, and of what tends to happen when one nation conquers another "for its own good" speak against allowing such an account of "just cause."[11]

An aversion to altruistic war and a retreat to a more narrow conception of defence against aggression reflect something like the attitude behind the imposition of "total fire bans" in Australia on hot summer days. One can certainly make out a case for an experienced bushman cooking himself a lunch or boiling a billy in the bush (Australian idiom for making tea by boiling it in a tin over an open fire) even in very hot, dry weather conditions, but the general benefits of a total ban and the dangers of allowing exceptions that are all too likely to be exploited or abused are so great that even the bushman must abide by the rule. This seems to have moral force as well as legal weight. Considerations of this sort lie behind attempts by rule utilitarians to develop a version of utilitarian theory that justifies strict adherence to moral rules because of their utility, but whether one is a utilitarian or not, there are clearly some moral rules or policies that can be given this sort of justification. Similarly with war: the evils of war are so great that restricting it to cases where the justification for resort to lethal violence is obvious and overwhelming is likely to have much better consequences than allowing a wider range of justifications that can easily be open to misinterpretation and abuse.

I think that this provides a powerful objection to altruistic reasons for war, but the fact remains that there can be some extreme cases that create a worry for this view, just as some specific dire situations can challenge a rule like the fire ban. Walzer treats the Indian invasion of Bangladesh in 1971 as such a case, an intervention to prevent the massacre of a population by what was nominally its own government. He thinks it important that the Indians were in and out of the country so quickly and that there was such palpable evil being perpetrated. The Vietnamese invasion of Cambodia may be a similar case, as may the Tanzanian invasion of Uganda, though the unhappy subsequent histories of those nations need to be considered in an overall assessment. The disaster in Rwanda is the most cited recent case. Anscombe's example of the use of violence in a "first blow" fashion to attack "the man-stealing business" seems another case that has good claims to exception from the ban, but this is in part because Palmerston's crusade was not directed against particular nations or peoples but against criminal groups who were often operating in defiance of national laws. Indeed, the British government was careful to arrange treaties with other countries that

---

[11] See, in this connection, Walzer's analysis of the U.S. intervention in Cuba in 1898 (Walzer, *Just and Unjust Wars*, pp. 102–103). Nor is the turmoil in the aftermath of the war in Iraq that deposed Saddam Hussein consoling for those who favour altruistic war.

gave the UK the legal right to board slavers operating under those other flags, and most such boardings were nonviolent.[12] Attempts to deal with piracy on the high seas or, in modern times, the hijacking of aircraft are somewhat similar phenomena.[13]

I should make it clear that I do not want to deny that there may be some exceptional circumstances in which a just cause for war may go beyond self-defence, even generously interpreted, toward the defence of desperate others. My concern, rather, is to dampen the enthusiasm for altruistic war that has gathered pace in recent years amongst many whose humane instincts I otherwise share. In recent times, the cases of Bosnia and, most significantly, Rwanda seem to qualify as such exceptional circumstances.[14] The Rwandan disaster has understandably given a powerful boost to the case for armed intervention. It was a case of widespread civic breakdown in which the country's government was promoting the massacre of large numbers of its people. If it were true that a limited military response by outsiders could have nipped the slaughter in the bud, as the Canadian officer on the spot, General Romeo Dallaire, claimed, then this would give a powerful boost to the case for humanitarian intervention.[15] But Rwanda is something like the exception that proves the rule, and it should not be taken, as it often is in some quarters, to provide fuel for an enthusiasm for humanitarian war that ignores both the value of limiting the scope of legitimate causes for war and the powerful prudential barriers to the prospects for such interventions. In Chapter 3, I warned against the dangers of moralism, one of which is the tendency to substitute high-mindedness for hard practical attention to realities on the ground such as the difficulties of achieving humanitarian objectives by military invasion. Moralism, for instance, often leads to misunderstanding the cultural and political realities of the country to be invaded. An extreme example, but one that embodies many typical features of interventionist thinking, is President McKinley's avowed reasons for the U.S. annexation of the Philippines at the end of the nineteenth century. Believing the Filipinos "unfit for self-government," McKinley thought America had

---

[12] See James Chambers, *Palmerston: The People's Darling* (London: John Murray, 2004), Chapter 7.

[13] See Robert C. Ritchie, *Pirates: Myths and Realities* (Minneapolis: University of Minnesota Press, 1986), for an interesting short overview of traditional piracy; Roger Villar, *Piracy Today: Robbery and Violence at Sea Since 1980* (London: Conway Maritime Press, 1985), for more recent developments; and Barry H. Dubner, *The Law of International Sea Piracy* (The Hague: Martinus Nijhoff, 1980), for legal perspectives.

[14] Many would add Kosovo to the list, but for a variety of reasons I am doubtful of the intervention against Serbia on behalf of the Albanian Kosovars. But it would be a distraction to canvass that case thoroughly here.

[15] See Romeo Dallaire, *Shake Hands with the Devil: The Failure of Humanity in Rwanda* (New York: Carroll and Graf, 2003).

"to take care of them, and educate them and Christianize them."[16] The fact that they had been Christians for centuries (though no doubt the wrong kind for McKinley) did not impinge on the president's lofty perspective. Nor was he concerned, when the idea of annexation "came to [him] one night," that the Filipinos had sought political independence for years, with martyrs, exiles, and widespread support. The United States' humanitarian takeover was unsuccessfully resisted with arms for two years and, sadly for the Filipinos, the "taking care" lasted for fifty years.

It needs to be insisted that invasion is what military intervention, in the strict sense, standardly involves. Intervention is essentially something that is contrary to the will of the government of the nation on the receiving end of intervention. Where nations invite other nations to their shores, we have nothing like the scale of problems that intervention typically involves.[17] I would not therefore call the Australian-led military support for East Timor, with all its problems, an intervention in the relevant sense. Of course, the matter is complicated in the case of "failed states" where there is no government, or nothing worthy of the name, but we should be cautious about affixing that label too readily.

One of the most problematic aspects of humanitarian intervention concerns satisfaction of the JAB criterion of prospect of success. This will be discussed more fully in Chapter 5, but we may anticipate here the conclusion that there is often a difficulty deciding between different understandings of success. In the present instance, should we think of success in a short-term way as saving these lives now, or as restoring these people to their homeland? Or should the criterion of success embrace longer–term objectives such as ensuring political stability and enduring safety for any in the area threatened with the same kind of persecution? Clearly, both accounts of success have their attractions, but equally clearly they are in tension. In particular, the shorter-term objective is compatible with – and, in some respects, suited to – military procedures, whereas armed forces alone are unlikely to deliver the longer-term objectives.

Advocates of the short-term view will say that at least we saved these people's lives now, but the long-termers will say that this is small comfort if our intervention merely delays the catastrophe or helps to create a new one. Furthermore, if you are going for the longer term, you will need more than mere violent intervention. Some longer-term solution is ideally preferable in

---

[16] Quoted by Henry Steele Commager, "Ethics, Virtue, and Foreign Policy," in Kenneth W. Thompson (ed.), *Ethics and International Relations*, vol. 2 (New Brunswick, NJ: Transaction Books, 1985), pp. 127–137.

[17] For fuller development of this definitional point, and indeed for a more sustained treatment of the perils faced by humanitarian intervention, see my "War for Humanity: A Critique," in Deen K. Chatterjee and Don Scheid (eds.), *Ethics and Foreign Intervention* (Cambridge and New York: Cambridge University Press, 2003), pp. 274–295, and *The Ethics of Humanitarian Intervention* (Washington: United States Institute of Peace, 2002).

both the domestic and the international spheres, since most short-term solutions risk futility. But the "longer term" cannot be too long. An intervention must avoid escalating into a colonial saga or even an enduring protectorate.

Yet even sensible longer-term solutions that might avoid these perils require many things that are not readily available. First, they require non-military techniques and personnel; second, they require a commitment of will over a relatively long time; and third, they require the dedication of financial and other resources for an unglamorous long haul. They necessitate, in short, what Thomas M. Franck has called a "holistic approach" to humanitarian rescue.[18]

The Sovereignty Question

It is often argued that the opposition to military intervention or war for any purpose other than defence against aggression (or causes closely related to it) is based upon the modern concept of sovereignty arising from the Peace of Westphalia, which put an end to the European wars of religion.[19] Simplifying somewhat, we may say that this concept prohibited states from intervening militarily in matters that were the concern of other sovereign states, and gave the sovereign states themselves the right to govern and to decide upon the use of force internally for control and externally for defence. This constituted the recognition of a form of "absolute sovereignty." It is then argued that this concept is dangerously outmoded, since the idea of sovereign power has been eroded by the economic and informational processes known as "globalization" and by the development of cosmopolitan political processes, such as the UN and the various global NGOs. Moreover, it is said that the concept was always flawed insofar as it left citizens at the mercy of their governments, with frequently alarming consequences. The nation-state must now be regarded, therefore, as having "conditional sovereignty," that is, sovereignty which is conditional upon some minimal level of respect for the human rights of its citizens. The critique and rejection of aggressive resort to war needs to be viewed against this background, and therefore amended appropriately.

There is undoubtedly something to this line of critique. The modern nation-state and its pretensions are by no means sacrosanct. Nonetheless, the reigning paradigm is not so easily dismissed. The opposition to intervention, even for the purposes of doing good, is based on deeper insights

---

[18] Thomas M. Franck, "A Holistic Approach to Building Peace," in Olara A. Otunnu and Michael W. Doyle (eds.), *Peacemaking and Peacekeeping for the New Century* (Lanham, MD: Rowman and Littlefield, 1998), pp. 275–296.

[19] For an influential argument related to this, see J. Bryan Hehir, "Intervention: From Theories to Cases," *Ethics and International Affairs* 9 (1995), p. 6. See also Henry Shue, "Conditional Sovereignty," *Res Publica* 8, no. 1 (1999), pp. 1–7.

than the needs of a seventeenth-century political settlement, even though these insights had relevance to that settlement. There are two sorts of insight involved. The first, which I have argued earlier, concerns *the need to limit resort to war*. This puts an emphasis upon restricting the impulse to resort to violent solutions to political problems and does so by allowing such resort only in the most palpable circumstances of justification – for example, self-defence. The second concerns the *right to national self-determination*. Here, it is not Westphalia that is significant, but a combination of the much earlier insight that jurisdiction should have a strong local and popular element (which need not mean democracy) and the much later developments associated with decolonization that gave prominence to the ethical-political value of national self-determination.

These insights are in danger of being forgotten in the renewed enthusiasm (amongst those who are enthusiastic!) for altruistic war. Both insights are moral though they have prudential components. The first needs no further explanation here, except to note that the concern to limit war extends beyond the nonaggression paradigm to the other just war restraints. The second insight needs some expansion under both elements of the combination. Colonialism got its bad name not merely from the explicitly repressive policies of the colonial powers, grim though they commonly were, but also from the inherent difficulties foreigners face in understanding their subject peoples, in properly comprehending their religious, cultural, and historical circumstances. Colonialism is also intrinsically committed to certain attitudes of inequality built into the idea of imperial rule and encapsulated in McKinley's patronising remarks about Filipinos. The theme of "unfitness" is found even in so enlightened and profound a thinker as J. S. Mill, whose famous essay on nonintervention made an exception for the case of "uncivilised" peoples.[20] It was a theme of the far less noble-minded Spanish conquistadores in South America: paganism allegedly deprived the Indian peoples of any right to self-government. This proposition was decisively undermined by a number of courageous Spanish theologians, notably Vitoria, Las Casas, and Montesinos who argued for a natural right of self-government possessed by peoples whatever their religion. The American Indians, said Vitoria, "undoubtedly possessed as true dominion, both public and private, as any Christians."[21]

---

[20] See John Stuart Mill, "A Few Words on Non-Intervention," in his *Collected Works, Vol. XXI: Essays on Equality, Law and Education*, ed. John M. Robson (Toronto and Buffalo: University of Toronto Press, 1984), pp. 118–120. Mill's wholehearted defence of British imperialism and the civilizing mission of the English also invokes what might well be called "English exceptionalism." By comparison to other civilized nations, England is "a novelty in the world" (p. 111).

[21] Francisco De Vitoria, "On the American Indians," in his *Political Writings*, ed. Anthony Pagden and Jeremy Lawrence (Cambridge and New York: Cambridge University Press, 1991), pp. 250–252. Vitoria thinks that if it could be shown that the barbaric state of the

The self-government argument needs supplementation by some account of what is meant by a "people" and "self-government." For the first, the idea of "a nation" when cashed in ethnic terms is surely too narrow; and when cashed in terms of state identity, it tends to beg the question. For the second, the requirement of democracy seems too strong, though it indicates the ideal; and absence of rebellion seems too weak. This is not the place to explore fully the contours of the difficult ideal of self-government, but it is important to stress that this norm is not identical with the value of "absolute sovereignty," and hence the critique of the latter is in danger of ignoring or demeaning the value of the former. The critique of sovereignty has some merit, but it surely suffers from the remarkable fact that enthusiasm for conditional or qualified sovereignty is often asymmetrical. Many of those who are keenest on the conditional sovereignty of others resist strenuously the slightest diminution of their own sovereign rights. The ghastly horrors of the American Civil War might have presented a case for humane military intervention by outsiders, but as William Shawcross put it: "If the prospect of having their conflict 'managed' for them by foreigners (however well intentioned) would have been unwelcome to the American people then, why should it be more acceptable to other peoples in the world today just because the motives of those who believe fervently that 'something must be done' are often decent?"[22] This indicates that the value of self-government is connected to some form of sovereignty, and this in turn should caution against any revived enthusiasm for benign imperialism whether in the form of humane rescue or advancing democracy.

These issues about sovereignty are connected to the worry that critics of the self-defence model have about the way the model seems to sanctify the international status quo in an objectionable way. It puts a protective wall around existing national state arrangements without regard to the way states treat their own citizens. Critics ask: Why should *these* boundaries and *these* states be given such respect? Why should a tyrannical state have a moral right to use violence in its own defence? The question is given added force by the ways in which colonisation and then decolonisation have often created states with whimsical boundaries and with populations that have often been artificially aggregated or divided. On the other hand, the question of origin cannot be equated with that of legitimacy. Most states have immoral, arbitrary, or idiosyncratic elements in their beginnings. Conquest, colonialism, ethnic persecution, and nationalist fantasies have all played a part in

---

Indians was such that they could be regarded as virtually mad, then they might have to be governed by others for their own good (though certainly not for the profit of those others), but he considers this prospect merely "for the sake of argument" and palpably does not believe the madness premise.

[22] William Shawcross, *Deliver Us from Evil: Peacekeepers, Warlords, and a World of Endless Conflict* (New York: Simon and Schuster, 2000), pp. 30–31.

creating contemporary states. A basic question is how this has been absorbed into an acceptance or tolerance of current arrangements by those governed. Here, a prudent pragmatism is more important than considerations of tribe, race, or social contract. Reasonable prosperity, social need, and the dangers of alternatives can provide the sort of cement that constitutes the basis for legitimacy, or if not legitimacy (which may be too big a word for what we need here) at least the sort of allegiance that will reasonably resent foreign military incursion. If this allegiance is wedded to democracy and a respect for basic human rights, so very much the better. I do not deny that historic or current grievances can destroy the acceptance; this has evidently occurred in recent years in the break-ups of the former Yugoslavia and the former Soviet Union, though political opportunism played a major part in fanning some of those grievances. But delegitimation or disintegration is not an inevitable consequence of understanding the peculiar circumstances of origin or history. Indeed, the broadening of acceptance is possible in spite of historic divisions and animosities, as the European Union, with all its problems, shows. Moreover, where acceptance breaks down it need not do so violently, as the separation of Czechoslovakia demonstrates. When violent remedies are proposed, there is a strong pragmatic case for respecting existing boundaries and state jurisdiction in spite of their dubious origins. The benefits of civic order and the realities of local attachments should not be too readily disparaged, even in states that have arisen capriciously and in which the government is marred by numerous blemishes.

Walzer's Position and Luban's Critique

Several of Walzer's critics nonetheless see his and the UN's version of the defence against aggression account of a just cause as providing too great a protection to those existing states, whatever their origins, that are denying their citizens basic human rights. The critics argue that theories such as his offer existing states a guarantee that other states will not prevent their depredations against their own people.[23] Of course, Walzer does allow for some interventions. In addition to those mentioned in Chapter 3, he grants that in extreme humanitarian emergencies, where governments are engaged in genocide, ethnic cleansing, or other extreme attacks upon their own population or significant parts of it, the defence of self may be extended to defence of others. In a Preface to the third edition of *Just and Unjust Wars*,

---

[23] See Gerald Doppelt, "Walzer's Theory of Morality in International Relationships," *Philosophy and Public Affairs* 8 (1978), pp. 3–26; David Luban, "Just War and Human Rights," *Philosophy and Public Affairs* 9 (1980), pp. 160–181; Richard A. Wasserstrom, "Review of *Just and Unjust Wars*," *Harvard Law Review* 92 (1978), pp. 536–545; see also Charles R. Beitz, "Bounded Morality: Justice and the State in World Politics" *International Organization* 33 (1979), pp. 405–424.

he has made this even clearer, but even so, the critics would be more permissive because they take a more sceptical view of the relationship between states and their peoples and its significance. Walzer allows that there are three types of circumstances in which the sovereignty of an existing state may be disregarded:

a. When a particular state includes more than one national community – an empire or a multinational state (for instance, Yugoslavia) – and when one of the communities is in active revolt, then foreign powers can come to their aid to assist in secession or national liberation. This is a case where Walzer thinks there is a clear lack of "fit" between *government* and *community*.

b. When a single community is disrupted by civil war, a foreign power can intervene to balance another state's interventions.

c. When a state is engaged in the massacre or enslavement of its own population, or possibly in the mass expulsion of certain groups of citizens. Here again, Walzer thinks that this shows that there is a radical lack of "fit" between the community governed and the state governing. By contrast, there is no case for intervention to prevent "ordinary" oppression, which has gone on in most states anyway for most of history.

Condition (c) is the most relevant to our present concerns. This is not to say that (a) and (b) are straightforward; it is not at all clear that achieving a "balance" is the sort of thing that by itself confers a right to intervene. If one side in a civil war is winning a fight to free slaves or defend itself against ethnic cleansing and is supported militarily by a foreign power, it would be strange to allow that this gives other foreigners a moral right to nullify their success. Nor is it clear that efforts at violent secession by a "community" automatically provide a licence for foreigners to intervene supportively. But condition (c) is our primary concern here. It allows for humanitarian intervention, and it suggests that we might see the dispute between Walzer and his critics more clearly if we were to view them as departing in different ways from the simple model of the self-defence justification.

Walzer departs from the simple model in his theory of justified intervention (and in some other ways), but this is because he thinks that states can lose their rights by losing the natural "fit" between government and community. His critics depart from it because they are much more sceptical about this fit. Walzer moves, as we saw, from the rights of individuals (including the right of self-protection and defence) to the rights of states via what he calls the "metaphor" of the social contract. Sharing a common life, a common soil, mutual benefits, a language and a set of cultural-religious traditions, a group of people form a community by this implicit bonding together in a "social contract." They generate or employ a government that is obliged, among other things, to defend them against foreign attack. The *union* of people and government forms *the state*. This union can come apart (as when the government tyrannises over the people), and then the state loses *legitimacy* and the people may morally rebel. But Walzer thinks that outsiders are usually in no position realistically to deny this sort of legitimacy. Indeed, because of this, he thinks that there are two types of legitimacy, one internal and one external or international. A state can therefore be illegitimate domestically but remain legitimate in the international order. (As Walzer says, "The doctrine of legitimacy has a dual reference," though he also puts the distinction in terms of states' being "actually legitimate at home" and "presumptively legitimate in international society.")[24] He writes that foreigners must "in the first instance" make "a morally necessary presumption: that there exists a certain 'fit' between the community and its government and that the state is 'legitimate'.... This presumption is simply the respect that foreigners owe to a historic community and to its internal life."[25] *But* there can come a time when the lack of "fit" is "radically apparent" even to foreigners, who can then declare the state in question *illegitimate* even in the international order.

Walzer's critics deny that the fit between people and government is normally so cosy, and they tend to identify the state with the government, the coercive apparatus. David Luban talks of Walzer's commitment to "the romance of the nation-state."[26] They think that he exaggerates the degree to which nations and peoples are identified with and served by their actual governments. In particular, for Luban, where it is clear that a government is denying its citizens "socially basic human rights," then a case exists for a just war waged by foreigners in defence of those rights. "A socially basic human right" is *one whose satisfaction is necessary to the enjoyment of any other rights* – for example, security rights (not to be subject to killing, assault, torture, etc.) or subsistence rights (to healthy air, water, food, shelter). So Luban defines a just war in these terms: "A just war is (i) a war in defence of socially basic human rights (subject to proportionality); or (ii) a war of self-defence against an unjust war."[27]

We can see these criticisms as rejections of the transition made by the domestic analogy from the individual's right of self-defence to the state's right of self-defence. This transition has also been subject to sustained and even more radical criticism in an impressive recent impressive critique of the self-defence justification by David Rodin. Let me begin, however, with Luban's objections.

---

[24] Michael Walzer, "The Moral Standing of States: A Reply to Four Critics," *Philosophy and Public Affairs* 9 (1980), p. 214.

[25] Ibid., p. 212.

[26] David Luban, "The Romance of the Nation-State," *Philosophy and Public Affairs* 9 (1980), pp. 392–397.

[27] Luban, "Just War and Human Rights," p. 175. On the other hand, a war is unjust, according to Luban, "if and only if it is not just" (p. 163).

Luban's definition of a just war goes beyond licensing humanitarian intervention (in addition to legitimate self-defence) in one way, and possibly in two. In the first place, he would allow for what he calls "economic war." His prime example concerns two neighbouring countries, A and B, of approximately the same military capacity that are separated by a mountain range that contributes to very different climatic conditions in the two countries. A has a flourishing natural environment, whereas B is semiarid. One year a lack of rain causes a severe famine in B at a time when A has a food surplus, but "for a variety of cultural, historical and economic reasons" A makes none of this surplus available to B. Luban thinks that B is entitled to go to war with A.[28] The second way in which Luban's position seems to depart from the standard case for humanitarian intervention (and from Walzer's) is in its apparent countenancing of intervention to prevent "plain repression" or the denial of security rights and not solely in circumtances of catastrophic persecution.

Luban's first way represents an alarming departure from the restrictive impulses of the defence-against-aggression model. As this abstract example is structured, it is perfectly clear that A has some moral obligation to provide help to B, but granted this, in the real world there are numerous factors that would militate against the morality of the resort to war by B. For one thing, appeals could be made to other nations and international agencies that have shown themselves willing to help with famine relief. For another, the prospect of B's succeeding against A given the great disparity of provisions between the two armies is surely bleak. Luban stipulates that they are equal in military strength, but this equality is certain to be short-lived if one side's troops are soon to be starving or, at least, undernourished. Another factor is that A has no responsibility for the conditions that have created the crisis in B: that is why the proposed attack is not a case of self-defence. Nor is it motivated by altruism, but rather by something like self-preservation. Licensing war to remedy natural ills or disasters when the war is against those who have done nothing to produce the evils (even though they might have done something to remedy them) is a regressive step in the drive to restrict the evils of war.

Luban's second way is his version of the humanitarian intervention scenario, and it is open to an interpretation that is more permissive than those commonly offered, most notably that offered by Walzer. It is hard to be certain of the interpretation that he intends, because he sometimes writes as if he has in mind a condition in which a foreign government is engaged in wholesale violence and massacre, while at other times it is merely "highly visible signs that it does not enjoy consent," "plain repression," "violations of security rights," or the illegitimacy of the government. One or more of these phrases would license military invasions by strong nations into a great

---

[28] Ibid., pp. 177–178.

number of states in the contemporary world, and the spread of the attitude behind these phrases amongst the powerful nations in the world is itself likely to have catastrophic results for world peace and for international stability. Such stability can of course be overrated; it is one of the problems of realism that it puts too high a value on it; but nonetheless it has a significant value, as the consequences of the Iraq invasion make clear. Luban accuses Walzer, with some justice, as being seduced by "the romance of the nation state," but he shows a tendency himself to be seduced by "the romance of the human rights crusader."

In a much later article, Luban has retreated from this more permissive stance on humanitarian intervention, arguing that he was wrong to set the threshold for humanitarian intervention so low. He also abandons the emphasis on consent and political legitimacy, since both are compatible with severe human rights abuses.[29] Instead, he urges the merits of the recognition of "barbaric evil" as a trigger for legitimate intervention. He elucidates the notion of the barbaric by reference, naturally enough, to civilization, but admits that the distinction between the civilized and the barbaric is "fluctuating and fraught with relativism."[30] Luban's discussion is rich and suggestive, but his relativising of the legitimacy of judgments of barbarity to cultures is, I believe, a retrograde step. Certainly, it makes his ultimate position seem more unstable than he wants it to be. He admits that Western Europeans have abandoned the death penalty as uncivilized (and not just Europeans, of course; it is abolished in Australia and New Zealand and elsewhere), whereas the United States retains it. Where other nations regard the death penalty as barbaric, would this entitle them, had they the power, to launch a humanitarian intervention against American barbarism? I certainly regard the death penalty, in all normal circumstances, as barbaric; but even were such an intervention prudential, I would reject such a case for intervention. Clearly, more needs to be said about the concept of barbaric evil, but there is no space for it here. Enough to note that Luban's later position is very close to Walzer's own.

Abandoning Self-Defence?

David Rodin is not principally concerned to defend humanitarian intervention or to extend the self-defence model: his doubts about the self-defence model are more radical still. Rodin argues *inter alia* that the state's right to self-defence must ultimately rest upon its defence of individual rights, and

---

[29] David Luban, "Intervention and Civilization: Some Unhappy Lessons of the Kosovo War," in Pablo de Greiff and Ciaran Cronin (eds.), *Global Justice and Transnational Politics: Essays on the Moral and Political Challenges of Globalisation* (Cambridge, MA and London: MIT Press, 2002), pp. 79–115.

[30] Ibid., p. 105.

specifically the right to life. Hence where the right to life of a large portion of the community is at stake, the state may legitimately call on self-defence as a ground for resort to war.[31] Yet the standard accounts of a state's right to self-defence are much broader than this. Standard accounts are based on a strong understanding of state sovereignty and permit the resort to war to defend territory and political autonomy where the threat to citizens' lives may be minimal or nonexistent. This takes us far from the domestic model, since that concentrates only upon the right to defend your life with violence against violent attack. Surely, you would not be entitled to maim or kill someone who was preventing you from getting to the polls to vote or even stealing your property.[32] There is certainly some force in Rodin's criticism, especially when we consider the readiness with which states resort to violence in reaction to insults, incursions, threats, and invented "attacks"; and I have already argued against Walzer's idea that aggression is an undifferentiated offence that always requires a warlike reaction. If this were the standard view, then Rodin would be right to reject it. Nonetheless, the form his rejection takes tends to ignore or belittle goods that political community makes possible in ways that are not accessible to the individual in the one-off domestic analogy. An invading state bent upon eliminating your political autonomy is normally not simply going to prevent your voting on a particular occasion (assuming you live in a democracy) or substitute one form of democracy for another; it is more likely to dramatically circumscribe or eliminate your right to vote altogether, and along with it your rights to many other goods, such as freedom of speech and association. Along with this are likely to come significant unjust penalties and persecutions for many people simply because the new political order is so different from the old, all of this being sustained by the violence that brought about the changes in the first place. Similarly with the property issue: if the example is that of a thief not merely stealing some valuable item of property, but permanently taking over part of your home along with several of your children, who are thereafter forcefully kept in the thief's care, surely the matter looks somewhat different. Of course, if this sort of thing happens in a stable state, you will have recourse to the police and the law, and there are good reasons for not wanting individual citizens to take the law into their own hands. But the domestic analogy envisages some

---

[31] David Rodin, *War and Self-Defense* (Oxford: Clarendon Press, 2002), pp. 139–140. Rodin's book is a rich and subtle critique and contains other objections to the self-defence model that I will not discuss, principally because their target is a standard view many elements of which I do not support.

[32] See ibid., pp. 134–138, for the discussion of threats to property and its relation to national defence, and pp. 47–48 on threats to liberty, such as freedom to vote or freedom of expression. As Rodin notes, Richard Norman takes a similar position on the limitations of the domestic analogy. See Richard Norman, *Ethics, Killing and War* (Cambridge: Cambridge University Press, 1995), Chapter 4.

version of the state of nature (or a temporary simulation of it) where that recourse is not available. Here it is much less clear that Rodin's insistence that you have no entitlement to violent defence of property or political rights is plausible.

It might reasonably be objected that I have loaded the critique of Rodin unfairly because I have taken the example of a nondemocratic state invading a democratic one, and that things would be different if the invader were the democratic state and the target nondemocratic, or even tyrannical. Certainly that makes a difference, but the question is how much difference. People who live in politically unsatisfactory regimes will often have a variety of reasons for preferring the relative stability of these regimes to foreign rule, and at least some of these reasons may be good ones. Many Americans view their intervention in Iraq as an attempt to do good for the Iraqi people, but even had this been a major motivation in the intervention, which I doubt, the disruptive violence used by the invading coalition in the regime change and its aftermath has provided some of the reasons for the armed resistance, and it is plausible that such reasons might legitimate armed resistance. Some of the insurgents want Saddam back, but many who hated Saddam want to get rid of the occupiers as well. Or, to change the example, some of the Russians who fought for their land and community against the invading Nazis had little or no regard for the villainous regime of Josef Stalin. I am not arguing that defence of one's homeland and associated rights is a complete justification for armed resistance, because the other conditions of the JAB need to be addressed as well, but I think that even in the case of a nondemocratic regime, or even, sometimes, a tyrannical one, an armed invasion threatens far more substantial goods than Rodin recognizes. In defence of dictatorial post-colonial regimes, it was sometimes said by their victims: "He's a monster, but he's our monster!" This oversimplified too many issues, as slogans tend to do, but it suggested some significant values that are endangered by foreign rule.

I have argued that the values of self-government and of some form of political sovereignty cannot be lightly dismissed, even by the resort to the legitimate concern for human rights. I cannot provide a full account of these values here, but the arguments of Rodin and the other critics at least raise an acute problem for Walzer's analysis in that the "fit" between a community and its government is seldom as snug as Walzer's picture suggests, and even where it is, this is not always a good thing. Frequently it is not so much a natural as a contrived connection, which often suits the interests of those in power. Marxist analysis of societies as scenes of class conflict is no longer fashionable and was certainly oversimplified and distorting, but it rightly stressed the way in which social institutions and government itself often serve baser interests than those professed by the rhetoric of common goals or proclaimed purposes. Theorists like Walzer *at least* need to argue more for the fit and its virtue.

Second, in practice, Walzer's and his critics' positions on when to go to war don't finally differ as much as one might think. Walzer agrees that foreign intervention may have been justifiable in South Africa at the height of the apartheid regime. In the end, the underlying model of self-defence and aiding other-defence can in principle be extended to defending communities that are not represented by states when those communities are facing extreme enough threats – it is really just a difference on *presumption* about *states* as the bearers of rights and duties in the international order rather than peoples. Here, despite the important development of international agencies and significant cosmopolitan pressure groups in recent years, and despite the often-ambiguous effects of globalisation, it must be stressed that nation-states are the major players in the international order and are likely to remain so for a long while to come. This must be factored into any account of the conditions for humanitarian intervention.

Third, though the critics seem to me to be more nearly right about the philosophical issue regarding the nature of state sovereignty, Walzer is nearer the truth on the pragmatic, practical questions. The case he makes for the dangers of intervention is, I think, persuasive, and my own arguments earlier can be seen as elaborations of such a case. In addition, I think that the critics, in their anxiety to stress the overriding importance of basic human rights, are insufficiently attentive to various values of self-government that may survive even in illiberal or oppressive regimes. These values are not such as to rule out external criticism and pressure or internal resistance or even rebellion, but they do provide a hurdle to righteous, violent intervention. The "just cause" of national self-defence may nonetheless be defeasible, in the sense that it becomes unavailable to a state that exhibits a very considerable or total lack of the "fit" Walzer speaks of between government and community, or even where there is some high degree of fit but the government and most of its community are bent upon genocide or enslavement of some subgroup. This opens the way to the possibility of legitimate humanitarian interventions. Even so, the hurdle creates a substantial barrier, and it combines with the prudential considerations outlined earlier, many of which are related to the other conditions of the JAB to be examined in the next chapter, to create a powerful case against abandoning or dramatically extending the self-defence model.

5

Justice with Prudence

The US has broken the second rule of war. That is, don't go fighting with your land army on the mainland of Asia. Rule One is don't march on Moscow. I developed these two rules myself.

Field Marshal Montgomery, commenting on
the American war in Vietnam.[1]

The previous two chapters have focussed upon the interpretation of the just cause condition of the JAB. In this chapter, we shall examine those conditions of the JAB that are more concerned with the exercise of prudence in approaching the decision to wage war. This raises issues having to do with the consideration of expectations and consequences and the judgement and balancing of the weight and relevance of such matters. Emphasis on the broadly non-consequentialist nature of the just war tradition can give rise to the thought that this form of thinking cannot be concerned at all with consequences. This is a foolish thought, though it can be encouraged by some of the starker oppositions that philosophers sometimes make between consequentialist theories and those that are contrasted with them. No moral theory and no moral thinking can afford to ignore entirely the assessment of the consequences of action. Where intrinsicalist theories part company from theories like utilitarianism is in their refusal to treat the assessment of consequences as the whole task of moral thinking.[2] Once certain negative duties are established or the importance and nature of adherence to certain virtues is assured, then there will usually be considerable room for arguing the merits of some course of action on the basis of its likely good or bad outcomes. A further, less often remarked departure is in the way in

---

[1] Alun Chalfont, *Montgomery of Alamein* (New York: Atheneum, 1976), p. 318.

[2] I prefer the term "intrinsicalist" rather than such expressions as "deontological," since it has broader scope than a reference to rights or duties and covers all theories or theorists that are committed to intrinsic rights and wrongs, other than the failure to maximise goods or minimise evils.

which consequences are considered, since intrinsicalist thinkers will be less concerned to assess consequences in a spirit of mathematical maximising. This is not the place to elaborate in more detail on the contrasts; our principal concern is merely to indicate that moral theories underlying just war doctrines allow for the relevance of consequences in just war thinking.

The point about this relevance is connected to debates in philosophy about the supposed opposition between morality and prudence. When this opposition is proposed, it is usually done by treating prudence as essentially a matter of self-interest. For my part, I am reluctant to contrast morality and prudence sharply, since properly understood, prudence is, it seems to me, part of morality. Such proper understanding needs to reject the common philosophical identification of prudence and self-interest. For one thing, you can exercise prudence on behalf of others; but more generally, prudence is concerned with the judicious, feasible, and efficacious implementation of moral principles and virtuous injunctions as well as plans and objectives. In this sense, prudence is no more likely to conflict with moral requirements than courage or temperance. Yet self-interest certainly can conflict with morality, even if such conflict is not as endemic as some puritan moralists would insist. As we noted in the discussion of political realism in Chapter 3, the promptings of self-interest and of morality will often enough converge, but they can also part company, whether the self in question be an individual or a nation. By contrast, prudence is an integral part of morality.

Just Cause – Some Further Thoughts

In the previous chapter we considered the "defence against aggression" model of just cause at some length and examined some proposed modifications to and departures from it. Another dimension of the just cause debate, more directly related to the virtue of prudence, also needs to be stressed. We might approach this by recalling the old debates about whether both sides can have just cause in a war. This is discussed by theorists like Vitoria and Suarez, and the common answer is that objectively it is impossible for both sides to be in the right, though it is clearly possible and indeed invariably the case that both sides will think that they are in the right. It is also clearly possible that both sides will be in the wrong, as when one imperial power has brutally acquired a colony that was previously independent and another imperial power attacks the colony in order to supplant the first invader.

There is obviously good sense in this analysis of the possibilities. The comments about the objective aspects of the question are meant to mirror logical features of discourse more generally – the logical laws of noncontradiction and excluded middle are clearly present in the background of the debate. True, some logicians have challenged both of these, if not their validity, at least their scope. But for our purposes they would have great force in this connection. If the issue of just resort to war can be assimilated to the model

presented by "If X is true then not-X cannot be true," then surely the case
would be settled. But is it so easy?

Part of the problem is that the question of who is in the right depends for
its answer on asking the further question, "About what?" For in any political conflict between states, or for that matter between states and nonstate
groups, there will usually be a constellation of grievances and perceived
wrongs on both sides that go to make up the *causus belli*. Some of these will
be mere pretexts, but there will often remain factors in the behaviour of
both sides that constitute contributory wrongs in the political situation that
seems to require war as its solution. So, Iraq's supposed possession of some,
and apparent search for more, weapons of mass destruction was a bad thing,
but so was the earlier complicity of the United States and several of its allies
in Iraq's militarization. So also were the shocking effects of the sanctions
regime against Iraq, which was largely sustained by U.S. pressure at the UN,
though Saddam's own complicity in the sufferings of his people was another
factor. Israel's war against the Palestinians, in its latest phase, can cite the
dreadful acts of the suicide bombers as its "just cause," but they can hardly
be considered in isolation from the unjust Israeli "settlements" in Palestinian land, along with other acts of Israeli belligerence that have served in
part to provoke them. These complexities mean that the judgement of "just
cause" is a perilous one, and they suggest caution in the rush to judgement
about the justice of one's cause. The eventual determination that one has a
just cause will be an outcome of preponderating judgement and should be
hedged about by the awareness of complexity and uncertainty, both moral
and factual. This in turn must remind us of the fact that "just cause" is no
more than a necessary, though preeminent, condition for resort to war and
should turn our attention to the significance of the prudential checks upon
such resort.

We should also be wary of conflating the justice of our cause with the
real or supposed superiority of our political system or ideology to that of
the foreign power against whom we have a grievance. Even were Christianity
superior to the animist religions of the Congolese, this would be irrelevant
to the verdict on the rapacious wars of Christian Belgium in the Congo in the
nineteenth century. Nor does the superiority of democracy over dictatorship
as a political ideal mean that democracies automatically have a just cause
in conflicts with a nondemocracy or even a dictatorship. This is an obvious
enough point, but it is remarkable how influential the conflation can be in
the context of political crises. Indeed, the mantle of respectability that even
a half-way decent democracy can convey will often blind its citizens and
leaders to the evils it can commit, both domestically and internationally.
The discussion of the faults of moralism in Chapter 3 is relevant here. The
conviction that "we're the good guys" is a powerful recipe for folly at the
least and self-righteous vice at the worst.

Last Resort: Exploring the Alternatives

The just war provision of "last resort" contains many puzzles and ambiguities, especially those that raise semantic and logical problems concerning what it can mean to call something a last resort. There will always be *something* that might be tried as an alternative to violence, but if there is a great evil to be prevented we cannot be expected to wait upon every possibility other than effective violence. Clearly, some considerations of feasibility are required to screen the realistic availability of alternatives to violence. And it needs to be remembered that waiting to try numerous such options may actually reduce the likely effectiveness of the military option when it is tried.

Nonetheless, bearing these difficulties in mind, the criterion has a commonsense interpretation in which it functions as a reminder that the resort to violence must be, to a significant degree, reluctant. Hence, the condition might better be described as "genuinely reluctant resort." It enjoins us to make serious efforts at peaceful resolutions of our political problems before resorting to the sword. The term "peaceful" is itself open to varied interpretations, depending on how rich or thin a notion of peace is in play, and we shall examine this more carefully in Chapter 13.[3] Here it should include a comprehensive range of nonviolent methods which may certainly involve pressure and coercion. In the case of intervention, the emphasis needs to be put upon such nonviolent efforts, including coercive interventions of an economic and political nature.

These may involve what has been called "coercive diplomacy" or "forceful persuasion" by Alexander George.[4] George's definitions of this phenomenon are a little loose, but they are meant to cover threats of violence and certain forms of deprivation, as well as the combination of these with concessions, promises, and other "carrots" or positive inducements. Threats to withdraw existing support, such as aid, trade status, or diplomatic recognition, or threats not to proceed with economic or political aid that has been anticipated, are coercive interventions in domestic affairs in that they exercise power by seeking to constrain the choices of national agents. The imposition of economic sanctions constitutes an extreme form of such coercion, and this can shade into violent measures, as when a sanction regime is enforced by military means. Clearly, there are more problems with some of these options than with others. Sanctions, in particular, were once viewed as a clean alternative to violent intervention, but can now be seen often to have very harmful effects upon the least guilty, and only minimal impact upon

---

[3] Jeff Ross and I sketch some of the relevant distinctions in C. A. J. Coady and Jeff Ross, "St. Augustine and the Ideal of Peace," in the special issue on St. Augustine, *The American Catholic Philosophical Quarterly* 74, no.1 (Winter 2000), pp. 153–161.

[4] Alexander L. George, *Forceful Persuasion: Coercive Diplomacy as an Alternative to War* (Washington DC: United States Institute of Peace Press, 1991).

the primary agents of the evil they were intended to prevent or restrict.[5] Of course, there are sanctions and sanctions. One of the most successful forms of sanction, only partially economic, was the sporting sanction imposed on South Africa, which had a great imaginative impact on a fanatically sports-loving society and politically hurt the predominantly oppressive white community more than the black, though it did not cause starvation and death. The other problem with sanctions is that they are sometimes difficult to operate and frequently take time to have an effect; but in many cases military intervention and other military enterprises are also protracted (witness the miscalculations about how long the bombing of Serbia would need to go on, and, more dramatically, the U.S. misjudgement about the scope and duration of its involvement in Vietnam). Both persuasion and certain non-violent coercive measures should be employed in the early stages of a crisis, or as a crisis looms, when opportunities for prevention or mitigation may present themselves, or can be constructed.[6] This sort of prevention is likely to be less costly and less damaging than the military response to the head-line grabbing disaster, though it is a curious quirk of human psychology that it is easier to create support for very expensive, dramatic military efforts – especially where the risks to the interveners appear low – than for cheaper nonviolent activities aimed at prevention.

Michael Walzer's advocacy of the merits of resort to "force-short-of-war" instead of war proper was briefly discussed in Chapter 1, and is relevant here. Walzer's talk of "force" rather than "violence" inherits many of the problems I discussed in Chapters 1 and 2, and this is illustrated by the diverse sorts of things he groups under "force-short-of-war." He gives as "one possible example of this use" the containment regime of 1991–2003 in Iraq.[7] This regime, however, included several of the various types of coercive diplomacy just discussed, as well as the palpable violence of the persistent bombing. Walzer lists three elements in the "regime": the arms embargo, the UN inspection system, and the "no-fly zone" bombing.[8] Only the third directly involved violence (and, unlike the other two, was not endorsed by the UN), though embargoes can require implied or threatened violence that is occasionally realised. Walzer claims that all three involved "the use of force," but this is not true of the inspections regime, nor of all uses of the embargo on arms supplies. Even stopping ships at sea, which Walzer cites as a use of force, can be done without violence, and often is, though the threat of violence is usually in the offing.

[5] See Joy Gordon, "Cool War: Economic Sanctions as a Weapon of Mass Destruction," *Harper's Magazine*, November 2002, pp. 43–49.

[6] This was again an emphasis of Kofi Annan's address published as *The Question of Intervention* (New York: United Nations, 1999).

[7] Michael Walzer, "Regime Change and Just War," *Dissent* 53 (2006), p. 106.

[8] Ibid., p. 105. Walzer here claims that the containment regime was "UN endorsed," but this is only true of the embargo and the inspection elements.

Concentrating, however, on the no-fly zone bombing campaign, and taking it to be justified as a measure for preventing Saddam's attacking his internal opponents, we should ask whether violence-short-of-war should not be conditioned by last resort. Walzer says, "Despite the French argument at the UN in 2002 and 2003 that the use of force must always come as a last resort, force-short-of-war obviously comes before war itself."[9] So described the point is indeed tautological, but the French need hardly be disturbed by this. The crucial point is whether force-short-of-war, where it is violence short of war, should allow us to relax the requirements of just war theory, especially that of last resort. Walzer thinks it should, and he believes we need a new theory of *jus ad vim* to supplement *jus ad bellum*; the new theory should not be "overly tolerant or permissive" but "more permissive" than just war theory.[10]

On the contrary, where it is really political violence rather than coercive diplomacy that we are talking about, we do not need some more permissive theory quite distinct from just war thinking. As pointed out in Chapter 1, the no-fly zone bombing was a very significant resort to violence, and its justification should certainly have invoked considerations such as prospects for success, proportionality, and last resort. I argued earlier in this section that "last resort" draws attention to the need to seek realistic solutions to political problems that are less damaging than resort to political violence. Political violence of any sort should require satisfaction of the genuine reluctance constraint. What is true, of course, is that there are greater and lesser degrees of violence and of war, and what truth there is in Walzer's claim resides in that fact, since there should be greater reluctance to engage in wholesale invasion than, for example, to send in a small armed unit to effect a minimal objective such as a rescue of captives. Nonetheless, there are dangers in the latter, as the botched U.S. attempt to rescue its captive diplomats in Iran during the Carter presidency demonstrated, and even small–scale killing and destruction – as against available, feasible alternatives that are less damaging – needs justification.[11]

Another form of sanction short of violence that is in the process of development and needs further encouragement is the criminal sanction of law. War crimes tribunals, the International Criminal Court, and even foreign domestic courts have deterrence potential as well as retributive power; although their processes are slow, they target only individuals and have difficulty getting those they indict to appear, their political impact is significant

---

[9] Ibid., p. 106.

[10] Ibid.

[11] In fact, the alternative of negotiation was successful in releasing the captives in Iran, though it had to wait for Ronald Reagan's assumption of the presidency to succeed. That it had to wait was, we now know, the result of an unscrupulous deal between the Reagan Republicans and the Iranian leadership that was intended to derail Carter's presidency.

and likely to increase. Indicted political and military leaders may be secure for a time in their own countries, but (as the Pinochet case showed) they will be at risk when travelling abroad, and they can have no confidence in immunity if the leadership in their own nation changes, as eventually it is very likely to do.

These nonviolent approaches are not guaranteed to work, and they need imagination and political acumen in their implementation if they are to be successful, but both these points apply to the use of violence as well.

The Prospects for Success

This criterion, like that of last resort, is partly motivated by concern that the horrors attendant upon war not be unleashed capriciously or without sufficient regard for outcomes. But that is also a condition upon rational action of any sort. In this latter aspect, it is part of acting for an end that one thinks about how probable it is that the proposed means will achieve that end. Understood in these two ways, this criterion is clearly an important prudential constraint upon war making. It is particularly significant in providing a dampener to the unbalancing effects of enthusiasm, outraged feelings, and triumphalist fervour that often precede the decision to go to war.

That said, there remain complexities about the application of this criterion. Success depends not only on one's efforts, but also upon how one's ends are defined. Indeed, part of the importance of this test is that it forces concentration upon the clarity and importance of one's purposes in contemplating resort to war. Clausewitz rightly emphasised the idea that resort to war should be guided by political ends, but this is merely a necessary condition upon ends, since the subordination of military means to political ends is not sufficient to establish that it is right to employ them. The political ends must themselves be reasonable and morally acceptable. Talk of "victory," "crushing the enemy," "defeating evil," "making the world safe for democracy" may serve certain motivational purposes, but will usually fail to provide feasible, attainable objectives for war.

Here, there can be a tension between aims that are limited and achievable but fall short of fully remedying an evil, and those that would remedy the evil but are ambitious and full of risk. It is hard to say anything helpful in the abstract about this, since so much turns on the particularities of the concrete situations that arise, but where lives, civic order, and human infrastructure are put at grave risk with very uncertain prospects for success, there is surely a presumption in favour of more modest goals. This is especially indicated when we consider the innumerable follies that lofty military fantasies have produced. Military overreach is just as common, and even more damaging, than political or economic overreach. It might be objected that the more modest path was observed strictly in the Gulf War, with the result that Saddam Hussein remained in power. Even so, it is not at all clear what the internal political consequences of external military overthrow of Hussein would have been, given the divided opposition forces, the ethnic hostilities, and the religious oppositions in Iraq. Indeed, the subsequent war in Iraq is providing grim lessons in the hazards of seeking to achieve by military means such grandiose goals as the democratisation of Iraq and the Middle East.

A further problem that has emerged in recent years and deserves treatment here is that of "cost-free intervention." It is a significant element in the current debate about humanitarian intervention that the various guidelines laid down by Western governments considering the problem insist upon conditions for intervention that are profoundly self-regarding. In some respects this is merely prudent, but there is reason to believe that the emphasis on interventions that will be cost-free to the interveners in terms of risk to their own forces (though not so much in terms of money expended) has become excessive because it leads to a disproportionate response to the problem. It is very understandable that interveners want to minimise risks to their own forces: the concern for one's own troops represents a moral advance over many military policies of the past, such as the treatment of one's own soldiers as the merest cannon fodder in the trenches of World War I. In democracies, there is also a question of the political costs of acting in defiance of widespread public fears.[12] Nonetheless, if the saving of foreigners from massacre or mass expulsion from their homelands is a worthy cause for war, then governments and commanders must be prepared to put troops in harm's way.

The refusal to do so inevitably leads to the reliance upon remote forms of air power and technological wizardry that tend to shift the damage onto largely blameless civilian populations, as happened to some degree in the bombing of Serbia. The damage in terms of immediate killing of civilians, estimated by the London *Times* to be in the order of 1,500 deaths,[13] is significant enough; and Amnesty International considered that such NATO killings "may have violated international humanitarian law."[14] But in

---

[12] As several commentators have pointed out, it is not clear that there is quite as much public opposition to humanitarian military operations (including interventions) that involve genuine risks to the lives of troops as is commonly believed. At least this seems to be the case prior to intervention and in its early stages. But what worries politicians is public opinion when the body bags start arriving.

[13] "The War So Far," *The Times* (London), World Wide Web edition, May 23, 1999.

[14] *Amnesty International Annual Report* 2000, <http://web.amnesty.org/web/ar2000.nsf/58f967 f150817f77802568f500617d07/445feb9f97b52b9e802568f200552985!OpenDocument>. AI gives a figure of 500 civilians killed by NATO, though it is somewhat unclear from the report whether this is meant to be civilians in Kosovo alone, as the context seems to indicate. Estimates of the number of civilians killed by Serb forces in Kosovo, vary dramatically, though the U.S. State Department claims that "probably around 10,000" Kosovar Albanians were killed in the Serbian purge. See the U.S. Department of State report "Ethnic Cleansing in Kosovo: An Accounting," Archive Site (January 20, 2001),

addition to this, the bombing of what are called "dual-purpose" targets (especially power, water, and transport facilities) clearly created a serious humanitarian problem for the Serbian civilian population and for many others beyond the borders of Serbia, for example, in the disruption of the Romanian economy. (The problems raised by the category of dual-purpose targets will be examined more directly in a later chapter.) In addition, the possibility of successful warfare that carries little risk to your own forces, and hence little domestic political cost, can make the resort to war seem an easier option than it should be.

Proportionality

The notion of proportionality is employed extensively in just war theory, both in the context of the resort to war in the first place and, as we shall see in Chapter 7, in the context of the legitimacy of incidental collateral damage. Yet its employment is often a curious combination of the natural and the theoretically opaque. It seems natural in that there is obvious intuitive sense to the requirement that we should rule out the use of violence that is disproportionate to the ends that supposedly legitimate it. Unleashing a nuclear bombardment in response to persistent violation of fishing waters would be an obvious example. Yet what is it to be disproportionate or proportionate? Certainly, there are few developed accounts of what such proportionality amounts to, and it is impossible to settle the problems that surround this notion here, but some brief comment on the complexities is necessary.[15]

It is tempting to think that there is a simple utilitarian or consequentialist construal of the concept available: violence is proportional if it brings about more overall benefits than harms, disproportional if not. But this seems false both to the just war tradition and to our intuitions about particular cases. For any but the most dedicated utilitarian, it cannot be that the concept invokes the quest for answers to the question whether this particular action is more likely to bring about the optimal state of the world, all things considered, than any of the available alternatives; but, if not, what can it be doing? Any answer must lie in the direction of what might be called middle-range assessment. What we need to ask is broader than the question, "Will

<www.state.gov/www/global/human_rights/kosovoii/homepage.html#exe>. This is at the high end of estimates and does not distinguish civilians from Kosovo Liberation Army combatants. Moreover, the vast majority of these killings occurred during the dreadful expulsion of Kosovar Alabanians by Serb forces, *after* the NATO bombing campaign began.

[15] For the best recent discussion of proportionality as a tool of just war analysis, see Thomas Hurka, "Proportionality in the Morality of War," *Philosophy and Public Affairs* 33, no. 1 (2005), pp. 34–66. Hurka's subtle analysis still leaves, as he acknowledges, many questions unanswered.

this offensive drive the enemy back and allow us to occupy the ground he now occupies?" But it is also narrower than the question, "Will this offensive make the world safe for democracy?" Of course, the first question is absurdly local and should be inadequate by strategic military canons as much as by moral standards; and the second is ridiculously lofty. Nonetheless both have played their parts in disproportionate military campaigns, ranging from some of the battles of World War I through to the follies of Vietnam. The idea of proportionality calls upon us to assess the proclaimed necessities of military means to military ends against the tragic human certainties of death and injury to combatants and noncombatants (on both sides) and the moral and political purposes of the conflict. Assuming, for instance, that the Gulf War was a morally legitimate undertaking for the purpose of decisively removing an aggressive force from Kuwait – about which assumption doubts may well be raised – we may nonetheless judge that the killing of so many routed Kuwaiti soldiers, as they fled the battlefield weaponless, was disproportionate.[16] To do this is to judge those deaths to have been recognisably excessive for achieving that aim, but it is not of course thereby to assert that they would have been unnecessary for some other aim, such as the toppling of Saddam Hussein's government and the establishment of an independent Kurdish state. The problem with these further calculations is, first, that the war was not publicly justified and endorsed on such grounds in the first place and very likely could not have been so justified morally given the sort of valuations thereby involved; and second, that the prospects for establishing such outcomes by such methods (even were the outcomes, in all their complexity, morally desirable) are far too remote and uncertain to be worth the deaths of so many people and the further political ramifications of occupation. Nor is this simply a matter of epistemic uncertainty, important as that is. There are some good outcomes that may be highly probable but seem nonetheless irrelevant to the judgement about appropriate violence: the fact that a war against some minor offender (over, say, a border incursion) would increase international economic activity in a way that would bring considerable benefits to the world cannot make resort to war proportional.[17] It would seem that proportionality cannot be invoked where the beneficial outcomes are merely possible or speculative (as against the certain or highly probable harms foreseen) nor where the benefits aren't sufficiently related to the justifying conditions for the resort to war in the first place. Clearly more needs to be said about proportionality, but whatever is said, it seems certain that the determination of what is proportional will leave a great deal to concrete, circumstantial judgement rather than the application of

---

[16] There is serious room for dispute about the numbers killed in this way, or indeed more generally in the war itself.

[17] Hurka, "Proportionality in the Morality of War," p. 40.

some hard-and-fast rule.[18] Here, as elsewhere in philosophy, we are clearer about the truth of various concrete judgements of disproportionality than about our analysis of the concept of proportionality embodied in those judgements.

Legitimate Authority and Right Intention

I turn now to two conditions that generally receive less attention in modern treatments of the just war than the conditions so far examined. The condition of legitimate authority has its rationale in the concern that the licence to resort to war be restricted to political agents who might be expected to exercise more responsibility than private agents or criminal groups. As we have already seen, however, legitimacy is itself a contested notion and even when unambiguous it may not put as great a brake on self-interest, folly, impulsiveness, or indeed criminality as the framers of this condition had hoped. Still, it is plausible to think that it provides something of a restriction on the types of conflict that could count as just wars. It should not, however, be construed as ruling out entirely the idea of a just revolution or insurgency, since legitimate political authority is at least capable of being extended to nonstate groups. Armed struggle against colonial or domestic oppression faces many problems of justification, but conditions like last resort, prospect of success, and proportionality (assuming that just cause is satisfied) pose more acute difficulties than legitimate authority. Nonetheless, the latter does pose problems, mostly having to do with the degree of political control that the leadership of the struggle can exercise over their followers. This is inevitably more fluid and subject to "splintering" than the political authority of a stable state. Against this, it must be conceded that many states are not all that stable, and that those that are do not have complete control over the behaviour of their troops in time of war. I shall return to some of the problems raised by legitimate authority in the discussion of terrorism in Chapter 8.

As for right intention, it has suffered some neglect as a separate condition because much of what it appears to encompass seems contained within the other conditions of the JAB or the JIB. Pursuit of a just cause, regard for proportionality, respect for noncombatant immunity, all seem to be part of what should count as a right intention in waging war. This is so, but it might

[18] There is a further problem with applying the proportionality test of the doctrine of double effect to those who are waging an unjust war. It is not at all clear that those whose cause is unjust can defend their unintended but foreseen killing as proportional to their military and political objectives where these are unjust. Even so, there may be a derivative sense in which it is good that they avoid killing that is disproportional to their military objectives, even where these are themselves illegitimate. The problem here is related to the problem discussed in Chapter 3, and more fully in Chapter 6, of the relations between the JAB and the JIB.

be responded that the right intention condition still serves the purpose of calling attention to the internal orientation of the potential combatants. Such orientation should naturally mirror the external conditions that must apply, but the internal and external conditions could come apart, as, for instance, when a just cause to go to war obtains but the ruler whose state has suffered the injury goes to war for reasons unrelated to it. The ruler might aim at eliminating a trade rival or expanding his state's domination of a region rather than merely repelling an invader. In such circumstances, the just cause serves as something of a pretext for reasons that should not justify resort to war. Thus understood, the condition insists that the war aims of the justified violence should be directly under the guidance of the just cause condition. With respect to the other conditions, the right intention clause merely stresses what is surely implicit in them, that proportionality or immunity of noncombatants, for example, should not merely be accidental features of the conduct of war but part of deliberate policy.

The idea that war aims are intrinsically connected to just cause and constrained and controlled by it is very important and is related to some of the issues discussed in Chapter 13, but room needs to be allowed for the possibility that the war may itself generate purposes that may be legitimately pursued even if they were not part of the initial war aims, and even where they may not have justified resort to war in the first place considered by themselves. An obvious case is the purpose of disarming a defeated invading enemy sufficiently to ensure that they are not in a position to engage in further aggression. In the absence of their actual aggression on this occasion, going to war to disarm them would not have been a legitimate cause for war, but it is a licit further aim once the war has legitimately begun. Here, and in many such cases, the further purpose is clearly related to the initial just cause; it is, as it were, under its guidance.[19] But there are other possibilities more remote from the initial just cause. Consider the situation where nation A fights a justified war of self-defence against a vicious invader nation B and in the course of repelling the invader finds that the enemy has set up concentration camps for members of an ethnic minority in their midst. The prisoners have done nothing to deserve their imprisonment. Surely, nation A is entitled to use violence to release the prisoners and to take steps to see that they are well treated, though releasing them might not have been in itself sufficient to justify war in the first place. Here, the justification is, or

---

[19] Jeff McMahan and Robert McKim make a similar point, using the terminology of "sufficient" and "contributing" just causes, in "The Just War and the Gulf War," *Canadian Journal of Philosophy* 23 (1993) pp. 512–513. Their distinction is also adopted by Thomas Hurka in "Proportionality in the Morality of War," p. 41. I prefer to count only sufficient just causes as just causes at all (though they are not properly sufficient unless the other conditions of the JAB are satisfied as well) precisely because "contributing" purposes can do no work in initially providing just cause for a war. They may, as Hurka argues, contribute as beneficial outcomes toward satisfying the proportionality condition of the JAB.

might be, remote from the just cause of self-defence, since the concentration camps need have nothing to do with the initial aggression of A against B. Yet once the justified war has been embarked upon, it seems that the alleviation of great suffering and the restitution of major human rights can be a legitimate accompanying purpose of the war, given that it is not in conflict with the justifying war aims and satisfies other prudential constraints such as proportionality. The more clearly the waging of the war conforms to just cause and right intention, the easier it will be to defend the pursuit of subsidiary humanitarian objectives.

Preemption and Prevention

Finally, there is the question of legitimate preemption. This returns us to considerations about the scope of just cause, but the topic also raises significant prudential considerations. The classic natural law presentations of just war theory by Vitoria and Suarez make no reference to war for anticipated injuries, but the context of their discussion seems to exclude its legitimacy entirely. Suarez distinguishes between legitimate wars that are strictly defensive and those that are aggressive in terms that restrict the former to responses to injuries that are in the process of occurring, whereas the latter respond to injuries that have already taken place. His comments provide no defence of preemption, but are mainly notable for the use of the term "aggression" to describe wars that modern sensibility and usage would clearly regard as defensive. Some later theorists, especially those enamoured of the "balance of power" doctrine in international affairs, have been more sympathetic to justifying war in terms of anticipated injuries.

It is worth recalling Michael Walzer's useful distinction between preemptive and preventive war. In Walzer's version of just war theory in *Just and Unjust Wars*, it seems that preemption is sometimes legitimate and prevention is not. Broadly, he reserves the term "preemption" for those cases where one side strikes the first blow in anticipation of an imminent attack, whereas preventive war is aimed at forestalling a longer-term prospect of harm, related, for example, to anticipated changes in the political or military balance of power. I say "broadly" because the clarity of Walzer's discussion is blurred by his desire to show that the Israeli anticipatory attack on Egypt was legitimate, even though he admits that it occurred "in the (probable) absence of any immediate intention [by Egypt] to launch such an attack or invasion."[20] He admits that this constitutes "a major revision" of the legalist paradigm regarding preemption that he had previously taken himself to be expounding. His position seems to be that this case of an Israeli first strike is in a grey area between preemption and prevention, though nearer to preemption. Noam Chomsky objected, in a review of Walzer's book, that

---

[20] Michael Walzer, *Just and Unjust Wars: A Moral Argument with Historical Illustrations*, third edition (New York: Basic Books, 2000), p. 85.

this revision was the primary innovative feature of the book and that it was a testament to the "special place of Israel in Walzer's 'moral world.'"[21] It is certainly a curious exception, since the tenor of Walzer's previous discussion would have lead one to expect an outright condemnation of Israel's aggression.

More recently, in a discussion of the Bush administration's plans for invading Iraq, Walzer used his distinction to cast doubt on the moral legitimacy of such an invasion.[22] He argued that, in the circumstances then prevailing (in late September 2002), the proposed war would be, at best, preventive and not preemptive, and hence "neither just nor necessary."[23] Even so, Walzer claimed that if such an invasion did come, in the wake of real or alleged failures by Iraq to help the UN inspection efforts, he and other critics would probably end up, "very reluctantly, supporting the war the Bush administration seems so eager to fight."[24] Here, again, it appears that the record of Israel is at least influential in his thinking, since he cites with approval the Israeli preventive strike against Iraq's nuclear reactor in 1981. This is adduced as an illustration of what seems a further "revision" of his earlier account. He now says that "the old argument for preventive war did not take into account weapons of mass destruction or delivery systems that allow no time for arguments about how to respond. Perhaps the gulf between preemption and prevention has now narrowed so that there is little strategic (and therefore little moral) difference between them."[25]

Yet weapons of mass destruction and rapid delivery systems really do nothing to repair the defects in the "old arguments" for preventive war. These were well sketched earlier by Walzer, and even earlier by the great nineteenth-century moral philosopher Henry Sidgwick. As Sidgwick pointed out, even legitimate preemption

... easily passes over into anticipation of a blow that is merely feared, not really threatened. Indeed this enlarged right of self-protection against mere danger has often been further extended to justify hostile interference to prevent a neighbour growing strong merely through expansion or coalescence with other states.[26]

We might add that the resort to preventive war by one nation provides a pattern for other strong nations to emulate, so that the dangers instanced by Sidgwick are multiplied.

[21] Noam Chomsky, "An Exception to the Rules" (review of *Just and Unjust Wars* by M. Walzer), *Australian Outlook* 32, no. 3 (December 1978), p. 363, originally printed in *Inquiry*, April 17, 1978, pp. 23–27.

[22] Michael Walzer, "No Strikes: Inspectors Yes, War No," *The New Republic*, September 30, 2002, pp. 19–22.

[23] Ibid., p. 22.

[24] Ibid.

[25] Ibid., p. 21.

[26] Henry Sidgwick, "The Morality of Strife," in his *Practical Ethics* (London: Swann Sonnenschein and Co., 1898), p. 101.

Once we get beyond immediate threat of attack by an enemy, we are pretty much in the realm of untrammelled speculation. Another nation's development of weapons, including weapons of mass destruction, may create various worries and uncertainties, but there is so much that can come between that development and its hostile use that we should not risk the hazards of war on behalf of the alarming prediction. After all, numerous nations now have such weapons, especially nuclear weapons, and so far only the United States and Iraq have used any of them, and both (at least at the time of this writing) have subsequently refrained from employing them. Moreover, the existence of rapid delivery systems does not eliminate the space for arguments about response, since these arguments will have been canvassed long before any attack. Widespread knowledge of military potential has become as swift and comprehensive as the speed of delivery systems, though fallibility still attaches to both.

Walzer's revisions seem to me clearly to take us too far towards the dangers of preventive war. Indeed, his invocation of Israeli examples merely highlights some of these dangers, when we consider the contribution of Israel's dubious military policies to Middle Eastern instability in the past thirty or more years. In the context of the world of the early twenty-first century, the revival of a taste for preventive war, under the guise of preemption or otherwise, is truly alarming. This is not to deny the need to stop the development, storage, and ultimate use of so-called weapons of mass destruction (WMD). Such weapons are indeed morally disturbing, and we shall discuss them in Chapter 12. But there are several things that it is important to note about their presence in our world.

One is that prevention is currently invoked as avowed policy by a power that already has an abundance of nuclear weapons, retains at least the capacity to produce chemical and biological weapons, and has already used nuclear weapons against civilian populations. Moreover, in addition to its nuclear arsenal, the United States has massive military superiority over the rest of the world; in the face of that superiority, it is hardly surprising that lesser powers that do not trust American intentions abroad should seek to arm themselves with very powerful weapons. Nor can it be assumed that mistrust of the international policies and doctrines of the United States is always misplaced or, worse, a sign of perfidy or evil. The history of empires and of lesser states shows, to put it mildly, that overwhelming power does not always bring overwhelming wisdom. The great powers have long promoted the doctrine of deterrence; they should not be surprised to find others invoking it. It is one thing for Iraq, Iran, and North Korea to seek or to possess weapons of mass destruction; it is another for them to present a *real and present* threat of using them. Given the nature of such weapons, and the hazards of deterrence, their proliferation should be discouraged, but that effort can be effective only if it is accompanied by the similar disarmament of those already in the WMD club. To take only nuclear weapons, the club includes (at least) America, France, Britain, Pakistan, Israel, India, and China, several of which are already involved in political and military situations that could be described as precarious. Further movement away from WMD armaments by members of the club, combined with further inducements to participation in nonproliferation treaties and regimes of neutral inspection, provide much better prospects than military intervention.

Against this scenario, namely, one of negotiated prevention of WMD proliferation, weapons inspection regimes, and eventually general WMD disarmament, it might be argued that there is a better, and even more realistic, course. This is to make use of the massive military might of the United States to prevent the spread of such weapons by taking or threatening military action against those who are suspected of ambitions to develop them, have begun to develop them, or have recently come to possess them. America's more belligerent posture in world affairs since the election of George W. Bush has made this option a live one, whereas earlier U.S. leaders would not have contemplated it. The advantage of this course of action is that U.S. military superiority, especially in its technical aspects, is now so great that the costs of preventive war seem to be much lower than critics like Sidgwick could have envisaged. But most of this is mere appearance, and there are great and evident disadvantages as well. Much of the appearance of low-cost warfare is related to the low costs to the attackers of the wars in Serbia, Afghanistan, and Iraq, but these are not of course the only costs of those wars, since they have together taken a human toll that very probably exceeds 100,000 deaths. In the case of Iraq, the cost in lives to the invaders, initially low, has gathered momentum with the development of insurgent warfare. Moreover, the financial cost is soaring and seems to have no clear horizon, and, whatever the intervention may have prevented, it has clearly stimulated terrorist activity in the region and beyond.

The traditional justification for preemptive war turned on the idea that the harm to be dealt with was grave and imminent, and Walzer's distinction between preemption and prevention is principally made in terms of the test of imminence. David Luban has recently argued that imminence should be seen as a special case of high probability (highly probable and temporally near), and he uses this to allow for preventive wars in special cases against "rogue states" whose nature is such that they are "all but certain," to engage in an attack, even though such an attack is not imminent.[27] Although Luban is right that imminence is a special case of probability, his extension of the test beyond temporal imminence is fraught with danger, and his resort to the fashionable but dubious notion of "rogue states" compounds the problem. The point about imminence is that it is excellent evidence that an attack is "all but certain," whereas other indicators such as the character of the regime, its public rhetoric, and even its past record are

---

[27] David Luban, "Preventive War," *Philosophy and Public Affairs* 32, no. 3 (2004), p. 230.

much less secure. A considerable gap in time between bellicose behaviour or past wrongdoing or other alarming indicators still allows plenty of room for hesitation, reconsideration, or reform on the part of the potential aggressor, and for nonmilitary efforts at diplomacy or other interventions short of war. What Luban calls the "rule consequentialist" objection to preventive war still has force against his proposed extension.[28] Indeed, the talk of rogue states makes this even clearer. It has been argued by Michael Klare that the currency of the category of "rogue states" originated in the Pentagon's desire to resist spending cuts and other reductions as a result of the ending of the Cold War.[29] Whatever the truth of this claim, the category has proved an elusive and dangerous tool of world politics. The description was originally applied to Libya, which has now graduated to respectable status, in part through a shrewd renunciation of its ambitions to obtain nuclear weapons, and is still applied to Cuba, which has no such ambitions. The idea has been given additional impetus by the attacks of September 11, though the Bush doctrine of an "axis of evil," predating those attacks, is also part of the same mindset. The fact is that the September 11 attacks had nothing to do with designated "rogue states" such as Iraq, North Korea, or even Iran, and it is unlikely that the Taliban government of Afghanistan had anything directly to do with the attacks. Luban defines a "rogue state" as having the following "important characteristics": "militarism, an ideology favouring violence, a track-record of violence to back it up, and a build-up in capacity to pose a genuine threat." All of these palpably apply to the United States itself, a society with a huge military budget, a unique gun culture, a record of military adventurism in various parts of the world, and an ever-increasing military capacity that many other states view, not unreasonably, as threatening. There will, of course, be numerous other countries beyond the "axis of evil" that might plausibly fit the category, including China and Israel; some regimes are worse than others on some of the indicated criteria, and there is much room for debate and interpretation. But these facts themselves indicate how obscure and dangerous an instrument the concept of a rogue state is, especially in the context of a discussion of preventive war.

[28] The idea is that we should have a rule against preventive war because such a rule would have the best overall consequences; in particular, it would prevent the sort of bad consequences that I have discussed earlier. I prefer not to speak of rule consequentialism in this context because that suggests that the justification of rules by reference to consequences is somehow the preserve of consequentialist philosophers, whereas it is obviously available to any moral theorist to make use of consequences, while believing that this is not the only resort available. See Luban, ibid., p. 225.

[29] Michael Klare, *Rogue States and Nuclear Outlaws: America's Search for a New Foreign Policy* (New York: Hill and Wang, 1995). The category is taken more seriously by Robert Litwak in *Rogue States and U.S. Foreign Policy: Containment after the Cold War* (Washington, DC: Woodrow Wilson Center Press; Baltimore: Johns Hopkins University Press, 1999).

I have concentrated upon the likely bad consequences of preventive war, but, real as these are, there is a deeper, though connected, objection. That is the objection that the horrible recourse to war needs as a justifying cause the commission of some wrong. This is the intrinsic problem with the preventive project, viewed as an exercise that comes under the scope of justice. Within the state, the need to deal with wrongdoers may extend occasionally to those who are about to commit a crime or actively conspiring to do so, but it is unjust for the state to exercise "the right of the sword" against those whom it suspects might become wrongdoers sometime in the future. In the international order, the same principle applies. Unless the wrongdoing or attack is palpable and imminent, there can be no justification for unleashing the horror of war. In this respect, there is something deeply misleading about Clausewitz's dictum that war is "the continuation of political activity by other means."[30] As mentioned earlier, one useful point he is trying to make is that resort to warfare must, in a broad sense, be governed by nonmilitary objectives, since there is no moral sense in merely pursuing victory or conquest as an end in itself. These governing objectives must, in a broad sense, be political, but, again as remarked earlier, this governance can only be a necessary condition for the legitimacy of resort to war, since only appropriate political conditions can provide the right sort of justification. Clausewitz's dictum makes the justification look too easy, since there are all sorts of circumstances in which political activity is unsuccessful or stalemated and we just have to live with it, rather than resort to the mayhem of war. Few worthy objectives can constitute specific just cause for war, and the worthy objective of removing conditions that might lead to future crimes is not one of them.

Against this, it has been argued that preventive war may be legitimate when it is seen as a response to a crime that is already in progress: the analogy with domestic crimes of conspiracy or attempt has been cited by Allen Buchanan in this connection.[31] Buchanan thinks of such deeds as "wrongful impositions of dire risk." The attempt analogy is hardly relevant, since an attempt is an action that is fully under way in the appropriate sense but fails of its objective. The traditional doctrine of legitimate preemption allows that defensive violence may be used when an attack is actually being attempted. But the conspiracy analogy is more interesting and pertinent. Certainly in domestic legal contexts it can make sense to criminalise the planning of crimes, but, as Buchanan is aware, the analogy with the international order limps in several ways. For one thing, since conspiracy is a charge that is manifestly open to abuse by prosecuting agencies, it is more than usually

---

[30] Carl von Clausewitz, *On War*, ed. and trans. Michael Howard and Peter Paret (Princeton, NJ: Princeton University Press, 1976), p. 87.
[31] Allen Buchanan, "Institutionalizing the Just War," *Philosophy and Public Affairs* 34, no. 1 (2006), pp. 9–11.

important that allegations of conspiracy be tested by authoritative, independent tribunals, especially where the conspiracy involves political issues. Yet this is exactly what is conspicuously lacking on the international scene, though present, with some fragility, in the more constitutionally stable domestic jurisdictions. Given the temptations of national leaders to spring to conclusions about the conspiratorial behaviour of other states, using the conspiracy model to reject the criticism that preventive war wrongly responds to possibilities of offence rather than actual offences is hardly compelling. Buchanan realises that there are dangers in the model, but thinks them merely contingent, so that preventive war against a conspiracy is not *necessarily* a violation of the rights of those targeted. This emphasis (the italics are Buchanan's) may be thought a typically philosophical one, and small comfort for those whose rights are highly likely to be violated in the real world. In fairness, it should be stressed that Buchanan regards the consequentialist and prudential objections to preventive war as decisive in the world as it now is; his position is that empirical work is required to establish whether institutions might now be developed that would make resort to preventive war (and indeed war to establish democracy) immune to these powerful objections. As he puts it:

My aim is not to show that the institutional approach outlined here is likely to be adapted [sic] by the most powerful states either at present or in the future. If it turns out that the institutional demands for morally permissible decisions to engage in preventive self-defence or forcible democratization will not be met, then my argument supports the conclusion that preventive self-defence and forcible democratization are not justifiable.[32]

Buchanan's institutional approach is interesting though highly speculative, and it has some relevance to the discussion of pacifism in Chapter 13. In the world as it is, and is likely to remain for the foreseeable future, the moral case against preventive war is compelling.

[32] Ibid., pp. 35–36.

6

The Right Way to Fight

The old distinction maintained in civilized warfare between the civilian and combatant populations disappeared. Everyone who grew food, or who sewed a garment, everyone who felled a tree or repaired a house, every railway station and every warehouse was held to be fair game for destruction.

H. G. Wells, writing of World War 1[1]

To any but those consumed with warrior lust, it must make sense to ask, as we asked in Chapter 3: "when, if ever, is it right to go to war?" In the broadest interpretation of morality, this is a moral question, since, as noted earlier, those who look solely to national interest, even national aggrandisement, or to the balance of power will invoke moral or ethical concepts in the course of answering it. They have, they will declare, as leaders of their people (or even as politicians) an obligation to pursue the national interest, since that is what they have been entrusted to do. The national or imperial interest so pursued will produce a certain sort of global harmony, or at least betterment; the resort to political violence in sober pursuit of the national interest eliminates the dangerous consequences of moralistic motivations driving nations either to complacent inaction or to ideological warfare; the balance of power is a recipe for stability and a certain type of peace. Many of these justifications, as we saw in the discussion of realism in Chapter 3, are debatable, if not downright confused: certainly, the idea that a general pursuit of national self-interest alone will promote the general international good seems to rely upon an even more mystical "invisible hand" than the equivalent idea in economics. Moreover, the poverty of the moral vocabulary employed clearly leaves a lot to be desired. Nonetheless, there is no doubting the operation of recognisable elements of moral thinking in the arguments offered. These elements suggest that even the most tough-minded feel the need to make a moral case for resort to war.

[1] H. G. Wells, *A Short History of the World* (Harmondsworth: Penguin, 1922), p. 256.

Yet when we turn to the conduct of war, we often encounter a quite different moral climate. The difference is partially explicable by the facts that war is a zone of human activity in which the end – victory – is overwhelmingly urgent, and in which the experience of battle is supremely horrible. These facts can be combined to produce a doctrine of "military necessity" so severe as to exclude any but the most minimally utilitarian, or at least consequentialist, moral reasoning. Since "War is hell" and victory urgent, the swift ending of the hell on terms that honour the significance of the original moral commitment to the fight can seem the only relevant imperative. The idea of codes and honour in war often went with a romantic picture of the realities of combat, and Hobbes is in part reacting against this when he says, as cited earlier, "Force and fraud, are in war the two cardinal virtues." The American Civil War general, William Tecumseh Sherman's profound understanding of the horror of war led not only to his eloquently honest outburst describing it as "hell" but also to his disregarding the rules of war in order to speed its end in his infamous march through Georgia. It is worth quoting his denunciation of the glamour of war:

I am sick and tired of war. Its glory is all moonshine. It is only those who have neither fired a shot nor heard the shrieks and groans of the wounded who cry aloud for blood, for vengeance, for desolation. War is hell.[2]

Yet this cannot be the whole story, since, as Michael Walzer shows so well, the vocabulary in which soldiers, politicians, and ordinary people discuss war and criticise their enemies is replete with moral terms that seem to commit them to right and wrong ways of conducting hostilities.[3] The concept of an "atrocity," for instance, is at the centre of such discourse. The unsentimental airman Chuck Yeager quoted in Chapter 1 showed himself aware of it and its moral reverberations. We need only a few examples to remind us of its significance. Here is one, concerning the treatment of prisoners of war, narrated by an Australian veteran of the Malaysian counterinsurgency:

We attacked a terrorist prison camp, and took a woman prisoner. She must have been high up in the party. She wore the tabs of a commissar. I'd already told my men we took no prisoners, but I'd never killed a woman. "She must die quickly. We must leave!" my sergeant said.

The Australian could not bring himself to shoot even though the woman (whom he described as "magnificent") taunted him for his evident nervousness.

"I gave my pistol to my sergeant, but he just shook his head. . . . None of them would do it, and if I didn't I'd never be able to control that unit again.

"You're sweating Mr. Ballentine," she said again.

"Not for you," I said.

---

[2] Quoted in Lieutenant Colonel Dave Grossman, *On Killing: The Psychological Cost of Learning to Kill in War and Society* (Boston: Little, Brown, 1995), p. 74

[3] Michael Walzer, *Just and Unjust Wars: A Moral Argument with Historical Illustrations*, third edition (New York: Basic Books, 2000), pp. 11–16.

Whereupon he blew her head off to the congratulations of his Malay platoon. But the interview with him makes it clear that he was still disturbed years later by the episode, and still seeking a justification for his act ("I'd never be able to control that unit again").[4]

Nor is the idea of an atrocity something derived solely from Christian sources and hence subject to the Nietzschian strictures against the softness of the Christian moral legacy. The Chinese philosopher Hsun Tzu, writing in the tradition of Confucius 300 years before the Christian era, is clearly aware of the need to put constraints on the conduct of war. In his essay "Debating Military Affairs," Hsun Tzu says,

The king's army does not kill the enemy's old men and boys; it does not destroy crops. It does not seize those who retire without a fight, but it does not forgive those who resist. It does not make prisoners of those who surrender and seek asylum. In carrying out punitive expeditions, it does not punish the common people; it punishes those who lead the common people astray. But if any of the common people fight with the enemy, they become enemies as well. Thus those who flee from the enemy forces and come in surrender shall be left to go free.[5]

Even Winston Churchill, who so enthusiastically embraced the terror bombing of German cities in World War II, was reluctant to admit publicly its true purposes and came belatedly to see some of it as morally suspect. Along the way, however, he offered the following glib comment on the erosion of moral restraints against direct attacks on noncombatants that his policies had required: "it is absurd to consider morality on this topic.... In the last war the bombing of open cities was regarded as forbidden. Now everybody does it as a matter of course. It is simply a question of fashion changing as she does between long and short skirts for women."[6] We must examine whether there are more profound bases for the prohibitions of the JIB than this; there are certainly more profound consequences of violating them than accrue from disdaining the restraints of fashion.

The Principles of the JIB

We would do well to begin such an investigation by returning to the simple domestic analogy used in a previous chapter. The axe attacker is again your problem, and you have been forced to reach for the confiscated gun. Now suppose that in the course of the struggle your gun is pointing not at the attacker but across the street at a small child who is staring in amazement

---

4 Grossman, *On Killing*, p. 201.

5 *Hsun Tzu: Basic Writings*, trans. Burton Watson (New York: Columbia University Press, 1966), p. 67.

6 Quoted in Stephen A. Garrett, "Political Leadership and Dirty Hands: Winston Churchill and the City Bombing of Germany," in Cathal J. Nolan (ed.), *Ethics and Statecraft: The Moral Dimension of International Affairs* (Westport, CT: Greenwood Press, 1995), pp. 80–81.

at what is going on. You reason that if you shoot the child, her screams will distract the attacker and perhaps attract others to the scene who can offer you help. Are you entitled to shoot the child? Surely not. The child is not attacking you, nor is she complicit in the attack. It is the prosecution of the aggression that gives you the right to direct violence against those who are attacking or positively assisting the attack – not against others, even if maiming and killing others would help your cause. Or, to change the example a little, suppose you are attacked not by a strong man with a sharp axe, but by an enraged child with a light plastic toy golf club. You may well be entitled to defend yourself with some force, but resort to the confiscated gun would be "overkill" indeed. Or you have shot the axe attacker and he lies bleeding, groaning and out of action. You produce some confiscated thumbscrews from your pocket and proceed to torture him for some time and then shoot him dead. You have, to put it mildly, gone beyond the reasonable requirements of self-defence.

Though there are many specific rules and detailed conventional accords in the various legal and quasi-legal provisions of the international law of war and in the codes of military conduct that, to some degree, reflect them, there are two central moral principles that underpin much of the legislation, and which are illustrated by our example and its variants. These are:

The Principle of Discrimination (including the Rule of Noncombatant Immunity)
This is basically concerned with the legitimacy of targets and targeting plans (though some important distinctions will arise here in connection with deterrence theory). As the simple fable illustrates, not everything that will promote your war aims is morally legitimated by your just cause, just as not everything that promotes the protection of your life is legitimated by your right of self-defence. The "bystander" child across the street is a model of the ideal noncombatant. Things are more complex in war and revolution, particularly in so-called total war, but where the distinction between combatant and noncombatant can be made, it should be respected. Nor does the mere fact of membership in the enemy's national community make a difference, for it would make no difference if the child across the street were the attacker's daughter or sister. It might make a difference, however, if the child were bringing a replacement axe. There are deep waters here into which we will later plunge.

The Principle of Proportionality
According to this principle, the fighting you do should inflict damage that is not out of proportion to what is required to right the wrong that entitles you to go to war in the first place. This is illustrated by the child attacker in the fable. It also applies most importantly to the problems raised by the idea of "collateral damage," since there seem to be occasions on which it is permissible to attack a military target where it can be foreseen as highly

probable that "incidental" harms will be caused to noncombatants. If this is permissible, it can be only if the associated deaths or injuries to innocents are proportional to the good advanced by the attack upon the military target.

Proportionality applies, of course, in both the JAB and the JIB, as we saw in Chapter 3, since the decision to go to war in response to an injury may be disproportionate, just as much as the continuing decisions to fight the war in this way or that. As we shall see, although there is real point in distinguishing between the JAB and the JIB for certain purposes, total logical separation of the two sets of criteria is dubious for a number of reasons. We shall examine this more closely later.

Some applications of the discrimination principle concern such things as the requirements of surrender and the treatment of captured prisoners, but a major role for the principle is the support it provides for the immunity of noncombatants from direct attack. This is a key point at which utilitarian approaches to the justification of war tend to part company with the classical just war tradition. Either they deny that the principle obtains at all, or, more commonly, they argue that it applies in virtue of its utility. The former move is associated with the idea that war is such "hell" and victory so important that everything must be subordinated to that end. Yet even in utilitarian terms, it is unclear that this form of ruthlessness produces the best outcomes, especially when it is shared by the opposing side. Hence, the more common move is to argue that the immunity of noncombatants is a useful rule for restricting the damage wrought by wars. A clear statement of this position is given by R. B. Brandt.[7] Nonutilitarians (I shall call them "intrinsicalists" because they believe that there are intrinsic wrongs, other than the failure to maximise goods) can agree that there are such extrinsic reasons for the immunity rule, but they will see this fact as a significant additional reason to conform to the discrimination principle. Intrinsicalists will argue that the principle's validity springs directly from the reasoning that licenses resort to war in the first place. This resort is allowed by the need to resist perpetrators of aggression (or, on a broader view, to deal with wrongdoers), and hence it licenses violence only against those who are agents of the aggression.

This is the point behind distinguishing combatants from noncombatants, or, in another terminology, wrongdoers from innocents. In this context, when we classify people as noncombatants or innocents we do not mean that they have no evil in their hearts, or that they totally lack enthusiasm for their country's policies; nor do we mean that the combatants have such evil or enthusiasm. The classification is principally concerned with the role the individual plays in the chain of agency directing the aggression or wrong-doing. And it is agency that is important, not mere cause: the soldier's aged

---

7 R. B. Brandt, "Utilitarianism and the Rules of War," in Marshall Cohen, Thomas Nagel, and Thomas Scanlon (eds.), *War and Moral Responsibility* (Princeton, NJ: Princeton University Press, 1974), pp. 25–45.

parents may be part of the causal chain that results in his being available to fight without their having any agent responsibility for what he is doing. The combatant may be coerced to fight, but he or she is still prosecuting the war, even if the greater blame lies with those who coerce. On the other hand, the young schoolchild may be enthusiastic about her country's war, but need not be prosecuting it. Neither is the farmer whose products feed the troops, for he would feed them (if they'd buy) whatever their role.

It is important to stress that I am interpreting the combatant/noncombatant distinction rather broadly, so that it is not equivalent to the soldier/civilian distinction even though they overlap considerably. As indicated earlier, I think of combatants as those involved in the chain of agency directing the perceived aggression or wrongdoing. This involvement need not require wearing uniforms or carrying weapons. Some civilians will be legitimate targets (and hence "combatants" in my sense) if they are actively directing or promoting unjust violence. The fact that political leaders and senior public servants who are planning and controlling war are not themselves in uniform or bearing arms is no barrier to their being legitimate targets. Nor, as we have seen recently in Iraq, is the designation "civilian contractor" a barrier to combatant status. We shall have more to say of such contractors in the discussion of mercenaries in Chapter 10. There is nonetheless a broad pragmatic justification for the common tendency to treat *most* civilians as noncombatants and *most* soldiers as combatants. There may well be soldiers who are pacifist conscripts determined not to shoot when the battle begins, just as there may be elderly civilian women who are dedicated political agents taking some very active part in the war campaign. But here, as elsewhere in the discussion of public morality, the idea of reasonable expectation is important, and absent specific information to the contrary, it is reasonable to view soldiers with guns as engaged in prosecuting the attack and elderly civilian women as not. Definite knowledge that opposing troops are reluctant conscripts, or that a group of elderly civilians are engaged in prosecuting the war, should make a moral and prudential difference to how one treats them. Risks could be taken to induce the surrender of the former, and precisely targeted attacks upon the latter would, at least in theory, be licit.

The complexities here may be helpfully clarified by considering the following categories of people as candidates for the status of legitimate target:

1. Those who are on any account totally innocent of knowingly and freely intending harm or indeed of harming at all. They have no malice towards the other side and exhibit none. These include babies and small children as well as objectors to the war who take no part in its conduct (they may be in prison or gone underground). Call them "perfect bystanders."

2. Those who support the war in their hearts but do little or nothing to exhibit their support. They take no serious part in the war effort, perhaps because they are too infirm or too timid or too young (older children, for example). Call them "imperfect bystanders."

3. Those who, like imperfect bystanders, support the war, but who go further and do such things as writing letters to the press supporting the war, march in demonstrations in support of it, urge others to do their "patriotic duty," buy war bonds or otherwise give money to the cause. However, they don't bear arms and don't have an executive role in the war effort (as a minister for defence or a defence scientist would), nor do they work directly in war-related industry (like a munitions factory). Call them "cheerleaders."

4. Those who resemble cheerleaders but who go further still and volunteer to work (or are cheerfully conscripted to work) in explicitly and significantly war-related industries. They do no fighting, but they are willing parts of the chain of agency directed to prosecuting the war. Call them "willing ancillaries."

5. Those who are coerced into playing an important (enough) role in the war effort, such as captured enemy soldiers forced to work in building military installations or military roads. We might call them "coerced ancillaries."

6. Those who are coerced into fighting, such as conscripted soldiers who would not have fought had they not been subject to conscription. Call them "coerced fighters."

7. Those who are not coerced into fighting or into playing an important role in the prosecution of the war, but who fight or assist because they are nonculpably ignorant of the justice or injustice of the war. Call them "deluded fighters" and "deluded ancillaries."

8. Those who freely choose to fight and understand pretty well the nature of the war. Call them "outright fighters."

This list clearly presents a range of very different potential targets for lethal violence. As we move from (1) to (8), it becomes clearer that we are moving from the clearly illegitimate at one end to the clearly legitimate at the other, with some more debatable cases in the middle. Leaving aside, for now, issues of "double effect," it is evident that the reasoning that licenses resort to armed violence in certain cases gives no licence to attack perfect bystanders (category 1) in those circumstances. Nor should it license attacks upon imperfect bystanders, since they really do nothing substantial to advance the evil against which the violence is (presumptively) legitimately employed. Attacking them for their thoughts or feelings is unfeasible and unjustifiable. Cheerleaders are getting nearer to the status of legitimate targets in that they *are* doing something to further the national war effort, but what they do is sometimes susceptible to different interpretations (those buying war bonds may just be finding a place to park their money in unsettled times, a motive that may not be very praiseworthy, but is hardly warlike in itself), and in any event it will usually be practically impossible for an adversary to pick them out for attack. They will normally be side by side with perfect and imperfect bystanders whom it is illegitimate to attack.

This leaves coerced, deluded, and willing ancillaries, and coerced, deluded, and outright fighters. Willing ancillaries are directly contributing to the war effort by making weapons, building military bridges, or assessing military intelligence. They may wear civilian clothing, but their willing roles are military ones. This granted, the status of coerced ancillaries turns on whether their being coerced into the role is a condition that makes targeting them illegitimate. This question also arises in a slightly different way for the category of coerced fighters. Coercion is generally treated in law and morals as an excusing condition; it does not render agents incapable of acting otherwise, but it puts such pressure on them to act in a particular way that it may be deemed difficult or even unreasonable for them to resist the pressure. There may indeed be extremes of coercion that make the agent's wrongdoing almost impossible to avoid, as when instant execution or extreme torture is the penalty for disobedience. Even here, especially when the wrongdoing is grave, there is still room for agency, since the person coerced can choose to endure the penalty in conformity with the Socratic dictum that "doing wrong is worse than suffering wrong."[8] In other cases, the coercion may be considerable but less extreme, less excusing, so that the coerced actor retains a more substantial degree of agency even though acting under pressure. But if heavily coerced persons, such as slave labourers, have only very minimal agency, then it is primarily their role plus the agency of those who control them that could make them legitimate targets. Where that role is significant enough, it seems that lethal violence may be directed at them, though with great regret. The fact of that regret makes it imperative that ways of eliminating the dangerous activity without eliminating the coerced people themselves should be explored. Certainly, where possible, attacks upon those who are doing the coercing has moral priority over attacking the coerced. Something similar applies to the category of coerced fighters, though here the fact that the fighters are directing violence against you or your compatriots or allies, or standing ready to do so, makes their agency more palpable, and usually makes their role more immediately threatening

It will be clear that my use of the combatant/noncombatant distinction departs somewhat from the use made by some writers in the just war tradition and in much discussion in international law, where the distinction is

[8] Plato, *The Gorgias*, trans. Walter Hamilton (Harmondsworth: Penguin, 1960), 473a, p. 59.

equivalent to "soldier/civilian" or something very close to it.[9] Yet although this difference in interpretation is philosophically and morally important, I would not want my interpretation to contribute to any dramatic extension of the category of combatant. Indeed, I would urge great caution about recent proposals to radically extend or reinterpret the range of agency in this area. This is for three reasons. First, it will generally be very difficult to show that civilians without a pretty direct connection with advancing the war, or committing the offences that are believed to make it legitimate for others to wage war in response, are sufficiently responsible for the war or some part in it to make them valid targets of lethal violence. It is sometimes urged that voting or other indicators of compliance with a government are enough to make people legitimate targets.[10] Yet those who support a government or vote for it do so for many complex reasons, and one cannot simply read off the appropriate degree of support for the government's war from voting or other endorsement patterns. This is especially so when the price of opposition is very high, possibly fatally high, as is often the case in authoritarian or unstable regimes. Even in democracies, voting patterns are too inconclusive since they do not indicate which policies have attracted which votes, and other forms of support for a government may likewise be based on the attraction of policies unrelated to its war efforts, or on the lack of viable oppositional alternatives.[11] Second, there is considerable danger that any such extension will lead to a widening and intensification of the war, since it is likely to shift or solidify civilian support in the enemy nation

[9] The UN Charter, for instance, in Article 43 of the 1977 additional protocol declares that "[M]embers of the armed forces of a Party to a conflict (other than medical personnel and chaplains covered by Article 33 of the Third Convention) are combatants, that is to say, they have the right to participate directly in hostilities." It is true that this seems to state a sufficient rather than a necessary condition for combatant status, but in the context it would appear to be aimed at exhibiting both.

[10] A recent attempt to extend the scope of legitimate targets to include those who "deserve their governments" is that of Barry Buzan in his article "Who May We Bomb?" in Ken Booth and Tim Dunne (eds.), *Worlds in Collision: Terror and the Future of Global Order* (New York: Palgrave, 2002). Igor Primoratz also plays with something of the sort, though less permissively than Buzan, in his "Michael Walzer's Just War Theory: Some Issues of Responsibility," *Ethical Theory and Moral Practice* 5 (2002), pp. 221–244. Primoratz, I understand, would no longer defend this position.

[11] A particularly egregious set of confusions about the agency responsibility of voters (and taxpayers) can be found in one of Osama bin Laden's attempts to justify wholesale attacks upon U.S. civilians. He says: "The American people should remember that they pay taxes to their government, they elect their president, their government manufactures arms and gives them to Israel and Israel uses them to massacre Palestinians. The American Congress endorses all government measures and this proves that the entire America is responsible for the atrocities perpetrated against Muslims. The entire America because they elect the Congress." Osama bin Laden as interviewed by Hamid Mir, November 9, 2001, at <http:www.dawn.com/2001/11/10/top1.htm>.

for their regime. Third, it establishes a precedent for the enemy to extend its understanding of legitimate targets on your side in the current conflict, as well as establishing a precedent for opposing sides in future conflicts. These considerations apply even more emphatically to the idea that the net of legitimate targets should be extended even to failures to act in opposition to war policies.[12]

Much more could be said about this, and I am not denying that there are grey areas. What, for instance, should we say of the readily identifiable active political supporters of a regime, those who enthusiastically endorse its war aims and make a substantial contribution to the war effort? Examples might be government film production units making effective propaganda movies for the regime, or industrialists who donate large sums specifically for financing the war. The objections already raised maintain some of their force even here, but perhaps not enough to rule out, for instance, an attack upon the production studios of the propaganda film unit. The objections would, however, clearly rule out attacking an independent TV crew from a neutral country whose news reports are unpalatable to "our" side.[13] But what of a rally specifically in support of Hitler's war by declared Nazi Party members? A lot would turn on how effective such rallies are, and how we know that these are genuine supporters rather than a crowd of the coerced or curious. Whatever is said, there are clearly many epistemological, conceptual, and moral problems lurking.

Doubts about Immunity

There will be those who greet these qualifications and elaborations with impatience. Their doubts about the immunity principle extend well beyond its application to various difficult categories of person such as slave labourers coerced to work in munitions factories; they doubt that it has any relevance at all to the highly integrated citizenry of modern states. Many people say that it is surely anachronistic to think of contemporary war as waged between armies; it is really nation against nation, economy against economy, peoples against peoples. It is collectives that wage war and are liable to attack. But although modern war has many unusual features, its "total" nature is more an imposed construction than a necessary reflection of a changed reality. Even in World War II, not every enemy citizen was involved in prosecuting the

---

[12] Buzan's argument falls victim to all three of these objections; in addition, it fails to recognise the degree to which, by his own criteria, citizens of democracies like the United States will be more open to legitimate attack than citizens of dictatorships like Iraq, Iran, and North Korea. For a fuller treatment of this issue, see my discussion in "Terrorism and Innocence," *Journal of Ethics* 8, no. 1 (2004), pp. 37–58.

[13] This seems to have been what happened in the U.S. missile attack upon Al Jazerha's news unit in Baghdad that killed one of their reporters, though the American military authorities declared it an accident.

war. In any war, there remain millions of people who are not plausibly seen as involved in the enemy's lethal chain of agency. There are, for instance, infants, young children, the elderly and infirm, lots of tradespeople and workers, not to mention dissidents and conscientious objectors. This sweeping challenge to the distinction requires there to be no discernible moral difference between shooting a soldier who is shooting at you and gunning down a defenceless child who is a member of the same nation as the soldier. The conclusion is perhaps sufficiently absurd or obscene to discredit the argument. Moreover, in the case, for instance, of Germany against the Allied powers, the argument would count the persecuted German citizens of the totalitarian Nazi regime as equally part of the German collective, and equally responsible for the war and liable to attack. Nor is it plausible to maintain that the distinctions required are mere academic constructions, inapplicable by soldiers in the heat of battle. Consider, for example, the American helicopter pilot Hugh Thompson, who, at the age of twenty-four, arrived at the scene of the My Lai massacre in the midst of the slaughter and courageously confronted American troops who were threatening Vietnamese villagers. He ordered his gunner and crew chief to shoot any Americans who opened fire on the civilians, and then called for a helicopter gunship to rescue the peasants and evacuated one of the boys in his own helicopter. Thompson, who died only recently (2006), may not have read any just war theory, but his moral revulsion expressed the basic idea of the principle of discrimination. As he put it: "I didn't want to be part of that. It wasn't war."[14]

In passing, it is worth remarking on an ironic aspect of the attempt by supporters of state violence to undermine the combatant/noncombatant distinction. Some supporters of revolutionary violence who have learned a lesson from this attempt argue, equally speciously, that in revolutionary struggle it is impossible or wrong to distinguish between combatants and noncombatants amongst the "enemy." Here the supposedly unified enemy is sometimes a class rather than a nation, but in either case the notion of "collective guilt" or "collective combatant status" is very dubious. Interestingly, in the debate about the vexed question of "German guilt" for the Holocaust, many intellectuals who survived the Nazi death camps flatly rejected the use of the idea of collective guilt. No doubt they recalled the way the German army had ruthlessly enforced the immoral doctrine of collective guilt, not only in support of racist extermination policies, but also in their vicious hostage policies whereby families, villages, and whole towns were killed in retaliation for Resistance attacks upon German soldiers. These people most commonly had nothing to do with the Resistance attacks, but the German armed forces had evolved formulae for the number of co-nationals they

---

[14] Quoted from the *New York Times* obituary notice, reprinted in the Melbourne *Age*, January 12, 2006, p. 14.

would kill to terrorise the occupied population.[15] Many of the death camp survivors saw too great a parallel between the group-think of the Nazi murderers and that of the retributive advocates of wholesale German guilt. Primo Levi put it this way: "I cannot tolerate the fact that a man should be judged not for what he is but because of the group to which he happens to belong."[16] And Bruno Bettelheim claimed even more strongly, "when we select a group of German citizens, show them the concentration camps, and say to them, 'You are guilty', we are affirming a fascist tenet."[17]

I do not say, as some philosophers do, that the idea of collective responsibility or collective guilt makes no sense. There has arisen in recent years amongst philosophers an interesting debate about the proper understanding of this notion, but it would lead us too far afield to address it fully here. A few points, however, need attention. There are clear cases of group responsibility where all the members of a group are agents of the deed in question even though they play different parts in its performance. Four criminals who decide to rob a bank, jointly evolve a plan to do so, and then play assigned roles in the robbery are joint agents in the crime, share responsibility for it, and can each be blamed or punished (though perhaps not identically, depending on role and circumstance). This has some parallels with the group responsibility of an armed force. But it is far removed from the sort of group responsibility sought by those who want to abandon the combatant/noncombatant distinction. They want to catch the members of large groups, particularly nations, within the liability net simply because of their group membership. But this attempt to make all citizens share responsibility for the crimes committed by the governments of the nations to which they belong is a huge stretch from the cases of criminal gangs and armies.

Greg Kavka, who has made this extension by trying to "loosen connections" in the attribution of liability in the context of discussion of nuclear deterrence, calls enemy citizens "partially innocent" and compares them in this respect to mad attackers; but most of them are not attackers at all. Indeed, vast numbers of them are not doing anything to contribute to the wrong their government is doing or planning. Kavka seems to recognise as much when he says that "organisational decision procedures and group pressure can often funnel individually blameless inputs into an immoral group output."[18] Furthermore, many of the so-called inputs may never get

[15] For an excellent account of the deliberate policy of hostage murders and associated moral dilemmas attending Resistance activity, see Rab Bennett, *Under the Shadow of the Swastika: The Moral Dilemmas of Resistance and Collaboration in Hitler's Europe* (London: Macmillan, 1999), especially Chapter 5.

[16] Primo Levi, *The Drowned and the Saved*, trans. Raymond Rosenthal (New York: Vintage, 1989), p. 174.

[17] Bruno Bettelheim, *The Informed Heart* (Glencoe, IL: Free Press, 1960), p. 288.

[18] Gregory S. Kavka, *Moral Paradoxes of Nuclear Deterrence* (Cambridge: Cambridge University Press, 1987), p. 91.

into the funnel at all; but Kavka is really concerned with something else. It is the prospect that respecting the traditional immunity of noncombatants will mean that those who want to control behaviour will "largely lose the ability to influence group acts by deterrence."[19] This reflects the context of Kavka's article, which is primarily concerned with nuclear deterrence policy, but there seems no reason why the point should not be generalised to the delivery of violence as well as the threat of it. But now the question urgently arises as to what makes the citizens of some nation so different from bystanders that they are liable to violent destruction for what their government has done. Kavka simply takes it that citizens somehow form part of the group entity that engages in the offending acts for which retaliatory (or perhaps preventive?) violence is legitimate. The most he produces in support is an argument from efficiency that we must now consider.[20]

This argument turns on an account of the point of attributions of moral responsibility. The idea is that we have the concept of moral responsibility because it allows us to influence behaviour in certain desirable ways (there are echoes here of some classical soft determinist accounts of responsibility). Kavka does not put the matter quite like this because he is concerned with liability more broadly rather than with moral responsibility alone. But he thinks that holding people morally responsible gains its point from the functions served by attributing liability. As he puts it, "The basic purpose of holding people liable for risks and harms is to protect people, by deterring and preventing dangerous and harmful acts. It is generally most efficient to control such acts by holding liable those morally responsible for them."[21]

But this externalist perspective on responsibility and liability is surely faulty. It makes questions of personal desert far too instrumentally dependent upon social engineering. The "efficient" control of behaviour is indeed important, at least up to a point, but our interest in immunities from harm is primarily motivated by the concern not to inflict injury or harm on those who don't deserve it. This is why agency can limit or annul immunity where social policy cannot (or at least where it needs to make a very special case to do so). As Kavka notes, in the case of minor matters some legal systems are, for reasons of utility, prepared to deliver small punishments on the basis of "strict liability." This usually refers to the fining of those who break some law without knowing that their act was illegal even in circumstances where that knowledge was hard to come by. (Actually, Kavka speaks of "vicarious liability," and this is confusing, since it may refer to holding liable those who

---

[19] Ibid.

[20] Actually, Kavka does produce another argument of sorts when he uses analogies between various types of "innocent threats" and enemy noncombatants in order to help the project of "loosening connections." These are, by themselves, distinctly unpersuasive without the argument addressed in the text. I have discussed his strategy more fully in "Terrorism and Innocence," cited earlier.

[21] Kavka, *Moral Paradoxes of Nuclear Deterrence*, p. 90.

have no agency connection whatever to the proscribed acts. I shall return to this later.)

I think we should be cautious about equating the accepted practices of legal systems with the requirements or legitimate permissions of morality, even where these systems are our own, and it is worth noting that there are many critics of the practice of "strict liability." Other legal systems have sometimes thought it efficient to punish family members very severely for crimes committed by their relatives, even where the family members knew nothing of the behaviour and would have deplored it. This is what is normally meant by "vicarious punishment," and even those who accept strict liability in some cases have generally opposed this. Indeed, the efficiency criterion leaves it open that "we" might find it "generally most efficient" to hold vicariously liable all manner of people who are unconnected to the harming. It is surely a contingent matter how such efficient community management might best proceed. As Paul Ramsey once suggested, in a subversive comment on nuclear deterrence, the most efficient way to prevent road carnage might be to strap babies onto the front of motor vehicles.[22] As noted, Kavka is anxious to preserve the immunity of the mere bystander, but where utilitarian manipulation to prevent harm is the criterion for immunity, the bystander's lack of agency connection to the harm is no guarantee of immunity.

"Loosening connections" for the sake of efficiency in controlling behaviour is fraught with peril in two directions. The first is that involved in expanding the categories of people caught in the loosened web of connections. We have already explored this. The second danger is the way in which the loosened connections are likely to carry the same grave consequences as the tighter connections. Kavka notes of strict liability that it is acceptable only where the penalties are light. As he puts it in speaking of domestic legal liability: "Where the penalties are not severe, and the efficiencies are relatively large, we are not greatly bothered by such loosening of liability conditions. When penalties are more serious, such as imprisonment, death, or risk of serious injury, we generally believe that tight standards of liability should be employed."[23] But when we are dealing with war and the immunity of noncombatants, "loosening the connections" means allowing the most severe of harms to be visited upon them. If there is any story about strict or vicarious liability that makes it morally acceptable, it surely cannot reach to consequences like these.

---

[22] Paul Ramsey, *The Just War: Force and Political Responsibility* (Lanham, MD: University Press of America, 1983), p. 171. Ramsey comments on his proposal: "That would be no way to regulate traffic *even if it succeeds* in regulating it perfectly, since such a system makes innocent human lives the *direct object* of attack and uses them as mere *means* for restraining the drivers of automobiles." I doubt that the babies would usually be objects of attack exactly, but Ramsey's point about their efficient use not making the use legitimate is surely right.

[23] Kavka, *Moral Paradoxes of Nuclear Deterrence*, p. 90.

Clearly, more is needed to show that the sort of membership in a group that citizenship involves is enough to make you a legitimate target of justified violence provoked by your government. (To be fair to Kavka, he shows some nervousness at extending the range of legitimate targets and talks of noncombatant citizens as "partially innocent." He also thinks that considerations of "proportionality" should operate to reduce the vulnerability to attack of the "partially innocent." But the dominance of the efficiency test surely operates to undermine the significance of this concession.)

The virtual elimination of the combatant/noncombatant distinction was used by Osama bin Laden and his supporters in purported justification of the killings of September 11, 2001. Those who say that any combatant/noncombatant distinction is meaningless in interstate conflicts are clearly in danger of depriving themselves of a central moral objection to such acts of terrorist violence. Nonetheless, interesting and rather tricky questions are raised by transferring the notions of combatant and noncombatant from the context of formal international war to the area of less formal conflict within the state or of violence directed against the state by nonstate agents. We shall discuss this more fully in Chapter 8.

In fact, there has been a remarkable change on the issue of noncombatant immunity in the strategic doctrines and military outlooks of many major powers since the end of the Cold War. It is now common to pay at least lip service to the principle, as evidenced by a certain restraint shown during the first Gulf War and in the bombing of Serbia, and by the widespread condemnation of Russian brutality in Chechnya. The rhetoric, at least, of the U.S.-sponsored war in Afghanistan and then the invasion of Iraq has also been respectful of the distinction. This change in rhetoric, and to some degree practice, may be attributable to several different causal factors. A very significant one is the growing realisation of how much damage modern warfare does to civilians. Purely in terms of the number of people killed, there has been a staggering shift in the ratio of noncombatant deaths to soldier deaths. According to one source, the ratio of soldier to civilian casualties shifted in the course of the twentieth century from 9:1 to 1:9.[24] Not all of this has resulted from direct targeting, but much of it has. The real question is not so much whether it is immoral to target noncombatants (it is), but how "collateral" damage and death to noncombatants can be defended. This is a matter to which I will turn in the next chapter.

If one takes the principle of noncombatant immunity to invoke an absolute moral prohibition, as just war thinkers have commonly done, then it is always wrong to violate it. Yet many contemporary moral philosophers, supportive of or sympathetic to just war thinking, are wary of moral absolutes. This is a natural thought for utilitarian and other consequentialist thinkers

---

[24] The figures are cited in John Stremlau, *People in Peril: Human Rights, Humanitarian Action, and Preventing Deadly Conflict* (New York, Carnegie Corporation, 1998), p. 25.

who hold all moral prohibitions and principles hostage to the calculation of certain sorts of consequences. Their only absolute is the utilitarian or consequentialist principle itself. But many theorists hostile to consequentialism also draw back from what they see as too stringent an adherence to the prohibition on attacking the innocent. They would treat the prohibition as expressing a very strong moral presumption against the targeting of noncombatants (and hence, as we shall argue in Chapter 8, against terrorism), but allow for exceptions in extreme circumstances. So Michael Walzer thinks that in conditions of "supreme emergency" the violation of the normal immunity is permissible in warfare, though only with a heavy burden of remorse. He thinks the Allied terror bombing of German cities in World War II (in the early stages) was legitimated by the enormity of the Nazi threat. John Rawls has recently endorsed this view while condemning the bombings of Hiroshima and Nagasaki.[25] I note their position here and postpone a fuller discussion of it to Chapter 14.

The moral objection to targeting noncombatants can sometimes make it seem as if there can never be anything wrong with targeting combatants. This appearance is misleading for several reasons. One reason is that there are wrong ways to treat combatants, even when your cause is just. We shall discuss this interesting question in Chapter 9. Another reason is that all those who are killed or harmed by unjust warriors are thereby gravely wronged. There is a clear sense in which those who are waging an unjust war are not entitled to kill the troops who are justly in the field against them. Polish troops who were killed by German invaders in the attacks that sparked World War II were unjustly victimised. Given this, it may seem that we have some reason to make light of any distinction between the targets selected by unjust aggressors. After all, if a war (or a revolution, for that matter) is unjustified, then any killing it promotes, whether of combatants or noncombatants, is wrong.

The Independence Issue and "Moral Equality"

There is a point of connection here with the question of the independence of the JIB and the JAB. Michael Walzer has, for instance, claimed that the "two sorts of judgements are logically independent. It is perfectly possible for a just war to be fought unjustly and for an unjust war to be fought in strict accordance with the rules."[26] I have argued against the first kind of independence elsewhere.[27] I shall now merely reaffirm that it is imperilled

---

[25] Walzer, *Just and Unjust Wars*, Chapter 16; and John Rawls, "Fifty Years after Hiroshima," in Kai Bird and Lawrence Lifschultz (eds.), *Hiroshima's Shadow: Writings on the Denial of History and the Smithsonian Controversy* (Stony Creek, CT: The Pamphleteer's Press, 1998), pp. 474–479, originally published in *Dissent* 42, no. 3 (1995), pp. 321–331.

[26] Walzer, *Just and Unjust Wars*, p. 21.

[27] See C. A. J. Coady, "The Leaders and the Led," *Inquiry* 23 (1980), p. 286.

by the idea that what the JAB justifies is a certain course of action *the nature of which* is partially specified by the means which are proposed or involved, and which in turn fall under the judgement of the JIB. We need room for the thought that a war that begins as a just response to aggression or some other grave wrong can turn into a morally indefensible enterprise or be prosecuted from the beginning in an unjustifiable fashion. This is possible in a variety of ways, as when the legitimate war aims are expanded into illegitimate areas (thus shifting the criteria of success and the content of just cause), or when disproportionate damage is sought (perhaps in a spirit of vengeance), or when indiscriminate attacks upon noncombatants become a standard feature of the conduct of hostilities. This last possibility is not usually mentioned in elaborations of the conditions for the JAB, though it might just be encompassed by the condition of right intention. Nonetheless, it is an important issue for further participation in or support for a war that has begun as justified. We would not want to characterise a war *tout court* as unjust if there were occasional atrocities committed in its conduct. Regrettable as that is, it would be unrealistic to think that a just war must be immune from the fog and madness that afflict all war. Critics of war, including pacifists, are right to point to this aspect of war as a discouragement to war making; it is certainly an objection to militarism and bellicose romanticism. But when atrocity becomes policy, then it is surely right to see the war as no longer just (or as never just when such a policy is built into its beginning).

One might seek to preserve the independence thesis by holding that when war aims expand illegitimately, or when other policies are adopted that can coherently be brought under the provisions of the JAB, then what we have is a different war, and similarly with changes in policy that involve persistent violations of the principle of discrimination. There is some plausibility in this, since our tendency to talk of "the war," as in the Second World War or the Gulf War, tends to obscure the fact that any given war will contain many different stages or phases that each might well merit the description of "a war." This is acknowledged to some extent by the terminology common in World War II of "the war in the Pacific," "the war in the desert," and so on. So it might be argued that the JAB needs to be reapplied sensitively to the different phases – some campaigns, stages, and so on will be just, and others not. I am not entirely hostile to this suggestion, though it faces the problem that the degree to which these different phases can be seen as part of the one overall enterprise inevitably raise the question whether that enterprise can remain justified when its unjustified stages are taken into account. This is a particularly pressing question for the troops prosecuting the enterprise. In any case, the manoeuvre does little to answer the question with which we began about whether persistent violations of the JIB can affect the judgement of justification under the JAB. A different move might appeal here to defenders of the independence thesis. They might separate the question of the *overall* justification for the war (or for any given stage of it) from the independent verdicts given by the JAB and the JIB. War X may be a just war by the standards of the JAB and nonetheless unjust in its methods by the standards of the JIB, yet because of the gravity of the latter verdict, it may be judged unjustified overall.[28] It may be possible to operate with this schema, but it has an inherent clumsiness, since the question of overall justification seems, on the face of it, precisely the question that the JAB is designed to answer. When we ask the question "Is resort to war here justified?," we are surely asking for an overall justification of the war. If we are interested in the justice of war, this is the question that the JAB is supposed to answer.

So much for the problems inherent in any idea generated by the independence thesis that would allow persistent violations of the JIB to leave the status of the JAB untouched. But our earlier discussion about combatants unjustly killed puts the focus on the second kind of independence, the idea that an unjustified war can be fought in accordance with the moral rules of the JIB. There is a sense in which this is clearly possible, both for a war and for a revolution, but there is also a sense in which, as I have already said, *all* the killing done by warriors whose cause is unjust is itself unjustified, so that the suspicion can easily emerge that the victims in uniform are as much sinned against as any civilians killed in defiance of the *jus in bello* and the war conventions associated with it.

Is this suspicion correct? Almost, but not quite. There is substantial truth in it, but it tends to obscure something important, namely, that whatever the objective facts about a given state's justification for going to war, its soldiery are likely to believe that they have good moral reason for trying to wound or kill enemy soldiers, whereas – even subjectively – they will not be in the same position vis-à-vis most of the enemy's civilian population. This consideration has quite wide scope, for it ranges from matters to do with trust in one's national leaders to quite specific issues to do with shooting back when you are shot at. All of these involve important questions of responsibility with which I cannot now deal, but, taken in conjunction with the fact that it may often be difficult for anyone to determine which, if either, side in a war is justified in fighting, they make it intelligible that, in the case of warfare, at least, we should continue to insist upon some moral differentiation between killing combatants and killing noncombatants, even by those who are waging an unjust war. Such an insistence should not, however, be at the expense of the genuine insight contained in the idea that the killing of combatants by those waging an unjust war is morally problematic.

At this point, it is necessary to say something about certain attempts to make much more of the right to kill combatants than the account given here. Michael Walzer's idea of "the moral equality of soldiers" can be our point

---

[28] This possibility was suggested to me by Igor Primoratz in conversation.

of entry. Opposing soldiers are moral equals, on Walzer's view, because they are in the grip of a shared servitude: they are not responsible for the war they wage, although they are responsible, to a degree, for the way they wage it. From this equality stems the mutual right to kill and the restrictions upon it, such as the prohibition on the killing of prisoners and noncombatants, the rights of quarter and restrictions upon the behaviour of captured soldiers who have, for instance, a right to try to escape but no right to kill a guard in order to escape.

For the most part Walzer writes as if the "shared servitude" is that of military conscription but he also extends the courtesy to serving officers (such as Rommel) and other professional soldiers, and I think he would count volunteers as well, at least those who see themselves as serving their country. In fact, the moral equality of soldiers turns out to be based in part upon a surprisingly narrow view of political obedience. The soldier is merely a servant of the state and is not responsible for its wars; his responsibility is restricted to the way he fights the war. As Walzer puts it: "The atrocities that he commits are his own; the war is not. It is conceived, both in international law and in ordinary moral judgement, as the king's business – a matter of state policy, not of individual volition, except when the individual is the king."[29]

It is not at all clear to me that Walzer is echoing "ordinary moral judgement" here, but, in any case, such judgement is unlikely to be decisive in a matter like determining the reach of moral responsibility for war fighting. I shall directly treat of Walzer's detailed account of this responsibility in Chapter 11 (on "Objecting Morally"), but some issues surrounding the mutual right of combatants to kill opposing enemy combatants need to be addressed here.

Walzer's reference to the case of Rommel is significant because we cannot think of Rommel as either too ignorant or too coerced to have any responsibility for the war he fought in, over and above responsibility for the way he fought it. Referring to Rommel's honourable conduct in refusing to obey Hitler's order to kill Allied prisoners, Walzer asserts that it would be "very odd" to praise him for this unless we also "refused to blame him for Hitler's aggressive wars. For otherwise he is simply a criminal and all the fighting he does is murder, or attempted murder, whether he aims at soldiers in battle or at prisoners or at civilians."[30] Here, as elsewhere, the concern with praise and blame tends to obscure the central moral issue. If we suppose

---

[29] Walzer, *Just and Unjust Wars*, p. 39. Walzer's view is echoed and indeed treated as the merest common sense, by Paul Christopher in *The Ethics of War and Peace: An Introduction to Legal and Moral Issues* (Englewood Cliffs, NJ: Prentice-Hall, 1944), pp. 96–97. Christopher says that "soldiers can never be responsible for the crime of war, qua soldiers. Resort to war is always a political decision, not a military one" (p. 96).

[30] Walzer, *Just and Unjust Wars*, p. 38.

that Rommel knew full well that he was conducting (part of) an unjust war, then I see no oddity at all in blaming him for that while praising him for the courage and restraint needed to keep his criminal activities within certain boundaries. It is very misleading to talk of being "simply a criminal," for there are many different types of criminality and even important moral distinctions within the one category of crime. A justly imprisoned convict who kills an armed guard who is impeding his attempt at escape is a murderer, but his crime is very different from that of a similar escapee who shoots and kills unarmed bystanders in order to create a diversion. Rommel's situation is, to take another analogy, like that of a bank robber who kills the armed guard who is using morally permissible violence to try to arrest him, but who spares the bank staff and clients and another guard who "surrenders," even though his leader is urging him to kill them all.

Walzer may think that Rommel has no responsibility for the unjust war because he is a professional soldier, and it is true that the existence of massive standing armies in modern nation-states has produced a professional class whose primary business (ultimately) is killing, maiming, and destroying. There is an understandable tendency for these professionals and those who support their existence to remove any possible stain of criminality from their "work." But where they are voluntary and senior professionals, they should not be allowed to treat the morality of their work as solely a matter for "the king." Walzer will not allow this for their relations with noncombatants or prisoners, but their killing of soldiers who are in the field only because they are defending themselves against unjust attack is treated as no responsibility of theirs.

I have argued that the moral equality thesis is false but that its falsity does nothing to erode the importance of the moral prohibition on attacking noncombatants. Just combatants may legitimately attack and kill unjust combatants, but they certainly have no licence to do the same to noncombatants. Unjust combatants may not legitimately attack and kill just combatants, but it is even clearer that they have no moral licence to do the same to noncombatants. This is principally because there is not even a presumptive case that the noncombatants are using violence to promote grave injustice. But in rejecting the equal right to kill enemy combatants, don't I need to say more about this difference in "presumptive case"? For there does seem to be a presumptive case that opposing soldiers are entitled to kill each other in combat – to defend themselves, yes, but also to initiate attacks. But what can this case be, since there is no substantive moral argument that could allow an unjust warrior to attack and kill a just one? The more that needs saying partly concerns the nature of just war thinking, partly the significance of self-defence, and partly the relevance of excusing conditions. The just war tradition is, according to my account of it, geared towards restricting the use of lethal violence in the political arena to those who have a just cause and fulfil, in the first instance, the other conditions of the JAB. Nonetheless, there will inevitably be political leaders who wrongly avail themselves of its tenets in the belief that their cause does indeed satisfy the conditions of the JAB, and they will persuade or coerce their citizens or followers into fighting in that cause. Once arrayed against the enemy's troops, those fighters will often see themselves as entitled to use lethal force against those troops because they believe their cause is just and sometimes in order to defend themselves against enemy fire. Their belief in the justice of their cause is false, but its falsehood will often be contentious, as matters of political policy so commonly are. What moral case there is for the existence of standing armed forces rests on the idea that nations must be prepared to fight just wars and that at least some citizens have a duty to fight in them. Against this institutional background, it is not surprising that many people will willingly serve in what are in fact unjust or dubiously just wars, and, of course, others will be coerced to do so. The role morality imposed by institutions that have a legitimating purpose will operate to provide people with "justifications" for behaviour that is objectively wrong, and is indeed not legitimated by the designated purpose. This does not justify the killing and harming of enemy combatants, but in certain contexts it may partially excuse it, and it certainly makes it morally intelligible. Moreover, in the heat of battle, a primary objective of many soldiers is self- and group preservation, a motive that has been claimed by some philosophers, most notably Thomas Hobbes, to justify killing an attacker whatever the circumstances.[31] If those circumstances, however, include the fact that you have unjustly initiated a violent conflict and are now responding to the defensive violence of your victims, it is far less obvious that you are entitled to continue with self-protective violence. Nonetheless, self-protection will in practice remain a powerful, if not overwhelming, motive.

What I have called the moral intelligibility of the "presumptive case" constitutes a legal or regulative recognition of these realities. The equal right to kill is not a deep moral fact about the equal status of combatants on opposing sides. It is the acknowledgment of an uneasy compromise between the profound moral fact that unjust combatants have no objective right to kill just ones and the empirical, institutional, and subjective facts created by the realities of war itself and the attempt to formalise moral and legal regulation of it. Where intelligent citizens of good-will, including intellectuals who have informed themselves of the relevant facts, can disagree about the justice of a war, we have a situation in which judgements about the moral legitimacy of soldiers deploying lethal force against enemy soldiers are bound to lack the same force as judgements about violence against noncombatants. It is a further consequence of these facts that attempts to enforce legal condemnation

---

[31] Thomas Hobbes, *Leviathan*, ed. C. B. Macpherson (London: Penguin, 1968), especially Chapters 13 and 14. See also Jenny Teichman, *Pacifism and the Just War: A Study in Applied Philosophy* (Oxford: Basil Blackwell, 1986), p. 85.

of the killing of enemy combatants by warriors deemed unjust are likely to be counterproductive. Such warriors and their leaders, seeing that they are under total condemnation whatever they do to forward their military cause, may well throw off all restraints in the conduct of the war, and so, as Vattel says, "the quarrel will become more bloody, more calamitous in its effects, and also more difficult to terminate."[32] When it comes to the legal regulation of warfare, therefore, a rule that criminalizes the killing of enemy combatants by unjustified warriors lacks feasibility.

This unfeasibility marks one of those points at which law and morality come apart, or more accurately, at which there are good moral reasons for not enforcing legitimate moral condemnations. Such conclusions can be, and perhaps should be, morally uncomfortable, somewhat parallel to the uneasiness created by the "peace and reconciliation" processes that grant amnesties to brutal murderers and torturers. This is the sense that I would give to the presumption that warriors are entitled to use direct lethal force against opposing warriors where they have some warrant for seeing them as wrongdoers or attackers, without there being any such case for attacking noncombatants. This presumption is primarily political, in a broad sense, though it draws upon facts relevant to morality. The distinction and the connection are similar to those made by Vattel when he distinguishes between the basic law of nature (or "eternal rules of justice") that must govern the conscience of those determining whether to resort to war and the "voluntary law of nations" that concerns the "external effects" of the natural law. The latter is itself determined by morality (for him, the natural law) but less directly.[33] Even so, the presumption is much weaker, even rebuttable, in cases where the enemy troops are palpably in the right or offer no serious threat. Here there is room for public condemnation of the unjust leaders and their troops, and there may well be room for some legal penalties against them, depending on circumstances. Whatever the politico-legal case, the moral case against unjust warriors killing just warriors also remains significant as a consideration for leaders contemplating resort to war and for citizens who face the choice whether to participate. We shall discuss this issue more fully in Chapter 11.

Unequal War

There is a point of connection here with some recent writings that seek to elucidate what is wrong with the phenomenon called "asymmetric warfare."

---

[32] Emmerich de Vattel, *The Law of Nations or The Principles of Natural Law*, trans. Charles Fenwick (Washington, DC: Carnegie Institution of Washington, 1916), Book 3, Chapter 12, para. 188.

[33] Ibid., para. 189. Vattel thinks that the pure verdict of the law of nature applies its condemnations and approvals only to the sovereign, whereas I shall argue in Chapter 11 that it must also apply to individual citizens.

This term refers to the kind of war that is waged between rivals with disproportionate standard military capacities. Since it also refers to the dissimilarity of tactics used by different sorts of enemies (often because of this disproportion), it may be better to use the term "unequal war" to describe situations where one side can inflict damage on the other with impunity, and hence where the presumed equality of soldiers totters insecurely on the shoulders of massive destructive and physical inequality. The primary case of this, of course, in the early years of the twenty-first century is any standard military conflict involving the United States (solely or in concert with its allies), since the armed might of that country is massively superior to that of any potential enemy. Hence, we have the spectacles of "no-risk wars" such as the Gulf War to expel Iraq from Kuwait and the bombing into submission of Serbia, in both of which massive airpower was deployed against relatively defenceless enemies with the result that there were virtually no casualties suffered by the superpower. One aspect of this is the tendency that such a situation has to create unconventional violent responses such as terrorism and guerrilla war. Another aspect is the undermining of the chivalric appeal of the moral equality thesis by eliminating the idea that war is a form of "fair fighting" between mutually respectful warriors. This idea is connected with the notion of chivalry and honour between foes, perhaps seen at its most vivid in the mutual attitudes of opposing war pilots in World War I, and dramatised in Jean Renoir's classic film *Grand Illusion.*

Paul Kahn has argued that the right of opposing combatants to kill each other is predicated on a rough equality of power.[34] There are some echoes of Walzer's position in his argument, for Kahn also thinks that there is a moral equality of soldiers, but he takes it as a corollary of this equality that there must be a rough equality of power between the opposing forces. In his account, the equal rights of opponents to injure exist only "as long as they stand in a relationship of mutual risk."[35] He thinks this "rule of reciprocal self-defence" stands "as its own first principle within a circumscribed context in which individuals act in politically compelled roles."[36] Where this equality of power is absent, the equal right to kill is cancelled. Asymmetrical (as unequal) warfare is not really warfare at all; he believes it most resembles (on the part of the powerful justified side) a police action, but he thinks there are certain problems with regarding massive armed events in the present international arena as police actions.

There are images associated with this account that certainly have some force. First, there is the idea of a "fair fight" and its violation, as in contests

---

[34] Paul Kahn, "The Paradox of Riskless Warfare," *Philosophy and Public Policy Quarterly* 22, no. 3 (2002), pp. 2–8. See also, Paul Kahn, "War and Sacrifice in Kosovo," *Philosophy and Public Policy Quarterly* 20, no. 3 (1999), pp. 1–6.

[35] Kahn, "The Paradox," p. 3.

[36] Ibid.

between ill-matched knights or boxers, and Kahn makes something of the way in which asymmetric war erodes chivalry; second, there is the picture of the powerful bully beating up the weaker victim. The first of these assumes that the framework is a consensual contest between parties to which justice of cause is largely irrelevant, the only problem being that disproportionate power vitiates the framework because it makes consent, even "idealised consent," implausible. The second takes it that the more powerful agent (the bully) is actually engaged in an unjust offence. The first image may have had some application in the past, as in the case of the pilot combatants of World War I mentioned earlier. It appeals to the idea of war as a sort of sporting contest, albeit one with high stakes. Nonetheless, I doubt that it has applied very widely in the past, and it has no plausibility now as a framework for any modern war, even between initially well-matched foes. As for the second, it trades on the idea that where one vastly more powerful protagonist is contending violently with a much weaker foe, the more powerful must be in the wrong. This is a natural thought, because we wonder why the much weaker is engaging in the battle at all unless they have been unjustly attacked. It would be irrational for them to initiate a war of aggression. Nonetheless, nations, like individuals, often enough engage in irrational behaviour or in behaviour that looks rational at the time but involves some crucial miscalculation. Moreover, sometimes the situation of weak against strong can be brought about by the weak's imprudent aggression against an even weaker victim, an aggression to which the very strong responds by way of support. Saddam's invasion of Kuwait is a good example, since he had reason to think that he could get away with the invasion through his superior strength. His confidence was buttressed by apparently reliable information that the United States would turn a blind eye. So the first massively asymmetrical war of the United States and its allies against Saddam was arguably a just war of the very strong against the quite weak, and here vastly superior strength surely affords no reason for moral qualms.[37] Kahn sometimes treats the asymmetry as entailing that the combatants on the weaker side do not constitute a threat, but this is by no means clear, since, even though they are unlikely to win, they may be able to do some damage, and it may be damage to those who do not deserve to die.[38] It is true that when the threat no longer exists the war should be stopped, but this follows from just war principles that need no resort to the moral equality thesis.

Kahn might well object to the use of the Kuwait example because he thinks that where a very powerful country intervenes in an existing symmetrical struggle on the right side, the asymmetry created doesn't affect the status of

---

[37] What qualms do exist concern other matters, such as whether the last resort condition was fulfilled, and whether the massive power superiority was deployed in disproportionate fashion.

[38] Kahn, "The Paradox," p. 5.

combatants and the equal right to kill.[39] This seems to me a mysterious claim, since the equal-fair-fight story is dramatically altered by the intervention of the great power. If it matters that the interveners are supporting the just side, then it should also matter in cases where they are not interveners but defending themselves against a weaker opponent in a just cause. Riskless warfare poses many problems, as does hegemonic military power, but the fair fight story isn't one of them. If anything, it merely distracts us from considering the real problems. Such a consideration need invoke no "new" moral theory of war, for the elements needed to discuss it are already present in the just war tradition.

[39] Ibid., p. 7.

7

The Problem of Collateral Damage

The world will not help us; we must help ourselves. We must kill as many of the Hamas and Islamic Jihad leaders as possible, as quickly as possible, while minimizing collateral damage, but not letting that damage stop us.
"Enough," editorial in the *Jerusalem Post*, September 11, 2003, p. 8

I recognized beforehand that someone might be...bringing their kid to work.... However, if I had known there was an entire day-centre, it might have given me pause to switch targets. That's a large amount of collateral damage.
Timothy McVeigh, interviewed by reporters for *The Buffalo News* about his attack upon the Alfred P. Murrah Federal Building[1]

We have been examining the principle of discrimination, in particular, its prohibition of intentional attacks upon noncombatants. But there remains an important area of contention, even if all I have argued in Chapter 6 about the immunity of noncombatants is accepted. This area is that often covered by the military euphemism "collateral damage."

This phrase is one of those catchwords that help to sanitise the horrible reality of war and other employments of political violence. It has taken its place along with "surgical strike," "revisiting the area" (i.e., renewed bombing), and "neutralising assets" as part of the linguistic camouflage that contemporary war fighters often use to disguise the human and moral costs of what they do. Perhaps the most astonishing military euphemism is that recently coined to describe a bomb that missed its ostensible target in Kosovo and hit a residential area: "seduction off the target"![2] This delightful touch

---

[1] "Dead Children Called 'Collateral Damage,'" *St John's Telegram*, March 29, 2001, p. 41. According to the reporters, McVeigh's only regret was that the children's deaths proved to be a public relations nightmare that undercut his cause.

[2] This appeared in a report by John Davison published in the British newspaper *The Independent* on April 10, 1999. Davison was reporting a NATO admission (correcting an earlier denial) that their bombing in the Kosovo capital, Pristina, had killed civilians and badly

not only helps the speaker disclaim responsibility, but manages to shift the blame onto the victims, who have somehow managed to "seduce" the bomb into killing them.

This extreme case illustrates something that is nonetheless present less idiotically in other military euphemisms. So it is that many uses of the term "collateral damage" suggest both an excuse and a belittling. The excuse: these deaths and maimings are not really what we wanted to happen. The belittling: these sufferings and killings are a very small part of a big picture. The *Jerusalem Post* editorial appeals to both with its talk of minimising the damage and its resolute plea for desperate measures of self-help in an emergency. In what follows, I want to examine the legitimacy of the excuse and the significance of the belittling.

Noncombatants are often killed or injured in warfare even when such harms are not intended. This is sometimes accidental and sometimes incidental. It is accidental when the deaths or injuries are unforeseen, and here the moral question is basically whether they should have been foreseen. Negligent and reckless acts are common in war and deserve even more censure than in peacetime, though the sad fact is that they seldom get it. The harms are incidental when they are unintended but foreseen.

This latter category has puzzled many people, including philosophers, because it requires the idea that an agent can know that his primary action will have a particular consequence, but can still go ahead with the action not intending that consequence. (The verb "know" should be interpreted flexibly here to include the strong and reasonably grounded belief that the consequence will follow.) Some philosophers, such as Jeremy Bentham, and some legal systems hold that the agent must be held to intend the known consequences of his or her action. Even here, it is noteworthy that Bentham acknowledges some need for a distinction by talking of "oblique intention," whereas those he opposes want to talk of "foreseen but unintended consequences." There is an extensive literature on this topic that we cannot explore here, but it is clearly connected with such issues as the validity of the doctrine of "double effect," the significance of "negative responsibility," and the relative importance of the character of an act or an agent compared to the action's good or bad outcomes. In certain cases, at least, it seems that there is both point and moral relevance to the idea that certain outcomes can be foreseen but not intended. I may know with practical certainty that if I refuse a gangster's invitation to murder a colleague, the gangster will

damaged homes in the context of the NATO bombing of Serbia. The admission was made by Air Commodore David Wilby, who said that the attack was aimed at the main telephone exchange in Pristina, which he claimed to be a legitimate target because it was being used for communications between Serbian forces in Kosovo and Belgrade. The full quote from Wilby is: "One bomb appeared to be seduced off the target at the final moment. Close inspection of imagery indicates that it landed some 200 to 300 metres away in what seems to be a small residential area." (*The Independent*, April 10, 1999, p. 2.)

murder two other people who stand in his way, but it would surely be very strange to describe me as intending, by my refusal, the deaths of the other two. Here there is the will of another involved in the outcome, and perhaps that is enough to vitiate the idea that it is even a "consequence" of my action of refusal. But this is at least disputable, and, in any case, there are other examples that do not involve the mediation of another's will. For example, suppose I am walking along a footpath and am aware of another pedestrian walking behind me. A runaway truck comes into view and is careering toward me with the driver dead in the cabin. In the instant I have left, I leap aside in the full knowledge that the person behind me will be hit and probably killed. Surely it is clear that I did not intend by my self-preserving action to inflict injury and death on that person, even though I could reasonably have foreseen that outcome.[3] Or consider my plight as a surgeon in a war zone who must choose who amongst the wounded to aid with scarce lifesaving drugs. In choosing to save Brown and Smith with the foreseeable consequence that Black, Jones, and Grey will die, it surely makes sense to describe me as intending to save Brown and Smith with the foreseen but unintended consequence that the latter three die, rather than as intending to save Brown and Smith while intending to kill Black, Jones, and Grey.

For my purposes, we need not assume that this defence of the category is unequivocally successful. The point of this discussion is principally to explain the initial appeal of the category and thereby to make comparative sense of the way it might be explicitly employed, or implicitly relied upon, in discussions of the morality of "collateral damage." As we shall see, there are ways in which this initial plausibility can be stretched and even eroded in those discussions.

The Accidental and the Incidental

Let us call the form of collateral damage that requires the idea of foreseen but unintended damage "incidental damage" by contrast with the other form of "accidental damage." First let us consider the moral problems associated with accidental damage. Demonstrating that some effect of one's actions is "accidental" does not automatically excuse or eliminate the need to justify it. It shows that the effect was not intended, and moreover that it was not aimed at under any description available to the agent at the time. As far as your intentional control is concerned, the effect was the product of chance. As J. L. Austin pointed out long ago, there is a distinction between "mistake" and "accident." Like all distinctions, this has blurred edges, and Austin doesn't

---

[3] If it is urged as a defect in the example that the person behind will be killed whether I jump aside or not, we could amend the example so that my staying put will save the other's life. Instead of a truck, it is a maniac with a spear whose thrown spear will kill only me if I don't move, and only the other person if I do.

bother to give an account of it, but it is, roughly speaking, the distinction between going astray because of something wrong with one's thought processes or perceptions and getting it wrong because of some mishap in the "outside world."[4] But, for ease of exposition, I will collapse this distinction and treat mistaken damage under the same heading as genuinely accidental damage. In both cases, for different sorts of reasons, the agent does not know that the damaging effect will occur, at least under the relevant description. If the American authorities are to be believed, the bombing of the Chinese embassy in Belgrade during the NATO attack upon Serbia was a mistake – they meant to hit that building but didn't mean to hit the Chinese embassy, because they didn't think it was the Chinese embassy. On my last trip to China, I could find no Chinese who believed the American claim of mistake, and my European colleagues sneered at my naiveté in accepting it. (By contrast, I was surprised that they were all convinced that the CIA would have reliable maps of Belgrade!) But if the mistake story were true, it would provide the beginnings of an acceptable excuse for the deaths and damage that ensued. Similarly with the bomb that went off target in Kosovo. Unless the residents of the Pristina suburb exercised some magical power to bring about their own destruction ("seduced off target"), then the NATO explanation aims to provide the excuse of accidental deaths and damage. In both cases, the question that needs to be answered is whether the mistake and the accident were the result of negligence or recklessness. Although a primary interest in moral assessment is a concern for intentional actions, that concern does not exhaust the scope of moral assessment. People who do not intend the deaths of others but who do not take reasonable steps to guard against accident or mistake are morally culpable, even if the culpability will often be of a different order from that borne by those who set out to kill and maim. Accidental deaths, injuries, and damage are to be avoided if they can be. If the American military could have known by taking reasonable steps to discover it that the building they planned to attack was the Chinese embassy, then they are guilty of the deaths and damage. If the NATO bomber command, or some relevant figures in the chain of command, could have known that they were using defective weapons, then the same applies to them. In both cases, if they couldn't have known at the time, then the episodes may provide grounds for more care in the future about the reliability of targeting and weaponry.

The general point behind the morality of accidental damage is that unintended actions that accidentally or mistakenly kill people you are not entitled to kill have done great harm to those people (and a real but lesser harm

---

4 See J. L. Austin, "A Plea for Excuses," in his *Philosophical Papers* (Oxford: Oxford University Press, 1961), p. 133, note 1. Here Austin illustrates the distinction at work with the example of two different donkey scenarios in one of which the donkey is shot by mistake and in the other by accident.

when it is not a matter of killing but of damaging their property). This harm becomes a wrong when the accident or mistake could reasonably have been avoided. Hence we have a place for the moral and legal categories of negligence, recklessness, and due care. It is incumbent upon people not to put themselves in positions where accident and mistake are liable to eventuate in the death or injury of others or in damage to their property. This point can be obscured, especially in war, by the otherwise perfectly legitimate concentration upon preventing intentional killing of the innocent. Murder is a dreadful thing, but we cannot congratulate ourselves on avoiding it if we are casual about manslaughter and negligent homicide.

Of course, it would be too much to insist that war may proceed only where all possibilities of accident or mistake have been eliminated. Any large-scale undertaking will involve unavoidable accidents and mistakes, or accidents and mistakes that could have been avoided only at too great a cost to the enterprise. If we assume that there are some just wars, then some such accidents or mistakes may be a regrettable accompaniment to their successful prosecution. Even here, however, the just war requirement of proportionality may be in play. If in the course of a war it becomes clear that the weapon systems are heavily prone to accident or mistake, then the verdict may have to be that the harm done may well outweigh the good that the war is expected to achieve. But at this point the awareness so created moves us into the category of incidental rather than accidental damage.

The incidental killing of noncombatants has always been a problem in just war theory, often solved by resort to some form of the principle of double effect. This allows for the harming of noncombatants in some circumstances as a foreseen but unintended side effect of an otherwise legitimate act of war. The "circumstances" include the proportionality of the side effect to the intended outcome. Not everyone agrees with the principle, but the conduct of war in contemporary circumstances is morally impossible unless warriors are allowed knowingly to put noncombatants at risk in certain circumstances. Some modification to the immunity principle to allow indirect harming seems to be in line with commonsense morality in other areas of life and to be necessitated by the circumstances of war. If it is not available, then pacifism, as Robert Holmes has argued, seems the only moral option, at least for anyone uncommitted to some strong version of direct utilitarianism (or consequentialism).[5]

In discussing incidental killing, it is important to distinguish different types of foresight. Sometimes the agent can see that there is some chance of noncombatants being killed; sometimes he or she has reason to believe that their deaths are probable or highly probable, sometimes that they are practically certain. These varying degrees of epistemic judgement raise

---

[5] Robert L. Holmes, *On War and Morality* (Princeton, NJ: Princeton University Press, 1989). See especially pages 193–203.

the moral stakes considerably, since they change the issue from being one of entitlement to put the innocent at risk to one of confidently envisaging their deaths. An awful lot of our ordinary legitimate practices put the innocent at some risk, as when we drive children to school. We do what we can to minimise such risks, but consider them sometimes worth taking for the benefits involved or the evils avoided. In the context of war, there is a world of moral difference between bombing a military facility believing that there might be one or two noncombatants (a visiting child, some prisoners of war) who are thereby placed in grave danger, and bombing it in the certain knowledge that a group of noncombatants, say, coerced nonenemy sex slaves, are permanently housed there or very nearby and certain to be killed. Both scenarios should give pause, but the latter should raise acute concern.

The Intricacies of Double Effect

It is worth stressing in this connection (and in others) that the doctrine of double effect (DDE) does not hold that incidental damage is acceptable merely because it is incidental to intent. The usual conditions are:

1. the action at issue must not itself be morally bad, nor should any intended effect of it be morally bad;
2. the anticipated bad effect must be genuinely unintended and not merely secondarily intended (e.g., intended as a means to a further end);
3. the harm involved in the unintended outcome must not be disproportionate to the moral benefit aimed at in the act.[6]

There is another condition (or, as I would prefer, precondition) that I will discuss later. For now, I want to say a little about these three conditions. The first simply specifies that the moral utility of the DDE arises only when what is intended by the agent (the outcome that has the unintended but foreseen bad consequence) is a benefit that is either morally neutral or morally good. The second condition is aimed at precluding what Elizabeth Anscombe once called "double think about double effect."[7] As we saw earlier, people faced with the difficult choices about what tactics to use in their war efforts will often adopt a simple utilitarian or consequentialist stance about the means they will employ. But where they don't adopt such a stance, there is a strong temptation to stretch the DDE in order to gain maximum tactical advantage in the deployment of violence. So it may be argued that the real intention

---

[6] These conditions are expressed differently by different authors. This list is my distillation of the sense of those treatments I have read.

[7] G. E. M. Anscombe, "War and Murder," in Richard A. Wasserstrom (ed.), *War and Morality* (Belmont, CA: Wadsworth, 1970), p. 50.

in attacking a day care centre is to win the war, not to kill the children and their caregivers. Admittedly, this is an extreme in sophistry, since it blatantly ignores the fact that having an ultimate purpose for some action does not exclude having an intermediate purpose that requires fulfilment in order to achieve the ultimate objective. Generally speaking, someone who intends an end also intends the means chosen to that end. But there are philosophical manoeuvres that seek to complicate this.

Consider one propounded by David Lewis in connection with arguments about nuclear deterrence. A political leader, call her Jones, who has suffered a nuclear attack on one of her cities, considers launching a nuclear attack on an enemy city as a response in order to dissuade the enemy commander-in-chief from further attacks. Lewis argues that she need not intend the massive civilian deaths and casualties that "result" from her action. How so? Well, according to Lewis, Jones does not intend the deaths and casualties since she needs only to affect the reasoning of the enemy commander and so needs only the flight path of the missile and the flash of light as the city explodes to figure as premises in the reasoning the commander will engage in. The commander will reason from the detected flight and subsequent fireball to the conclusion that the city has been destroyed and be persuaded to desist from further attacks. He does not need the later, more direct information about deaths and devastation in order to come to his conclusion. So Jones intends the flight and flash, but the massacre is an unintended though foreseen consequence.

Quite apart from the fact that such "persuasion" has a somewhat tenuous hold on probability of success, this argument of Lewis (which echoes one made by Jonathan Bennett) shows the way in which double-think about double effect can lead even so humane and intelligent a man as David Lewis into what is surely sophistry. Of course, Lewis himself does not endorse the DDE, for he has a largely consequentialist approach to the problem of collateral damage. He is merely arguing that a countervalue attack to obliterate a city, if that is the only way to prevent massive nuclear devastation, does in fact comply with the DDE. (Lewis in fact opposes countervalue attacks because they are more disproportionate than his preferred option of finite counterforce) To this extent, his argument is a sort of reductio: if the DDE will let you get away with this, we might as well forget about it.[8] But the problem surely resides in Lewis's treatment of Jones's intention, rather than in the defects of the DDE. A philosophical account of intention is fraught with complexities, but whatever account we give it must respect plain thinking about what someone does and what they mean to do. And the idea that Jones doesn't intend to devastate the city when she carefully plans the missile's trajectory and explosive capacity to that very end and wants that

---

[8] See David Lewis, "Finite Counterforce," in Henry Shue (ed.), *Nuclear Deterrence and Moral Restraint* (Cambridge: Cambridge University Press, 1989), pp. 112–113, note 45.

destruction and death to figure in the enemy commander's reasoning and response, is just dotty. It is simply irrelevant to this attribution that the enemy commander can reason from certain features of the action, other than direct observation of the devastation, to the fact of the devastation. Perhaps Lewis thinks, as Bennett does at one point, that the fact that Jones might be happy were a "miracle" to occur such that the flight and flash occurred without the devastation but the enemy commander was nonetheless persuaded shows that Jones does not intend the devastation. But again this is simply confused. There are many things that we intend as means to some good end that we don't feel pleased about, but we intend them nonetheless. The "miracle" device could be cheerfully and absurdly employed in every case to show that we don't intend them. In the case of the city's destruction, Jones can infer that the enemy commander will come to his conclusions on the basis of reports (or direct observation) of flight and flash, but she needs the deaths as well, since a later report that the flight and the flash were, say, cunning visual deceptions will mean that the commander's reasoning will not go through.

The DDE requires that we think in commonsense ways about what people intend and foresee. This means that there are various disentanglements of the parts of an action that we cannot really allow. Consider someone who has a great hatred of flies. To his horror, he finds a fly in his apartment, and the only swatting implement to hand is a big, heavy hammer. The fly is very hard to keep up with, but it eventually settles on the bald head of his best friend, where it is clearly visible against the bald surface. If he smashes the hammer down upon the fly and the head it rests on, fully aware that he will thereby kill or severely injure his friend, it would surely be absurd for him to plead that he did not intend his friend's death or injury. The remark, "I only intended to kill the fly; my friend's death was a foreseen but unintended side effect of my action," just doesn't make sense. (Of course, if it did make sense, it would still be no excuse under the DDE because of the proportionality requirement, but the more important point here is that we cannot take apart the smashing of the fly and the smashing of the head.)

Grossman gives a good real-life military example of this double-thinking evasive mindset. It concerns illegitimate attacks upon combatants rather than noncombatants, but the mode of thinking is similar. He records a conversation he had heard amongst U.S. troops who had just completed a training exercise about treatment of prisoners of war. Several of the soldiers held straightforwardly barbaric views, such as that POWs should be marched through an area saturated with persistent nerve gas or just killed outright. Another suggested using them for minefield clearance. The chaplain intervened to cite the Geneva Conventions, and one of the soldiers reported that in training school they had told him that the Geneva Conventions forbade firing white phosphorus at troops, "so you call it in on their equipment." Here is convenient double-think with a vengeance. The equipment happens to be attached to the people (or nearby), and so attacking it achieves your real objective of attacking them, but you can disavow this with a verbal device.

I am not suggesting that the DDE is immune from defects, merely that these evasive devices will not work. I think, for instance, that the notion of "means" that the doctrine employs requires more attention, and, as mentioned earlier, that the DDE is much more plausible where the foreseen effect is risk to noncombatants rather than certain death, but this is not the place to engage fully in the very extensive and complex debate about the doctrine. This debate has been carried on intensively in recent years – often, of course by critics of the doctrine who are consequentialists and hence disposed to find no significance in the ways that good or bad consequences are brought about. More interestingly, many non-consequentialists are questioning the DDE and sometimes seeking other ways of maintaining the possibility of a moral defence of some forms of collateral damage. Alison McIntyre, for instance, in an important and comprehensive critique, wants to reject the DDE but keep the moral significance of the distinction between intention and foresight, or some parallel distinction that preserves a non-consequentialist outlook regarding collateral damage.[9] Frances Kamm seems to have a similar project in view. Kamm, in one characteristically intricate discussion, explores the superiority of a doctrine of triple effect and argues that an unintended side effect of one intended action may be a means to another legitimate and intended outcome, thus rejecting the view that one must intend the means to one's intended end.[10] Kamm's discussions in this area, though always philosophically penetrating and challenging, sometimes involve such recherché examples and such complex mental states that their relevance to the issues we are concerned with must remain unclear.

In another paper, for instance, she disputes the importance of intention to permissibility by comparing two scenarios.[11] In one, an attack is made on an important military target with the foreseen but unintended consequence that some legitimately proportionate number of noncombatants is killed. In the other, the very same outcomes occur, but the attack is carried out by a "Baby Killer Nation" that intends the deaths of the noncombatants but chooses this incidental method for the killing because the real purpose can then be hidden behind the cloak of collateral damage. Kamm thinks both acts are the same and hence that both are permissible, even though the DDE would permit the first and not the second. My reaction to the example is twofold. First, there is an external sense in which the two actions are the

---

9 Alison McIntyre, "Doing Away with Double Effect," *Ethics* 111 (2001), pp. 219–255.

10 Frances Kamm, "The Doctrine of Triple Effect and Why a Rational Agent Need Not Intend the Means to His End," *Proceedings of the Aristotelian Society*, supp. vol. 74 (2000), pp. 41–57. Further references to this work will be abbreviated as "The Doctrine of Triple Effect."

11 Frances Kamm, "Terrorism and Several Moral Distinctions," *Legal Theory* 12 (2006), particularly pp. 29–36. There are many other interesting issues raised in this recent paper that I cannot discuss here.

same, but another in which they are different, precisely because the second scenario is deliberate murder and the first is not.[12] (We might mark this by talking of identical acts but different actions.) Similarly, a movement of my elbow when I reach out to greet someone may accidentally knock over your valuable porcelain vase and smash it, whereas in other circumstances the same set of movements may constitute an act of malicious damage because they are performed with that intent. In Kamm's more complex case, I would say that when we understand the two scenarios as different actions, then it is clear that the first is permissible and the second is not, even though "externally" the performances and outcomes are the same. And this is not just a point about the blameable motives of the agents in the second scenario, since we are rightly concerned to condemn murderous actions and not merely to blame the agents, no matter how the actions are disguised. This is in part because, given the firm intentions of the leaders of Baby Killer Nation, we have no guarantee that they will not shift tactics to more direct and massive attacks upon innocents when, for example, their real motives can no longer be disguised behind the cloak of collateral damage. Kamm insists in a footnote that, for the purposes of her discussion, we should ignore such factors.[13] If we are concerned with realistic possibilities that have to do with war, I think that this advice has limited utility, though her example does point to the interesting fact that what we may be happy to see done can come loose from what we think it wrong to do. If a Nazi prison guard murders another guard in order to steal his money and avenge some slight, but thereby provides an opportunity for a death camp prisoner to escape, we would not (in Kamm's phrase) "require him to refrain."[14]

The issue of realistic possibilities raises a second problem with critiques of double effect, namely, that they are geared to bizarre scenarios that are arguably too remote from the real contingencies of warfare to throw light upon the utility or disutility of the DDE in those contingencies. Consider one of Kamm's discussions of the well-known trolley problem in which an agent is on a runaway trolley that is approaching a fork in the track where one side contains five innocent people strapped (perhaps) to the rail, and the other side contains only one.[15] Kamm treats the case as one involving the DDE, whereas I would be inclined to treat it differently, but that does not affect the point I want to make. Following Judith Thomson, Kamm considers a version of the example, known as Loop, where the rail beyond the fork

---

[12] Kamm considers something like this point when she discusses Thomas Scanlon's claim that two such acts can be said to have different "meanings." See Thomas Scanlon, "Intention and Permissibility," *Proceedings of the Aristotelian Society*, supp. vol. 74 (2000), pp. 301–317; and Kamm, "Terrorism and Several Moral Distinctions," p. 35. Kamm is uncertain about the force of Scanlon's proposal but insists, in any case, that both acts are permissible.

[13] Kamm, "Terrorism and Several Moral Distinctions," p. 29, note 9.

[14] Ibid., p. 34.

[15] Kamm, "The Doctrine of Triple Effect," pp. 21–39.

loops around and joins up. If we choose to turn the trolley in the direction of the one person, it may be that we need that person to be struck, since that is the only way that the trolley will fail to complete the loop and hit the other five. This raises some interesting questions about intention; but, not content with this variation, Kamm goes on to consider (amongst others) an Extra Push case, a Track Trolley case, a Double Track case, and then an Unintended Good case to further fine-tune the possible intentions of the agent. Along the way, she utilises the idea of an agent who does not want the five hit from the right side (because she doesn't want their faces damaged) but is indifferent to whether they are hit from behind by the looping trolley, and an agent who correctly turns the trolley in the direction of the one in order not to hit the five, but who doesn't intend to hit the one because she intends to attempt a rescue, reasoning that if her running after the speeding trolley fails, then the five are saved, and if it succeeds, then the five are no worse off than they would have been if the trolley had not been turned toward the one.[16] Speaking for myself, I find at this point, if not before, that my grip on intuitions about intentions and their relevance to real moral problems becomes quite insecure.[17]

It is, however, worth repeating that unless the DDE, or some other principle that serves a similar purpose, is allowed, then the possibility of waging a modern war that respects the immunity of noncombatants is vastly reduced. This is because there will be many situations in which noncombatant deaths and injuries can be foreseen with certainty or probability as a result of attacking important military objectives, and without something that acknowledges a moral difference between intended outcomes and unintended but foreseen outcomes, these attacks will be ruled out by the immunity of noncombatants. Whether acknowledgement of this and abandonment of the DDE (or some similar principle) would lead to less restrained warfare or to pacifism depends on many other factors, but I should think that the former is more likely.

Other Aspects of the DDE

Instead of pursuing the critique of the DDE's viability further, I want to emphasise an aspect of the DDE that is easily overlooked. It is related in spirit to a direct qualification to the usual statements of the DDE that has been suggested by Michael Walzer. I shall look at Walzer shortly, but the

---

[16] Kamm, "The Doctrine of Triple Effect.": for Track Trolley, see p. 24; for Extra Push, p. 28; for Double Track, p. 36; for Unintended Good, p. 37; and for the Rescue device, pp. 28–29.

[17] In "Terrorism and Several Moral Distinctions," Kamm has another Trolley variation that parallels the structure of Baby Killer Nation. This is "Bad Man Trolley," where the agent positively wants to kill the one, who is his enemy, and cares nothing about the five, but nonetheless acts externally in just the right way. See p. 32.

aspect I want to stress is more a precondition for the application of the DDE. This precondition is that where there are other feasible ways of achieving the good end that do not involve the harmful side effects or involve fewer or less grave such effects, the agent should choose them. And this holds even where the alternatives involve somewhat higher costs to the agent. I call this a precondition because the spirit of the DDE remains restrictive, even where it has a permissive form. In the case of war or political violence more generally, the protection of the innocent remains a primary value of the *jus in bello* and hence dictates that incidental injury or killing of the innocent is to be entirely avoided where possible. Of course, the "where possible" needs unpacking in the particular setting; it will include such things as the degree of risk to one's troops and to one's prospects of success, but a serious commitment to the protection of innocent people requires giving their safety a high priority. Michael Walzer treats something like this as part of the condition specifying that the apparent effect be not really a means to the intended goal. Walzer's version goes as follows: " . . . aware of the evil involved, he seeks to minimize it, accepting costs to himself."[18] This is in the same spirit, but it seems to ignore the possibility that means might be available, and should be sought (other things being equal), that avoid the incidental damage altogether. (Perhaps Walzer means his talk of "minimizing" to include the limit of zero evil.)

This precondition is very important because it reinstates the value of avoiding the deaths of innocent people, a value that can be obscured by the DDE. It can be obscured because, if the legitimate goal is important enough, the innocent casualties can be too lightly discounted by the idea of proportionality. This comes out very clearly in the tone of the quotation at the head of this chapter from the *Jerusalem Post*. There is the breezy reference to minimising collateral damage, but this is immediately followed by the assertion that such damage must never stand in the way of the killing of the leaders of Hamas and Islamic Jihad. This looks like trying to have your cake and eat it. It suggests that the talk of minimising is simply a ritual gesture toward morality or world opinion. There is no suggestion that the intentional killing may have to be abandoned altogether if the minimising is not sufficient. There is no sense that alternative ways of killing the enemy that might create no incidental damage should be sought. Here, the understanding of what the DDE might licence is remote from the spirit of such just war theorists as Vitoria, who says: "It is never lawful to kill innocent people, even accidentally & unintentionally, except when it advances a just war *which cannot be won in any other way*"[19] (my italics). As I read Vitoria, he

---

[18] Michael Walzer, *Just and Unjust Wars: A Moral Argument with Historical Illustrations*, third edition (New York: Basic Books, 2000), p. 155.

[19] Francisco de Vitoria, *Political Writings*, ed. Anthony Pagden and Jeremy Lawrance (Cambridge and New York: Cambridge University Press, 1991), p. 316.

is saying that the killing of the innocent in war can be licit only when it is done either accidentally or unintentionally (i.e., when it is foreseen but not intended), but even then, it is licit only when there is no alternative to it. Thus put, the precondition expresses an idea that is somewhat parallel to the last resort condition of the JAB.[20] Other ways of achieving the military objective without the high risk of injury or death to noncombatants should be the first priority. And this applies not only to the war at large, as the quote from Victoria might seem to say, but also to particular campaigns and battles (etc.) within it.

The trouble with the DDE expressed without the precondition can be seen if we imagine a scenario in which clearly identified enemy troops (or terrorists) are moving in a crowd of people – a procession, perhaps – and can be shot while in the crowd with the foreseen result that some few of the innocent civilians will be injured or killed. As long as their deaths are unintended and the need to kill the terrorists is grave enough, the DDE (without the precondition) will allow the shooting. But suppose we know or have good reason to believe that the terrorists are going to part company with the crowd at the next intersection, where our troops will have a clear shot at them without the risk of any civilian deaths. The troops who ignore this option and shoot into the crowd have done a grave wrong, and the DDE would be defective if it applied to excuse them. And even if the army authorities don't know precisely when they will otherwise get a shot at enemy soldiers or terrorists, surely a genuine respect for noncombatants would counsel the seeking of alternatives to attacking them when they are surrounded by noncombatants and not engaged at that time in any armed offensive. The Israeli army was clearly in horrible violation of this counsel when they used a one tonne bomb to blow up a block of flats in order to kill a solitary Hamas leader, Sheikh Salah Mustafa Shehada, with the result that eight children (one of whom was two months old) were killed in the bombing. Indeed, not only is this action in probable violation of the precondition, but it has distinct similarities to the hammer example used earlier. As in that example, it is hard to see how the action could be so disentangled as to claim with any plausibility that the bombers intended *only* to kill the Hamas leader, and even were this plausible, the considerations of proportionality would also defeat the excuse.

Is the precondition the same as Walzer's additional subcondition? Walzer makes the agent's intention to minimise the harm to noncombatants, accepting costs to him or herself, a part of his third condition of the DDE (in effect, my second condition). But the intention to minimise the evil of noncombatant deaths and injuries is itself a consequence of the precondition that requires avoidance, where possible, of even incidental noncombatant

[20] I owe the suggestion of this parallel to Igor Primoratz. My thanks to him also for pointing out the reference to Vitoria.

deaths. If we are enjoined to avoid, wherever we can, getting into a situation where we cause collateral damage of the incidental kind, then it seems to follow that when we cannot avoid it, we should take positive steps to minimise the casualties.

Some of the considerations discussed in connection with what I have been calling "the precondition" are related to the third condition of the DDE concerning proportionality. We have considered proportionality in an earlier chapter, but there are significant issues to do with the idea of proportionality as applied to collateral damage that we must now address. An important one concerns whether proportionality is at all relevant to the collateral damage done by unjust warriors. Here, as in the discussion of unjust warriors killing just ones that we pursued in Chapter 6, there is intellectual pressure in two opposed directions. On the one hand, it seems that there cannot be symmetrical application of proportionality to the incidental killing or harming of noncombatants, since such proportionality should be morally assessed only with regard to the military aims of a just enterprise, and the enterprise of the unjust warrior is, by hypothesis, unjust. Hence all killing done by unjust war fighters is unjust, including the incidental killing deemed to be proportional to their war aims. On the other hand, there is surely a moral distinction between attacks on military targets that reflect a concern that incidental killing be proportional to military objectives and those that don't – whichever side shows that respect. In line with the solution adopted in Chapter 6, I want to agree that any incidental killing done by unjust warriors is objectively morally wrong, but continue to distinguish for moral and regulative reasons between the incidental killing (or other damage) they do that is proportional to the "ordinary" military objectives they seek and incidental harm that is quite disproportional. The reasons are readily adaptable from our earlier discussion in Chapter 6, and concern issues having to do with likely perceptions of justification and responsibility, as well as the need to promulgate rules to restrain and regulate the conduct of parties to warfare that are more likely to be adhered to because viewed as even-handed. Just as it may be wrong for unjust warriors to kill enemy combatants who are fighting in a just cause, but even worse for them to kill enemy noncombatants, so a similar point applies to incidental killing. It may be wrong for unjust warriors to kill some small number of noncombatants incidentally, but it is even worse for them to kill a large number incidentally *and* unnecessarily. Moreover, the wrong of the latter should be clearer to them, less contaminated by mistaken views of the justice of their cause, than the former.

A further problem with proportionality concerns the tendency to treat it as a merely consequentialist balancing of benefits and harms. Instead of talking of the good achieved "outweighing" the harmful effect, as though summing a totality of goods against a totality of harms, and thus potentially making the DDE more permissive than it is meant to be, we might do better to think in terms of the weight of the moral reasons for taking the action that has the harmful consequences. McIntyre thinks this a more satisfactory route, but judges it too vague and thinks the search for more precision unsuccessful.[21] Clearly, there is more work needed on the role of this concept in the DDE and related principles, though it does seem to have some intuitive plausibility.

Dual-Purpose Targets

There are other ways in which the idea of "collateral damage" can be abused in either its accidental or incidental forms. Curiously enough, one is by loudly proclaiming a commitment to noncombatant immunity as a way of disguising one's contempt, or marginal respect, for it in practice. Another is the expansion of the permissible scope of the category of collateral damage by expansion of the scope of legitimate military targets. This is the strategy of targeting "dual-purpose" facilities, a practice that has become increasingly familiar in recent U.S. military practice, though it has an ancient lineage. The war against Serbia over Kosovo provides many examples, as does the recent attack upon Iraq. The case of the Pristina telephone exchange, mentioned earlier, may (if we set aside the magical possibilities of "seduction off target") have been a mistake, but had it been a case of dual-purpose targeting, we should have to pay due regard to the significance of a telephone exchange for civilian life. The destruction of a central telephone exchange is, in the modern age, a massive blow to civilian well-being, given all the services in a contemporary city that depend upon modern communications. There may indeed be many cases in which an institution or facility principally serving noncombatant purposes may also serve some subsidiary military purpose. Other examples would be bridges, electricity grids and other power supplies, dams, communications facilities, and many features of daily civic life that we might call "infrastructural."

I do not want to deny that sometimes a grave enough case may exist to treat some subsidiary military purpose as sufficient to permit such an attack. But the mere existence of a dual purpose is not itself enough to legitimate an attack and to treat the damage to noncombatants as permissible "incidental" injury. Enemy soldiers often use the same water supply as civilians, but this will hardly license the destruction of water supplies and the deaths from thirst and disease that will ensue. A particular problem with the current vogue for dual-purpose targets is the idea that it is sufficient to determine that some proposed target has *some* value for the enemy's military purposes in order to legitimise an attack upon it. This is defective in ignoring the proportionality requirement by focussing wholly on the military advantage, no matter how minor, and disregarding the harm to noncombatants, no

---

[21] McIntyre, "Doing Away with Double Effect," p. 223ff.

matter how great. Even international law is currently too permissive in this respect, since it rules out dual-purpose targets only where the objects proposed for destruction cause incidental damage (in my sense) that "may be expected to leave the civilian population with such inadequate food or water as to cause its starvation or force its movement."[22] Proportionality may have difficulties of interpretation, but it certainly requires attention to more harms than this. Malnourishment, disease, and a range of other serious deprivations are simply ignored, while the balancing of the military advantage against these and other harms to noncombatants is passed over.[23]

Where the respect for noncombatant immunity is rejected or ignored as a moral constraint on fighting, it will be natural to target not only civilians and their property but also the infrastructure that directly supports their lives or more indirectly gives those lives meaning. Hence the dam-busting raids of World War II were a natural accompaniment to the area bombing of German cities. But once it is accepted that restraint must be exercised in the targeting of civilian populations, attacks upon infrastructure immediately become more problematic. A casual attitude toward the destruction of infrastructure needs careful scrutiny as it may really reflect a disregard for the rights and protections that should be accorded noncombatants.

The doctrine of dual-purpose targets can easily be adapted to the aim of demoralising enemy populations so that their pain or protest will weaken the leadership's will to continue resistance. When the bombing of bridges, water supplies, electricity generators, and even media quarters is openly justified in terms of their military significance, and when this is done in the broad context of inducing "shock and awe" – as the American leadership put it in connection with the recent invasion of Iraq – or of crushing the enemy's will to resist, then the dual-purpose nature of the targets will often reflect a dual-intention strategy in the attackers. The fact that one intention is licit does not sanctify the other illegitimate purpose. There is indeed a double effect, but both effects are intended and desired. Indeed, in many cases it is hard to resist the conclusion that the military justification for the targeting is spurious and incidental. The primary purpose is to harm civilians.

This point is connected with the fact that, whether we are dealing with war or terrorism, much discussion of collateral damage has, understandably, focused upon the *killing* of noncombatants. But there are many other harms, damages, and sufferings that can be inflicted that do not result in

---

[22] Article 54, paragraph 3, of Protocol 1 of the Additional Protocols to the Geneva Conventions.

[23] There is an excellent discussion of the limits of dual-purpose targeting and of the state of international law and military practice in Henry Shue and David Wippman, "Limiting Attacks on Dual-Use Facilities Performing Indispensable Civilian Functions," *Cornell International Law Journal* 35, no. 3 (2002), pp. 559–580. The article contains detailed proposals for new approaches to the problem.

immediate death. The dual-purpose strategy tends to involve viewing the infrastructural features of an enemy population as connected with short-term military gain and short-term civilian discomfort, but the moral gaze needs to be broader than that because, especially in modern societies, the infrastructures are increasingly crucial to well-being, survival, and some-times even to life itself. Something like this point can be extended to the problems raised by direct or incidental damage to the natural and human environment of the enemy's country. Forests, rivers, architectural and artis-tic creations and the like can be viewed both as valuable in themselves and as part of the significant life of the enemy's civilian population, or indeed as part of the broader human heritage (hence the outrage at the Taliban's destruction of ancient statues of another faith). The protection of such cultural and environmental values from the ravages of war has been recog-nised in various international legal instruments such as the 1954 Hague Convention for the Protection of Cultural Property in the Event of Armed Conflict, later incorporated into the humanitarian laws of the Geneva Con-ventions. Of course, such destruction is often more direct than collateral. There is a sad history of intentional destruction of enemy cultural and envi-ronmental values dating back to ancient times. From the razing of Carthage by the Romans to the destruction of mosques and churches during the Bosnian conflict of the 1990s, the deliberate attempt to obliterate the mem-ories and cultural identities of enemy peoples has been a persistent feature of war.[24]

More broadly, whatever the problems with the DDE, there are moral attitudes behind the different approaches to collateral damage that are re-flected in the application of the DDE that are themselves of clear significance in the prosecution of war. These fall into (at least) four camps:

1. Sadistic contempt for noncombatants' lives and well-being, leading to the intentional killing of them.
2. Instrumental disdain for them, leading again to the intentional killing of them.
3. Indifference to their lives and well-being, leading to a casual attitude to collateral damage.
4. Concern for their lives and well-being, leading to attempts to avoid or limit collateral damage.

However we work out the formulae that allow for some foreseen but unin-tentional killing of noncombatants, it is the moral superiority of (4) over (1), (2), and (3) that gives significance to the attempt. We have already dis-cussed in Chapter 5 some of the difficulties involved in giving an adequate theoretical account of the proportionality that can justify some collateral

---

[24] See Robert Bevan, *The Destruction of Memory: Architecture at War* (London: Reaktion Books, 2006).

damage to noncombatants, and it will, I think, always involve an element of concrete judgement in situations of uncertain outcome and the pursuit of debatable goods. The difficulty of making these decisions, and the costs involved, are reasons for not resorting to war, revolution, or insurgency in the first place. But assuming that wars and other resorts to political violence can sometimes be justified and that politicians and peoples will continue to make that judgement, no matter how mistakenly, we need to allow for the feasible prosecution of a just war, or one believed to be just, while giving moral priority to protecting the lives of noncombatants. Disallowing intentional targeting of them is an important step forward. Producing a frame of mind that will limit collateral damage is a good next step.

Innocent Shields and Other Complications

The issue of the innocent shield is an old one in war fighting and indeed in other contexts, and it raises another set of acute and complex questions about incidental and direct killing of noncombatants. Just as criminals use innocent people as hostages or shields in attempting to escape capture, so soldiers have always been tempted to resort to the same device. In Ken Loach's film about the Spanish Civil War, *Land and Freedom*, a group of POUM militia attack a village held by Fascist Falange troops. Some of the Fascist troops fight the attackers from the security of the local church, and, at one point, two of them issue forth shooting and protecting themselves by using two of the village women as shields. The POUM militia are reluctant to shoot back and suffer losses. One of these losses is a man who has run out of ammunition and begs his comrade for more bullets but is refused because the comrade is afraid the man will kill the women in order to shoot the soldiers. Instead, the man is shot by one of the Fascist soldiers while shouting at his comrade to hand over the bullets. Eventually the Fascist soldiers are killed, as is one of the women. Interestingly, Loach's dramatic scene echoes one in Conrad's novel *Lord Jim*, which may indicate just how ubiquitous the innocent shield device is.

It is clear that those who use the innocent shield are doing wrong, though in desperate situations of self-defence their behaviour is at least understandable. (Hobbes would presumably have regarded it as justified *in extremis* as an act of self-preservation, but this seems to be a point at which his exaltation of the primacy of self-preservation loses its moral, as opposed to psychological, plausibility.) What is philosophically interesting about the case, and about others we will consider, is that those who use innocent shields are *relying* upon the moral prohibition against killing the innocent. The innocent shield problem represents an inescapable aspect of moral prohibitions: namely, the way in which the unscrupulous can exploit the adherence of the scrupulous to moral standards. This aspect is particularly alarming in war, where the stakes are so high, but it is present in other moral contexts.

In Hitchcock's thriller *I Confess*, Montgomery Clift's priest is bound by the confidentiality of the confessional when he hears the confession of someone who has killed a man who is blackmailing the priest. The killer then uses the priest's principled silence to throw suspicion upon him for the killing.

The general point is that adherence to morality can be exploited by those who don't adhere to it in order to damage the adherent. So the Fascist soldiers think they have a chance of escape just because their enemies are morally constrained not to kill the innocent shields. Of course, the POUM troops might well be constrained by self-interested considerations alone or as well. They might, for instance, be anxious to gain or keep the political support of the villagers. But moral beliefs, if deeply held, are less likely to shift and so provide more secure ground for malevolent manipulation. If resistance to killing the innocent were based purely on self-interest, then the innocent shield tactic would be less likely to work, since it directly threatens major interests of those against whom the shield is used.

The fact that the innocent shield problem exhibits a general feature of morality – its exploitability by the unscrupulous – shows that its possibility is inherent in morality rather than being wholly externally generated. This contrasts with the possibility that morality might not guarantee you happiness, since (on ordinary construals of happiness) much of the prospect for happiness depends on luck. Perhaps the connection of morality with happiness is not as distant as that envisaged by the American humorist Garrison Keillor, who has one of his staunch Protestant characters rebuke another with, "We weren't put on earth to be happy, we are here to do the right thing." But even Aristotle, who links virtue with a certain sort of happiness, insisted that it was absurd to claim that the good man must be happy even on the rack.[25]

Yet doesn't the fact that morality necessarily puts you in a position to be exploited by the unscrupulous challenge the very idea of morality? This might be said by someone who believed that the moral life must leave one invulnerable to the malice of others, but there is surely no reason to think this. Alternatively, the thought might be that the practice of morality itself should never be exploitable by the malicious, but again it is not obvious why this should be so. Perhaps Hobbes gets us closest to the idea that such exploitation is somehow logically or conceptually paradoxical. He does this by making the very rationale of morality turn upon the rationality of self-preservation, so that you can never be morally required to suffer being

---

[25] "For possession of virtue seems actually compatible with being asleep, or with lifelong inactivity, and, further, with the greatest sufferings and misfortunes; but a man who was living so no one would call happy, unless he were maintaining a thesis at all costs." Aristotle, *The Nicomachean Ethics*, trans. David Ross (Oxford: Oxford University Press, 1998), Book 1, Chapter 5, p. 7.

placed in a position of grave vulnerability. But surely loyalty, compassion, and fidelity remain strong moral motivations involving requirements and obligations even when self-preservation is at serious risk.

There remains the question whether one is ever justified in killing an innocent shield. The shield is like the coerced ancillary, discussed in Chapter 6, in being involved unwillingly in the aggressor's acts, but usually dissimilar in lacking any form of agency no matter how tenuous. What agency the shield might have would be geared to frustrating, rather than advancing, the cause of the aggressor. There is no parallel to this in the case of coerced fighters or ancillaries, except for those rare cases where they try to sabotage the war effort in which they are engaged. So the innocent shield is even more problematic a target. Clearly, one's hope is to kill or disable the aggressor without harming the innocent shield, and every effort should be bent in that direction. But what if this is impossible?

One consideration that is important is the probable eventual fate of the shield at the enemy's hand. Sometimes we will have no way of knowing this, but occasionally we will have good reason to believe that the shield is doomed whatever we do. Had it been possible to know of the plans of the September 11 hijackers and to intercept their flights on the way to their lethal destinations, then the decision to destroy the hijacked planes in the air would have been a decision to kill the innocent passengers along with the terrorists. A burdensome decision, but it is made more acceptable by the fact that the passengers are doomed anyway. One might try recourse to the DDE here, but it seems to me implausible to maintain that we intend to kill only the hijackers; it is more pertinent that the passengers are already doomed and that, moreover, they can be presumed to prefer these slightly earlier deaths, since the events that kill them will thwart the evil that their later deaths would have been part of.

Absent such knowledge (or reasonable belief) about the fate of the shield, it seems wrong to kill the shield to get at the enemy. This judgement may be readily defensible in many cases, but what if you can be certain that the enemy thus shielded will kill a number of innocent people? Perhaps you know that the enemy is grabbing the shield precisely so that he can attack other innocent people. Obviously, you should do everything possible to kill or disable the enemy without harming the shield, and you are entitled to risk injury to the shield when aiming at some exposed part of the enemy, but there may be little time or scope for such options. This is an agonising situation, and it raises several important, though rather opaque, moral considerations that seem to blunt the force of the prohibition on killing the innocent. One is that you may know that the shield would prefer to be killed rather than be used as an instrument of destruction against the innocent. Indeed, the shield may call upon you to shoot regardless of his or her fate. Another is that there is an argument to say that the responsibility for the shield's predicament is the enemy's and that if you kill the shield to prevent the enemy's evil purposes, the shield's innocent blood should be laid at the enemy's door. As for the first point, the consent of the shield seems to me to make a significant difference, since it brings the case closer to such categories as assisted suicide, or, more accurately in this case, assisted self-sacrifice. The shield would sacrifice his or her life to frustrate the enemy's purposes if that were possible, but outside assistance is required. Some (those who are totally opposed to euthanasia in any form, for instance) would say that consent can never make a difference to the permissibility of killing the innocent; others might allow that individuals themselves can make the sacrifice but that no one can presume to assist. Intuitions are likely to vary on this, but my own view is that such consent makes an important difference. As for the second point about responsibility, this is more difficult. We do not want to open the gates to absolving agents of responsibility for morally dubious actions simply on the grounds that others have created the situation in which the action seems necessary. Japanese warmongers were responsible for the Asia/Pacific part of World War II, but this doesn't mean that it would be right to shift the responsibility for the bombing of Hiroshima and Nagasaki solely onto them. Nonetheless, the innocent shield cases do seem to belong to a category in which responsibility for the outcome must lie heavily with those who force a choice between bad outcomes onto others. A classic case is the awful predicament of Sophie in William Stryon's novel *Sophie's Choice*, where a Nazi officer at a death camp forces a mother (Sophie) to choose which of her two children will be sent to extermination and which will live. If she doesn't choose, both will die. Such a choice will, as in the novel and the film based on it, haunt the agent for life, but it is fair to say that the Nazi officer is wholly to blame whatever the outcome of the situation. If Sophie chooses one rather than the other, she is not responsible for that child's death, and if she refuses to choose, she is not responsible for the double death. The Nazi's attempt to involve her in the responsibility for his hideous decision is a vicious sham. Perhaps the user of the shield who violently puts the shield in the way of lethal attack should be treated in the same way.

Finally, one of the most important issues with respect to the damage that war does to noncombatants is that of mines and antipersonnel weapons generally. This category includes all but the most precise of bombs. In very recent times, attention has turned to land mines and the devastating and irresponsible damage that they do, and continue to do long after hostilities are finished, to noncombatants as well as to former combatants. A related issue is that of the airborne mines, that is, the bomblets spread by the ubiquitous "cluster bomb," often called the workhorse of antipersonnel weapons. In a letter to the *New York Times* of January 21, 1994, Suzy Kane, who says she is writing a thesis on the Gulf War, writes that the U.S. army munitions command supplied her with the information that the United States alone during the hostilities had "dropped 28,595,724 of these bomblets – 1.5 bomblets for every man, woman and child in Iraq." A great number of these lie menacingly unexploded (as she says). Such a use of cluster bomb technology exhibits a contemptuous attitude toward civilian immunity and the values that underpin it. Practices such as this make a mockery of any defensible idea of collateral immunity. Attempts to justify this sort of practice smack of intellect in the service of evil.

8

The Morality of Terrorism

Throwing a bomb is bad,
Dropping a bomb is good;
Terror, no need to add,
Depends on who's wearing the hood.
          Roger Woddis[1]

Terrorism intrigues and disturbs policy makers, the media, and the public even more in the infancy of the new millennium than it did in the last quarter of the twentieth century. And although this fact no doubt delights terrorists themselves, and consoles them for the apparent ineffectiveness of much terrorist activity in achieving ultimate political goals, it is nonetheless surprising that the phenomenon has commanded such attention. Prior to September 11, 2001, the death and damage done by what are commonly called terrorist attacks in any single year had been mostly insignificant compared to the annual road toll in the United States, or to the "collateral" death and damage caused by the NATO bombing of Serbia in just one month of 1999. Even the September 11 attacks were small-scale compared to the destruction wrought by other dramatic attacks, such the bombing of Dresden and the atomic destruction of Hiroshima and Nagasaki in World War II. These might well qualify themselves as terrorist acts, and indeed I shall argue that they should, but most of the contemporary anxiety about terrorism is focused on the activities of substate agents whose successes have been nowhere as spectacular. The explanation of what can seem a disproportionate concern with substate terrorism is sometimes said to lie in the random and unexpected nature of the attacks, but this cannot be the whole story, since most road deaths are, if anything, even more random and unexpected, though of course they are not usually "attacks."

---

[1] Roger Woddis, "Ethics for Everyman," in Kingsley Amis (ed.), *The New Oxford Book of Light Verse* (Oxford: Oxford University Press, 1978), p. 292.

Part of the explanation has, I suspect, religious roots, especially in the United States, where the anxiety about terrorism probably runs strongest (and did so even before September 11) and where religion and its sinister (often unwanted) bedfellows of superstition and religiosity are more influential than anywhere else in the industrialised world. In the United States, the level of religious profession and observance is high, religious cults and sects are thick upon the ground, and an amazing number of people think that they have been abducted or contacted by alien beings from outer space. Against this background, the terrorist stands out as a satanic figure or at least a representative of an evil religion, the religion of terrorism. As such, the relatively insignificant impact of substate terrorist activities tends to fade into the background while the demonic creed and its hidden powers occupy our attention in the foreground. Naturally, this picture is given added colour and emphasis when the terrorists can be linked, as they sometimes can – for example, in Northern Ireland and the Middle East – to an explicitly religious cause.

I want to argue that we get off on the wrong foot by treating terrorism in anything like this fashion. The religious element reinforces a strong tendency commonly present in the scholarly and subscholarly literature on terrorism to treat it as something like an ideology or a comprehensive, belief-driven outlook. There is an equally strong tendency to treat it as always immoral. These tendencies were clearly evident in the aftermath of September 11, where the good-versus-evil divide was massively invoked in the rhetoric of "the war on terror," and Biblical and Koranic analogies were freely deployed in different quarters. Such tendencies go hand in hand with a considerable degree of muddle about the meaning of the term "terrorism." Indeed, it has been estimated that there are well over a hundred different definitions of terrorism, many of them contradictory, in the scholarly literature.[2] This disarray reflects the highly polemical contexts in which the term is used, so that the act of defining can become a move in a campaign rather than an aid to thought. I shall try to dispel this unclarity, and, against the first tendency, I shall argue for a more definite and, I think, more persuasive analysis of terrorism that will show the way in which the second tendency raises issues of inconsistency, and even hypocrisy.

The tendency to think of terrorism as an ideology is no doubt encouraged by superficial verbal resemblances – so many expressions ending in "-ism" are words for ideologies, religions, or systems of belief – but reflection indicates that the "-ism" here may refer to no more than the relatively systematic nature of a method or a tactic. This, in any case, seems to me the healthiest and most realistic way to conceptualise terrorism. If we do this, we can dispel

---

[2] Alex Peter Schmid, *Political Terrorism: A Research Guide to Concepts, Theories, Data Bases and Literature* (Amsterdam: Transaction Books, 1983), pp. 119–58, as cited in Walter Laqueur, *The Age of Terrorism* (Boston: Little, Brown, 1987).

the illusion that the terrorist is a special sort of representative of an alien religion or ideology, and instead see him or her as a representative of this or that political, or politico-religious, grievance or program, with a range of tactics at his or her disposal, just like the rest of us, and, just like the rest of us, resorting from time to time to morally dubious or outrageous tactics. This gestalt shift would also have the advantage of sidelining the dubious academic industry of psychological investigation of the terrorist personality, the fruits of which have been pretty unappetizing. But these are promissory notes. Let us start, unlike so much of the literature on terrorism, with some statements from terrorists themselves, or at any rate from those who would commonly be regarded as terrorists.

In Their Own Words

(1) Carlos Marighela, the Brazilian revolutionary who had such a strong influence on the development of urban guerrilla warfare in South America, devotes only two paragraphs to what he calls "terrorism" in his *Handbook of Urban Guerrilla Warfare* published in 1969, the year of his death. His definition is rather restrictive. "By terrorism," he writes, "I mean the use of bomb attacks."[3] Although distinctly narrow, the definition picks out a central terrorist technique and makes it clear that it is a means to political objectives. Elsewhere, when discussing other techniques such as kidnapping and execution of informers (which would probably be called "terrorist" by others, certainly by the media), Marighela makes it clear that such acts are meant to serve the wider political objectives of the revolution. It is a weakness of his and other such writings that they do little to show that the various paramilitary techniques will actually promote these wider objectives, but that is another matter; it is clear that Marighela believes that they will. Talking of executions, for instance, he says: "We should use the death penalty for such people as American spies, agents of the dictatorship, torturers, fascists in the government who have committed crimes against patriots or tried to capture them, police informers."[4] It is apparent from this quotation that the killing of these categories of person is viewed by Marighela as a kind of judicial punishment to be justified in whatever way such punishments are justified, especially in times of war.

(2) Another important theorist and spokesman for South American revolutionary movements, Régis Debray, wrote of what he called "city terrorism" in his book *Revolution in the Revolution?* as follows:

---

[3] Carlos Marighela, *Handbook of Urban Guerrilla Warfare*, collected in Carlos Marighela, *For the Liberation of Brazil*, trans. John Butt and Rosemary Sheed (Harmondsworth: Penguin, 1971), p. 89.

[4] Ibid., p. 87.

Of course city terrorism cannot assume any decisive role and it entails certain dangers of a political order. But if it is subordinate to the fundamental struggle, the struggle in the countryside, it has, from the military point of view, a strategic value; it immobilizes thousands of enemy soldiers, it ties up most of the repressive mechanism in unrewarding tasks of protection. . . . the government must, since it is the government, protect everywhere the interests of property owners; the *guerrilleros* don't have to protect anything anywhere.[5]

We can see from these extracts that far from being an ideology, or a long-range goal of action, terrorism, or what many people would regard as terrorism, is treated as a technique in the service of such a goal. This is hardly surprising, for terror is a form of violence, and violence is primarily a means. It must of course be conceded that just as there are those who treat the violence of warfare generally as *almost* an end in itself, so there are those who do the same with terrorism. Our earlier discussion of romantic militarism in Chapter 3 indicates as much. Some of the responses in Great Britain to the outbreak of World War I present this welcoming face to violence. Consider, for instance, the English poet Julian Grenfell, whose much-anthologized poem "Into Battle" expressed so well the intoxication with war that so many of his generation seem to have had. Grenfell, a sensitive and intelligent man, wrote to his mother from the front saying, "I *adore* war. It is like a big picnic without the objectlessness of a picnic. I've never been so well or so happy."[6] Grenfell was awarded the DSO for crawling into no-man's-land and almost into enemy trenches in order to snipe at Germans. It was his own idea, and he killed three Germans. Afterwards, he made two entries in his game book; they come after an entry for October 1914 of "105 partridges" and read: "November 16th: 1 Pomeranian; – November 17th: 2 Pomeranians."[7] Similarly, with some terrorist operations it may be that the terror itself has assumed something like the status of an end, so that terrorism has become a sort of ideology, the wreaking of havoc itself a value that needs little or no justifying purpose beyond it.

I shall acknowledge, then, that there are warriors who treat war as self-justifying and terrorists who treat terror as self-justifying, but I shall ignore them as aberrational. It may be possible to argue that those who begin by treating war or terror as means inevitably finish up treating them as ends; this is an important line of moral criticism, but it contains the implicit concession that the activities can seem justifiable as means, and since this is how they are usually defended, this is how they should, in the first instance, be examined.

---

[5] Régis Debray, *Revolution in the Revolution?*, trans. Bobbye Ortiz (London: Monthly Review Press, 1967), p. 75.

[6] Quoted in Nicholas Mosley, *Julian Grenfel: His Life and the Times of His Death* (London: Weidenfeld and Nicolson, 1976), p. 239.

[7] Ibid., p. 243.

This usefully helps locate our concern for terrorism within the framework of just war theory outlined earlier.

The Tactical Definition

Our definitional search has initially located terrorism as a method, but what method? It is clear from the earlier references to Marighela's views that the term "terrorism" (or just "terror") can be used more or less narrowly, and it is unlikely that the term in ordinary political parlance has any particularly definite sense, since it has arisen and continues to be employed in contexts of a highly emotional, partisan, even hysterical nature. The semantic confusion generated by such contexts seems about equally distributed between supporters and opponents of terrorism, but it is possible to discern in the welter of accusation, complaint, and exposition an outline on which the different concerns and anxieties converge. I shall attempt to bring this outline into focus by defining the concept in terms which capture much of what seems to exercise people in their worries about terrorism and which allow me to continue my exploration of analogies between warfare and other forms of political violence. I think that this approach also does justice to the historical evolution of the term as it has been well summarized, for instance, by Laqueur and Lineberry.[8] The definition used by Jan Schreiber in his book *The Ultimate Weapon: Terrorists and World Order* will be my starting point.

Schreiber defines terrorism as "a political act, ordinarily committed by an organized group, involving death or the threat of death to noncombatants."[9] Although on the right path, this needs amending in certain obvious directions: as it stands, it is misleadingly unspecific about the kind of causal nexus indicated by the word "involving." It should at least be made clear that the political act *intentionally* produces death or the threat of death to noncombatants, otherwise loud applause at a political rally which distracted a passing (civilian) motorist, causing him to crash into a pole and die, would count as an act of terrorism. As indicated in Chapters 6 and 7, I use the term "intentional" in such a way that it is possible for there to be foreseen consequences of one's acts that are not intentional. The designer of a freeway, for instance, may have good statistical reason to expect that some people will be killed in consequence of its being built, but he does not intentionally bring about their deaths. I take it to be in the spirit of Schreiber's discussion to treat the "involving" as of the (directly) intentional kind.

The other modification to Schreiber's definition is to widen it a little, since a terrorist act can be aimed at severe injuries other than death. Torture

---

[8] Walter Laqueur, *Terrorism* (London: Weidenfeld and Nicolson, 1977); R. C. Lineberry, *The Struggle against Terrorism* (New York: Wilson, 1977).

[9] Jan Schreiber, *The Ultimate Weapon: Terrorists and World Order* (New York: Morrow, 1978), p. 20.

or the threat of torture would surely do the trick, and so would lesser but still severe injury. By the same token, certain types of severe attacks upon property would probably count, for most people, as terrorist – for example, the destruction of homes or of civil airplanes – even without any danger to human life. As amended, then, the definition of a terrorist act would go as follows: "A political act, ordinarily committed by an organized group, which involves the intentional killing or other severe harming of noncombatants or the threat of the same or intentional severe damage to the property of noncombatants or the threat of the same."[10] The term "terrorism" can then be defined as "the tactic or policy of engaging in terrorist acts." I shall call this the "tactical" definition.

As so defined, terrorism stands condemned under the moral principle of discrimination enunciated as part of the JIB. Note that my definition does not smuggle such condemnation into the terms of the definition. If one rejects the principle of discrimination, then there is room for accepting terrorism. It all depends on your attitude toward just war theory. We have already examined some of the problems with this principle in Chapter 6 and shall explore more of those that are specific to revolutionary violence later in this chapter.

One critic who takes a dim view of just war theory generally, and who particularly objects to its employment in connection with terrorism, is Robert Goodin. Goodin has recently attacked tactical definitions, and one of his complaints is that on such definitions terrorists "have done nothing worse than ordinary murder" and that terrorism "seems worse than that, somehow."[11] But on my account, terrorism is not "ordinary" murder, since it is a form of murder committed for political purposes by (normally) an organised group. Goodin thinks that the tactical definition makes the terrorist no different from "a common or garden lunatic gone on a (highly successful) killing spree," but terrorism as defined here clearly has ramifications that naturally give rise to a very different sort of concern for terrorist murders.[12] Goodin's appeal to our intuitions here sits uneasily with his highly counter-intuitive definition of terrorism as "acting with the intention of frightening

[10] The definition treats threats as essentially intentional so that the specification "intentional threat" would be pleonastic. If the reader believes that there can be unintentional threats, then he or she should read the relevant part of the definition as referring to intentional threats. There is an argument that threats should not be included in the definition, since it is better to focus on the actual delivery of violence rather than the offer of it, and the threat to do X is generally not a case of doing X, except in special cases like the threat to threaten. I was tempted by this argument in another place. See C. A. J. Coady, "Defining Terrorism," in Igor Primoratz (ed.), *Terrorism: The Philosophical Issues* (Hampshire and New York: Palgrave, 2004), pp. 3–14. But, on balance, I think the inclusion of threats of violence to noncombatants in the definition better squares with common intuitions.

[11] Robert Goodin, *What's Wrong with Terrorism?* (Cambridge, UK, and Malden, MA: Polity Press, 2006), p. 10.

[12] Ibid.

people for political advantage," a definition that has *no* reference to violent means of any sort and makes terrorists of Green politicians who frighten people (rightly) with talk about global warming in order to get elected and try to prevent ecological disaster![13]

Other critics have objected to the inclusion of property damage in the definition. It seems to me clear that destruction of noncombatant property strikes most people as terrorist and also falls under the principle of discrimination, since noncombatant homes and belongings are not legitimate targets.[14] Nonetheless, the sort of condemnation appropriate to killing usually differs strikingly from that appropriate to property damage. So there will be some terrorist offences that are not as grave as others. Indeed, minor property offences may even be justifiable in certain circumstances, attacks upon noncombatants lives are not. This relates to the issues concerning stringency explored in Chapter 14.

A further point about the terms of the definition concerns the reading that should be given to the intention specified in it. Terrorists must intend to harm noncombatants, but of course some terrorists do not believe that their targets are genuinely noncombatants or innocents. Does this belief matter for the characterisation of their acts as terrorist? In philosophical jargon, this is the question whether in such sentences as "The IRA intended to kill those innocent people" the context governed by the verb "intended" is to be read as opaque or transparent. More colloquially, does terrorist status turn on the objective facts about the nature of the target or on the attacker's subjective belief? Where an attacker mistakenly believes his targets to be somehow combatants, does this mean he or she is not a terrorist? (This is not the same as asking whether the attack is justified or excusable, though there are connections between the two questions.) Here, as elsewhere in discussions of intention, the nature of the mistake is important. In short, I would hold that if the mistake is factual then the attack is not terrorism, but if it is conceptual then the attack is. If a soldier shoots an innocent civilian who has been forcibly dressed in an enemy uniform and shoved into the line of fire as a decoy, the soldier's action should not be called terrorist; but someone who shoots babies because he regards all the enemy as collectively guilty is palpably a terrorist. In the former case, the agent's action involves an ordinary (if tragic) factual mistake; in the latter case, the agent (if sincere) is conceptually confused, and the confusion should not be allowed to infect our characterization of the type of action. There will of course be grey areas in the application of the factual/conceptual distinction, but it provides sufficient guidance for clarifying the tactical definition on this point.

---

[13] Ibid., p. 156. Goodin's other complaints about just war theory are similar to those discussed elsewhere in this book.

[14] One critic who complains about the property inclusion is Jenny Teichman. See *Pacifism and the Just War: A Study in Applied Philosophy* (Oxford: Basil Blackwell, 1986), pp. 91–92.

Another issue connected with intention has to do with whether attacks that are not intended to kill or injure noncombatants or their property but are negligent, reckless, or insufficiently concerned about damage to noncombatants should be classified as terrorist. This issue is linked to the discussion of collateral damage in Chapter 7, and my view (as elaborated there) is that such attacks deserve moral condemnation, but I think that the tactical definition rightly rules them out as terrorist. My reasons are similar to those used in Chapter 2 to oppose attempts to widen the definition of violence. Though the motives for such definitional expansion are understandable, the outcome is likely to be both confusing and practically counterproductive. What is true is that attacks that cause unacceptable collateral damage share something of the spirit of terrorist attacks, but their form and effects are very different. To capture what is similar, we might refer to them as neo-terrorist.

With these initial clarifications noted, we must turn to certain other consequences of the tactical definition.

Effects, State Terrorism, and Other Definitional Matters

My definition makes no explicit reference to some features of terrorist activity that commentators have regarded as important – for instance, the sort of wider effects it typically aims to produce, such as publicizing a forgotten cause, provoking an overreaction from the enemy, intimidating some group that may or may not be the group under direct attack, and so on. These features are important, but I do not propose to treat such specific political objectives as part of the definition. The more general reference to a "political act" is here advantageously vague because it does not restrict the political uses to which the terrorist tactic may be turned, and it rightly allows for empirical investigation to determine what various groups use terrorism for. We can illustrate this by taking the motivation of publicity, which has seemed sufficiently compelling to many commentators to build it into the understanding of terrorism as a necessary component. Such commentators are impressed by terrorism as communication, theatre, or symbolic act. But recent developments in the phenomenology of terrorism have made it plausible that the publicising of a forgotten or neglected cause is not as central to the analysis of terrorism as it once seemed.

The emergence of what was often called "silent terrorism" in the 1990s presented the curious phenomenon of terrorists who would not claim responsibility for their deeds. When terrorists make no effort to claim their deeds, it is hard to see publicity for their cause as part of the motivation for their acts. That being the case, we are wise to make it no part of the definition. Of course, it remains puzzling that silent terrorists avoid this sort of publicity, simply because of the opacity of motivation this seems to engender. But this very fact provides a challenge for investigation, a challenge that would have been precluded by a definition incorporating the publicity motivation. I will not conduct such an investigation here (especially since silent terrorism has not been so prominent in the new millennium) beyond suggesting that the failure to claim personal or group responsibility may be aimed at adding to the target's country's nervousness by creating some uncertainty about which of their enemies is responsible, with the additional bonus that retaliatory responses by the target country will be enmeshed in problems created by that uncertainty. Deniability may also help your relations with your host nation when you belong to an organisation that is domiciled in a foreign country. As to publicity, you get publicity for your cause anyway, because your group will probably be one of "the usual suspects." Another possibility is that silent terrorists are interested not in publicity, but in demoralising their opponent and causing the opponent to engage in counterproductive retaliation that tarnishes the opponent's image.

It might, however, be claimed that there is one very general effect of terror tactics that deserves to be written into the definition, namely, the intended effect of fear.[15] The distinctive point of terrorism as a tactic, it will be said, is that it aims to terrorize, to spread fear and so destabilize social relations. This is as true of silent terrorism as of acknowledged terrorism. This fear emphasis contains an important insight into the sociology of terrorism, but I do not think it should be made a matter of definition.[16] My reasons are twofold. In the first place, stress upon this intended effect tends to preclude any serious concern with the more intrinsic issue of the type of method used (as it may be) to generate the fear. This tendency is clearly at work in Martin Hughes's treatment of the topic, and more recently in Robert Goodin's.[17] Second, as already mentioned, we are prejudging an empirical investigation into the specific motives of those who choose to attack noncombatants. Indeed, it is surely plausible that some terrorist attacks are aimed at creating anger rather than fear, since anger may lead to the sort of escalated response that can help to alienate neutral groups caught up in the conflict and drive them into the terrorist camp, as well as to enlist international support in the face of such escalation.

I do not, of course, deny that the tactic of deliberate attacks upon noncombatants is commonly perceived as being aimed at the creation of the sort of fear that produces panic, demoralization, or misjudged retaliation, and, moreover, it can be admitted that the perception is often correct. The

---

[15] Inclusion of the fear effect is only plausible as an intended effect. If we defined terrorism as a tactic which actually had that effect, then terrorist attacks which gave rise, not to the spread of fear and demoralization, but to defiance and a strengthening of resolve would not be terrorist, even if they deliberately killed scores of children!

[16] Here I side with Paskins and Dockrill against Martin Hughes. See Barry Paskins and Michael Dockrill, *The Ethics of War* (London: Duckworth, 1979), p. 90; and Martin Hughes, "Terrorism and National Security," *Philosophy* 57 (January 1982), p. 5. My agreement with Paskins and Dockrill is only partial, however, since they want to restrict the application of "terrorism" to contexts of evasive warfare and not apply it to full-scale interstate wars.

[17] Goodin, *What's Wrong with Terrorism?*.

tactic is, after all, called "terrorism." Yet, for the reasons given, I would prefer to make no reference to such motivation in the definition. The philosophy of language has made us familiar with situations in which the referent or extension of a term may be fixed by a predicate which does not determine the nature of the reality so indicated and which, if true at all of it, is so contingently. It seems to me that something similar holds of the link between terrorism and the motivation of creating fear. Yet there is here some genuine ground for definitional dispute, and I do not want to be dogmatic on a point that inevitably involves a degree of stipulation. Those readers who agree with me that the attack upon noncombatants is the crucial definitional feature but are more impressed by the fear-creation motive than I am could amend the definition to include a subsidiary reference to the common presence of such motivation. The phrase "and commonly involving the intention to create or maintain widespread fear" could then be inserted after the phrase "an organized group." Such a guarded and secondary reference to the fear effect would not materially affect the course of our discussion. I shall further discuss some of the issues raised by the relationship between fear and terrorism at the end of this chapter.

As defined, terrorism is not a tactic restricted to revolutionaries and other nongovernmental groups. Doubtless many people would be surprised at the idea that governments and authorized governmental agencies do or can use terrorist methods for their political purposes, but such surprise is quite often the product of naiveté or prejudice. If we see terrorism as a particular kind of employment of political violence (and this seems a central strand in all the varied and often confused uses of the expression), then we should surely be impressed by analogies and identities among the methods used rather than by dissimilarities among the powers and standings of the agents using them. Otherwise we run the risk of treating the term "terrorism" the way some people treat the term "obstinacy," as a state into which only others can lapse, the parallel state in their own case being described as "strength of purpose." It is worthy of comment in this connection that Winston Churchill himself used language appropriate to the characterisation of terrorist policies when expressing belated doubts about the Allied policy of city bombing late in World War II. Writing to Sir Charles Portal after the British firestorm destruction of Dresden on February 13, 1945, in which estimates of casualties vary from a conservative 35,000 deaths to a radical 200,000, Churchill wrote:

It seems to me that the moment has come when the question of bombing of German cities simply for the sake of increasing the terror, though under other pretexts, should be reviewed. . . . I feel the need for more precise concentration upon military objectives such as oil and communications behind the immediate battle zone, rather than on mere acts of terror and wanton destruction. However impressive.[18]

[18] Quoted in Noble Frankland and Charles Websater, *The Strategic Air Offensive against Germany 1939–1945*, vol. 3 (London: Her Majesty's Stationary Office, 1961), p. 112.

It is interesting that in 1940 Churchill's predecessor, Neville Chamberlain, had denounced such "blackguardly" bombing proposals as "mere terrorism."[19]

Some would defend their restriction of the use of the term "terrorism" to nonstate agents by locating terrorism as a phenomenon, or as an object of concern, in the arena of civic order and presenting terrorism as a threat to the civic order maintained by states.[20] Some of the definitions in the literature point in this direction, and when they do, they tend to invoke the idea of legality or legitimacy and its violation. So the FBI defines terrorism in this spirit when it declares: "Terrorism is the unlawful use of force or violence against persons or property to intimidate or coerce a government, the civilian population, or any segment thereof, in furtherance of political or social objectives."[21] Although not explicit about restricting terrorism to nonstate agents, the implication of the definition is clearly in that direction. More explicit, and even more restrictive, is Walter Laqueur's statement: "Terrorism is an attempt to destabilize democratic societies and to show that their governments are impotent."[22] Laqueur does not intend this as a definition, since he thinks a definition is impossible, and certainly unnecessary, but he later endorses the restriction his statement announces by denying that any form of oppression by the state can count as political terrorism.[23] What we have at work here, and in other places that could be cited, is what could be called a political status definition rather than a tactical definition. It should be clear that I find this conceptual locution less satisfactory than the one I have provided. It has a strong tendency to collapse the possibility of a distinction between legitimate and illegitimate violent threats to civic order, between just and unjust revolutionary violence.[24] It does this because no state will countenance the idea that there could be legitimate acts of violence against its legally established order. It also renders illegitimate certain obvious complaints that revolutionaries (or, for that matter, innocent third parties themselves) can make in the vocabulary of terrorism against certain violent activities of state authorities. It is natural to speak of state terrorism when the state attempts to stamp out revolutionary activity by threatening, harming, or killing those peasants, intellectuals, workers, or villagers who are not themselves engaged in violence. They may be perceived as sympathetic to those who are, or as simply insufficiently sympathetic to the government.

---

[19] See J. F. C. Fuller, *The Conduct of War, 1789–1961* (London: Eyre Methuen, 1972), p. 280.

[20] See Laqueur, *The Age of Terrorism*.

[21] Quoted by the Terrorism Research Center Inc., viewed June 17, 2002, at <http://www.terrorism.com/terrorism/def.shtml>.

[22] Walter Laqueur, "Reflections on Terrorism," *Foreign Affairs* 65, no. 1 (1986), p. 87.

[23] Ibid., p. 89.

[24] Some proponents of political status definitions, or outlooks, would allow for just revolutions against oppressive nondemocratic regimes, but never against democracies. This seems to be Laqueur's position, and Paul Wilkinson's in his *Political Terrorism* (London: Macmillan; New York: Halsted Press, 1974).

There is, of course, no need to deny that the use of terror by nonstate groups rather than by the state raises special theoretical issues, and I shall have something to say about this later.

Following Schreiber, I have used the term "noncombatant" where some may think the term "innocent" more appropriate. Each term has its advantages and disadvantages, as discussed in Chapter 6. I prefer the term "noncombatant" at this point for reasons of convenience in exposition, since the term "innocent" may be even more likely to mislead, but "innocent" will do as well if we keep in mind the distinctions discussed in Chapter 6.

I have made no use of the notion of indiscriminate violence that often figures in definitions or discussions of terrorism. I have avoided this because I think that it is confusing. There is a sense in which I agree with the idea that terrorism involves indiscriminate violence; namely, the sense in which it fails to discriminate between combatant and noncombatant targets. This is all that Paskins and Dockrill, for instance, mean by "indiscriminate."[25] On the other hand, many writers use "indiscriminate" to convey the idea that terrorism is quite irrational in that the terrorist weapon is used in an undiscriminating way, as it were, wildly and pointlessly. This need not be true at all of attacks upon noncombatants or their property, and there is sometimes a good deal of thought and selection going into the terrorist technique employed.

Talk of "indiscriminate violence" does, however, raise another issue. Some readers who agree with me on the importance of the combatant/noncombatant distinction and its relevance to the definition of terrorism may nonetheless prefer to define terrorism more widely as any violation of the *jus in bello*.[26] In other words, any use of political violence that stands under moral condemnation because of the type of violence used rather than its relation to the political goals of the users would then count as terrorist. I suspect that there is some linguistic warrant for this wider usage, but on the whole, I think we do more justice to the concerns usually articulated by the term "terrorist" if we operate with the narrower definition I have proposed. If a revolutionary group adopted the immoral but not uncommon military policy of taking no prisoners ("yielding no quarter") or even of killing their prisoners after interrogation, then although the behaviour deserves moral condemnation, it does seem to require somewhat different treatment than a direct attack upon the uninvolved. This is so even if the condemnation in both cases goes beyond utilitarian considerations. In any case, employing the wider concept of terrorism will not greatly affect the broad purposes of my discussion.

A final definitional clarification concerns the phrase "for political purposes." To this it has been objected that some terrorism is conducted for religious or ideological rather than political purposes. Here I should say that

---

[25] Paskins and Dockrill, *The Ethics of War*, p. 89.
[26] I am indebted to Michael Stocker for drawing my attention to this possibility.

the reference to the political is aimed at demarcating the scope of terrorism so that it does not encompass areas such as ordinary criminal violence, no matter how reprehensible and no matter how damaging to innocent people. Such a distinction seems plausible as an extrapolation from ordinary talk about terrorism. But my reference to political motivations is not meant to be so narrow as to include only secular or pragmatic outlooks. When religion or ideology employs violent means to undermine, reconstitute, or maintain political structures for the further transcendent ends of the religion or ideology, then that counts as "political purposes." War is a paradigm political activity, despite its ugliness, and it would be strange to say that the medieval crusaders, for example, were not involved in politics when they invaded the Holy Lands. Modern counterparts of the crusaders and their enemies struggle for political supremacy even when their motives involve religious or idealistic commitments to theocracy or Islamic fundamentalism, on the one hand, and democracy, free markets, or Christian fundamentalism on the other. It should be added that the borders of the merely criminal and the fully political constitute a broad and fuzzy area. Criminal activities can become involved with the political, even in the matter of violence, as happened with the criminal drug lords in Colombia some years ago; and groups whose rationale is basically political may indulge in ordinary criminal activities, such as bank robbery, to finance their operations. Still, the broad distinction is clear enough.

Terrorism, Revolutionary Violence, and Consistency

Many condemnations of terrorism are subject to the charge of inconsistency, if not hypocrisy, because they insist on applying one kind of morality to the state's use of violence in war (international or civil or anti-insurgency) and another kind altogether to the use of violence by the nonstate agent (e.g., the revolutionary or insurgent). For one's own state, a utilitarian or consequentialist standard is adopted which morally legitimates the intentional killing of noncombatants, so that such acts of state terrorism as the bombing of Dresden are deemed to be morally sanctioned by the good ends they supposedly serve. The same people, however, make the move to higher ground when considering the activities of rebels or revolutionaries and judge their killing of noncombatants by the intrinsic standard. In the case of the revolutionary or insurgent, the thought is that even if the cause is just and the revolution legitimate, the methods are morally wrong because of what they are or involve. In the case of the state and its instrumentalities, this thought is quietly abandoned and replaced by those utilitarian considerations which are denied to the revolutionaries.

Consistency may be achieved in one of two ways: by adopting either the outcome response to both kinds of case or the intrinsic response to both kinds of case. I would myself urge the second type of consistency and object to the technique of terrorism as immoral wherever and whenever it is used or proposed.[27] But this presupposes that we can in both contexts make a distinction between combatants and noncombatants. I have defended this supposition at some length in Chapter 6 and will not repeat the argument here. I want instead to examine the specific difficulties that arise for the distinction in the context of revolutionary violence. It is worth noting again, however, an ironic consequence of the attempt by supporters of state violence to undermine the combatant/noncombatant distinction. This is that some supporters of revolutionary violence have learned from them and argue, equally speciously, that in revolutionary struggle it is impossible to distinguish between combatants and noncombatants amongst the "enemy."[28] (Recall the comments of Osama bin Laden cited in Chapter 6.) Those who say that the distinction is useless in war should be more sympathetic to at least the form of the revolutionaries' theoretical position than they are. Nonetheless, there are interesting and rather tricky questions raised by transferring the notions of combatant and noncombatant from the context of formal international war to that of conflict within the state. Before looking more fully at this, however, there is one further point that should be briefly discussed.

It may be urged against much of what I have said that it assumes – especially in its parallels between war and revolution – that a revolution can be morally justified. It is this assumption that is highly debatable, for it may be said that citizens can never be morally justified in bringing violence to bear against their rulers. In reply, I would urge that *if* it is possible for some wars to be morally justified, then it is hard to resist the extension of the justificatory patterns to the case of revolution. Certainly, some regimes seem to have committed such wrongs against their own populations or against subgroups within those populations as to create at least a prima facie case for violent redress. Nazi Germany and Uganda, under Amin, seem to present such cases; moreover, armed underground resistance to Nazi occupation forces in countries like France, whose leaders signed a formal surrender treaty, seem to bring us close to the revolutionary pattern, and this was

---

[27] As noted in Chapter 6, it seems possible to espouse a less absolute form of intrinsicalism in which some actions can be seen as wrong from an intrinsicalist perspective but, regrettably, have to be done, at least in part because of the awful consequences of not doing them. Many contemporary philosophers, including Michael Walzer, are attracted to such a view. This issue is discussed in Chapter 14.

[28] The tenor of Frantz Fanon's *The Wretched of the Earth* seems to commit him to this position, and Sartre's Preface to the volume is more explicit still, though written in a highly rhetorical way. Speaking of French "believers in nonviolence" who are not themselves direct combatants, Sartre says: "But if the whole regime, even your non-violent ideas, are conditioned by a thousand-year-old oppression, your passivity serves only to place you in the ranks of the oppressors." *The Wretched of the Earth*, trans. Constance Farrington (New York: Grove Press, 1963), Preface, p. 25.

generally approved of by many people who are opposed to revolutionary violence in other contexts. It may be said that a moral case for revolution against a dictatorship can exist, but never against a democracy. As a convinced democrat, I am sensitive to the force of this rejoinder but find its force blunted by two considerations. The first is that many basically nondemocratic political societies have democratic trappings. South Africa in the apartheid era, for instance, was frequently classed as a democracy because it had democratic forms for a portion of its population, but the restricted franchise surely disqualified it from the protection of any argument against revolution based upon politically relevant properties of democracies. The second is that, ever since Tocqueville, political theorists have been aware of the problems posed by majority tyranny over minorities and by the deep and serious injustices that democratic legal machinery can countenance – the historic background to the struggle in Northern Ireland is not irrelevant here. In any event, a good deal of revolutionary activity has taken place in countries, like several of those in South America in the not-so-distant past, that made small pretence of being democratic, or whose democratic practices tolerated extensive human rights abuses.

The general theory of the just revolution needs more development, but first I want to press the issue of how such revolutions should be conducted and, in particular, who the combatants and noncombatants are. Let me begin with the point that revolutionaries themselves do not always have trouble distinguishing broadly between combatants and noncombatants, though, of course, there are grey areas. To take an example used by Michael Walzer: Albert Camus' play *The Just Assassins* is based upon an actual episode in Russia early this century, in which a group of revolutionaries decided to assassinate a tsarist official, the Grand Duke Sergei, a man personally involved in the suppression of radical activity. The man chosen to do the killing hid a bomb under his coat and approached the victim's carriage, but when he got close he realized that the grand duke had two small children on his lap, so he abandoned the attempt. Camus has one of the man's comrades say, in accepting the decision, "Even in destruction, there's a right way and a wrong way – and there are limits."[29]

Similarly, if one reads Guevara's *Bolivian Diary*, one is struck by the care with which targets are discriminated, even to the point where captured government soldiers and agents are given a political lecture and then released (the guerrillas not having the facilities to imprison captives).[30] Again, in Régis Debray's *Revolution in the Revolution?* the only reference to terrorism is incidental and mostly critical; insofar as it is approved of, it is doubtful

---

[29] Walzer, *Just and Unjust Wars: A Moral Argument with Historical Illustrations*, third edition (New York: Basic Books, 2000), p. 199.
[30] Che Guevara, *Bolivian Diary*, trans. Carlos P. Hansen and Andrew Sinclair (London: Jonathan Cape/Lorrimer, 1968). For a few such incidents, see pp. 67, 77, and 92.

whether all that Debray calls terrorism would qualify on my definition. For instance, he approves of the role of city terrorism in that "it immobilizes thousands of enemy soldiers, it ties up most of the repressive mechanism in unrewarding tasks of protection: factories, bridges, electric generators, public buildings, highways, oil pipe-lines – these can keep busy as much as three-quarters of the army."[31] Certainly, he does not seem to have in mind any sort of killing but rather sabotage of property, which may or may not be noncombatant property and may or may not involve the risk of civilian deaths. The Cypriot revolutionary General George Grivas showed his sensitivity to the distinction in his memoirs when he wrote of the EOKA campaign: "We did not strike, like the bomber, at random. We shot only British servicemen who would have killed us if they could have fired first, and civilians who were traitors or intelligence agents."[32] Whether Grivas accurately described EOKA practice is less important for our discussion than his acknowledgment of the possibility and desirability of directing revolutionary violence at morally legitimate targets. A similar acknowledgement was made more recently in Yasser Arafat's condemnation of terrorism when he said that "no degree of oppression and no level of desperation can ever justify the killing of innocent civilians. I condemn terrorism, I condemn the killing of innocent civilians, whether they are Israeli, American or Palestinian.... "[33] Again, we may question the sincerity of Arafat's condemnation while recognizing the tribute it pays to the moral requirement of distinguishing combatants from noncombatants.

In a just revolution, then, who are the combatants from a revolutionary's point of view? To begin with, there are those who directly employ violence to perpetrate the injustices against which the revolution is aimed: the army or elements of it; the police or elements of it;[34] the secret police; foreigners directly involved in assisting the government forces in prosecuting the injustices; informers; and the politicians who are directing the "oppression" complained of. This list is consistent with my argument in Chapter 6 that the category of noncombatant is not equivalent to that of civilian. Let us suppose the IRA's revolutionary activity in Northern Ireland to have been justified. Its use of bombs on railways and in pubs would clearly be illegitimate and would count as terrorism, since such attacks necessarily fail to discriminate between combatants and noncombatants. Similarly with the killing of Mountbatten and the others on his boat, since not only were they innocent, but so surely was Mountbatten. Some years ago a visiting scholar at Melbourne

---

[31] Debray, *Revolution in the Revolution?*, p. 75.

[32] Quoted in Robert Taber, *The War of the Flea* (London: Paladin, 1972), p. 106.

[33] Yasser Arafat, "The Palestinian Vision of Peace," *New York Times*, February 3, 2002, p. 15

[34] The importance of discrimination here is illustrated by the example of the Jewish revolutionaries who assassinated Lord Moyne in Cairo in 1944 but refused to kill an Egyptian policeman whom they did not regard as an agent of British imperialism in Palestine, even though this refusal led to their capture. See Walzer, *Just and Unjust Wars*, p. 199.

University tried to include Mountbatten as a legitimate target by pointing out the amount of "Irish land" that he owned, but this seems to be a case in which an insufficient connection with a chain of agency has been established. By contrast, there is at least the beginning of a case for the assassination of the Conservative spokesman on Northern Ireland, Airey Neave – not, I think, sufficient but at least addressed to considerations which have some relevance. A more clear-cut case is provided by the kidnap-killing of the American public safety adviser Don Mitrione in Uruguay in 1970. Mitrione had been sent to Uruguay to assist in the suppression of the Tupamaros insurgency. There is considerable evidence that he had an important role in the torture campaign waged against Uruguay's political prisoners. It would be absurd to regard his position as that of an uninvolved civilian diplomat, though this was how he was initially portrayed in the Western media at the time of his death.[35]

Distinctions of this kind between targets of revolutionary violence are important not only for the revolutionaries from the point of view of how they should behave, but also for observers concerned with describing their behaviour. The fact is, of course, that most observers, and especially the media, tend to describe any revolutionary as a terrorist and virtually any revolutionary use of violence as terrorism, including even the killing of soldiers. At least this is so throughout most of the Western media with respect to revolutionary violence directed against established governments in what used to be called "the free world." The revolutionaries against Soviet occupation in Afghanistan, on the other hand, were seldom if ever referred to as terrorist in the Western press, though their tactics displayed hardly more concern for moral scruple than those employed in Belfast or El Salvador. The assumption underlying this linguistic habit is that revolutions against "our" ideological enemies are invariably justified, an assumption that is fortified when, as with the Mujahideen in Afghanistan, Western powers actively support and arm the insurgents. During the Cold War, a parallel assumption, with suitably adjusted referents for the indexical elements, guided the reporting of the Soviet bloc press.

Whatever the naiveté or cynicism of this assumption, it does raise interesting theoretical issues, since if we assume that some given revolutionary campaign is unjustified, then we would seem to have some reason to make light of any distinction between the targets selected by the rebels. After all, if a revolution or rebellion is unjustified, then its infliction of injury and death is unjustified, whether upon combatants or noncombatants. This point has already been dealt with in Chapter 6 in connection with unjustified war, and the discussion there applies directly to the present case. Our conclusion should be that there remain important moral and pragmatic

---

[35] For a sober assessment of allegations about Mitrione's role, see A. J. Langguth, *Hidden Terrors* (New York: Pantheon Books, 1978), especially pp. 250–254.

reasons for distinguishing between attacks upon combatants and attacks on noncombatants, even where both are in reality unjustified. Were Basque separatists to blow up a kindergarten, it would make plain sense to call what they did "terrorist" in ways that it wouldn't were they to defend themselves against Spanish troops or even attack them. This distinction is worth making whether the Basque cause is just or unjust. Hence we should continue to make a distinction between two broad types of revolutionary (or substate) violence: that which is directed at what would be legitimate targets if the revolution were justified, and that which is directed at noncombatants. We should reserve the term "terrorism" only for the latter, and it can be unequivocally condemned. Violence of the former kind stands or falls morally by the judgement of the overall legitimacy of the revolutionary activity.

Revolution and Legitimate Authority

Does this open the way to condoning far too many acts of political violence that understandably cause such widespread shock and distress? It all depends. If you think that violent revolutionary struggle is readily justifiable – an easy moral option – then you should be prepared for the consequences and have a realistic appreciation of what you are supporting. If, on the other hand, you think that violent revolution is sometimes, but only seldom, justifiable, then the killing you condone will be far more restricted. (You can vehemently condemn the killing of Aldo Moro without regarding it as terrorist.) My own view is that violent revolution, like war, is only rarely justifiable, though one's sympathies may often be more with the rebels because of their genuine and unlikely-to-be-remedied grievances. Those contemplating revolutionary or insurrectional violence need to be aware of the great evils that efforts at violent disruption of state order commonly unleash, even when the order is repressive and unjust. This is, of course, a central insight of Hobbes, who ruled out revolution in any circumstances. But, against Hobbes, the evils of rebellion may sometimes be outweighed by those inflicted by the repression, humiliation, and persecution that malignant state power can inflict. But a just revolution must also heed the other conditions of the JAB, especially those of reasonable prospect of success and last resort. Of course, this demand acutely poses the question: who should attend to these requirements? The short answer is: anyone contemplating initiating or participating in a revolution. This parallels the answer we have endorsed in the case of interstate war. But a longer answer must address what is probably the most difficult issue for the just revolution, namely, that of legitimate authority.

In the case of states, there is at least a preliminary answer ready to hand, since there will be an incumbent government with some presumptive authority. For revolution, this is much murkier because of the splintered form of so much revolutionary activity. But against this it must be said that "legitimate

authority" itself is a murky notion. Not only are theories of political legitimacy deeply contentious, we must also be wary of setting the standards
for legitimacy, especially in the context of the resort to political violence,
too high. There is a case for making democratic procedures and an associated respect for human rights conditions of political legitimacy, but perhaps
this should be seen as representing an ideal of legitimacy rather than strict
conditions for its existence, otherwise very few societies in history will have
had legitimate governments. Even if we are prepared to swallow this, it cannot capture the sense of legitimate authority embodied in just war theory,
since even tyrannical regimes are presumably capable of fighting a just war
in defence of their peoples, as Stalin's government did against the Nazi
invaders. This also suggests that the legitimacy in question need not be particularly stable. It may be called forth by the particular circumstances of
political emergency or grievance. In certain of those circumstances, revolutionary leaders may have more endorsement from and solidarity with their
people, or a significant section of them, than an incumbent government.
The JAB emphasis on legitimate authority is primarily aimed at ruling out
what the medievals called "private war" – of which feuding and brigandage
are good examples – rather than at endorsing violence between states as the
only candidates for just war.

It is perhaps this issue of legitimate authority, and doubts about the capacity of revolutionaries to satisfy its requirements, that leads many political
theorists and (often enough) ordinary people to operate with that different understanding of terrorism that I characterised earlier as a political
status definition. Some might defend any apparent inconsistency over state
terrorism by rejecting the tactical definition in favour of the political status definition. I have already discussed the defects of the political definition, but it is worth noting here that, like the tactical definition, it gains
much of its appeal from its ready connection to themes in just war theory.
Where the tactical definition links with the discussion of illegitimate targeting under the JIB, the political status definition links with the question of
legitimate authority under the JAB. Anthony Coates's discussion of terrorism, for example, seems primarily concerned to analyze terrorism in terms
of unauthorised violence in a political cause.[36] He believes that terrorists are
being conceded too much by those (like me) who think that their activities
should be defined and subsequently condemned in terms of the just war
principle of discrimination. His position makes it difficult for him to treat
revolutionary or secessionist violence as anything but terrorism, since the
primary paradigm of "legitimate authority" is a certain sort of state authority. Nonetheless, Coates recoils from categorizing all revolutionary violence
as terrorist. Even so, defining terrorism in terms of the resort to political

---

[36] A. J. Coates, *The Ethics of War* (Manchester and New York: Manchester University Press, 1997),
    pp. 123–128.

violence without "legitimate authority" surely stacks the odds too greatly against the possibility of a justified revolution. Coates wants to allow that just war thinking can apply to revolutions, and that there can therefore be a just revolution, but he has great difficulty specifying a sense of "legitimate authority" that can apply to units other than states. He is justifiably sceptical of romantic attitudes towards revolutionary violence, but his approach to terrorism takes him too close to the problems of the political status definition. In any case, if terrorism is defined in terms of the lack of "legitimate authority" alone, then those revolutions that do have legitimate authority cannot, by definition, employ terrorism. This is both counterintuitive and theoretically unsatisfactory. For we surely want to leave room for discussing the question whether a properly authorised revolution is nonetheless using terrorist tactics.[37]

Some Final Clarifications

My discussion of terrorism turns upon viewing it as a tactic, but it may be urged that the means/end model upon which I rely is not always appropriate to the realities. Sometimes revolutionary terrorism and, for that matter, governmental terrorism is employed not to achieve some definite end, nor as an aberrational end in itself, but as a piece of powerful symbolism, an act of self-assertion. Paskins and Dockrill seem to take this view of both war and revolutionary violence:

It is ... often difficult to answer the question whether war is useful or not. To look at the Allied bombing campaign as though it were a priori obvious that it was engaged in as means thought to be useful in the pursuit of some well-defined goal is, we argued, a very dubious proceeding. Many other explanations of the campaign are possible. The same is true of terrorism. One is apt to think of the terrorist as, however sympathetic, a ruthless figure prepared to use indiscriminate violence in pursuit of a well-defined goal. But there appears to us to be good theoretical reason to doubt all such stereotypes. Often, states wage war because they believe that they have no alternative; similarly with the terrorist.... To wage war because one thinks one has no alternative, or because one believes that war is the only way to show that one is in earnest is not necessarily to do something which one assumes is understandable, or justifiable, as means to some end.[38]

Although I think that some of this is confused, there is no doubt that the passage identifies a real motivation. The first thing to note about it, however, is that, although it provides us with a salutary warning against too crude a construal of the goals terrorism may serve, it does not invalidate the means/end model. Indeed, the talk of "having no alternative" needs to be construed in terms of certain goals and purposes in order to have sense made of it, since

[37] Ibid., Chapter 5.
[38] Paskins and Dockrill, *The Ethics of War*, p. 94.

there are usually other "alternatives" that are, however, inconsistent with certain values or ends it is believed that war or terrorism will promote or embody. Finland's war against overwhelming odds with the Soviet Union had alternatives, but none of them promoted or exhibited the values the Finns saw themselves as emphatically defending by their hopeless war. If such ends are thought to be too internal or constitutive for the usual means/end model, then I do not need to quarrel with the objector. The Finns were not engaging in war for its own sake but as a way to show their earnestness about their independence (on one possible account of their motives). Similarly with the parallel case of revolutionary violence, especially terrorism. We can understand how a community may become so downtrodden in its conditions of life and so threatened in its identity as to believe that the only really emphatic and appropriate way of asserting whatever dignity remains is to commit an act of terrorism. I do not think that in its pure form this is the typical case, but it is a possible case, and ingredients related to it may figure in the more common cases. We may admit that many terrorist attacks are expressive and symbolic, involving the affirmation of the attitude, "We are still here – take notice of us." Yet the expressive need not exclude the purposive. So terrorist acts can be, and usually are, both expressive and politically purposive. It is a further question whether these purposes are particularly realistic. The idea that terrorist acts are merely expressive is partly sustained by the belief that when viewed as purposive the acts are basically futile. The futility is often real enough, but purposive acts that are in fact futile abound.

This may be the point at which to discuss some related claims made by those concerned with a specific "terrorist psychology" who argue that we go wrong in thinking of terrorists as rationally concerned to achieve certain ends by violent means. They contend that the terrorist uses a very specific sort of "psycho-logic" rather than the logic used by the rest of us. Jerrold M. Post, for instance, in a discussion entitled "Terrorist Psycho-Logic: Terrorist Behavior as a Product of Psychological Forces," objects to the idea that "terrorists resort to violence as a *wilful* choice selected from a range of perceived alternatives. . . . [Rather,] *political terrorists are driven to commit acts of violence as a consequence of psychological forces*, and . . . their special psycho-logic is constructed to rationalize *acts they are psychologically compelled to commit.*"[39] One problem with this theory is that Post himself agrees with Martha Crenshaw that "the outstanding common characteristic of terrorists is their normality" and further admits that his own empirical research "does not reveal any major psycho-pathology" amongst terrorists.[40] This makes it somewhat

---

[39] Walter Reich (ed.), *Origins of Terrorism: Psychologies, Ideologies, Theologies, States of Mind* (Washington, DC: Woodrow Wilson Center Press and Cambridge: Cambridge University Press, 1990), p. 25.

[40] Jerrold M. Post, "Terrorist Psycho-Logic: Terrorist Behaviour as a Product of Psychological Forces," in Reich (ed.), *Origins of Terrorism*, p. 26; and Martha Crenshaw, "The Causes of Terrorism," *Comparative Politics* 13 (1981), pp. 379–399.

puzzling that they suffer from these compulsive drives, but in fact the psychology that Post goes on to describe is by no means as peculiar as his italicised excitement might suggest. Indeed, much of what he ascribes uniquely to terrorists is common to all sorts of other groups, including the politically committed wherever they are found. He cites, for instance, several authors who have apparently "discovered" that terrorists are "action-oriented, aggressive people who are stimulus-hungry and seek excitement."[41] Again, they "need an outside enemy to blame" – a need one might think common to many nonterrorists, including the governments of powerful states. Another such feature is an "extreme pressure to conform,"[42] which is surely as unsurprising in terrorist groups as it is in academic and military institutions. As Grossman says of ordinary soldiers: "Numerous studies have concluded that men in combat are usually motivated to fight *not* by ideology or hate or fear, but by group pressures and processes."[43] In short, there may be psychological causes for terrorist behaviour other than the operation of a strict means-end logic, just as there are in every walk of life (and death), but this is no reason to deny any significance to the idea that terrorism is at least a tactic for the achieving of certain goals. Here, as elsewhere in seeking to explain human behaviour, we need to avoid the twin fallacies of excessive rationalism and excessive psychologism. People do not always act rationally, nor when they act rationally do they always act according to the dictates of game theory; but neither does the discovery of other psychological pressures show that rationality has no place in what they do.

Finally, let me return, as promised, to the connection between terrorism and fear. Earlier, I questioned the suggestion that terrorism should be defined wholly or partly in terms of the creation or spread of fear, but there is no doubt that *one* of the reasons why people are so disturbed by terrorist activities is that they find such activities deeply undermining of social realities with which their lives are enmeshed and which provide a background of normalcy against which they can go about their ordinary living. (No doubt this is less important when their "ordinary" lives are already dominated by fear and oppression.) From my perspective, there is no reason to deny any of this. Indeed, my account of terrorism goes far towards explaining why this should be so, since the method of terror is to attack those who have reason to think of themselves as uninvolved. It is also true, however, that any form of covert warfare, no matter how discriminating, will tend to break down the conditions of normalcy, though not so dramatically as terrorism will. Any form of low-intensity warfare (to use the jargon) will make familiar figures such as policemen, soldiers, and politicians into targets; it will lead to the

[41] Ibid., p. 27.
[42] Ibid., p. 33.
[43] Lieutenant Colonel Dave Grossman, *On Killing: The Psychological Cost of Learning to Kill in War and Society* (Boston: Little, Brown, 1995), p. 89.

killing of apparently innocent people who are, in reality, informers, secret police, or foreign political advisers; it will result in some mistaken, accidental, or incidental killing or injuring of genuine noncombatants and itself create an atmosphere of suspicion. Here we have another potent source of the confusion between terrorism and other forms of revolutionary violence; but confusion it remains, however understandable, for the terrorist seeks to gain his ends by deliberately attacking those who are not morally legitimate targets.

This collapse of the categories of clandestine warfare and terrorism has been given renewed currency by Martin Hughes. Hughes simply defines terrorism as "a war in which a secret army spreads fear," and he claims that secret armies "must threaten everybody but their active supporters – and surely both lurking enemies and ambiguous, suspicious friends are quite frightening."[44] Hughes seems to think that clandestine warfare not only commonly creates the sort of fear discussed earlier but inevitably involves a policy of attacks upon noncombatants, so that there is no need for a distinct definition of terrorism in terms of such a policy. In this he is surely mistaken. Guerrilla wars which make little or no use of terrorist tactics are not only possible but seem to have occurred, though – notoriously – the facts are often hard to establish, in part because the reports and commentaries embody the sorts of confusions I am trying to dispel. One such "clean" revolution appears to have been Castro's insurrection against Batista; another (perhaps more contentious) was the EOKA campaign against the British in Cyprus. Hughes argues that it is too much to ask of resisters and revolutionaries that they attack only military forces as "great armies" are impregnable to such attacks. But in the first place, this greatly exaggerates the immunity of regular forces from attack by irregular resistance groups, as Cuba and Ireland and, more recently, Iraq have demonstrated; and second, it ignores the fact that orthodox military victory is not the usual aim of guerrilla attacks upon the enemy's armed forces; such attacks are intended primarily to produce political effects. In Vietnam, the Americans won the military victory in the Tet offensive, but it was nonetheless a political victory for the Vietcong and decided the destiny of Vietnam. One significant success of Palestinian resisters against Israel came when Hezbollah attacks on soldiers forced the Israeli army to leave southern Lebanon. Moreover, Hughes's argument at this point skates over the fact that the legitimate targets for a just revolution can go beyond men in uniform with guns.

Hughes does offer some concrete evidence for his view that covert wars must treat everyone but active supporters as the enemy, and it consists in the famous fate of Mrs. Lindsay. This, he says, "illustrates powerfully how necessary it is for revolutionaries to sap the courage of their civilian opponents. It seems hard to imagine how they could use any but very severe threats

---

44 Hughes, "Terrorism and National Security," p. 5.

for this purpose."[45] Curiously, Hughes merely cites Mrs. Lindsay's case and speaks of her "convictions and courage" without giving any details.

The facts are that she was an elderly woman who supplied information to the British forces in January 1921, which resulted in their surprising an ambush and killing two IRA men and capturing ten others, five of whom were later executed. She was subsequently kidnapped and shot by the IRA, who gave as their reason "the stern necessity to protect our forces." These details (provided by Townshend, on whom Hughes relies)[46] show that Mrs. Lindsay's fate was not that of a mere "civilian opponent" in the sense of one who disagreed with the IRA's aims and programme, but rather that of an informer, one who could plausibly be viewed as taking an active part in the war. The IRA may well have been wrong to kill her; they may have even been wrong to view her as an informer, for she may have acted to save British lives without realizing that she was condemning Irishmen; but whatever we decide about that, her fate does not illustrate the thesis that secret warfare must make targets of everyone but active supporters, that low-intensity warfare must be, in my sense, terrorist. Indeed, Townshend is able to report, shortly before discussing Mrs. Lindsay's death, that the IRA "did not show symptoms of the desperate terrorism which often marks guerrilla movements in decline. It continued to wage urban and rural war on roughly the same lines without resorting to indiscriminate attacks."[47] Townshend's source for the story of Mrs. Lindsay, incidentally, is H. C. Wylly's *History of the Manchester Regiment*. This makes for very interesting reading. Wylly describes Mrs. Lindsay as "a brave loyalist woman" who has shown "a great example of courage and devotion to the Empire."[48] After her disappearance, Lloyd George, during negotiations with de Valera, caused inquiries to be made amongst the rebels as to her fate. According to the rebel Parliament's minister of defence, she had been executed only after the British commander, General Strickland, ignored a letter from her pointing out that she would be killed if the British went ahead with the execution of five of the captured Irishmen. Five days after they were killed, so was she. Wylly makes no mention of the fate of her butler-chauffeur, Joseph Clarke, who was kidnapped along with her, but the absence of comment strongly implies that his captors regarded Clarke as basically a noncombatant and released him.

There is much more that could be said about terrorism, and of course about a related topic of some current importance, counterterrorism. Amongst these issues are questions about the supposed novelty of contemporary transnational terrorism and about the sort of legal status that should

---

[45] Ibid., p. 18.

[46] Charles Townshend, *The British Campaign in Ireland 1919–1921* (Oxford: Oxford University Press, 1975), p. 153.

[47] Townshend, *The British Campaign in Ireland*, p. 152.

[48] H. C. Wylly, *History of the Manchester Regiment*, vol. 2 (London: Forster Groom, 1925), p. 210.

be accorded captured terrorists. I have addressed the former question elsewhere, and have views about the latter that I cannot now spell out, except
to say that I favour giving them much the same status as other prisoners
of war.[49] The category "illegal combatants" or "enemy combatants," much
beloved of the Bush administration, largely obfuscates important moral and
legal principles, and I shall defer discussion of the issues connected with
this until the next chapter.

[49] For the novelty issue, see C. A. J. Coady, "How New Is the 'New Terror'?," *Iyyun: The Jerusalem
Philosophical Quarterly* 55, no. 1 (January 2006), pp. 49–65.

9

The Immunities of Combatants

The General

"Good-morning; good-morning!" the General said
When we met him last week on our way to the line.
Now the soldiers he smiled at are most of 'em dead,
And we're cursing his staff for incompetent swine.
"He's a cheery old card," grunted Harry to Jack
As they slogged up to Arras with rifle and pack.
* * * * * * * *
But he did for them both by his plan of attack.
                    Siegfried Sassoon[1]

Recent writings on war and violence by philosophers have understandably concentrated a lot of attention upon those provisions of the *jus in bello* that concern the immunity of noncombatants from direct attack and targeting. I say this is understandable because the history of so many twentieth-century wars tells of the staggering loss of non-combatant life, limb, health, and property, very much of it attributable to the tactic of aerial bombardment. It is one highly commendable achievement of the International Red Cross movement and the United Nations to have made the immunity of noncombatants an important element in the Geneva Conventions via its Protocols, so that where international law was once silent about the victimisation of noncombatants, it can no longer be so. The success of the movement to write these provisions into international law provides some evidence against the claim, discussed in Chapter 1, that just war theory is utterly ineffectual.

Modern just war theory has been exercised about the immunities of non-combatants ever since the full facts became available about the bombing policies of both sides in the Second World War. British and American

[1] Siegfried Sassoon, "The General," in his *Collected Poems 1908–1956* (London: Faber and Faber, 1961), p. 75.

writers were particularly concerned with the Allied terror bombing of German and Japanese cities, culminating in the nuclear destruction of Hiroshima and Nagasaki. Playing an important part in changing the moral climate of opinion on this issue were the writings of such people as the Jesuit John C. Ford (who courageously condemned the bombing of Germany in 1944 while the war was still in progress), Richard Wasserstrom (who criticised the failure of the international law of war to protect noncombatants), Elizabeth Anscombe, Peter Geach, Walter Stein, and other English Catholics (who made the status of noncombatants an important plank in their critique of nuclear deterrence).

Concern for Combatants: The Background

Yet it is worth remembering that the Geneva Conventions and numerous other modern attempts to bring moral and humane concerns to bear upon warfare began in a compassionate response to the plight of soldiers, not civilians. When Henry Dunant found himself on the plains of Lombardy in the vicinity of Solferino in 1859, he saw thousands of wounded soldiers left to die by their leaders, and from his compassion for the victims and his revulsion from the callousness shown to them came the impetus for the formation of the International Committee of the Red Cross and eventually the work of the various Geneva and Hague conventions. In earlier centuries, with medicinal and organisational opportunities so much less available, compassion for the dismal plight of the wounded could take more terrible and paradoxical forms, as Ambroise Pare, one of the founders of modern military medicine, reveals in writing of his experiences entering Milan with the French army in 1536. There he saw three soldiers hideously burned by gunpowder and was asked by an old soldier who viewed them "with pity" whether there was any means of curing them. Pare said there was not, so:

At once he approached them and cut their throats gently and, seeing this great cruelty, I shouted at him that he was a villain. He answered me that he prayed to God that when he should be in such a state he might find someone who would do the same for him, to the end that he might not languish miserably.[2]

Understanding the horror that so often accompanies life and death in violent conflicts has come far in the last decades of the twentieth century and continuing into the present century, but it is significant that the conflict which did so much to undermine the romantic image of war and the version of militarism associated with it (discussed in Chapters 1 and 3) was World War I, a war in which, although noncombatant immunity was certainly violated in many villages of France, the principal immoralities concerned the

---

[2] Quoted in John Keegan and Richard Holmes, *Soldiers: A History of Men in Battle* (London: Hamish Hamilton, 1985), p. 146.

carnage amongst the combatant troops on both sides. Images of the Somme and Paschaendale, Ypres and Gallipoli fuelled antiwar sentiment as very little before had done; and much of the revulsion and moral outrage sprang from the futility of the trench warfare and the sense that the generals on both sides had too little concern for the human lives committed to their responsibility. It was probably a more "literary" war than any before or since, and, for all its problems as an aesthetic, Wilfred Owen's remark that "the poetry is in the pity" expressed much of the motivation for the literary output the war occasioned. Of course, some of the emotion, especially the anger, was directed at the war's having been fought at all. Many believed at the time that this war was unjustified, and, with the benefit of hindsight, many more believe it now. But part of what the hindsight contributes is knowledge of the extraordinary casualties, and certainly much of the rejection of World War I as unjust stems from the wholly intelligible belief that the costs were so disproportionate. As we saw earlier, the criterion of proportionality tends to span the JAB and the JIB, and this is one of the contexts in which the methods of waging the war cast doubt upon its overall legitimacy.

The final irony of World War I for the argument presented here resides in the often-overlooked fact that the massive casualties amongst the troops on both sides and the consequent moral revulsion from this type of war – a war of attrition – were instrumental in developing and popularising the techniques of aerial bombardment. These techniques have contributed much to the widespread destruction of civilian life and property that has marked most subsequent warfare in the twentieth century. The leading military historian and strategic thinker of the period between the two world wars was Sir Basil Liddell Hart. While Liddell Hart played a powerful role in promoting the idea that wars should be fought against the enemy's civil population, his campaign for air warfare was fuelled by humanitarian motives. He believed that aerial bombardment of the enemy's civilian population would crush the enemy's will to resist and thus end war more quickly with far fewer casualties. Writing in 1925, he deplored what he characterised as the "Napoleonic theory of absolute war" whereby the objective of war was the total destruction of the enemy's troops.[3] Liddell Hart thought that this distracted attention from the major political and strategic object of war, which was to subdue the enemy nation's will to continue fighting, and that it gave rise to the inordinate bloodshed and agonising stalemate so characteristic of World War I. Discussing the Napoleonic theory, he wrote:

Thus mechanical butchery becomes the essence of war. To kill, if possible, more of the enemy troops than your own side loses is the sum total of this military creed, which attained its tragi-comic climax on the Western front in the Great War.[4]

[3] B. H. Liddell Hart, *The Memoirs of Captain Liddell Hart*, vol. 1 (London: Cassell & Co., 1965), p. 142.
[4] Ibid., p. 140.

By contrast, he thought, a sudden decisive blow at the enemy's heartland would better serve the interests of all concerned:

Aircraft enable us to jump over the army which shields the enemy government, industry and people, and so strike direct at the seat of the opposing will and policy. Provided that the blow be sufficiently swift and powerful there is no reason why, in a few hours, or at most, days, from the commencement of hostilities the nerve centre of one of the contending countries should not be paralysed.[5]

Yet despite the horrendous consequences of attention to his ideas in the years that followed, it is clear that Liddell Hart's suggestion was advanced from recognisable moral and prudential perspectives. Mostly he writes of the benefits to one's own nation in reducing the personal costs of war, but he also has some sense of the significance of the costs to the enemy, and sees these considerations as complementary. So he says:

But self-interest as well as humane reasons demand that the warring nations should endeavour to gain their end of the moral subjugation of the enemy with the infliction of the least possible permanent injury to life and industry, for the enemy of today is the customer of the morrow, and the ally of the future.[6]

Liddell Hart's perspective is vitiated by an excessive consequentialism and, even within that framework, a profound misjudgement about the psychology of civilian populations and their governments, as well as by a failure to foresee the scale and intensity of damage that bombardment could wreak upon populations, economies, and nature. (It also depends upon a metaphysical conception of "will" that has been extremely influential in thinking about war, but is no less suspect for that.) Nonetheless, it is worth quoting his analysis partly because it does reflect the importance of a concern for combatant sufferings that has been somewhat obscured by the realisation that he, and those he influenced, were so wrong about noncombatant sufferings. It also expresses certain arguments to which we shall later be attending.

Combatants, Necessity, and Proportion

These background facts deserve initial mention because they help to dispel the otherwise powerful idea that, while it is wrong to make the un-involved a target of your violence, enemy troops are fair game for any form of lethal attack. The object of war is to win by maiming and killing the opposition's armed forces, and there cannot be any question about the means of so doing except as those means affect noncombatants. Moreover, this intuition often extends to the use of one's own troops as means. But this powerful idea is defective in several directions. The first is the point made by so

---

[5] Ibid., p. 141.
[6] Ibid.

tough-minded a theorist as Hobbes, and noted in Chapter 1, about unnecessary cruelty. Weapons and tactics that inflict suffering and death beyond what is necessary for military success stand condemned by the simplest rational reflection and are certainly contrary to any just war theory that could be generated by attention to the domestic analogy discussed in earlier chapters. The doctrine of "military necessity," which is often thought to restrict the application of moral categories to war, may itself be appealed to here to point up the immorality of much practice that has, in fact, been common in war, such as slaughtering those who have surrendered or are otherwise *hors de combat*.

"Necessity" in time of war can be interpreted to mean many different things, and certain moral dilemmas can arise from this. A common one concerns what to do with captured enemy troops when they are impeding one's progress in a risky way, or when they are about to be freed by enemy forces and used against you. But this is a moral problem that can be confronted on its own terms. A more serious defect of the idea of military necessity is that its interpretation clearly depends upon some prior grasp of the relevant military purposes that the necessity is to serve. What is required is that such purposes have themselves a political and moral legitimacy, for otherwise any goal that is dictated by mere triumph of arms will find some necessity that endorses the most appalling means. It may, for instance, be a military objective, in this sense, to try out some new military technology even though the battle can be as effectively won by other means involving vastly fewer deaths and, for that matter, much less devastation to the environment. Or certain tactics may be required to win this battle, while the sanest moral and political judgement is that it is better to negotiate an end to the war without contesting the battle at all. This recalls Clausewitz's important idea that military objectives are not self-supporting but need subordination to broader political objectives, though (for reasons already discussed) we should be less reluctant than Clausewitz to invoke a moral perspective as well as a political one. These sorts of reasons should not only make us cautious about too ready or simplistic a resort to "military necessity," but also point up some of the advantages of talking instead of "proportionality." Winning some particular battle may involve casualties, risks, or foreseeable long-term political consequences that are out of proportion to the immediate benefits of the victory.

As we saw in an earlier chapter, proportionality is a puzzling notion in some respects, but it should be apparent that any sort of morally sophisticated understanding of necessity in the context of proportion will rule out such operations against enemy combatants as excessive killing or maiming (and at least serve to raise the question whether these particular killings and maimings are excessive) and will also prohibit deliberate infliction of cruelty on those whom it is legitimate to disable or kill. In addition to such full-bloodedly intentional harmings, it will also rule out reckless or negligent infliction of the same or related wrongs upon the enemy and, very significantly, upon one's own troops. Let us take these in turn. It might be thought that you can only wrong the enemy intentionally, but it is plausible to suppose that in normal circumstances we have obligations of care and prevention of evil that enjoin us to avoid negligent and reckless harming of others. Such obligations may not be as stringent as obligations not to inflict such harms deliberately or intentionally, but we normally think that they have some weight. A passer-by who could easily prevent a baby from drowning in a puddle is under a moral obligation to do so, even if her failure to do so would not be a case of intentional killing. Wartime circumstances make a difference, of course – several differences, in fact, some of which tend to reduce responsibility and some to increase it. The peacetime "passer-by" will not normally be in frantic flight from great danger or rushing to secure some great good, as a soldier in disordered retreat or urgent attack may be; but, on the other hand, she will not usually have contributed to the plight of the stricken victim, in the myriad ways that the combat soldier or his colleagues may have done. So although the moral point applies differently, it still applies. Where enemy troops are not in a position to attend to their own casualties, then simply leaving enemy wounded to die in agony when they could be assisted without major individual risk (such as that posed by minefields), and without serious disadvantage to the prosecution of the war, would be wrong. And duties of care apply even more obviously to one's own troop casualties.

The point about responsibility for one's own troops may be thought too evident to mention, though history suggests that it needs emphasis, and it was indeed stressed by the Chinese philosopher Hsun Tzu 2,300 years ago when he said: "Do not press too hard for victory and forget about defeat. Do not be too stern with your own men and despise the enemy."[7] Part of the widespread moral revulsion from the dreadful conflict of World War I is produced by the perception that there was a callous disregard by the general staff of both armies for the well-being of their own troops. I lack the expertise to be confident about the validity of this perception, though I suspect that it is accurate. Certainly, the generals seldom got close enough to the conflict to gain any sense of what their policies were inflicting upon the men, and they displayed an attitude toward the wastage of human life that suggested they viewed their troops as mere cannon fodder. It has been claimed, in their defence, that the frightful stalemate of trench warfare, in which a few yards of apparently useless ground were gained in one horrendous battle and lost again a little later in another, was forced upon them by circumstance and that no other tactics were available to fight the war. I doubt that this

---

[7] Hsun Tzu, "Debating Military Affairs," in *Basic Writings of Mo Tzu, Hsun Tzu, and Han Fei Tzu*, trans. and ed. Burton Watson (New York and London: Columbia University Press, 1967), p. 65 (of the Hsun Tzu selection).

is so, and indeed I think that the situation illustrates the important point that the limits of possibility are set in part by what is considered morally impossible. Had the general staff viewed the wastage of life as the moral enormity it has subsequently come to seem, they would have exercised more imagination in trying to find other ways of fighting. Financial restrictions, personnel restrictions, and weaponry restrictions impel imagination and intellect towards previously undreamt strategic and tactical options, and the same should be true of moral restrictions.[8] On the other hand, if no other methods were available or devisable, this surely constituted a reason to make urgent efforts to negotiate a settlement. Nor did the conduct of particular manoeuvres, forays, and attacks inspire great confidence, as Sassoon's poem at the head of this chapter indicates.

Other cases from the history of war could also be cited where military leaders showed a callous indifference to the life and limb of their own troops, and where they made morally inexcusable blunders that cost lives needlessly, though seldom their own. Norman Dixon's vigorous and refreshingly irreverent book *On the Psychology of Military Incompetence* contains some hair-raising examples.[9] General Townshend's infamous campaign in Mesopotamia during World War I, for instance, culminating in the siege of Kut, was a sorry saga of incompetence fuelled by overwhelming ambition that left no room for concern for the lives of the human beings entrusted to his and his fellow generals' command. Townshend had been sent to protect a British oil pipeline but decided (along with other senior officers) to adopt a more belligerent role, even to the point of attacking and capturing the city of Kut and then making an attempt upon Baghdad with an absurdly inadequate force. Townshend's blundering strategies cost 7,000 casualties in his efforts to reach Kut, a further 1,600 dead during the siege, a further 23,000 casualties amongst the forces seeking to lift the siege, and finally 7,000 deaths amongst the 13,000 troops taken by the Turks when he surrendered them into captivity. By contrast, Townshend and all his senior officers (with the honourable exception of Major-General Mellis) chose not to share the conditions of their men, but were wined and dined by the Turkish high command in Constantinople. Townshend spent his confinement in a comfortable villa on a fashionable island resort, while his troops were starved and brutalised.[10] Dixon is probably right to think that Townshend's casual attitude towards his responsibilities at least partly requires a psychiatric explanation, but there are also other considerations (equally stressed by Dixon)

---

[8] In fact, there were other strategies and tactics available, most notably tank warfare, which was introduced at Cambrai but used inappropriately. For a discussion of the role of tanks at Cambrai, see Norman Dixon, *On the Psychology of Military Incompetence* (New York: Basic Books, 1976), Chapter 7.

[9] Ibid.

[10] Ibid., pp. 105–106.

that are more relevant here. These include factors such as careerism and, relatedly, the acceptance of an order in which the workings of the military machine assume a validity somehow independent of what it is for. Dixon calls this latter phenomenon "militarism."[11] Townshend, it is true, defied superior orders, or at least exceeded them, but, in so doing, he was driven by a picture of the military role which had more to do with fame, glory, and career advancement than a sane and morally balanced understanding of the purposes of military activity.

Forbidden Weapons

Returning at this point to the discussion of proportionality, we should note that the requirements of proportionality also help explain something that might otherwise be puzzling, namely, the moral objections to certain sorts of weaponry. This has been a persistent concern of the various conventions on war in their efforts to extend and clarify the international law of war and the associated body of regulations often called international humanitarian law. The most famous such restriction in modern times has been that on the use of poison gas, a restriction that has recently been extended to chemical and biological agents more generally. In the past, there were debates about and denunciations of various innovatory weapons, such as the crossbow and the dum-dum bullet. The fact that some of these debates about particular weapons no longer occur does not mean that the moral issues underlying them have gone away.[12] This is sometimes merely a testament to the vastly extended technological capacities for cruelty and unnecessary carnage that we have developed, capacities that can make the best of past cruelties or excesses seem tame. It is instructive to look at the recent attempts in international law to outlaw certain weapons. The ban on poison gas and other chemical and biological weapons is not in fact explicitly part of the Geneva Conventions or Protocols, but there has recently been widespread

---

[11] Ibid. Dixon's treatment of militarism runs throughout the book, but see especially Chapters 15 and 16. See also Andrew Alexandra, "Militarism," *Social Theory and Practice* 19, no. 2 (Summer 1993), pp. 205–224.

[12] Even the most anachronistic of debates in the discussion of war can turn out to be instructive – for example, the medieval debate about whether war could be waged on the Sabbath or other holy days. These debates seem so strange to modern secular ears because the religious importance of such days no longer resonates for many in today's world, but one need only recall the outrage caused in Israel by the Arab war of 1973, which began with an attack on the holy day of Yom Kippur. Israelis were of course angered by the war's occurring at all, but for many of them, including a surprising number who were not religious, there was a special outrage at the violation of the holy day. Aquinas, be it noted, thought that you could fight on such days when the necessary defence of the community made it imperative. See Frederick H. Russell, *The Just War in the Middle Ages* (Cambridge: Cambridge University Press, 1975), p. 272, for reference to *The "Summa Theologica" of St. Thomas Aquinas* (London: Burns Oates & Washbourne Ltd., 1916), 2–2, q. 40, art. 4.

international agreement on the dangers of such weapons under the aegis of arms control agreements.

The Geneva Protocols contain a general and rather vague reference to a prohibition on "weapons, projectiles, and methods and materials of warfare of a nature to cause superfluous injury, particularly those which are intended to cause, or can be expected to cause widespread, long-term and severe damage to the natural environment."[13] In the 1980s, however, the matter was taken further by the UN when it drew up the cumbrously titled "Convention on Prohibitions or Restrictions on the Use of Certain Conventional Weapons which May Be Deemed to Be Excessively Injurious or to Have Indiscriminate Effects." This places "prohibitions or restrictions" on the use of the following weapons: (a) those the primary effect of which is to injure by fragments which escape detection in the human body, thus preventing treatment of the wounds caused; (b) mines, booby traps, and other such devices (which in the past have killed and injured numerous civilians, often long after the end of hostilities); and (c) incendiary weapons (which have caused great suffering to human beings as well as enormous damage to the environment).[14]

Some of these prohibitions are related to the effects of such weapons on noncombatants, as in the case of (b), and this will generally be a powerful criticism of the development of essentially indiscriminate weapons or methods. Nonetheless, part of the wording raises a somewhat different issue. The reference to weapons with long-term effects upon the environment expresses an interest that is not quite the same as a concern for combatants or noncombatants considered in the usual way. It looks to the longer-term interests of the enemy population as a whole, present noncombatants and future post-combatants and others yet unborn. It also looks to the interests of all those, of whatever nationality, who are likely to be affected by the damaged natural environment and who also must survive in an habitable environment after the war is over. Land mines have recently become a focus of international concern because of the dreadful damage they continue to do long after a war is over; they present a particularly difficult problem because they are seductively cheap to manufacture, difficult to detect, and tremendously expensive to remove. In poor countries like Cambodia, this last consideration makes for the certainty of continuing tragedy for generations to come. International convention specifies patterns for the laying of mines so that clearing minefields after a war can be made easier, but these patterns are not always adhered to, and even where they are, the clean-up is still expensive and dangerous. (Interestingly, Iraqi forces did adhere to

---

[13] *Basic Rules of the Geneva Convention and Their Additional Protocols* (Geneva: International Committee of the Red Cross, 1987), p. 24.

[14] This account of the provisions of the convention is taken from Francoise Bory, *Origin and Development of International Humanitarian Law* (Geneva: International Committee of the Red Cross, 1982), pp. 29–30.

the rules in the minefields they laid in Kuwait during the Gulf War.) [15] Nor do land mines pose the only long-term threat of this nature to the human and natural environments of the countries in which wars are fought. Airborne mines, most notably the bomblets dispersed by the militarily popular cluster bomb, also pose similar problems and are even more easily delivered than land mines. According to one source, as mentioned in Chapter 7, the United States dropped 28,595,724 of these bomblets on Iraq during the Gulf War, or 1.5 bomblets for every man, woman, and child in Iraq. [16]

Other issues that look beyond the standard categories of combatants and noncombatants are concerned with the damage done to the cultural fabric of a society. Protocol I, article 53 (which echoes a protection in the 1954 Hague Convention) seeks to guard against attacks upon "cultural property" such as historical monuments, works of art, and places of worship "which constitute the cultural or spiritual heritage of peoples." [17] The attempt to limit damage to outstanding works of the human imagination goes beyond a concern for the physical health and well-being of the enemy's noncombatants and combatants, and extends not only to their cultural and psychological existence, but also to the common human interest in the preservation of such irreplaceable creative achievements.

Another important moral restriction concerning dealings with enemy combatants is that which relates not directly to how they may be killed, but rather to how truthfully we must deal with them. This is a matter with a long history of discussion amongst the theorists and practitioners of war, and it was an acute problem for those medieval theologians who, following St. Augustine's rigorist prohibition on lying in any circumstances, worried about the various forms of falsehood and deceit that the successful prosecution of war might involve. Aquinas, for instance, allowed ambushes on the grounds that we could not be obliged to declare all our purposes to everyone, and especially not to an enemy; indeed, he didn't even think that ambushes fell into the category of deception. On the other hand, he believed, as part of a rigorist view of lying, that it was always immoral to lie to the enemy. [18] This seems far too strong a view, though it is consistent in its rigorism. Like Augustine and later Kant, Aquinas is not prepared to allow an exception against lying even for the case where a lie is, or is rationally believed to be, the only way to deflect a potential murderer from his victim, so he is not prepared to do it for the collective case of the example, necessary defence in a just war. Hobbes's dictum that in war "force and fraud are the two cardinal

---

[15] For discussions of the land mine problem, see the *New York Times* editorial of December 27, 1993, and the letters column for January 13, 1994.

[16] This figure is cited in a letter by Suzy Kane to the *New York Times*, January 21, 1994. She gives the U.S. army munitions command as the source of the information.

[17] *Basic Rules of the Geneva Convention and Their Additional Protocols*, p. 37.

[18] Thomas Aquinas, *The "Summa Theologica" of St. Thomas Aquinas*, 2–2, q. 40, art. 3.

virtues" at least has considerably plausibility at the descriptive, if not the normative, level, inasmuch as the use of fraudulent and deceitful strategies seems to have been an essential element in most actual wars. Surely a central part of just warfare is the morally legitimate use of guile, to keep the enemy guessing, to have him wrong-footed, to use your "knavish tricks" to foil his. Some of these tactics may not involve lying, or even direct deception, but others, such as the use of spies, for instance, inevitably will. It may therefore seem particularly futile even to raise a question about the moral necessity to be honest with one's military adversary.

There is indeed, as I have conceded, a certain amount of truth in this, but moral theorists and military traditions (including codes of conduct) have long insisted that the licence to cheat, trick, and deceive the enemy has its limits. This insistence is enshrined in recent international conventions as the prohibition on perfidy, and the need for belligerents to have some degree of trust in each other's word has long been recognised, and often honoured. In the simplest and most obvious case, it is necessary for both sides to respect a flag of truce, or to keep their word in safeguarding the immunity of a negotiator. This is a reflexive obligation in that, for instance, those operating under a flag of truce may not use their immunity to mount an attack. Given the degree to which trust inevitably breaks down during a war, and must have broken down considerably for a war to have begun in the first place, it becomes all the more important to try to sustain some degree of trust during the conduct of hostilities. Unless this is so, personal honour and virtue are further undermined, and, more pragmatically, the conditions required to bring the war to a rational end may not exist. Another important consideration about the dangers of too-tolerant an attitude towards the licensing of lying and deception in war is the way in which enthusiasm for deceiving the enemy under the heading of necessity so readily translates into an equivalent enthusiasm for deceiving your own population. The habit of lying is difficult to confine. Just in connection with the United States, we may recall Roosevelt's lies to the American people about how involved the United States was in World War II before the official declaration of war, the ongoing saga of "body counts" in the Vietnam War days, and the lies surrounding the Tonkin Gulf episode, not to come any closer to the present day. To put it mildly, this sort of development has bad effects upon the values and procedures of a democracy and makes rational control by citizens of even justified war-making vastly more difficult.

The issue of limitations on deception of the enemy leads naturally to discussion of another restriction that has been subject to some erosion in practice in recent times, and also subject to philosophical criticism. This is the requirement that combatants be identifiable as such, usually by the wearing of distinctive dress "recognisable at a distance" and/or by the open carrying of arms. As late as 1977, Protocol I of the Geneva Convention insisted on this requirement, though it allowed "in exceptional cases" that combatants may be released from the dress requirement as long as they carry arms openly "during the engagement and during such time as they are visible to the adversary while engaged in a military deployment preceding the launching of an attack in which they are to participate."[19] Some critics have treated this requirement as an archaic obsession with fancy dress and uniforms and see it as having no relevance to modern military conditions; others have seen it as an attempt to impose unfair conditions upon guerrilla or insurgency forces who must rely upon concealment and anonymity in a way that regular armies need not or perhaps cannot.[20]

It is common for such critics to treat the identification requirement as unfairly weighted in favour of the established powers as against insurgents. What is basically the argument from military necessity surfaces in these discussions and, ironically, is used by those who sympathise with insurgency warfare in a way that they would be the first to condemn were the argument used to justify various military policies pursued by incumbent authorities. But, as we saw in Chapter 6, argument from military necessity cannot succeed in allowing the state to wipe out unaligned villagers in order to terrorise the rest of the population into loyalty to the government, nor will it license insurgents to murder captured troops just because they have nowhere to keep and feed them. So why should it allow insurgents to violate the identification requirement? Well, it will be said that the dress code, unlike the prohibition on killing prisoners or on attacking noncombatants, does not embody a basic moral insight. It is a mere agreement to facilitate certain interests of states.[21] But this seems simply to misunderstand the underlying point of the identification requirement, which is chiefly to protect noncombatants. Unless it is, in principle, ascertainable who are the legitimate targets for lethal violence, then the prospects of noncombatants being attacked and killed are greatly increased. Of course, the identification need not be flaunted; the requirement is not one that prevents concealment or camouflage. Michael Walzer has argued that the moral acceptability, in some popular revolutions, of fighting from ambush and wearing camouflage shows that these attempts at requiring distinctive dress can hardly be treated with full moral seriousness. If the people rise en masse, "they are not required to put on uniforms" and can hardly be expected to display their weapons. What is really morally objectionable, he claims, is the "use of civilian clothing as a ruse and a disguise."[22] Yet whether or not the insurgents aim at deceit or treachery, the

[19] See Protocol I, Article 67 as reported in *Basic Rules of the Geneva Conventions and Their Additional Protocols*, p. 23.
[20] See Sheldon M. Cohen, *Arms and Judgement: Law, Morality and the Conduct of War in the Twentieth Century* (Boulder, CO: Westview Press, 1989), Chapter 5, for a good review of the criticisms of the dress code and a defence of it along lines similar to mine.
[21] See, for example, Nicholas Fotion and Gerard Elfstrom, *Military Ethics: Guidelines for Peace and War* (London: Routledge & Kegan Paul, 1986), p. 213.
[22] Michael Walzer, *Just and Unjust Wars: A Moral Argument with Historical Illustrations*, third edition (New York: Basic Books, 2000), p. 183.

violation of the dress and arms convention is fraught with danger to non-combatants. The armed rising en masse is a dangerous paradigm here, not only because it is so rare, but also because its unusual comprehensiveness tends to obliterate the distinction between combatants and noncombatants. If literally everyone (women, children, the aged?) is marching and shooting, then there is no point to the restrictions, but this moral cannot be extended to the far more common cases of insurrectional warfare. As Cohen points out, the moral basis of the rules about uniforms is not that combatants cannot make use of surprise, or must make themselves easy to shoot at, but rather that they be distinguishable from noncombatants. A camouflaged soldier may be hard to tell from the foliage around him, but he does not look like a schoolteacher, a businessman, or a priest. Similarly, it may be legitimate to conceal one's troops and their weapons in a wood, but a part of a wood is not in itself an illegitimate target in the same way that noncombatants are.[23] The matter is more complex in the case of concealment in civilian houses. I am less certain than Cohen about the legitimacy of this, but a lot turns on the status of the town or city in which it occurs. In any case, the moral limits seem to be breached if a tank is disguised as an ambulance or an ambush is launched from a hospital. It may also be that some of the emphasis on identifiable uniforms is aimed as well at the protection of combatants themselves from a certain undermining of the tolerable psychological conditions of battle. The dress code prohibits not only doing battle disguised as a civilian, but also disguising oneself in the uniform of the enemy. The principal point of this is not to protect noncombatants, but to reduce the prospect that troops on the same side will be unable to trust one another, since they will be less able, in battle conditions, to tell who is friend and who foe. (This is not to deny any implications here for the safety of noncombatants.) The life of combat is hellish enough for all concerned without such uncertainties as these.

Another issue having to do with combatant status concerns the treatment of those who surrender or are otherwise captured. First, there is the question of the moral basis of the prohibition on killing prisoners. This basis is partly intrinsic and partly consequential. From the point of view of the primary justification for the killing permitted in a just war, those who have surrendered or been captured are no longer prosecuting the evil that justified lethal violence against them. They have laid down their arms and are defenceless; they are *hors de combat*. There may be a question about punishment, but this must normally be a matter for a tribunal. The status of surrendered combatants is different from that of enemy soldiers who are not, as it happens, attacking

---

[23] There are important respects in which the destruction of a forest or part of a forest raises significant moral issues to do with our duties of environmental care, so we cannot be casual about targeting the environment. The defoliation techniques of the Vietnam War rightly raised moral concerns. But I am thinking here of more limited attacks aimed, for example, at combatants who are attacking from the shelter of trees.

you at the time. It is sometimes raised as an objection to the moral significance of the combatant/noncombatant distinction that enemy troops stationed miles behind the lines and not engaged in hostile activities are effectively noncombatants and so should be immune from attack. This is then seen as a *reductio* of the significance of the distinction. But this is to take too static a view of combatant status. Although not for the moment actively engaged in harming, such troops remain empowered for and committed to the enterprise of harming against which (let us assume) violence may legitimately be directed. A captured combatant, by contrast, is disempowered and his commitment nullified. As for consequences, the knowledge that the enemy will not take, or will later kill, prisoners can remove or greatly reduce the motive to surrender. It also makes it more probable that the other side will reciprocate in its treatment of opposing prisoners. Both these implications increase the hazards of war and contribute to its persistence and cost in lives. These considerations would normally outweigh the advantages of not taking prisoners or of taking them and then killing them later. These have to do mainly with inconvenience, though the inconvenience can be great in certain contexts. Of course, there are problematic circumstances concerned with the difficulty and disutility of taking and keeping prisoners, as there are with the surrender process itself. These require judgement about whether people are genuinely surrendering, about what to do with those who have surrendered but whom you cannot afford to take with you, and so on.

Aside from killing, there are other important questions about the treatment of prisoners that have been the concern of international legal regulation for a long while, most notably the provisions embodied in the Geneva Conventions. The moral rationale for humane treatment is similar to that which underpins the prohibition on killing prisoners, and would need no further discussion here were it not for recent developments in the so-called war on terror, in which the dubious treatment of captives, alleged by reputable agencies to amount to torture, has been given some sort of legal "justification" by authorities in the United States by way of the dubious category of "illegal combatants." The issue of torture, and the revival of moral arguments in its favour, is beyond the scope of my book, but some brief attention must be paid to the "illegal combatant" story.

This is related to the question of uniforms discussed earlier, since that could be taken to raise a more comprehensive question about the nature of "legitimate" combatants. For most of my discussion in this chapter and elsewhere, I have been concerned with a distinction between combatants and noncombatants and its moral consequences. But there are further distinctions that could be and have been made within (and sometimes beyond) the category of combatants, as I have understood it. The Bush administration in the United States has made much of the category of "illegal combatants," and sometimes, weirdly enough, "enemy combatants," principally in order to avoid the obligations (or restrictions, as it sees them) of the Geneva Convention rules for the treatment of prisoners of war. Although the terminology is largely their own, the American authorities are relying in part on some distinctions that have had currency in UN documents and other international instruments, where the basic idea is that the term "combatant" not only removes certain immunities to attack but also confers certain privileges and permissions, such as the right not to be punished for killing other combatants in licit combat, the requirement to reveal only very limited information to one's captors and the right to silence beyond that, restrictions on the penalties that can be imposed on those who attempt escape, and the right not to be coercively interrogated. I do not intend a thorough discussion of the legal complexities surrounding the debate about illegal combatants and other matters, since my concern is with the moral and practical significance that the attempt to distinguish these categories might have. I have argued in earlier chapters that a distinction can be made between just and unjust combatants and that, strictly speaking, unjust combatants do not have the moral right to kill just combatants, and that this fact is important for the moral understanding of political violence in various ways. Nonetheless, I have also argued that, for a number of practical and political reasons with a moral dimension, this fact should not be translated into the legal regulation of war by way of distinguishing the rights and obligations of different types of combatants. This point applies beyond the issue of the right to kill (with which I was principally concerned in Chapter 6) and reaches even more clearly to the rights of captured prisoners. In particular, attempts to deny normal combatant rights to captured combatants who do not fight for a recognised state, or who have used terrorist tactics, or are mercenaries, or do not wear uniforms or otherwise properly distinguish themselves from noncombatants, seem to me misguided. Combatants who breach crucial rules of war certainly place themselves within the scope of legal prosecution as war criminals, and to this extent their treatment should, at least in principle, be different from that accorded those combatants who don't. Beyond this, however, I see no good reason to discriminate between them and good reason not to.

I have said that I do not want to adjudicate the many legal intricacies raised by the U.S. resort to this category, but my approach from the moral perspective is congruent with that of some recent legal theorists who have argued that the fuss about POW status raised by the U.S. attitude towards "illegal combatants" is misguided to a considerable degree on both sides, since the protections afforded "illegal combatants" in international law have increasingly come to resemble those given POWs. Derek Jinks, in particular, has claimed that the various Geneva Conventions and subsequent humanitarian law have reduced dramatically the significance of POW status on such matters as humane treatment, the right not to be tortured or coercively interrogated, the right to be charged with offences and treated with due process when tried, and so on.[24] As to liabilities, members of both categories may be prosecuted for war crimes and other violations of the laws of war. Their defiance of the JIB is culpable in both cases. Jinks argues that the principal difference in rights between illegal and legal combatants at present is that the illicit combatants can be prosecuted by the detaining power for their mere participation in hostilities, including, of course, the killing of their opponents, whereas the standard combatant cannot. He thinks that this should be abolished and that all combatants should be afforded what he calls "protective parity."[25] This proposal not only has the advantage of simplicity and consistency, but also has several other practical advantages. Chief amongst these, as Jinks points out, is the removal of a disincentive for illegal combatants to conform to the laws of war. If they are going to be prosecuted, and perhaps executed, for mere participation in combat, then they have less incentive to fight fairly or to respect noncombatant immunity. They will also have an incentive, though Jinks does not stress this, to treat their captured opponents with a similar lack of respect for their status. All in all, the best outlook is to treat all combatants equally with respect to status, permissions, and rights.

The "Innocence" of Combatants

The immunities of combatants is given additional point by certain ways in which the roles of combatant and noncombatant diverge from the simple domestic model we used in Chapter 6. In the first place, although it is plausible to view the enemy's soldiery as engaged in the violent prosecution of an evil attack that you are legitimately attempting to repel, nonetheless they may in fact be "morally innocent" of such activity under that description. In the terminology of Chapter 6, they may be coerced or deluded fighters. Indeed, given the twin facts of conscription and limited access to information, it may be that very many of the troops are acting under both duress and ignorance. Michael Walzer, as we have seen in Chapter 6, uses these facts to argue for the thesis he calls "the moral equality of soldiers," which effectively absolves combatants of moral responsibility for the wars they fight, though not of responsibility for the way they fight them. For Walzer, the JAB is no concern of theirs, but the JIB is. I have already objected to the Walzer view, and shall criticise this position further in Chapter 11, but here we can at least concede that the facts mentioned make some difference in the way we regard at least many soldiers in war, and some of the soldiers themselves acknowledge this difference by regarding enemy soldiers with a degree of sympathy as people whose plight is similar to their own. This

[24] Derek Jinks, "The Declining Significance of POW Status," *Harvard International Law Journal* 45, no. 2 (2004), pp. 367–442.
[25] See especially ibid., "Conclusion: Towards Protective Parity," pp. 440–442.

regard is sometimes very dramatically, even paradoxically, manifested in battlefield conditions, where soldiers themselves declare informal truces or refuse to fight each other in recognition of their common humanity and common plight. The episode in World War I where British and German soldiers fraternised in no-man's-land during the Christmas of 1914, and even exchanged presents, took photographs, and played soccer together, is well known, but there are many other similar episodes where institutionally sanctioned hostility has given way to recognition of common humanity and common bondage to the war machine. One such case, cited by Grossman, is worth quoting. Henry Metelmann, a German soldier on the Russian front during World War II, explains what happened when two Russians came out of their foxhole during one lull in the fighting:

> ...and I walked over towards them...they introduced themselves...[and] offered me a cigarette and, as a non-smoker, I thought if they offer me a cigarette I'll smoke it. But it was horrible stuff. I coughed and later my mates said "You made a horrible impression, standing there with those two Russians and coughing your head off."...I talked to them and said it was all right to come closer to the foxhole, because there were three dead Russian soldiers lying there, and I, to my shame, had killed them. They wanted to get the [dog tags] off them, and the paybooks....I kind of helped them and we were all bending down and we found some photos in one of the paybooks and they showed them to me: we all three stood up and looked at the photos....We shook hands again, and one patted on my back and they walked away.[26]

When Metelmann learnt, after a brief absence from the battlefield, that the Germans had overrun the Russian position, he found that he felt most concerned about what had happened to the two Russians, in spite of the fact that some of his friends had been killed. Upon learning that the Russians had indeed been killed, Metelmann describes his feelings thus:

> My feeling was very sad. I had met them on a very human basis, on a comradely basis. They called me comrade and at that moment, strange as it may seem, I was more sad they had to die in this mad confrontation than my own mates and I still think sadly about it.[27]

Military propaganda and training do their best to counter such possible bonding by using hate indoctrination, and one of the objectionable features of this is the way it ignores the force of the observation that many soldiers themselves are, to a degree, "victims" of war, or at least of some wars. This response can be overdone, as I shall argue later, but there is enough truth in it to offer support to the idea that some respect and concern is owed to enemy troops as human beings, and to make it plausible that this should be

[26] David A. Grossman, *On Killing: The Psychological Cost of Learning to Kill in War and Society* (Boston: Little, Brown, 1995), pp. 158–159.
[27] Ibid., p. 159.

embodied in restrictions on how they are to be treated, even when they are vital agents in unjust aggression.

We can see the point of this if we return to our original domestic model. The analogy begins with an individual attacked by someone wielding an axe and then rings certain variations on the example to arrive at a number of plausible moral judgements about the individual's entitlement to deploy violence and the limitations upon it. It is then suggested that our intuitions on the individual case are indeed those commonly, and understandably, invoked in the case of states, though of course there are many differences between the ontological status of individuals and that of states. Relationships amongst opposed soldiers return us full circle to the circumstances of the face-to-face analogy, but with a difference. It is as though the axe attacker bears you no particular ill will but has been convinced by plausible lies that you are a notorious hit man on your way to murder his sister; and there are two gunmen behind him who have threatened to kill him, or lock him up, unless he attacks you with his axe. (Perhaps he has been hypnotised or drugged as well, on partial analogy with the effects of media propaganda and ideological indoctrination.) You are still, it seems, entitled to defend yourself from him with violence, and lethal violence if need be, but if you know these facts about his state of mind, you are going to be more sympathetic to the idea that you should treat him as well as possible in repelling his attack. Philosophers who discuss the morality of self-defence have recently been much exercised by discussion of the category of what some have called "innocent threats." One colourful example of this is given by Judith Jarvis Thomson.[28] She imagines that someone bent upon your destruction seizes an innocent passer-by and hurls him (very accurately) over a cliff so that he will land on you as you are sunning yourself on your patio below and kill you. She asserts as a basic intuition that you are clearly entitled to deflect the unfortunate fellow to his certain death on the rocks below by using your sun-umbrella or whatever is to hand. In another variation of the case, you may have some sort of disintegrating gun and destroy the threat that way. I explored some problems related to this in the discussion of "innocent shields" in Chapter 7, and such shields constitute a sort of threat insofar as they threaten to block certain avenues for your self-defence or defence of others. I think that our right to destroy "innocent threats" is more debatable than often supposed in the literature, but in any case we need to distinguish cases more than is sometimes done in that literature. There may be important differences between "innocent threats" who in no sense intend your destruction (like Thomson's passer-by) and "innocent threats" who fully intend to kill you but do so under the illusion that you are a threat to them. There are further differences between those whose illusions are nonculpable and culpable.

---

[28] In Judith Jarvis Thomson, "Self-Defense," *Philosophy and Public Affairs* 20, no. 4 (1991), pp. 283–310.

Then there are those who act under some degree of coercion well short of being thrown at you. With respect to warfare, these sorts of distinctions and their significance were discussed in Chapter 6. Without fully recapitulating that discussion, we may say that enemy soldiers are very seldom "innocent threats" in quite such a full-blooded way as Thomson's passer-by (though the axe-man in our amended example was getting closer to it when we brought in hypnosis and drugs); most of them, after all, fully intend to attack and kill you or your compatriots. Nor, in spite of conscription, are they under the same degree of coercion as the passer-by in the innocent threat example. They may indeed be badly informed or deluded about your status, and it is an important question how responsible they can be held for their ignorance or delusion. But, if they are not full-fledged innocent threats, they might be thought of as coerced or deluded fighters, so that humane attitudes towards their fates would be required even if they had to be attacked and even killed.

It is certainly a fact that the belief that the enemy troops may be, at least partially, victims of their own governments can operate, at the psychological level, to reduce the appetite for cruelty and revenge. It may also work towards the generation of a concern for other harms we produce intentionally without such appetites and for harms that arise unintentionally from other actions of ours, such as highly infectious, or socially disastrous diseases or defects, like typhoid or sterility. Nor can the propensity to create such positive attitudes be viewed as morally irrelevant, since the idea that is so effective is at least closely related to the justificatory core of ideas in the JIB and the JAB. These ideas do not identify the concept range combatant/ noncombatant or the range morally guilty/morally innocent, but this is not to say that there is no connection at all between them. The idea that we are entitled to deal violently with those who are wrongly aiming at our destruction or at the destruction of others who do not deserve such destruction (and are innocent, in that sense) gets much of its force from the paradigm situation that presents this attack as something delivered by an aggressor who acts knowingly and freely. It is true that we also seem to be entitled to defend ourselves even to the death against attackers who are not fully or morally responsible for their attack, such as the insane or the nonculpably ignorant or the coerced. But whatever the interest of deluded and/or coerced assailants, the model for our moral intuitions about legitimate defence properly begins with a malicious attacker, and our intuitions may legitimately require some adjustment the further we get from this model. Indeed, many of the most plausible cases of innocent threats calling for lethal defence also involve standardly culpable agents who have produced the threat at one remove, for example, the politician who has created the threat by misinformation or coercion. When considering the prospect of facing an eight-year-old terrorist child carrying a bomb, our attitudes are understandably, and rightly, different from those we have in reflecting on a confrontation with a mature adult leader of the terrorist group, even if we believe that we are entitled to use lethal force against both in pursuit of protection.[29]

The Criticism of "Unrealism"

Much of the earlier discussion is based on the attempt to gain a deeper understanding of what it is to be a combatant, of the moral relations this might entail, and of the virtues relevant to this understanding and these relations. I can imagine that some might be dismissive of this approach, at least in the case of war and in the case of combatants in particular. A common complaint against what I say is that it is genuinely unrealistic to expect such attitudes to coexist with the prosecution of war.

What is and is not realistic about the provision of moral constraints on the conduct of war was discussed to some extent in an earlier chapter. The complaint of "unrealism" or unfeasibility is legitimate if it establishes that certain demands are literally impossible for human psychology to conform to, but this is a very difficult thing to establish. Even the most bizarre and self-destructive injunctions have found adherents who could, and did, act on them; witness members of religious groups who totally abjure sex, or suicide cults, or people who starve themselves to death. All of these think that some good is worth pursuing at the cost of the certainty or risk of great loss. On the other hand, if the complaint is that the moral constraints are unlikely to be adhered to by a specified group in a particular historical context, a natural reply would be that people are often reluctant to do what is right, but that does not show that it isn't right. There is, I think, a good deal in this natural reply, especially as applied to armies and their leaders; but when we are dealing with institutions, roles, and groups, a problem can arise with making this reply. Valuable institutions can, of course, be corrupted, or may be blinded to moral virtues or demands by historically contingent circumstances, and when corruption or blindness has taken hold, the likelihood that individuals within those institutions will respond to certain moral demands will be reduced. This constitutes no objection to the validity of those demands, though it may raise a partly political question about how best to achieve eventual compliance with them. But if it can be shown that it is in the nature of the institution to resist certain moral demands, and, in particular, that it is the very good the institution serves that creates and sustains that resistance, then this suggests either that the institution is not promoting an important enough good, or that the moral demand is, in some

---

[29] The example is no idle one, since the scourge of lethal children in contexts of political violence is very real, whether in terrorist or combatant-to-combatant settings. For a grim presentation of the problem, see Peter Warren Singer, *Children at War* (New York: Pantheon Books, 2005).

significant and undermining sense, unrealistic. We touch here upon part of the territory often referred to as "dirty hands." This is a territory that is hard to chart and difficult to define. Some see it as a region in which central claims of morality are subordinated to quite different and crucial rational claims; others think of it as a land in which morality is divided against itself. We cannot settle, or even advance, this matter here, though it will be addressed in Chapter 14, but in the case of war, the complaint of unrealism may be meant to indicate the way in which the legitimate imperatives of battle (in a just cause) rightly override the moral considerations presented here about the treatment of enemy combatants.[30]

These imperatives are most likely to take a consequentialist or prudential form (though, it should be noted, I do not think that "dirty hands" problems must involve a clash between duties and consequences; they can sometimes be between duties and duties). It may, for instance, be argued that it is possible to conduct war only if your troops have an attitude of hatred towards the enemy's troops, or, if this is too strong, an attitude of indifference to their well-being. An effective desire to incapacitate and kill will not cohabit with the concerns required by the moral attitudes supported earlier. Military training has often embodied this belief and has sought to counter the reluctance to kill by inculcating hatred of the dehumanised enemy, automatic responses to orders, and the conditioned capacity to deliver death on cue. The success of such training is clearly illustrated in the testimony of one Vietnam veteran:

I yelled "kill, kill" 'til I was hoarse. We yelled it as we engaged in bayonet and hand-to-hand combat drills. And then we sang about it as we marched. "I want to be an airborne ranger... I want to kill the Viet Cong." I had stopped hunting when I was sixteen. I had wounded a squirrel. It looked up at me with its big, soft brown eyes as I put it out of its misery. I cleaned my gun and have never taken it out since. In 1969 I was drafted and very uncertain about the war. I had nothing against the Viet Cong. But by the end of Basic Training, I was ready to kill them.

         –Jack.[31]

According to Grossman, the kind of desensitisation and glorification of killing that Jack was trained in has increasingly been used in combat

---

[30] I have discussed the problem of dirty hands in a number of places. See especially "Messy Morality and the Art of the Possible," *Proceedings of the Aristotelian Society*, supp. vol. 64 (1990), pp. 259–279; "Dirty Hands," in Robert E. Goodin and Philip Pettit (eds.), *A Companion to Contemporary Political Philosophy* (Cambridge, MA: Blackwell, 1993), pp. 422–430; "Politics and the Problem of Dirty Hands," in Peter Singer (ed.), *A Companion to Ethics* (Oxford: Blackwell, 1993), pp. 373–383; and "Dirty Hands," in Laurence and Charlotte Becker (eds.), *The Encyclopaedia of Ethics*, second edition (New York: Routledge, 2001), pp. 407–410.

[31] Grossman, *On Killing*, p. 306.

orientation training. Recalling his own basic training in 1974, Grossman gives an example of one of the running chants used then:

> Iwanna
> RAPE,
> KILL,
> PILLAGE'n'
> BURN, annnnn'
> EAT dead
> BAAA-bies[32]

The complaint that effective fighting requires the development of attitudes of contempt or hatred for the enemy certainly raises interesting psychological and moral issues, and it is hard to know how they should be addressed. I doubt myself that the psychological claim is wholly true. It seems to me more like the mythological thinking that sustains the idea that armies have to be so organised and constituted that ordinary soldiers must become unthinking automata, losing any entitlement to independent thought and action and any claim to democratic treatment. In any case, if the link between effective fighting and inevitable attitudes of contempt or hatred for the enemy were to be established, this might provide yet more ammunition (if I may be excused the metaphor here) for the pacifist's case. Traditional just war theory has always stressed that war must be waged with morally appropriate intentions, and that this must include a love of peace and, for Christians, the traditional love of one's enemies. Modern secular writers echo something like this thought. Thomas Nagel insists that "extremely hostile behaviour towards another is compatible with treating him as a person – even perhaps as an end in himself";[33] and he argues that extreme acts of hostility towards another should still involve certain sorts of moral relations, reference to which, he thinks, is part of the case against such weapons as napalm.[34] Support for the idea of sustaining respect amidst hostility is the argument that morality involves living a certain kind of life, a life of virtue, and so requires the development of strong habits of living well that need to be preserved in some recognisable form even in the extremities of warfare. Nor again is this a purely Western outlook, for it is a perspective that is powerfully present in classical Chinese discussions of ethics and war. (Recall Hsun Tzu's remarks earlier about not despising the enemy and his stress on the role in warfare of the benevolent ruler.) In addition to the loss of autonomy so characteristic of induction into today's armed forces, the physical and psychological dangers of battle, the necessity to kill and

---

[32] Ibid., pp. 307–308.
[33] Thomas Nagel, "War and Massacre," in Marshall Cohen, Thomas Nagel, and Thomas Scanlon (eds.), *War and Moral Responsibility* (Princeton, NJ: Princeton University Press, 1974), p. 14.
[34] Ibid., p. 21.

maim other human beings, and the uncertain benefits of the military outcome, there must now be added the necessity to cultivate vicious states of
mind. As indicated, my own view is that this necessity is largely a dispensable
part of military mythology, but if I am wrong, then we should first seriously
consider the possibility that morality demands that we dispense with the
institution of war rather than acquiesce in pervasively dirty hands whenever
we are drawn into battle. That the frenzied hate mentality is unnecessary, as
well as immoral, is suggested by the memoirs of the British soldier Colonel
Tim Collins, who gave a famous address to the troops under his command
just before they went into battle in Iraq in 2003. Tim Collins's pep talk was
certainly sternly realistic about the need to fight ferociously, but it explicitly disavowed any mindless motives of hatred. Although the speech was
impromptu, a British journalist present recorded it, and it is reproduced in
Collins's memoirs. After stressing that their mission was one of liberation,
not conquest, Collins went on:

> The enemy knows this moment is coming too. Some have resolved to fight and others
> wish to survive. Be sure to distinguish between them. There are some who are alive
> at this moment, who will not be alive shortly. Those who do not wish to go on that
> journey, we will not send; as for the others, I expect you to rock their world. Wipe
> them out if that is what they choose. But if you are ferocious in battle, remember to
> be magnanimous in victory.[35]

Collins goes on to stress that the enemy dead must be treated with respect
and buried with their graves marked, and he rejects "overenthusiasm in
killing" as well as cowardice. He emphasises that the enemy must be given
the right to surrender. These attitudes of a career soldier who served in
various conflict theatres with the SAS and the Royal Irish Regiment provide
striking evidence against the charge of unrealism we have been considering.

In any case, if there are consequentialist arguments against my position, it
can be responded that there are also consequentialist arguments in support
of it. Although I am far from being a consequentialist in ethical theory,
arguments from consequences nonetheless have a legitimate place in moral
reasoning; the consequentialist error is to see room for nothing else. Let
us begin with the treatment of one's own troops. It is surely plausible that
a commitment to respecting the value of the lives of one's own troops is
likely to pay off purely in terms of the loyalty and discipline one can expect
from those troops. It is true that other factors can make for loyalty, or at
least the behavioural equivalent of it, factors such as fear, class deference,
natural conformity, responses produced by drilling, and the irrational belief,
perhaps inculcated by propaganda, that officers are protective of your life
even where they are not. Nonetheless, it is hard to sustain these reactions in

---

[35] Tim Collins, *Rules of Engagement: A Life in Conflict* (London: Headline Book Publishing,
2005), pp. 131–132.

the face of evidence that the lives of troops are regarded lightly, especially when some of the factors, like class deference, have declined in power or disappeared. The practice of "fragging" officers in Vietnam, those who were perceived by ordinary soldiers to be too eager to take risks with their troops' (and sometimes their own) lives, suggests that armed forces can no longer rely on these other factors, or at least not exclusively. It is clear, moreover, that a casual attitude toward the lives of one's troops is grossly inefficient in purely military terms. Even where the killed and wounded troops are readily replaceable, their replacements have to be trained and equipped and are initially less experienced and skilled in combat techniques. Furthermore, the greater the wastage of lives in battle, the more devastating the economic, social, and cultural effects on civilian life are liable to be after the war. There are sometimes compensating effects, to be sure, but they are unlikely to be sufficient to balance fully the damaging consequences.

Even if it is conceded that these consequentialist considerations support a concern for the well-being of one's own combatants, it may be urged that they hardly provide support for a similar concern for the enemy's troops. But this is not so clear, as the quotations from Liddell Hart cited earlier have indicated, since even a relatively self-interested outlook on postwar reconstruction should produce an interest in making it easier for the defeated nation to reintegrate into the community of nations and achieve some degree of economic and political stability, and both of these aims are made increasingly difficult to achieve in proportion to greater levels of enemy combatant casualties. Similar points apply to the use of certain types of weapon that are likely to have long-term physical and psychological effects upon the population of the defeated nation. Biological weapons, for instance, that spread appallingly infectious diseases amongst the enemy's troops, are likely to produce a postwar society that not only damages dreadfully the life prospects of the innocent, such as children, but also creates a profound resentment that may take decades to surface and that may eventually be damaging to important concerns of the conquerors, as well as of others. Something similar is true of the use of land mines. Even where their purpose is principally to attack combatants, they leave an appalling legacy for the people of the country in which they are hidden, a legacy the enormity of which we are only now becoming fully aware. In 1995, the United Nations estimated that there were approximately 120 million land mines worldwide, with deaths and injuries from land mines in the previous few decades totalling in the hundreds of thousands. In Cambodia alone – where there are estimated to be two land mines for every child – more than 35,000 amputees have been injured by land mines. And there are indications that in Afghanistan there may be as many as 300 land mine casualties per month, with half of these being children under the age of eighteen.[36] Given that land mines

---

[36] Figures derived from the online resources of the International Committee of the Red Cross at <http://www.icrc.org>; the United Nations Mine Action Service (UNMAS) at

can lie dormant for decades, their use involves a malicious, enduring, and indiscriminate legacy.

It is difficult to be confident about consequentialist arguments concerning the effects of war policies upon future relations between previously hostile states, because so little is certain about the causes and effects of the complex sociological and psychological phenomena of modern warfare; indeed, we have only recently begun to understand the extent and character of the psychological illnesses that war seems to create in those who fight it. I advance these consequentialist arguments merely to meet some of the opposition on their own ground and to confront them with what I consider plausible considerations, supplementary to the others already advanced.

At this point, the objection needs to be faced that the need to respect the rights of one's own troops is a lesson that has been learned too well. In the debates over military intervention for "humanitarian purposes" in the 1990s, it became increasingly clear that powers with the military and financial muscle to contemplate rescue interventions will only attempt such rescues where there is a virtual guarantee that their own soldiery will suffer few or no casualties.[37] The distance travelled from World War I to Kosovo could not be greater. Certainly, it is true that the taste for indiscriminate sacrifice of the nation's young has changed dramatically, at least in those countries where a secure and relatively affluent life for most in the community has become the norm. In the United States and Western Europe, the opportunities provided by advanced weapon technology have made it possible to believe that significant political, and even ethical, objectives could be achieved without serious risks of casualties to one's own troops. Critics have complained both that this caution has made for too-reluctant a resort to military force in cases where it is morally appropriate and that it has caused the costs, where the resort is forthcoming, to be displaced onto civilian populations. The former problem is that posed by the Rwanda massacres, where, it is argued, an early swift resort to armed force via the supplementation of UN forces already on the ground could have prevented the slaughter of more than 500,000 people. The latter is posed by the relentless NATO bombing of Serbia in the spring of 1999 that resulted in some sort of victory on behalf of the Albanian Kosovars. I say "some sort of victory" because the implications of the Serbian capitulation for the political future of the people of Kosovo,

<http://www.mineaction.org>; and the International Campaign to Ban Landmines at <http://www.icbl.org>.

[37] The recent Iraq war might be thought a counterexample to the propensity for "riskless war," since, unlike the intervention in Kosovo, forces were committed on the ground, and coalition (especially American) troops have suffered relatively heavy casualties during the extended occupation. But the readiness to suffer greater risk to one's own troops is here connected with the widespread, though highly dubious, belief on the part of U.S. troops and the American public that the intervention was not primarily humanitarian but required as part of a defensive war against terrorism.

who are of Albanian, Serb, and Gypsy backgrounds, remain obscure, as do the consequences for regional stability.

The complaints of the critics have a certain weight, but this increased concern for the welfare of one's own troops is in itself surely to be welcomed. As so often, the problem is one of balancing competing values: in this case, the safety of one's troops and the need for preventive violence. My principal point throughout has been to emphasise the need for the rights of combatants to be properly weighed in the balance, since, far too often, they have counted too little in the past. If they sometimes weigh too much in some contexts today, this may require some reconsideration, especially as this bears upon the protection of people at risk who are distant in geography, culture, and appearance from those who may be required to protect them.

This leads to my final point. Aside from certain romantics about war (discussed in Chapter 3), most of those who address the question of war hold that peace is generally preferable to war, both morally and prudentially. As argued earlier, and as will be discussed more fully in Chapter 13, just war theory has to be understood in the light of the ideal of peace. It tells us not to engage in war unless certain hard-to-satisfy conditions are met, and when we do legitimately go to war or make a just revolution, we should be reluctant to act in ways that make peace less achievable and eventually sustainable. There are, of course, arguments against "peace at any price," but we should be anxious not to put needless obstacles in its path, and attitudes of hatred of, contempt for, or indifference to the good of the enemy's troops or civilians are such obstacles.

This point is particularly pertinent to the sorts of military engagements that seem increasingly to be on the international agenda. Recent UN and other collective military operations in disturbed parts of the world have highlighted the ways in which the standard training of soldiers, both in the ranks and in the officer corps, sometimes ill equips them for the role of peacemaking, or even peacekeeping; but they have also highlighted the need, or at least the potential, for troops to play such a role. In such engagements, the nature of "the enemy" is ill defined and hedged about by political, religious, and cultural complexities. If peacemaking is to have any chance of success, or even to make sense, the use of arms will have to have a strong moral component, and the troops who bear those arms (and the military thinkers who decide which arms to supply) will need to be trained in the importance of respecting the dignity of combatants as well as of noncombatants. This requires a complex set of attitudes and dispositions, for in these settings, as in others, a soldier must be trained and ready to kill if that is what is demanded.

10

Morality and the Mercenary Warrior

Mercenaries do nothing but harm.
                              Machiavelli[1]

Mercenary warriors have generally had a bad name over the centuries, and never more so perhaps than in the last third of the twentieth century. My purpose here is to examine both the name and the evaluation. I do this not only because of the considerable intrinsic interest of the topic, but also because I think that such an examination is likely to throw light upon wider issues in the theory of war, and especially upon the ethics of war and the morality of political violence in general. More specifically, closer attention to what is morally distinctive about mercenaries is likely to improve our understanding of the moral status and responsibilities of regular soldiers.

Both the name and the ill repute raise philosophical perplexities. There are underlying puzzles about what we are to understand by the term "mercenary," and there is a deal of obscurity about the source of the obloquy commonly heaped upon those who bear the name. Not that all evaluations have been negative: the supporters of mercenary soldiery include St. Thomas More, whose wise Utopians would do everything they could to avoid sending their own citizens into battle, and so "most of their fighting is done by mercenaries."[2] Indeed, mercenaries have been commonly employed in warfare throughout the centuries. To support or defend mercenaries, however, we need to have at least a rough idea of what they are.

Definition

Problems with the meaning of the word "mercenary" have plagued popular and technical discussions over the centuries and are reflected in much

[1] Niccolò Machiavelli, *The Prince*, ed. Peter Bondanella (Oxford: Oxford University Press, 1984), p. 43.
[2] Thomas More, *Utopia* (Harmondsworth: Penguin, 1974), p. 112.

contemporary debate, especially about legal measures to be taken against mercenaries. There is a strong tendency in the debate to oppose a definition (or an understanding) in terms of *motive* to one in terms of *affiliation*. Motivational definitions focus upon the monetary outlook built into the word, whereas affiliational definitions contrast the mercenary as an alien with the regular soldier as a citizen. For good measure, the motivational element may include a reference to blood lust, though this is usually thought of as a concomitant feature of mercenary psychology rather than as a definitional property.

It should be noted at the outset that the elements of monetary motive and foreign affiliation need not exclude one another. Indeed, the motivational element may be needed in order to distinguish among different sorts of foreign groups serving in a domestic force and thereby to form different moral assessments of them. We may need an element of this kind in order to distinguish, for instance, between the foreign brigades who fought in the Spanish Civil War and various foreigners who were later engaged in warfare in southern Africa. This is a matter to which I shall return. I want now to look at problems raised for the motivational element, problems that are sometimes insufficiently distinguished. There are three principal ones:

1. the difficulty of determining motive;
2. the difficulty of distinguishing between mercenary and regular troops by the motive test; and
3. the difficulty of mixed, complex, and ulterior motives.

The problem posed by (1) particularly exercises lawyers who write on this topic. The *Diplock Report* into the recruitment of mercenaries in the UK complained in 1976 that "any definition of mercenaries which required positive proof of motivation would . . . either be unworkable, or so haphazard in its application as between comparable individuals as to be unacceptable. Mercenaries, we think, can only be defined by reference to what they do, and not by reference to why they do it."[3] Burmester, who quotes this complaint, also endorses it.[4] Yoram Dinstein, discussing the Geneva Protocols of 1977, also objects to article 47 of Protocol 1, which deals with mercenaries, that "the definition hinges on the venal motivation," and he asserts that "this subjective element can rarely be established objectively: who knows what keeps an adventurer on the go? In the final analysis, mercenaries will be placed beyond the pale not because of their frame of mind, but because of that of their judges."[5]

---

3 Report of the committee of privy counsellors appointed to inquire into the recruitment of mercenaries, Cmnd. 6569, paragraph 7, August 1976.
4 H. C. Burmester, "The Recruitment and Use of Mercenaries in Armed Conflict," *American Journal of International Law* 72 (1978), p. 37.
5 Yoram Dinstein, "The New Geneva Protocols: A Step Forward or Backward?," *The Year Book of World Affairs* 33 (1979), p. 273.

In spite of this squeamishness, however, both legal enactments and the popular consciousness still seem impelled to make reference to a motivational element in the meaning of "mercenary." I think that this impulsion is both natural and justified, but my reasons for this will emerge later. For now, it is enough to make two points in criticism of those who dismiss the motivational element on grounds such as (1). The first is that it may be important for understanding our *moral* evaluations of mercenaries that they be characterised, at least in part, in terms of motivation, even if this creates difficulties for the *legal* implementation of whatever moral judgement it is best to make. The second point is that the complaint in (1), though understandable, is far too strong. Motives are not impossible to establish in ordinary life (or we would not be able to use the category as we do), nor are they in general excluded from the determinations of the law. The assessment of conscientious objection to warfare inevitably involves an attempt to determine motive, as do many important questions about mitigation and sentencing in the law at large. Many crimes are so defined that tribunals must determine matters that are either motivational or similarly "subjective," such as whether an accused *intended* to kill. Theft, for another example, is distinguished from related property crimes by the agent's "intent to permanently deprive," and although this may from time to time be difficult to establish, it is not impossible to do so, and the legal system is not excessively embarrassed by the difficulties.

Intentions, motives, and so on are indeed subjective in one sense, namely, that they are (like all other issues requiring *mens rea*) psychological, but this does not mean that they are always, or even often, hidden and mysterious, nor does it mean that they are "subjective" in any sense that implies that we cannot objectively determine their existence and nature from time to time. The legal worries about motive may spring in part from a lingering behaviourist suspicion of mental states and the related idea that anything mental must be a dubious article. This seems to be at work in Dinstein's final remark about "frames of mind." In one sense, it is trivially, and nonalarmingly, true that the frame of mind of a judge determines the outcome of a trial: if he is doing his job properly, he thinks, infers, assesses, and decides in an impartial frame of mind. In another sense, Dinstein's claim is more substantive and more contentious, in that he seems to be suggesting that the judicial determination of motives (or perhaps only of mercenary motives) must be biased. We can certainly imagine circumstantial arguments for this in the case of the trying of mercenaries, but since Dinstein gives none at all, he may well be relying on the confusions I have outlined.

The considerations in (2) are more serious. These allow motive to have been established but claim that it provides insufficient grounds upon which to distinguish mercenaries from regular soldiers. The basic point is just that many citizens may enlist in their national army for financial reward, especially when other opportunities for profit are scarce. Television advertisements for the army offering career and financial inducements seem to support this. It may nonetheless be possible to show that motivational differences of a somewhat more refined kind are capable in general of distinguishing between mercenaries and nonmercenary troops. Perhaps we could make some headway by citing such facts as that mercenaries are usually paid actually to fight, whereas the national soldiery are often paid merely to train and hope that they won't have to fight; and that after the war is over, the national soldiery are not motivated to go looking for another war, whereas the mercenaries characteristically are. Whatever the prospects for this line of inquiry, I will not pursue it further here, since it is at least more plausible initially to exploit my earlier comment about the nonexclusivity of the two elements, and so to conjoin motive and affiliation. We shall see that this needs further explanation as to *point*, but it seems to reflect usage to a considerable extent, since it enables us to make the standard distinction between mercenaries and nonmercenaries just where it is commonly made in historical and contemporary contexts.

The conjoined definition does not, perhaps, provide a perfect fit with usage, because there are certain cases which would be excluded but which would not be in common conversation. Colonel Mike Hoare, for instance, was not, it seems, in the killing business primarily for the money, though most of his military colleagues were. Hoare was supposedly moved by ideological considerations. Does this mean that, unlike most of his men, he was not a mercenary? It all depends. The definition of a concept like "mercenary" is bound to involve a degree of stipulation, since the concept has grown up rather in the way Wittgenstein describes in his discussion of family resemblance, where he talks of concepts developing in the way cities develop by the ramshackle addition of suburbs. We might well say that the conjunctive definition captures the core meaning of the expression, but we can allow that a certain overlapping effect will have Hoare count as a mercenary in ordinary discussions just because he led, recruited, sustained, and approved of genuine mercenaries. Even so, if we learned that he had no interest at all in the money, and was led entirely by ideology, we should be tempted to say, or to make ready sense of others saying, that he was not a true mercenary, but rather a (fairly regular) foreign volunteer. Again, if we accept the romantic picture of the French Foreign Legion as composed of men with criminal or disgraced pasts whose motive for enlisting is the desire to lose themselves and escape their pasts, then we will not classify them as mercenaries.

At this point, it is worth quoting the definition adopted by the Geneva Protocols:

A mercenary is any person who: (a) is specially recruited locally or abroad in order to fight in an armed conflict; (b) does, in fact, take a direct part in the hostilities; (c) is motivated to take part in the hostilities essentially by the desire for private gain and, in fact, is promised, by or on behalf of a Party to the conflict, material compensation substantially in excess of that promised or paid to combatants of similar ranks and functions in the armed forces of that Party; (d) is neither a national of a Party to the conflict nor a resident of a territory controlled by a Party to the conflict; (e) is not a member of the armed forces of a Party to the conflict; and (f) has not been sent by a State which is not a Party to the conflict on official duty as a member of its armed forces.[6]

This is a conjunctive definition in the spirit I have proposed, though it has rather a lot of conjuncts. The extra conjuncts are mostly no more than attempts to spell out what is implicit in the affiliation idea, and where they go beyond that they seem dubiously necessary. Condition (d), for instance, would rule out as a mercenary someone who is a national of state X and has lived abroad for some years but is so indifferent to his citizenship that he cheerfully accepts a lot of money to kill citizens of state X in a war, just as he would citizens of any other state. Such a person surely lacks the relevant affiliation, whatever the legal facts, and is a mercenary, even if he is also something of a traitor. Of course, if we are concerned with the law rather than with common usage, it may be well to distinguish him from other mercenaries for purposes of legal treatment. Condition (e) makes a certain obvious sense, but has in fact been circumvented by mercenary companies, such as Sandline in Papua New Guinea, who make their soldiers part of the recruiting countries' armed forces (in fact, Sandline/Executive Options declared their employees "special constables" in the New Guinea forces). In addition, it should be remembered that many nations, including France and the United States, have not endorsed the terms of article 47 of the Geneva Protocol. Nonetheless, for all of its difficulties, the Geneva definition can serve as a useful yardstick for discussion.

We must also allow weight to (3), which reminds us that individuals act for a variety of reasons, so that monetary interests can coexist with ideological and other more complex motivations. It is perhaps an implicit recognition of this that has the Geneva Protocols incorporating the idea of mercenaries' receiving material compensation "substantially in excess" of that available to normal troops. The idea might be that this guarantees that the monetary element will tend to dominate the other motives they have, or at least constitute a sufficient condition for their fighting. There are interesting causational questions here into which we cannot now enter, such as may arise where, in a particular case, the fighter has a mercenary as well as an ideological reason for fighting, each of which is sufficient and neither of which is therefore necessary for his performance. Cases such as this suggest that we should require a mercenary motive to be a sufficient rather than merely a necessary condition for the agent's performance. On the romantic

[6] Ibid., p. 272. See also "1977 Geneva Protocol I Additional to the Geneva Convention of August 12, 1949, and Relating to the Protection of Victims of International Armed Conflicts, Article 47," in Adam Roberts and Richard Guelff (eds.), *Documents on the Laws of War* (Oxford: Clarendon Press, 1989), p. 414.

interpretation of the Foreign Legionnaire, monetary considerations are not a sufficient condition for him. On the other hand, what do we say of the warrior who makes a lucrative career of independent war fighting, but will only fight on behalf of certain sorts of causes? The lucre is for him insufficient motivation by itself, but it is necessary. He will perhaps fight only on behalf of white racist regimes, but even then only if they pay very well. For the moment, let us say that he is not a mercenary, but return to him later. (It may be that the terminology of necessary and sufficient conditions, so beloved of philosophers, is a little crude for what must be said here.)

Furthermore, once a certain motivation is established as part of the definition of a mercenary, it will receive an institutional embodiment, since mercenaries characteristically have a group existence, fighting in their own corps rather than scattered about amongst regular troops, having a contract with their employers, and so on. This allows for a certain tension or even discordance between the motivations that an individual actually has for fighting and the motivations to which he has institutionally committed himself by publicly joining a mercenary force.[7] So we have the possibility of a variety of what I have earlier called "ulterior" motives actually dominating the monetary one. Consider the following cases.[8] (a) Jones, a wealthy man, joins a mercenary force because his own country is not at war and he is desperate to prove to his domineering father that (contrary to his father's belief) he is not a coward. He signs the mercenary contract for quite large sums but is indifferent to the financial rewards. (b) Smith, an idealist, joins a mercenary force in order to subvert it from within so that the third world country against which the mercenaries are fighting will be successful. In order to do so, he has to sign up and fight against those he is covertly supporting. (c) Brown, a cautious killer, decides that the best mercenary army to join is one that is offering a lucrative contract but, he calculates, very little prospect of actual fighting. Unfortunately, that unlikely prospect eventuates, and then he fights not really for the money but in order to protect his reputation or out of fear.

The institutional facts speak for classifying these men as mercenaries, even if the individual motivational facts do not. I think we should be tempted to say of case (b) that Smith is not really a mercenary, but is merely posing

---

[7] There are certain parallels with the philosophy of language. It is plausible to think that we can define various speech acts by the fact that a speaker intends to secure certain effects in an audience by a recognition of his intention to do so. We may also then try to define certain moods by saying that they either are used by a certain speech community to facilitate some speech act or express a specific communicative intention. But we must acknowledge that some performances of the speech act and some uses of the mood do not involve the relevant intention directly. I can occasionally ask a question without seeking information or speak in the imperative mood with no interest in audience compliance.

[8] My colleague Dr. Bruce Langtry drew a number of the examples that follow (or ones like them) to my attention. I am indebted to him for that, and for vigorous discussion of the conceptual issues generally. I do not know whether he would agree with my proposed solutions.

as a mercenary (especially if he contrives to fire in the air during conflict), though the institutional facts put us under some pressure to say that he has become a mercenary. It is less clear that this response is available in the case of (a), since Jones surely had many other ways of showing his courage, and his adoption of the mercenary style of life seems to involve an actual endorsement of the appropriateness of the motivation built into it, even if it means little to him. But suppose we learnt that he gave most of his income to a charity? As for case (c), the institutional facts do not allow us to say that Brown is not a mercenary since he was prepared, purely for the money, to put himself in a position where he might have to fight, even though other motives took over when the time came. His enlistment and readiness to fight are appropriately motivated. There is a parallel with ordinary soldiers, many of whom enlist in order to defend their homeland, but at times actually fight out of fear of showing cowardice, or for the glory of the platoon, or whatever. For such cases, I should like to say that the specific motive is under the control of the motive which put them into the position and which they have in no way renounced. Renunciation is one way in which such control may be lost, but there may be others.

The relevance of the institutional setting comes out in another way if we consider the example of someone who has the relevant motive but none of the institutional trappings. Green joins the regular army of a foreign power as a volunteer, but only because of the entrepreneurial opportunities that warfare will afford him. He expects to do very well by way of looting and by exploiting to the full other money-making opportunities not available in civil life. He is prepared to kill and maim in the course of doing so. Is Green a mercenary? His motivations tempt one to say that he is, but the lack of an institutional embodiment for them prompts a negative answer. It may also be unclear whether he is affiliated with the nation for which he fights in the appropriate way. I am supposing that he migrates and takes up so-called permanent residence but solely in order to pursue the commercial opportunities already mentioned, and maybe that satisfies the affiliation requirement. It is a further question, of course, whether what any of these people do is wrong.

Morality

Let us begin with Machiavelli, who provides several reasons for objecting to mercenary forces, all of which are moral in a fashion. One of his objections is that they are not sufficiently bloodthirsty for the high purposes of war. He claims, for instance, that the opposing mercenary armies in fifteenth-century Italy would not fight one another seriously. As he puts it in *The Prince*,

... they had used every means to spare themselves and their soldiers hardship and fear, not killing each other in their battles but rather taking each other prisoner without demanding ransom; they would not attack cities by night; and those in the cities would not attack the tents of the besiegers; they built neither stockades nor trenches around their camps; they did not campaign in the winter.[9]

Elsewhere he cites several engagements in which there were hardly any men at arms slain, although there were plenty of prisoners taken. (Prisoners could, of course, be ransomed for good money, though Machiavelli says that the mercenaries did not hold each other for ransom.)

It is interesting to contrast this objection with modern reactions to mercenaries. The modern aversion turns, in part, upon their monetary motivation, but it is not nourished by any belief that they are too pacific! Moreover, there is reason to believe that Machiavelli's factual claims about the nonbelligerent behaviour of the mercenaries of his day are largely false. Machiavelli asserts, for example, of the battle of Anghiari in 1440 that "one man was killed and he fell off his horse and was trampled to death," but modern scholars claim that the losses on both sides were in the vicinity of 900 dead. Of the battle at Molinella in 1467, Machiavelli claims that "some horses were wounded and some prisoners taken but no death occurred," whereas it has recently been argued that the losses were about 600 dead.[10] (If this is right, then Machiavelli may well be putting his theories into practice by disregarding the claims of the moral virtue of honesty in favour of advancing some important political values, i.e., the value – especially to a republic – of a citizens' army.)

Even were Machiavelli right about the relative nonbelligerency of mercenaries, it is not clear that this would constitute a decisive objection to their use. Of course, if a war is worth fighting in a legitimate cause, it is worth prosecuting vigorously with a view to victory. Yet even this has its limits, and that part of just war theory concerned with the conduct of war (the JIB) tries to specify such limits. A good deal turns upon one's general view of warfare, the nature and role of the state, and of political morality. Machiavelli's concern for republican nationalism, and the supreme value he attaches to the preservation of the state and the promotion of its glory, make it understandable that he criticises what he takes to be the inefficiency of mercenaries as agents of state military power. In fact, if one takes a dimmer view of the value and moral significance of war, and views from a wider perspective the effects even of "successful" war, then the fact, if it is a fact, that mercenary war is likely to be less bloody and wholehearted than war between citizen armies imbued with nationalist fervour could be seen as a virtue of it. The fact that the mercenaries had "a military code" arouses Machiavelli's scorn partly because this meant that they subordinated winning at all costs to considerations of how war should be conducted; but in light of the modern experience of warfare, these constraints have something

---

[9] Machiavelli, *The Prince*, p. 45.

[10] See Michael Mallett, *Mercenaries and Their Masters* (London: Bodley Head, 1974), for the citations and the conflicting historical evidence (especially p. 197).

to be said for them, even if there was an element of self-interest in their construction.[11] The horrors of World War I would have been considerably mitigated had commanders had more concern for the welfare and safety of their own troops and lived by a code embodying this concern, one that was shared by the enemy.

Another of Machiavelli's arguments is that, efficient or not, mercenaries cannot be trusted by their employers. If they are inefficient or incompetent, they cannot be trusted to conduct a campaign; if they are competent and efficient, they equally cannot be trusted because their victories will give them too much self-importance and power, and they will soon turn against their employers. Speaking of successful mercenary captains, he says, "you cannot rely upon them, for they will always aspire to their own greatness, either by oppressing you, their master, or by oppressing others against your intentions."[12] There is a good deal of shrewd judgement in this observation, but a problem for the view is that the political temptations of power and success are not restricted to mercenaries. History records many instances of citizen soldiers who have succumbed to them. Machiavelli acknowledges this and insists not only that there should be a citizen army but also that the prince must be at its head, or, in the case of a republic, a citizen, who should be replaced if incompetent, and restrained by laws if successful.[13] But a ruler being personally in charge of his troops in the relevant way has always been fairly rare and is virtually impossible in modern political conditions. The restraints of law offer better prospects in the case of a republic, but even there, the intoxication of power and the elitist mystique of the professional citizen soldier can overthrow them fairly readily, as the recent sad history of Fiji has shown. So, in the contemporary world, the difference between mercenary and other successful military leaders with regard to the temptation to abuse their office for political purposes may normally be insignificant.

Yet Machiavelli has another way of bolstering the claim about unreliability. He argues that the fundamental dispositions of mercenaries make them untrustworthy:

... they are disunited, ambitious, without discipline, disloyal; they are brave among friends; among enemies they are cowards; they have no fear of God, they keep no faith with men; and your downfall is deferred only so long as the attack is deferred; and in peace you are plundered by them, in war by your enemies. The reason for this is that they have no other love nor other motive to keep them in the field than a meagre wage, which is not enough to make them want to die for you.[14]

---

[11] Machiavelli, *The Prince*, p. 45. Machiavelli reports, for instance, that they put certain restrictions on night attacks, encouraged the taking of prisoners, and banned taking the field in winter.

[12] Ibid., p. 42.

[13] Ibid.

[14] Ibid. Virtually the same argument recurs in the *Discourses*, where Machiavelli says that "mercenary troops are useless, for they have no cause to stand firm when attacked, apart from the small pay which you give them. And this reason is not sufficient to make them loyal, or

This argument does, I think, cut rather more deeply, though it builds in certain debatable assumptions, and is open to the immediate retort that much could be remedied by the substitution of substantial for meagre wages. This will not make them positively *want* to die for their employer, but this desire is not particularly common amongst citizen soldiers either. Citizens, in certain circumstances, may be *prepared* to die for the state; more commonly they are *prepared* to risk their lives for it. Substantially rewarded, mercenaries may rise to the latter and might even, where their rewards can go to relatives, lovers, or whatever, rise to the former. In this connection, it is worth recalling that the Geneva Protocols definition quoted earlier defines mercenaries partly in terms of superior wages.

Nonetheless, Machiavelli's point is worth further development. Its fundamental thrust is that mercenaries necessarily lack or may be expected to lack some motive(s) appropriate to engaging in war. Machiavelli characteristically thinks of this motive as loyalty to the ruler or the republic, and a background assumption is that the nation's war will be morally legitimate and hence that the killing of the enemy and the risking of one's own citizens' lives will be justified – the only morally relevant question is how to guarantee loyalty to the cause.[15] But this perspective is contentious, to say the least, and reflects views about the justification of war and its methods that one need not adopt. From the perspective of most versions of just war theory, even those whose basis is entirely utilitarian, many nations have been, and will be, unjustified in resorting to war because their reasons are of the wrong kind (the right kind will be spelled out in the JAB), and quite frequently some of their ways of conducting the war, whether it was initially justified or not, will deserve moral condemnation (the basis of which is provided by the JIB). Against this background, a soldier should be motivated to fight by a reason that is at least consistent with the justification for war fighting provided by the theory. Even those who urge (mistakenly, in my view, as I have elsewhere argued)[16] that the citizen should not apply just war theory himself to determine the justness of a particular war in which he or she is called upon to fight, nonetheless concede as much because they typically argue that the citizen can assume that the ruler has done the application

---

to make them so much your friends that they should want to die for you." *The Discourses of Niccolo Machiavelli*, vol. 1, ed. and trans. Lesley J. Walker (London: Routledge, 1950), p. 311.

[15] This way of putting the point might be thought dubious in view of Machiavelli's views on the relation between morality and politics, but, for our purposes, a clarification of those views is unnecessary. Whatever precisely Machiavelli thought about morality, he certainly thought that political policies and actions could be judged as correct or incorrect, justified or unjustified. Unless we are ourselves Machiavellians, we do not have to operate with *his* qualms or abide by *his* reservations about *our* terminology.

[16] See Chapters 6 and 11 of this volume and also C. A. J. Coady, "The Leaders and the Led: Problems of Just War Theory," *Inquiry* 23 (1980), pp. 275–291. Michael Walzer is one of those urging the view that I criticise in that paper.

and can be trusted to have got it right. No doubt there are some differences between the motivations appropriate to ruler and citizens in the case of war waging, and that is why I have said "consistent with," though I am tempted to say, more strongly, "dominated by." There are murky waters here through which I do not see clearly enough. Consider someone who thinks that his country's war is just, and that citizens may fight in a just war, but fights himself only because he is conscripted. Does he have a morally wrong motive for fighting? If he would not fight in an unjust war, even if conscripted, then I think we should probably answer "no"; if he would, then perhaps "yes." The first answer, however, suggests that, contrary to the hypothesis, part of his motive for fighting is that the war is just. These considerations indicate that "consistent with" is too weak and that "dominated by" is too strong; the citizen's motives for fighting should at least be under the supervision of his considered belief that the war is just. Absent that belief, he will not fight; with it, he may or may not fight, depending on other motivations. Given these qualifications, we may proceed as though someone's motives for war fighting must include the complex of beliefs and desires that go with his considered judgement that the war is just. It is against this background that I will use such phrases as "lacking the motive appropriate to war."[17]

Someone who hires his gun to the highest bidder or, less dramatically, fights predominantly for money will typically lack the motive appropriate to war, as specified by just war theory. When a just war theorist like Vitoria objects to mercenaries, toward the end of the sixteenth century, this seems to be what he has in mind: "Those who are prepared to go forth to every war, who have no care as to whether or not a war is just, but follow him who provides the more pay, and who are, moreover not subjects commit a mortal sin, not only when they actually go to battle, but whenever they are thus willing."[18] Vitoria's reference to the mercenary not being a subject is very interesting here and echoes my point about affiliation. In his mind, it is probably connected both with the idea of right authority (though of course a ruler could declare a war and then hire mercenaries) and with the idea that a subject may be more concerned with the justice of the war, either directly or vicariously through his dutiful reliance upon the ruler's wisdom.

Whatever the merits of this thought, it is clear that a restrictive attitude towards just war thinking, such as that I have been defending in earlier chapters, will be concerned, like Vitoria, with those who follow the warpath solely for monetary reward. If, as much modern just war theory seems to maintain, the only legitimate justification for war is essentially defensive,

[17] I am again considerably indebted to Bruce Langtry for a discussion of these issues of moral motivation. The counterexample to the domination of the just war motive was suggested by him.

[18] Francisco de Vitoria, *De Bello*, in James Brown Scott (ed.), *Francisco De Vitoria and His Law of Nations* (Oxford: Clarendon Press, 1934), art. 1, para. 8.

then someone who is not a citizen of the state being defended against attack may be presumed unlikely to have the sort of solidarity with and stake in the well-being of the community under threat that would provide appropriate motive for killing on its behalf. Unlikely, perhaps, but not impossible. If we add that such a person fights principally for money, then we can be pretty sure that he lacks the motive appropriate to war. We then have a ready demarcation of a group of people whose participation in war is very likely to be immoral. Hence the point of our conjunctive definition. Of course, the mercenary motive by itself will theoretically pick out such a class, as will the blood-lust motive, but it is not surprising that we tend to give the benefit of doubt to a citizen who fights in a just war of communal self-defence, even though we may know that some are fighting only for money, and some for the joy of killing. So the conjunctive definition picks out a class of war fighters whose motivations are very unlikely to be morally appropriate to war, but it doesn't, of course, mean that they are the only category of immoral warriors. Volunteers who fight unpaid in order to slake a blood lust are under a similar condemnation, as are those whose motives are the concern for expansionist glory, though neither group count as mercenaries. The commercial motive is not the only one that can make participation in war suspect.

Moreover, there is an important caveat to be made in this connection about the significance of the affiliation condition, since membership in a nation, a state, or some similar political entity does not carry solely benign significance in the context of a discussion of appropriate motives for war fighting. We have been forcefully reminded of this in recent years by the ghastly phenomenon of "ethnic cleansing" in places such as Bosnia, Rwanda, and Kosovo. In all these places and others, nationalist, tribal, and ethnic zealotry have made mercenary motives seem almost agreeable by comparison. Certainly, nationalism and its relatives can provide a sort of absolutism about the waging of war that the mercenary motive usually doesn't: where the national or ethnic zealot demonises his enemies and seeks their total destruction, the mercenary may be less prone to the passions that drive such pictures and policies. This qualification about affiliation is important and shows that the moral force of the affiliation part of the conjunction underlying the use of the expression "mercenary soldier" is relatively weak, though it still carries some weight.

At this point, it is appropriate to shift focus a little, because my emphasis upon motivation and the subsequent orientation of the discussion towards the immorality of an individual's engaging in war fighting from certain motives may seem altogether too personal or individualistic a stress, especially when we are concerned with something as socially ramified and morally problematic as war. My emphasis is not, of course, accidental. It emerges naturally from the history of discussion of mercenaries and from the attempt to gain some conceptual clarification of that discussion, and it aims to show the moral point of the revulsion that is widely felt for those agents who are mercenaries. Nonetheless, I do not mean the analysis to be indifferent to more global concerns about the morality of war, such as the desire to limit the resort to war and to ensure that when wars are fought, one of the sides is justified in its resort to lethal violence. The connections are complex, but there are two strands that deserve special scrutiny here.

The first concerns the fact that an emphasis upon the moral motivations of ordinary agents should be crucial to the ethics of war. By "ordinary" agents I mean those who are not rulers but are called upon by rulers to fight the wars. There are grounds in general moral theory and in democratic political theory for being concerned that those who are called upon to fight exercise moral discrimination and judgement about whether they should respond to the call. They are, after all, being required to kill, maim, and to risk their lives and health, as well as to risk damaging important relations with their families and other dependents. I have argued elsewhere that it is a defect of much just war theory that it is addressed only to the rulers, and that there are good moral grounds for insisting that its appeal cannot be so restricted. The second strand insists that this concern with motivation and belief connects with the more global interest in limiting wars. It is surely plausible that the emphasis upon the need for an individual to have appropriate beliefs and motivations will also lead to less enthusiasm for the prosecution of wars that it is unjust to fight. At least this will be so if the individual is required to subject the beliefs that inform his or her motives to rational scrutiny, and if this requirement is an accepted part of the public culture, for this can be expected to mitigate the countervailing tendencies of righteous fanaticism that the rhetoric of "just cause" can sometimes provoke.

The move from the moral dubiousness of certain individual motives to the level of the social reality of war raises another interesting set of issues concerning the relation between the judgement and motives of the political leadership and those of the warriors they use. Some of these involve the problems of conscription and conscientious objection to be discussed in Chapter 11. More pertinent, in the case of mercenaries, is the situation in which the ruler (let us call her) has good reason to believe that a war is justified but has no means to fight it except by recourse to mercenaries. We may suppose that the ruler's small but wealthy state is about to be invaded by a ruthless and unscrupulous neighbour, bent upon taking over the country, enslaving its population, and acquiring its wealth. The target state has only minimal, ill-prepared defence forces, and the ruler is preparing for an heroic but doomed defence when her eyes light upon a copy of *Soldier of Fortune* magazine. She finds an advertisement of the "have gun and friends, will travel for money" variety. She has done a course in moral philosophy, and is persuaded by the sort of arguments presented earlier that it is wrong for mercenaries to engage in warfare; but, unlike Machiavelli, she believes that they would be effective, perhaps decisive, in fighting in what is objectively a just cause. What should she do?

It might be suggested that the reputable motives of the ruler sanctify, or otherwise ameliorate, the reprehensible motives of the mercenaries she employs. This seems to me a dubious route to take. The ruler's motivations are certainly good, on our supposition, but they do not *thereby* change or even affect the motives of the mercenaries she employs. What is more arguable is that the ruler's good intent makes irrelevant, for her, the bad purposes that move the mercenaries she employs. On the assumption that Machiavelli's worries about the inefficiency, treachery, and so on of mercenaries do not here apply, why should the ruler worry about their bad motives? Consider a parallel with a small-scale individual resort to self-defensive violence. I am being attacked by an aggressor with an axe, and am doing poorly in the struggle when a powerful passer-by offers to come to my aid for a large financial consideration. I may think him ignoble for not wanting to help me simply because I am an innocent under attack (which is, we may suppose, obvious), but why should I reject such aid, even if it is badly motivated? It is indeed true (to preserve the parallel) that he would as soon kill me for the money as my attacker, but that is not pertinent to my survival here, since I am doomed anyway. We are certainly entitled to take advantage of the wrongdoing of others in a variety of contexts – for instance, where my exposure of a political opponent's villainy will advance the good policies I invariably represent by showing that he is the wrong person to elect. The present case is more interesting in that I am actively contributing to an immoral performance by satisfying the suspect motive. I am knowingly providing an inducement to immorality.

One reason that we are unhappy to countenance such activity is broadly consequentialist: encouraging wrongdoing may here have a happy outcome, but on a more general view it's a bad idea. No doubt this more general view is pertinent to my predicament, but it may be thought hardly decisive. Returning to my ruler, she may similarly think that it is a bad idea to employ mercenaries, both for consequentialist and for other, more morally internal reasons, but when her country's survival (or my personal survival, in the individual case) is at stake, then the immorality must be endured. On this construal we have an interesting case of "dirty hands," and, one might think, a more plausible one than some in the literature. As I have presented them, the two examples may leave the impression that the individual and the ruler in their extreme situations need have no qualms whatsoever about their resort to the mercenary killer, and hence that their joining in a joint enterprise with those whose motivations are evil is a matter of no importance.

I think there are two thoughts that contribute to this impression. One is, of course, the overwhelming stakes of survival that are at issue, and the other is the fact that neither I nor the ruler is originating the corruption of our fellow agents. On the second thought, we may take it that if the mercenaries were not fighting in our just conflict, they would be off fighting other battles for money, and, given the scarcity of just causes, these would probably not have the justification that ours has. Even so, I do not think we can enlist their aid entirely without qualm, as the following considerations suggest. First, we may imagine that there are other fighters available who lack the suspect motives: these might be members of the organisation "Just Warriors Inc.," who fight for pay, but only in what they determine to be a just cause. Supposing them equal in efficiency to the mercenaries, the ruler should surely prefer them (just as, in the context of the axe attack, I should prefer the aid of the police). Or consider the sort of thing that arose at the height of U.S. Cold War hostility to Cuba, when the assassination of Fidel Castro became a priority for agencies of the U.S. government. Apparently, serious negotiations were begun with organised crime leaders with a view to hiring professional criminal hit men for the job. Assuming that assassination can sometimes be morally legitimate, and (more dubiously still) that Castro constituted such a legitimate target, can we go further and say that it is a matter of moral indifference whether the U.S. government has recourse to a criminal professional killer? I doubt it.

It is interesting to speculate on whether there is a more general moral lesson to be drawn from our exploration of mercenary motives. If mercenary motives undermine the moral significance and justification of soldiering, might they not do the same for other activities? I think that this is plausible for a whole range of human activities, though the undermining is less dramatic and perhaps less significant in some cases than in others. Let me suggest a few areas: sex, medicine, friendship, parenthood, and sport. Of these, the analogy between mercenaries and prostitutes, though limited in certain respects, has not escaped notice in the literature on mercenaries, though it does not seem to have been explored seriously.[19] The commercialization of sport has drawn some attention, and perhaps here, as in the case of sex, the undermining (if it exists) may be more that involved in the abandonment or deterioration of an ideal than in the destruction of a moral standard. What seems likely is that some relationships or activities can hardly exist in a mercenary form (witness friendship); others can exist but are morally blighted in their mercenary forms (witness war and possibly sex); others can exist and are not exactly morally blighted but are in some degree morally tainted by the dominance of the commercial motive (witness, I suggest, much of modern sport). I shall not explore these interesting issues here, though I have made a faltering start on the prostitution question elsewhere.[20]

---

[19] One book on mercenaries, for example, published in the 1970s, was called "The Whores of War." See Wilfred Burchett and Derek Roebuck, *The Whores of War: Mercenaries Today* (Harmondsworth: Penguin, 1977).

[20] C. A. J. Coady, "Mercenary Morality," in A. G. D. Bradney (ed.), *International Law and Armed Conflict* (Stuttgart: Franz Steiner Verlag, 1992), pp. 65–66. Recent philosophical writing on prostitution is relevant here. See especially Karen Green, "Prostitution, Exploitation and Taboo," *Philosophy* 64 (1989), pp. 525–534.

Further Complications

Returning now to mercenaries, I want to examine some complications to the picture of mercenary warriors that have arisen from recent developments in the area. These complications affect both our definitional and moral analyses. I spoke earlier of the institutional embodiments of the mercenary motivation, and these have of course been significant since ancient times – in the late medieval period, mercenary groups were often known as "companies." The international vogue, beginning in the 1980s, for construing all institutions on the model of the business corporation has had its impact on the phenomenology of mercenary warriors, many of whom are now likely to wear business suits rather than scruffy jeans or combat fatigues and to manage their conflict interventions from a suite of offices in London or Washington. The parallel late twentieth-century vogue for the privatisation and "downsizing" of all public institutions has also operated to produce mercenary companies that employ senior ex-military personnel from significant national forces who are very well connected with their own national military establishments, and often with several other national military establishments.[21]

Two preeminent examples of this trend are Executive Outcomes (EO) and Military Professional Resources Incorporated (MPRI). The former, based in the United Kingdom and South Africa, is basically a product of the changes in South African politics during the 1990s, which saw an exodus from the South African armed forces of highly trained soldiers who wanted to continue a military career but, for various reasons, were not able or willing to do so in the national forces of South Africa. Although EO was formally dissolved early in 1999, its disappearance was more apparent than real, since its functions have been largely devolved to companies that were previously constituents or associates of EO. This fact was overlooked by those who hailed the formal demise of EO as marking a decline in the influence of the modern mercenary corporation. MPRI is largely a product of Pentagon downsizing subsequent to the ending of the Cold War. These people see themselves as the complementary "private sector" to the governmental "public sector" in the provision of lethal services, much as private buses supplement public buses in the provision of transport services. One difference is that MPRI claims to offer only military training and support and does not admit to direct involvement in war fighting, whereas EO, though somewhat shy about making a full admission, has clearly been involved in fighting. The financial arrangements of the companies are quite complex, and EO is part of, or associated with, a web of companies that deal in energy

---

[21] The definitive contemporary analysis of the new mercenaries is Peter Warren Singer's, *Corporate Warriors: The Rise of the Privatized Military Industry* (Ithaca, NY: Cornell University Press, 2003).

and minerals. The existence of these sophisticated mercenary organisations has certain benefits for powerful states. Chief amongst these are the potential they provide for sponsoring military activities without endangering the safety of one's own troops, and a parallel capacity for "deniability" when sponsoring policies that may misfire. Accompanying the development of these corporate militias is some sign of an increased commitment to professionalisation, so that the mercenary motivation amongst their soldiery will often include the desire to perform well as a professional soldier, albeit operating in the private rather than the public sector.[22] How do these developments affect my discussion?

The principal effect is upon the affiliational condition. As already mentioned, its role in my discussion is relatively weak; it acknowledges that, in ordinary discourse, in addition to being seen as dominated by the money motive, the mercenary is seen as nationally unattached as far as his military commitments go, and it seeks to show that there is some moral point to this lack of attachment. But this is precisely where it is relatively weak. The point is simply that the national affiliation can help establish a legitimate motive for war fighting via the notion of national self-defence. But there are two reasons why this is morally weak. First, there may be legitimate war fighting that is justified by considerations other than self-defence, such as humanitarian interventions (discussed in Chapter 4); and second, to the degree that the private military sector becomes respectably institutionalized and professionalized, then to that degree it may become more susceptible to the idea that its "workers" should fight only for reasons that are dictated by just war theory. This raises the prospect that the moral force of an affiliational condition may be satisfied by attachment to the private organisation rather than to the nation. Indeed, one can imagine the situation, though it is hardly present yet, in which members of mercenary corporations are more likely to have just cause and fight justly than many members of tribal or national entities. One thing that makes this more plausible is that they are less likely to be exposed to the nationalist or tribal passions, mentioned earlier, that themselves militate against the appropriate motives for justified war.

A further shift in focus on mercenary activities prompted by the emergence of the "corporate warriors" is away from being concerned exclusively with direct participation in lethal activities and toward involvement in a variety of important military support roles. The private companies engage in such roles as engineering construction, provisions of meals, interrogation, intelligence gathering, and military training. MPRI, for instance, in spite of its public denials, is widely believed to have been behind the transformation of the Croatian army into an effective fighting force that defeated the

---

[22] For another excellent discussion of the new mercenaries, see David Shearer, *Private Armies and Military Intervention* (Oxford: Oxford University Press, 1998).

Bosnian Serb troops in 1995. MPRI's public reticence may be related to the
fact that the Croatian offensive "Operation Storm" was in violation of a UN
ceasefire, created 170,000 new refugees, and involved numerous human
rights violations that resulted in the indictment of Croatian commanders by
the International War Crimes Tribunal. MPRI was subsequently contracted
to train the Bosnian army and has training roles in Macedonia and Kosovo.

Moved by the fact that the corporate mercenary companies seem to be
here to stay and – aided by global economic, political, and military trends –
may well grow and consolidate, some voices that might normally be expected
to be critical of mercenaries have recently been raised on their behalf. David
Shearer, for instance, has argued that the "time has come to begin a policy
of constructive engagement with military companies. Doing so may create
possibilities for these companies to complement international and regional
peace-keeping efforts."[23] Given my earlier account of the moral implications of mercenary warfare, there must be some presumption against this
accommodation, but it is not an irrebuttable presumption, and some of the
considerations advanced earlier make the idea that mercenaries in their
modern form could be justifiably employed seem at least worth discussing.
Just as the idea that businesses exist only to make a profit and that therefore
their only moral responsibility (beyond the requirements of enacted law) is
to maximise profits for shareholders has come to seem profoundly inadequate as an account of the ethics appropriate to garden variety businesses,
so it may be that ethical criteria can be built into commercial soldiery. This
prospect may be made even more palatable by the fact that the modern mercenary has been trained as a professional in standing national armed services
and that, at least in many countries, this has imbued a sense of profession-
alism and some concern for the ethics appropriate to it. Certainly, in many
Western countries the training of officers has in recent decades become
more and more concerned with imparting a fairly broad general education,
and this frequently includes some exposure to the international laws of war,
just war theory, and other elements of military ethics. Shearer's proposal
may well be able to build upon this element to eliminate the residual moral
significance placed upon the affiliation requirement or to redirect it from
nations to the companies. In addition, whatever professional motivations
can be discovered in, or introduced into, the operations of such companies
will work to mitigate the negative ethical features noted by such theorists
as Vitoria. If so there may be certain practical advantages to the resort to
mercenaries in certain circumstances.

There are, however, many reasons for scepticism about this more accommodating attitude towards mercenaries. One reason is the relative absence
of legal restraints on the conduct of the new mercenary companies. Resort
to the restraining and controlling power of professional ethics makes sense

---

[23] Ibid., p. 76.

when professions operate against a background of legal regulation, the slack in which is taken up by professional codes and ethical training. Medical ethics is an important contributor to good medical behaviour, because laws can do only so much, and too much law can inhibit truly moral motivation. But with little or no legal framework to deal with palpable abuses, the efficacy of professional ethics in medicine or elsewhere would be greatly reduced. There are legitimate fears that the rate of proliferation of military outsourcing has now outstripped the reach of domestic and international law.[24] Part of this difficulty arises from uncertainty about the status of these outsourced operators who operate beyond the reach of normal military law, and this provides another reason for doubt about the more sympathetic moral view of modern mercenaries. The term "contractors" both symbolizes and adds to the confusion. In the occupation of Iraq following the invasion of March 2003, the invading forces employed contractors for a bewildering variety of tasks, many of them apparently innocuous (such as cooking) but all contributing directly or indirectly to the goals of the military occupation. Continued reference to these contractors as "civilians" obscures this fact and the moral status of the contractors in what is clearly a theatre of war. Some of the less innocuous tasks make this very clear, since contractors are employed for "security" purposes and are used to conduct interrogations. The U.S. company CACI International has admitted to involvement in interrogation work since the mid-1990s and has been implicated in the U.S. army's investigation into the notorious interrogation abuses at Abu Ghraib in Iraq.[25] It clearly makes a big difference to assessment of the morality of attacks on contractors in Iraq or elsewhere whether they are to be viewed as civilians or mercenaries or mere adjunct national soldiers (see below). Western press reports of such attacks usually treat the contractors as civilians, with the implication that they are noncombatants and that the attacks are terrorist atrocities. If they were genuine noncombatants, then, on my account of terrorism and of noncombatant immunity, the attacks would be rightly condemned. But if insurgents attack an interrogation team engaged in, or supporting, systematic torture of prisoners, then talk of "civilian contractors" merely obfuscates the moral facts. Nor is the distinction between "offensive" and "defensive" roles much to the point. The contractors in Iraq sometimes invoke this distinction in order to mitigate their role in the armed conflict, but providing armed security for what is a legitimate military target for insurgents can hardly make you a noncombatant.

A further reason for caution about the more sympathetic approach to modern mercenaries is the fact that many of these private warriors now work

---

[24] See, for instance, the comments of the Duke University law professor Scott Silliman reported in the Melbourne newspaper *The Age* (sourced from the *Baltimore Sun*), May 6, 2004, under the heading "Civilian Contractors Raise Doubts on Accountability."

[25] Ibid.

predominantly (or often enough) for their own governments. This means that they are just as likely to be exposed to patriotic or nationalist passions as their fellow citizens in the public army. This has two related consequences, one definitional and one moral. The first is that the affiliation condition is more plausibly satisfied as a national affiliation, so that we may (for the relevant conflicts) better view them not as mercenaries but as adjuncts of the standard military. The second is that, even if we continue to classify them as mercenaries, they no longer have any moral advantage based upon their not being subject to the nationalist passions that can militate against the appropriate motives for justified war. Moreover, as already noted, their twilight status means that they may be even less subject to the constraints of military codes and military law than the regular troops. Perhaps this situation could be improved in future, as Shearer hopes, but the prospects do not look bright. The recent exposure and prosecution of a private American group in Afghanistan who had set up their own "military" prison and were torturing inmates is a grim reminder of the difficulties involved in dealing with modern mercenaries. This case also raises in sharp relief the problem of official military complicity in such activities, since the mercenaries claim and the officials deny that U.S. authorities informally authorised the activities.[26]

The Law

I have no space for a full treatment of the way in which national and international law has attempted to deal with the problem of mercenaries, but let me briefly make a few all-too-general remarks. A very good discussion of the background facts and some of the theoretical implications may be found in Burmester's article cited earlier. As he argues, there seems to have been an interesting shift in the basis of legal measures against mercenaries in the second half of the twentieth century. Traditional treaty and other legal restrictions were generally aimed at preventing the recruitment or organising of mercenaries and imposed obligations upon states not to allow this to happen within their territories. Such obligations were rationalised as requirements of a proper neutrality, and extended beyond mercenaries to any armed forces.[27] More recently, the expression and rationale of such legal restrictions have made reference less to the requirements of neutrality and more to the perceived need to limit the resort to warfare altogether.

The experience of modern warfare and the influence of the changed attitude toward war contained in the UN Charter and various UN declarations and resolutions are probably responsible for this shift, and we noted

---

[26] Keith B. Richburg, "In Kabul, Private Jail Leads to Trial," *Washington Post*, August 16, 2004.
[27] See, for instance, articles 4 and 6 of the 1907 *Hague Convention Regarding the Rights and Duties of Neutral Powers and Persons in Case of War on Land.*

in an earlier chapter the different moral attitudes embodied in modern just war thinking and in Machiavelli and later raison d'etat theory.[28] A recent landmark decision that is clearly influenced by this shift in thinking is the International Court of Justice's findings in the case brought by Nicaragua against the United States. The court held that the U.S. government had violated a customary norm (corresponding to the nonuse of force norm in article 2 (4) of the UN Charter) prohibiting the use of force in international relations by, amongst other things, arming and training the contras. It also found that the United States had violated the principle of nonintervention in the internal affairs of a sovereign state by its support for the contras. The court's decisions were not unanimous, but they were overwhelming; on both the above-mentioned counts, the verdicts were twelve to three, with Judges Oda, Schwebel, and Sir Robert Jennings in the minority. It is unclear that all the contras were mercenaries, but the principles applied by the court are nonetheless relevant to the basis of national and international laws about mercenaries.

Two important issues about the legal treatment of mercenaries that arise in the legal literature and in practical politics are:

1. Should governments legislate directly against mercenaries themselves or restrict legislation to prohibiting recruitment, organisation, and so on?
2. How should mercenaries be treated under the laws of war?

With regard to (1), the British legislation in force on this matter, as far as I can ascertain, is still the 1870 Foreign Enlistment Act, which, unlike some modern legislation, does make enlistment as a mercenary a criminal offence. It has a number of anachronistic features, however, and does not prohibit recruitment activities. Lord Diplock's inquiry in 1976 produced a report that, *inter alia*, recommended abolition of the enlistment offence and replacement of it with prohibition of recruitment activities in the UK. The report has not to date been implemented. In the United States, it is an offence both to recruit (though not to advertise) and also to enlist; in contrast to the UK, however, enlistment is an offence only if it occurs within the United States. Recent Australian legislation is, in some respects, wider in scope than that of the UK and the United States. The Crimes (Foreign Incursions and Recruitment) Act of 1978 (Cth.), as amended by The Crimes Legislation Amendment Act 1987 (Cth.), prohibits both "incursions into foreign states for the purpose of engaging in hostile activities" and "recruitment" within Australia of persons who are to engage in such activities and

---

[28] An interesting discussion of changes in just war theory over the centuries and a comparison of just war theory in its different forms to raison d'etat and holy war theories is to be found in James T. Johnson, *Ideology, Reason and the Limitation of War* (Princeton, NJ: Princeton University Press, 1975).

of persons "to serve in or with an armed force in a foreign State."[29] These prohibitions are subject to various exclusions, and the exclusions as well as the debate in the commonwealth Parliament make it clear that "the need to preserve international relations" (as the then attorney-general, Senator Durack, put it in his second-reading speech)[30] rather than an emphasis upon neutrality was the basis for the legislation. It was, said Senator Durack, "a significant contribution to the Government's overall objective of dealing with all manifestations of terrorism and other resorts to violence whether in Australia or in other parts of the world."[31] One of the problems with legislation that attempts to proceed against the mercenaries themselves has been felt to be the danger of overly restricting the liberty of citizens. The Australian legislation expressly allows an Australian citizen to enlist in the armed forces of another country, though it prohibits anyone recruiting such a person to do so. The permission was granted, according to Senator Durack, because citizens "may wish to enlist and serve in the armed forces of another country because of a deeply held personal belief. To prohibit this generally would be a prohibition of individual freedom."[32] No doubt. But equally intrusive, presumably, is the prohibition on someone with deeply held personal beliefs *recruiting* others with such beliefs. Nor is it clear why such deeply held beliefs are entitled to respect only when they lead to enlistment in the armed forces of another country rather than in a revolutionary group, which may well have right on its side. The case of East Timor shows that such questions are of more than abstract importance. But liberal attitudes towards "deeply held personal beliefs" that produce military consequences have in any case come under increasingly strain since the events of September 11, 2001.[33]

As for mercenaries and their treatment under the laws of war, there has been a strong movement to exclude them from the category of persons to whom such laws apply. The Geneva Protocols, for instance, while extending the status of combatant and prisoner of war to favour guerrilla warfare, specifically exclude mercenaries from the benefits of categorizations such as POW status.[34] In line with my argument in Chapter 9, I regard this exclusion as a mistake. Apart from its dubious significance, given the protections afforded by other international instruments, it is likely to be counterproductive. If mercenaries behave particularly savagely now, it is surely plausible that their behavior will be even worse if they know that their opponents are determined to deny them legal rights that other fighters have. We should also be

[29] See Crimes (Foreign Incursions and Recruitment) Act, 1978 (Cth.), s. 6, 7, 8, 9.

[30] *Hansard Parliamentary Reports*, March 7, 1978, Senate, p. 363.

[31] Ibid., p. 364.

[32] Ibid.

[33] The fact that David Hicks could not be presented under Australian law for enlisting with the Taliban in Afghanistan is one reason for the Australian government's inertia concerning this Australian's prolonged incarceration at Guantanamo Bay.

[34] Geneva Protocols, article 47 (1).

clear that the exclusion of mercenaries from the category of "combatant" is not intended to include them in the category of "noncombatant." Under the *jus in bello*, this would be to give them more privileges, not fewer, than combatants. It is better to treat the combatant/noncombatant distinction as both exclusive and exhaustive in the domain of warfare (no matter how hard it is to decide borderline cases). Talk of mercenaries as "mere criminals" does not seem to be sufficiently enlightening here, because there is a good case for saying the same of ordinary soldiers who violate the laws of war or who knowingly and willingly fight in a war that their nation or group is waging unjustly. There are some parasitic figures in warfare who need to be treated as "mere criminals," such as looters, black marketeers, and some arms dealers, but these clearly fall into a different category than the fighters themselves, whether regular troops, guerrillas, or mercenaries.

11

Objecting Morally

His power of choice he thrust on the police
As if it burnt his hands; he gave the banks
His power to work; then he bestowed with thanks
His power to think on Viscount Candlegrease. . . .

Strong in his impotence he can safely view
The battlefield of men, and shake his head
And say, "I know. But then what can I do?"
John Manifold, "The Deserter"[1]

Michael Walzer has argued that membership in the political community entails in certain circumstances an obligation to die for the state.[2] In this, he follows Hobbes, and to a greater degree Rousseau, though like Hobbes, but for somewhat different reasons, he is uneasy with the obligation and, in the upshot, hedges it in various ways. Hobbes and Rousseau are not (unlike Walzer) conspicuous contributors to, or advocates for, just war theory, and this is, I believe, significant, since adherence to just war theory makes it difficult to maintain an unqualified commitment to the obligation. Indeed, some of the most significant challenges to at least the scope of the obligation have come from conscientious objectors who do not reject war altogether, and often rely upon a just war perspective to legitimate their refusal of service. In what follows, I shall examine some of the problems raised by the idea that governments should legally accommodate such challenges in a nonpunitive way. Let us begin with Hobbes's discussion of the alleged obligation to die for the state.

[1] The Australian poet John Manifold wrote this poem during World War II. It is included in Victor Selwyn (ed.), *The Voice of War: Poems of the Second World War* (London: Michael Joeseph, 1995).

[2] Michael Walzer, "The Obligation to Die for the State," Chapter 4 in his *Obligations: Essays on Disobedience, War, and Citizenship* (New York: Simon and Schuster, 1970).

Hobbes and War

We might expect Hobbes to be enthusiastic about the citizen's obligation to take up arms in defence of the social contract, and he certainly does list this as an obligation stemming from a law of nature. As he puts it: "every man is bound by nature, as much as in him lieth, to protect in war the authority, by which he is himself protected in time of peace."[3] But this listing comes as a sort of afterthought in the last chapter of *Leviathan*, entitled "A Review, and Conclusion," and is in some apparent tension with other strands in Hobbes's thought. This final chapter is explicitly written as an attempt to address certain problems of apparent inconsistency, one of which is that his system seems to require that individuals possess an impossible combination of personal characteristics, especially courage and fear. Hobbes thinks that this is a great difficulty, but not an impossibility, since education and discipline can reconcile such opposites by directing them at different objects (fear the law, but courage in battle). It is an interesting question whether this reply is adequate; it seems initially somewhat superficial, since the fear of the law is a mere instance of the deeper fear that is a foundation stone in Hobbes's system, namely, the fear of death and injury that goes with the basic drive to self-preservation, and that fear is very much in play when it comes to the obligation to risk death for the state. In fact, Hobbes is so aware both of the power of this fear and the rationality of heeding it that, in his earlier discussion of "the liberty of subjects" (in Chapter 21), he admits that a citizen commanded by the sovereign to fight against an enemy "may nevertheless in many cases refuse, without injustice."[4] Hobbes does not elaborate "the many cases," merely giving the one rather engaging example of substituting "a sufficient soldier" in one's place; but he does say that allowance should be made for "natural timorousness" not only in women but also in men "of feminine courage." He goes on to acknowledge with characteristic realism that there is much "running away" in battle, but he will not call this unjust, except for those who are professional soldiers and who have lost the excuse of a timorous nature by voluntarily assuming a military obligation. Nonetheless, Hobbes concludes by insisting that where warfare threatens the very basis on which loyalty to the state is founded, namely, the state's maintaining the protection of its citizens, then, given only that the help of all that can bear arms is required, "everyone is obliged" to respond.[5]

There are many interesting issues raised by Hobbes's discussion of these matters, but here I shall address only three. One is that although Hobbes

---

[3] Thomas Hobbes, *Leviathan*, ed. Michael Oakeshott (Oxford: Basil Blackwell, 1962), p. 461.
[4] Ibid., p. 142.
[5] Ibid., pp. 142–143.

is not a standard just war theorist and is notorious for his insistence that the sovereign cannot behave unjustly, he clearly treats the case of war as exceptional for citizen-sovereign relations.[6] A second is that even that part of Hobbes's discussion most favouring an obligation to fight for the state seems to leave room for the exercise of individual judgement, since the distinction between those cases where the individual may "without injustice" refuse to fight and those where "everyone is obliged" to participate rests upon a judgement about how grave the threat to the state's capacity to fulfil its role actually is. It is unclear whether Hobbes thinks of this threat solely as that posed by the external enemy or also as that posed by the refusal to serve itself, but in either case it would seem that individuals must assess this for themselves.

A third consideration is that, for Hobbes, the gravity of the war issue is related to the dominating place that the rationality of self-preservation occupies in his system, and hence the primary personal consideration against military service is the danger it poses to oneself. Operating with a less monistic approach to morality and political justification, one might more realistically accommodate another moral motivation, namely, the objection to being called upon to endanger, injure, and kill others. Certainly, this prospect is something that many people, before they become combat-calloused, view with horror and misgiving. If it can be justified at all, it requires powerful legitimating reasons. Furthermore, if we are prepared to be even slightly more expansive than Hobbes in our understanding of human nature and its connection with the sources of morality, we must include a concern for the devastation that war does bring to the lives and well-being of other citizens (including family and friends) and to people beyond one's national boundaries, even where this devastation is not directly caused by oneself. Hobbes treats those whose refusal to serve is "without injustice" as subject to other vices, such as cowardice, but this reflects both the narrowness of his perspective upon the foundations of morality and his general (though not exclusive) subordination of the citizen's moral thinking to obedience to the law. From a different perspective, refusal to serve may be seen as driven by virtue rather than vice – by compassion, benevolence, and a concern for justice, rather than by cowardice.

Conscience and Just War Theory

A conscientious objection to war can be, and often is, based upon the total rejection of war. The moral theory (or set of insights) that backs this pacifist

---

[6] As argued in Chapter 1, Hobbes has some affinities with the just war tradition, in spite of appearance, and doesn't think that conduct in war is unconstrained by moral considerations (such as a prohibition on cruelty), nor that the sovereign may initiate war as he pleases. The sovereign cannot act unjustly, but can be guilty of "iniquity" when he violates the laws of nature. See ibid., Chapter 18, p. 116, and Chapter 30, p. 219.

rejection is often linked to a religious tradition, but this is not necessary. The enormity of the evils that any war involves, even where these are not strictly moral evils, is enough to provide plausible material for a secular morality that totally rejects resort to war. Indeed, there are "pragmatic" pacifists who accept some version of just war theory as applicable in principle to vindicate resort to war, but who hold that all actual (modern/nuclear/total) wars are ruled out by the theory. In what follows, although some of my discussion will be relevant to pacifist objections, I shall be less interested in how the state should deal with pacifist conscientious objection and more concerned with what is often called "selective conscientious objection" (hereinafter SCO), that is, a moral objection to participation in a particular war or type of warfare.[7]

From the perspective of just war theory, as defended so far, one might think it evident that the morality of one's involvement in war fighting should be determined by whether one is satisfied that the criteria of the JAB have been met. Where they are not, the strong presumption (to say the least) should be against serving. As we noted in Chapter 1, such criteria will not, of course, provide simple mechanical answers, uninfluenced by judgement and interpretation and indifferent to controversy over political and military facts. Furthermore, on any particuar occasion (or on all) it would seem perfectly possible for the citizen to come to a considered judgement of a war's legitimacy very different from that of the government of the day. Whenever the citizen is called on to act upon the government's judgement by taking up arms, the potentiality for conflict is very high. One way of resolving it is to deny the validity of the citizen's judgement in such a way that the obligation to fight is overwhelming. Michael Walzer has taken this path by insisting that moral responsibility for going to war rests entirely with the ruler and never with the individual citizen or soldier, though the individual must take a certain amount of responsibility for his own acts during war. As Walzer puts it: "The atrocities that he commits are his own; the war is not. It is conceived, both in international law and in ordinary moral judgement, as the king's business – a matter of state policy, not of individual volition, except when the individual is the king."[8] I have elsewhere argued in

---

[7] This disjunction is often marked by distinguishing between "selective" and "discretionary" objections, but we will not need to make that distinction here. For more discussion of classifications of types of objection, see Charles C. Moskos and John Whiteclay Chambers II (eds.), *The New Conscientious Objection: From Sacred to Secular Resistance* (Oxford: Oxford University Press, 1993), pp. 5–6.

[8] Michael Walzer, *Just and Unjust Wars: A Moral Argument with Historical Illustrations*, third edition (New York: Basic Books 2000), p. 39. Walzer's view is echoed, and indeed treated as the merest common sense, by Paul Christopher in *The Ethics of War and Peace: An Introduction to Legal and Moral Issues* (Englewood Cliffs, NJ: Prentice-Hall, 1994), pp. 96–97. Christopher says, "...soldiers can never be responsible for the crime of war, qua soldiers. Resort to war is always a political decision, not a military one" (p. 96).

detail against Walzer's view, which not only makes of international law and ordinary moral judgement too crude a guide, but also removes much of the point of just war theory by making most of it a matter of no concern to the people who are called upon to kill and maim on the basis of someone else's application of this crucial piece of moral thinking.[9] Walzer cites approvingly that part of the exchange in Shakespeare's *Henry V* between the disguised king and two of his common soldiers on the night before Agincourt in which the soldier Bates, responding to his companion Will's claim that they do not know whether the king's cause be just and his quarrel honourable, says: "we know enough if we know that we are the king's subjects. If his cause be wrong, our obedience to the king wipes the crime of it out of us."[10] Walzer's invocation of a moral outlook on political obligation perhaps appropriate to the relations between a fifteenth-century absolute monarch and his subjects as a model for contemporary democratic political theory is simply astonishing, and the wonder of it is compounded by his ignoring the complex dramatic ironies of the dialectic between king and soldiery. (This is particularly surprising in view of the fact that Walzer's own work is usually so sensitive to literary and historical context.) He goes on to argue that the citizen faced with a call to arms will be excused from responsibility on the grounds of both ignorance and duress, but again, if we are talking of modern democratic states rather than ancient autocracies, these factors can be (and are by Walzer) greatly exaggerated, and where the citizen is less ignorant and helpless than Walzer supposes, then the obligation to serve may be vitiated and a reaction of conscientious refusal may be required. In such circumstances, what response should a state make to this refusal, and what are the problems with it?

This question is given a particular urgency, and much of its modern form, by the existence of conscription for military service. Were the state to rely solely upon the voluntary participation of the citizenry in its wars, then one traditional problem of conscientious objection would not arise, or at least not in the form that I am considering it. A citizen could judge that all war is immoral, or that this particular war is immoral, and then act upon that judgement by not volunteering to serve. There would still be the question of what he should do about his government's engagement in what he considers an immoral enterprise, and the related question of how far the state should allow for conscientious demonstrations and public opposition to the war by concerned citizens.[11] These raise some of the same issues, but not with the same immediacy. For the state, what we might call the "efficiency" issues are similar; for example, the question of whether such protests damage

---

[9] See C. A. J. Coady, "The Leaders and the Led," *Inquiry* 23 (1980), pp. 275–291.
[10] William Shakespeare, *King Henry V*, act 4 scene 1.
[11] I use the male gender pronoun here because historically it has been mostly males for whom these questions have arisen directly.

the war effort (damage parallel to the supposed damage to the war effort of allowing conscientious objection in a conscription context). But other issues are different. On the side of the dissenting citizen, for instance, it can be said that you may well have an obligation to protest against your country's involvement in waging an unjust war and to do what you can to extricate it from the war, but that this is not quite the same as the obligation you might have to resist an invitation, or a legally sanctioned demand, to kill and maim or to be killed and maimed in an unjust cause. For one thing, your failure to protest someone else's vile action, even where the failure is culpable, cannot carry the same burden of guilt as direct involvement in the intentional planning and execution of that action. Even those who most enthusiastically criticize the moral significance of distinguishing between acts and omissions should not go so far. People who fail to protest about their neighbours badly beating their children may be defective neighbours and citizens, but they are not child abusers themselves and do not bear the same guilt. Refusal to serve in an unjust war, then, will normally have a more powerful, and imperative, moral motivation than a decision to protest against it; one may be obliged not to join in killing and maiming, where one is not obliged, or less strongly obliged, to protest at others doing it. Of course, there are more complexities that we will need to consider later.

One immediate complexity, however, deserves treatment at this point. This concerns the problem of conscientious objection in the case of professional soldiers. These are not conscripts; they are volunteers, in one respect, for they have chosen the profession of arms as a career, but they are not like those who volunteer in the context of war, since they are already committed to armed service on behalf of the state. This commitment involves them in a career, even a way of life, that makes them a warrior caste, even if many of them hope never to be engaged in actual warfare. Psychologically, at least, this puts them in a different position from that of an ordinary citizen who is considering whether to "answer the country's call." Their commitment has already done much to decide this question for them, and this makes a moral difference as well as a psychological one. But the commitment should not be seen as totally open-ended, even though this is how it is usually construed. In all professions, professionals owe duties to those they serve, and there will often be some presumptions built into that orientation about the legitimacy of the client's or the organisation's demands. But this still allows that the demands may be illegal or immoral, and in that case they should not be met, whatever one's prior commitment to client or organization. The point applies more powerfully still to the professional soldier who is called upon to engage in what he or she considers unjust killing. Even Walzer allows that the professional soldier must refuse orders to violate the JIB, but, as I argued earlier, there is no reason to believe that individual soldiers are absolved from consideration of the JAB. Indeed, conscientious objection or protest by regular military personnel and conscripted troops has now become a striking feature of wars waged by democracies in the twenty-first century. Israeli conscripts have refused to serve in the occupied territories because they believe that the occupation is (now) immoral.[12] And recently several members of the British forces in Iraq have refused service on the grounds of the war's illegality (by which they seem to mean both strict illegality and, more broadly, immorality). One of the these, Ben Griffin, was an SAS soldier who objected to further service in Baghdad because he regarded the war as illegal, on the grounds both of the reasons for fighting it and the immoral methods employed, especially (on his account) by American forces. Interestingly, Griffin was not court-martialed, but discharged with a favourable testimonial that described him as a "balanced, honest, loyal and determined individual" who has "the courage of his convictions."[13] Another protester, Flight-Lieutenant Malcolm Kendall-Smith, a Royal Air Force doctor, has had court-martial proceedings initiated against him after refusing to return to Iraq for a third tour of duty because he now regards the war as illegal.[14]

These various types of refusal or protest raise the question of how the state should respond to the challenge such objectors provide to its authority. In addressing this question, I shall principally consider the issue from the perspective of the conscientious objector to conscripted military service, but the discussion should also be viewed in the light of the comments made earlier about volunteers and professional soldiery, and my conclusions can be adapted to those other categories of objection to service.

The State and the Challenge of Conscience

There are many puzzles raised by this question. One is whether (as some have thought) this can be a problem only for the liberal democratic state, legitimated as it is by something to do with the moral involvement of the governed people in the principles of governance, or whether it is a more general problem for any legitimate state. (The two problems collapse into one if we hold that only the liberal democratic state has a genuine title to legitimacy. This may well seem too strong a view, but the alternatives have their own difficulties, as can be seen in John Rawls's attempts to characterise legitimate nondemocratic states in his essay on "The Law of Peoples.")[15] In what follows, I shall take it that at the very least the problem does arise for

---

[12] They offer reasons that involve both the JIB and the JAB, and many of them see a relation between them, thereby illustrating my contention that violations of the JIB can affect our judgement on the overall justice of the war. For more on this, see Coady, "The Leaders and the Led," pp. 275–291.

[13] Reported in *The Age*, March 13, 2006, p. 7, under the heading "SAS Soldier Refuses to Fight in Iraq, Saying US Tactics Illegal." Original report in the English newspaper *The Sunday Telegraph*, March 12, 2006.

[14] *The Age*, March 13, 2006, p. 7.

[15] John Rawls, "The Law of Peoples," *Critical Inquiry* 20, no. 1 (Autumn 1993), pp. 36–68.

liberal democratic states; I will explore some suggestions about whether such states have an obligation to provide a legal right of conscientious objection, and I will examine some of the difficulties surrounding this idea.

It is a striking fact, and one prima facie at odds with Walzer's picture of the received view on responsibility and war, that legal exemption from armed service for reasons of conscientious objection has been recognised in some modern democracies for much of the twentieth century and beyond. Indeed, it can be argued that such recognition is a sign of a certain political maturity and democratic confidence. I should perhaps confess at this point a modicum of patriotic pride in the fact that Australia was the first country in the world to enact continuing national legislation providing exemption from armed service for conscientious objection. This was done in 1903, only three years after the federal constitution was promulgated.[16] Less national and formal accommodations existed in other countries well before that – for instance, in various North American colonies in the seventeenth century – and Britain had extensive experience of conscientious objection tribunals during the First World War. Nonetheless, many modern nations, even some well-established democracies, have been legally and coercively intolerant of any room for such refusal of military service until quite recent times. France, for instance, took until 1963 to make any legal provision for conscientious objection, and really addressed the question seriously only in 1983.[17]

As is well known, the granting of such exemptions has historically been conditional on, or at least biased towards, the objector's establishing two facts: one, that the objection is grounded in religious belief, and two, that it is a total objection to all warfare. There has been pressure to change both conditions, though the former has actually seen much more change than the latter. Various strong forms of pacifism have been alive within Christianity from its earliest years, and modern Western governments, in times of conscription, have had to confront the reality that small groups among the citizenry, mostly associated with what were often called "the peace churches," were utterly opposed on religious grounds to their war ventures, whatever the circumstances. I will not attempt here to trace the complex history of, or offer detailed historical explanations for, the legal developments involved, but it seems plausible that both conditions had a rationale in the requirements of religious freedom to which modern pluralist democracies are rightly sensitive and in the evidentiary problems involved in establishing the conscientiousness of the dissenting belief and its depth. The former point is obvious enough, and the latter involved the idea that

---

[16] For details, see Hugh Smith, "Appendix A," in Moskos and Chambers (eds.), *The New Conscientious Objection*, pp. 209–211.

[17] Michel L. Martin, "France: A Statute but No Objectors," in Moskos and Chambers (eds.), *The New Conscientious Objection*, pp. 80–97.

commitment to a pacifist religious tradition provided a public test of the objector's sincerity and of the centrality of his pacifist belief to the core of his character and likely actions.

But the exclusiveness of both these considerations has been subject to erosion owing to the developing secularisation of modern Western societies and the general spread of antiwar thinking beyond the dogmas of particular sects. In the first place, modern liberal democratic theory is concerned to develop a principled place for the legal and political toleration not only of a diversity of traditional religious beliefs, but also of a variety of divergent outlooks on the world that are not religious in the standard sense (what John Rawls has called "conceptions of the good"). This has come to be reflected in the legal treatment of conscientious objection, even if it has sometimes involved a certain interpretive flexibility, as in the U.S. Supreme Court's extension of "religious conviction" to include the convictions of atheists as long as they are "purely ethical or moral in source or content" and occupy "a place parallel to that filled by the God of those admittedly qualifying for the exemption."[18] In the second place, the modern revival of just war theory, coupled with the specific horrors of modern technological warfare and the consequences of the ready conformity of German and Japanese citizens to their leaders' militarism in World War II, have made more plausible the idea not only that one might have a deep moral objection to particular wars waged by one's rulers, but also that it might be good for the world if such objections were treated with respect. This point connects with the idea, often raised about civil disobedience more generally, that the superiority of pluralistic democracies over dictatorships, theocracies, and other competitors resides not only in certain pragmatic advantages, but also in the respect they accord to the human dignity and moral integrity of citizens. Although the case will be made in different ways by different traditions, the various arguments converge on the value of the state's recognising the equal moral dignity of citizens and the value of their engaging in conscientious reflection on matters of significance for themselves and their communities. Such governments must be concerned with other matters as well, but their concern with this will be very much in play when the question is about coercing citizens against their deep moral convictions to endanger, maim, and kill other human beings and to risk such harms themselves. Democratic states should consider the good in conscientious objection even when their military cause is just, but a dispassionate consideration of the history of warfare surely shows in addition that states (even democratic states) all too

---

[18] These extensions are those provided by the decision in *United States v. Seeger* (1965) as amplified in *Welsh v. United States* (1970). See the discussion in James L. Lacy, "Alternative Service: The Significance of the Challenge," in Michael F. Noone, Jr. (ed.), *Selective Conscientious Objection: Accommodating Conscience and Security* (Boulder, CO: Westview Press, 1989), pp. 107–115.

frequently wage wars that are unjust. The selective conscientious objector reminds all of us, including the rulers, that our certainties about the rightness of our cause often need to be tempered by some scepticism. Where it is in fact an unjust war, then it is good that citizens conscientiously refuse to fight in it; where it is a just war, there is still value in the fact that some citizens conscientiously object to it and that the state honours their integrity by treating their objections with respect.[19] This is the good that has been recognized by the British army's civilized response, mentioned earlier, to SAS soldier Ben Griffin's refusal to fight in Iraq.

Here I should pause to consider an objection that may be raised to my procedure so far. This can be put in the form of a question: is the state obliged to provide special treatment or exemption for all forms of moral objection to its laws and policies? After all, there are many state laws, ranging from gun control to affirmative action and much in between, that arouse deeply felt opposition, a good deal of it based upon principles of one sort or another. I have been arguing that liberal democracies should have a particular respect for the moral dignity of their citizens and understand the importance of their engaging in moral reflection and basing actions upon it, but I do not doubt that there are problems in the idea that such respect and understanding should always translate directly into concessions for those who claim to be objecting morally. A full discussion of this would require a wider analysis of the debate about civil disobedience and the nature of conscience than is here possible, and would have to recognise the problems posed by mad and dangerous moral beliefs; but what I would claim about a conscientiously based objection to fighting in a war is that its moral significance is so much deeper and more central than most of the other cases that can be raised as to put it in a special category. Military conscription is a singular form of legal coercion; not only is it unique in coercing people into the public service, it also puts them into very dangerous circumstances both physically and morally. Because of this, and for the reasons given earlier, thoughtful people recognise that war is morally challenging and morally ambiguous, even when they support it for one reason or another. While it is possible, and even desirable, to empathise with moral objections to war (either total or selective) in the process of disagreeing with them, there is no such imperative for objections to political equality for women or to children's rights not to be beaten brutally for disciplinary reasons. In the latter cases and many others, we may need to understand motives, and it may be that this should make for some differences in response, but such understanding need not be oriented towards exemptions.

---

[19] There is a good discussion of the positive value of selective conscientious objection in John Langan, "The Good of Selective Conscientious Objection," in Michael F. Noone, Jr. (ed.), *Selective Conscientious Objection: Accommodating Conscience and Security* (Boulder, CO: Westview Press, 1989), pp. 89–106.

Nonetheless, these ideas about moral objection to warfare have had little success in persuading governments to legislate for the selective conscientious objector. Only in Australia has legislation been passed that permits exemption on grounds of conscience from particular wars or military operations.[20] In spite of the advocacy of the American Catholic bishops, such legislation has been rejected in the United States.[21] Dutch law has moved furthest in the direction of selective objection by allowing what is sometimes called "discretionary" objection, that is, objection to certain ways of waging war, such as nuclear war. The Dutch legislation seems to allow for a conscientious objection based upon considerations drawn more from the *jus in bello* than from the *jus ad bellum*, though the two cannot be kept totally separate, and the interpretive point is controversial. In practice, German law probably allows for selective objection, since it has a right to refuse military service enshrined in its constitution.

I do not propose spending time justifying the extension from purely religiously grounded objections to those based on "secular" moral belief. Not only has this ceased to be seriously contentious in most politically advanced societies, the idea that only religious people could have deep moral principles that might rightly or understandably compel them to political acts of dissent, disobedience, or refusal also has little to recommend it philosophically. The only possible argument for there being something special about religious conviction is the evidentiary test mentioned earlier, and I will examine this later. Let us turn then to the issues involved in granting legal standing, whether on religious or moral grounds, for selective conscientious objection, including in the scope of this term not only objection to the justice of a particular cause, but also objection to particular ways of fighting. Those who oppose granting such status point to several difficulties, some of which are also relevant to universalistic conscientious objection. I want to discuss three of these that seem to me most central to the debate. These are: (1) the threat posed to the state's right to wage just war, (2) the unfairness to compliant citizens of granting such exemptions, and (3) the impossibility of really determining that an objection is "conscientious."

Undermining the State's Right to Wage War

Many believe that the granting of conscientious objector status, especially selectively, is somehow at odds with the rights of the state. This style of objection takes various forms, ranging from the highly moral to the pragmatic. If a state is legitimate (so it is argued), then its remit must include the right to

---

[20] See Moira Coombs and Laura Rayner, "Conscientious Objection to Military Service in Australia," Research Note no. 31, 2002–03, Department of the Parliamentary Library of Australia, November 11, 2005, at <www.aph.gov.au/library/pubs/rn/2002–03/03rn31.pdf>.

[21] See Smith, "Appendix A," p. 211.

defend the community against external attack and the correlative right to enforce "the obligation to die for the state" upon citizens. It may be allowed that there can be a small number of citizens whose peculiar beliefs reject this right and obligation *in toto* and whose refusal to serve can be tolerated for various reasons, but the state's exercise of its right is imperilled by the idea that some citizens should be exempted from bearing arms because they disagree in particular cases with their legitimate government's considered policies concerning the protection of the realm.

There are several ways of responding to this difficulty. One is to point out that the claim of imperilment is implausible if construed at the level of likely immediate consequences. The existing statistics on conscientious objection do not suggest that it is an option that many will ever be eager to take, but it may be that widening the grounds to allow selective objection could lead to massive increases in the number of those seeking exemption. This raises a constructive dilemma that should be more worrying to the opponents of SCO than to its advocates: either the resort to war is genuinely and clearly necessary to the defence of the community, in which case (other things being equal, like the existence of some prospect of success in the defence) the extent of SCO is likely to be small; or it is not so necessary, in which case the extent of SCO may be greater, but is likely to be objectively justified, or so symptomatic of public disquiet about the resort to war as to make it politically unsustainable. Either way, the state's legitimate rights are likely to be more threatened by rejecting the right to conscientious objection than by conceding it. On the other hand, if the difficulty is supposed to be not that the government's authority is threatened with respect to this particular war, but that it is more generally undermined by its allowing SCO, then the response may plausibly be made, in line with the earlier argument about the distinctive value of democratic states, that its authority should be strengthened by its tolerance of such principled disagreement. Moreover, this point can be reinforced by the pragmatic consideration that the granting of conscientious objector status to those who object most strenuously to service keeps them within the ambit of the law rather than driving them into extralegal dissent or rebellion.

Another line of response to this difficulty is to point out that many wars do not involve defending the community against external attack. For the United States, the Gulf War and the Vietnam War (not to mention the invasion of Grenada) did not involve such self-defence, and the claim that the Iraq war did so (by preventing terrorist attacks on the United States) is highly implausible. It may be replied that the wars all involved the "security" of the nation, but the history of the concept of "national security" is now such as to make this recourse highly dubious. The disadvantageous effects on the United States of a communist victory in Vietnam or an Iraqi annexation of Kuwait or, later on, Iraq's supposed possession of (actually nonexistent) WMD were always speculative; if these interventions could be justified at all, it would have to be in terms broader than national self-defence. In earlier chapters we have discussed the legitimacy of such broader justifications, such as humanitarian intervention, and my view is that the case for even the most plausible of them is usually much harder to establish than that of serious self-defence. The supposed disastrous consequences of allowing SCO against wars for such causes are that much more dubious, and, in addition, the grounds for fighting, even where legitimate and demonstrated, are based upon moral considerations that may not have the compelling political weight that self-defence carries. The case for conscription in order to wage an altruistic war to save distant foreigners from persecution is morally weaker and lacks political feasibility compared to the case of self-defence. In any event, a self-defence model of just war theory will not be sympathetic to conscription, or, if sympathetic in some circumstances, need not be hostile, for the reasons given, to selective conscientious objection on the ground that it violates the rights of the state. On the other hand, a more internationalist and more interventionist version of just war theory is unlikely to ground its moral appeal upon state conscription; indeed, what form its political authority could take is still unclear.

The Issue of Fairness

Questions about the unfairness of allowing SCO are more difficult. Those who are conscripted to fight are exposed to great dangers, moral, psychological, and physical, and the long-term effects of that exposure can be very damaging. The conscientious objector (CO) is spared all this and enjoys the benefits, if any, of what the fighting of others achieves. Of course, traditionally the CO has often suffered indignities and other harms of a severe order (many grim examples from Britain in World War I are given by David Boulton),[22] but this has primarily been the result of abuse by others of his status or abuses attendant upon nonrecognition of that status, rather than a natural consequence of what should be involved in it.

Is the CO being unfair to fellow citizens who do not object to fighting? On the face of it, this seems a strange criticism. The SCO (in particular) does not claim a special privilege that other citizens are not to have. He or she wants SCO status to be available to all, and believes that, in principle, all have the capacity to claim it. The hardships that others suffer in fighting an unjust war result from their commitments to an immoral enterprise (though there may be reason to withhold judgements of guilt on many of them), and the SCO cannot be seen as shirking genuine duties and responsibilities that others have bravely shouldered. The SCO might accept that there is some sort of an obligation to die for the state, but only in what can be shown to

[22] See David Boulton, *Objection Overruled* (London: MacGibbon & Kee, 1967).

be a just war. Since this condition is, he believes, unfulfilled in the present case, there is no genuine obligation that he is unfairly avoiding while others accept it

This response seems to me to be strictly correct, but it fudges somewhat one aspect of the case that is important. This is the element of misjudgement that may be involved in many such conscientious decisions. I have known several Australians who were conscientious objectors during World War II, but later came to regret their decision when the full enormity of Hitler's regime and the awfulness of Japanese militarism were more clearly revealed. World War II may indeed have been an exception to the general run of wars, and it is also true that misjudgement is possible (some would say common) on the part of the majority who support any given war. Indeed, regret for such misjudgement on the part of those who rule or follow is also possible (though not very common), as Robert McNamara's belated mea culpa and its reception have shown.[23] SCOs admit that some wars may be just and so must concede that, in the unlikely event that this one is just, their refusal to participate relieves them of justifiable burdens that others will bear. (They could avoid this by denying the moral legitimacy of conscription even in a just cause. But I will not consider this move here.) These facts suggest that there is a principled, as well as a pragmatic, point to the provision of "alternative service" for objectors. Given the possibility that their judgement is astray, objectors should be prepared to show their good faith and their readiness to shoulder burdens on behalf of the community by making sacrifices to serve their fellow citizens in ways that do not violate their conscientious convictions. Given the certainty that their judgement on the war will be *perceived* as mistaken by the bulk of their fellow citizens, they have powerful prudential reasons for undertaking such service. Of course, there is room for further debate about what sort of service is appropriate; it may be difficult to find work that is not war-related, and where such work is available, the objector may not be particularly good at it. Indeed, the job he is already doing may serve the community better than any other, though his remaining in it is unlikely to satisfy perceptions of unfairness.

There is an interesting objection to the moral standing of the objector that could be seen as a very strong version of the unfairness claim. C. D. Broad has argued that the conscientious objector in a modern state is placed in a morally untenable situation by the fact that his objection is bound to be a minority affair. So even if your conscientious objection is correct, and you are right about the moral undesirability of participation in the war, you are nonetheless put in a "situation of one-sided dependence on what you must

---

[23] Robert S. McNamara with Brian VanDeMark, *In Retrospect: The Tragedy and Lessons of Vietnam* (New York: Times Books, 1995).

regard as the wrong actions of people who are less virtuous than yourself."[24] So the conscientious objector is fed and protected against what may well be great evils by the very people whose moral stance he rejects so emphatically. Broad regards this impasse as so significant that he thinks conscientious objectors should welcome the death penalty as a way out of it, and, failing that, he recommends suicide to them as a satisfactory resolution of their situation.[25] It is unclear how serious Broad is in his recommendations (the paper is the text of a talk given in polemical circumstances, and one of its targets was the left-wing belief that the coming war – namely, World War II – would be provoked by a reactionary British government in order to attack the Soviet Union), but the clash he supposes is an important one even if its significance is not as great as he maintains.

The conflict seems to be of the form: X is wrong and I am obliged not to do X, but by so refraining I find that my well-being is advanced (or my ill-being avoided) only because others do X. We may, I think, ignore Broad's claim about provision of food, since one's nation is not normally providing one with daily sustenance by the waging of war. Were there no war, this provision (insofar as it is the provision of the nation rather than of individuals in it) would continue in some form, perhaps more plentifully, and we are surely not obliged to co-operate with every governmental policy in order to be fed or to be entitled to be fed. But what about protection? Let us concentrate, as before, upon the conscientious objector to a particular war. (Some of the conclusions would apply to someone who objected to any war, others are perhaps less secure for such an objector.) Again, there is considerable exaggeration in Broad's description. Much of the protection the state provides the conscientious objector is merely what it provides anyway, against theft and other crimes, for instance. But the army he will not serve in is surely protecting him from the enemy he will not fight. This is complicated by certain facts that we will address later, but, for now, let us concede that were it not for the efforts of those of the objector's compatriots who are fighting the war, his own life would be endangered. There is then a sense in which he might plausibly be characterised as a "moral free rider" on the immoral efforts of others. Is there something wrong with this?

To answer this question, let us begin by considering what turns out to be an imaginary case. (I put the matter thus because in an earlier published version of material related to this chapter I put the example forward as fact, and I have since discovered it to be myth. I must apologise to anyone misled by my earlier account, which was based upon a misleading secondary source about the Quakers' dilemmas in Pennsylvania.) Imagine that the

---

[24] See C. D. Broad, "Ought We to Fight for Our Country in the Next War?," in C. D. Broad, *Ethics and the History of Philosophy: Selected Essays* (London: Routledge & Kegan Paul, 1952), p. 241.

[25] Ibid., pp. 241 and 242.

nineteenth-century Quakers in Pennsylvania, who thought themselves morally obliged not to take up arms, believed that they needed protection against "hostile Indians." They might have sought this protection from God alone, but, exercising a version of prudence in place of piety, they decided to employ others to fight for them. This would seem to be a situation in which the benefits of the immorality of others are not merely accepted; rather, their sinfulness is positively cultivated in order to gain those benefits. Admittedly, the sinfulness in question may be more "objective" than "subjective" inasmuch as the mercenary soldiers are presumably not themselves persuaded of the case for pacifism, and so may do no wrong by their lights. Yet, by the Quakers' own lights, they would certainly have been "objectively" wronging those they kill, even if the safety of the Quakers were thereby secured. But whatever we think of this (and it is close to the situation I discussed in Chapter 10 about the employment of mercenary soldiers by nonpacifists who believe in just war theory), the case of the conscientious objector is notably different. For the conscientious objector does nothing analogous to employing, inciting, or tempting his more belligerent fellow-citizens into fighting the war he will not fight himself. They are going to fight anyway, and all he does is reap unsought benefit (to counterbalance somewhat the numerous disadvantages he faces) from their doing so. There is no doubt a certain discomfort in benefiting from what you see as the objectively wrong behaviour of others, but it is unclear that it must always be wrong to do so. No doubt it will sometimes be wrong, but the circumstances in which this is so are not easy to spell out in general terms. If Nazis deprive Jews of their business or property and offer it to you, you would be complicit in their crime if you accepted the offer (unless, of course, you were coerced into it, but then you would be under some obligation to try to use the business to do some good for the deprived Jews).

But other cases are different. Consider, for instance, the case in which your rival for an important position suicides, thereby leaving the position to you. He would certainly have been preferred to you, and his suicide (by your lights at least) is palpably immoral – he had no thought for the dependents he left behind in straitened circumstances – but this does not taint your acceptance of the job. Just as the conscientious objector urges the government not to wage war, so you may have urged the rival not to suicide. Or consider a case in which your acquaintance Jones is bent upon attacking an innocent bystander because of something morally irrelevant about him, like his religion or skin colour, and you object to his proposal and reject his invitation to join him in his immoral adventure. In spite of this he goes ahead, but his attack is failing, and the bystander then counterattacks both of you (mistakenly believing that you are involved). Jones fights back and succeeds in chasing the bystander off. You have benefited from Jones's immoral attack in the sense that Jones's continued fighting has put you out of harm's way. Nonetheless, there seems little problem with your benefit, since the peril you have been saved from was precisely created by Jones's attack in the first place. This sort of case is clearly relevant to many conscientious objector contexts. The objector might well believe (and believe truly) that were it not for the war fighting of his own government there would be no need for the protection that is supposed to be morally suspect, since the enemy had no designs on his (or his countrymen's) lives prior to his own government's decision to go to war. It can hardly be denied that some (I would say many) war situations are like that.

One interesting issue here concerns whether it can be right to defend yourself from an attack that you have wrongly provoked. Is Jones, for instance, morally entitled to defend himself against the bystander? Put as baldly as that, the question does not, I think, admit of an unequivocal answer. If the bystander's violence is defensive, aimed basically just at repelling Jones's attack, then I do not think a good case can be made for Jones's right to defend himself. His morally gratuitous attack entitles the bystander to use defensive violence and cannot license Jones to continue the assault under the heading of self-defence. He should defend himself by flight or submission, not by injuring the innocent. Of course, the matter may change if the bystander refuses to accept submission or surrender, or uses more violence than is needed to defend himself. But contrary to Hobbes, and some of his modern supporters, the right of self-defence, as argued earlier in the book, is neither absolute nor primitive.[26] The SS killers in the Warsaw ghetto who were fired upon in self-defence by innocent Jews had no right to retaliate in self-defence. They had no business there with weapons at all, and it is a moral obscenity to talk of their right of self-defence in this context. In the Jones example, when the bystander extends his defensive violence to you, unaware that you are no threat to him and had no part in the attack, then it is more plausible to hold that you have a right to defend yourself, and, moreover, that Jones would have a right to defend you even if he had no right to defend himself.

Consequently, in the case of war, the conscientious objector (call him Smith) is in the position of being attacked or disadvantaged by the equivalent of the bystander who has been unjustly provoked by Jones, or at least that is how he should view the matter, given his conscientious judgements. If the enemy is doing things that will harm Smith in the course of legitimate self-defence (say, bombing a munitions factory near where Smith lives), then Smith should have mixed feelings about being protected by his national air force. He can certainly be pleased that he has survived an undeserved death or injury, though unhappy that just warriors have been killed by unjust to bring about the situation in which he is safe. Nonetheless, just as his harm would have been an unintended incidental harm, so his survival is also

---

[26] For a modern defender of the Hobbesian line (if a somewhat reluctant one), see Jenny Teichman, *Pacifism and the Just War* (Oxford: Blackwell, 1986).

an unintended incidental safety, since his national defenders are basically aiming to protect the munitions factory. None of this seems to add up to his being somehow guilty of anything.

On the other hand, if the enemy (though its cause be just) is engaged in immoral tactics, such as the terror bombing of civilian populations, then some of the benefits of military defence that the objector receives may be the product of uses of defensive violence that he can morally support, indeed that he could legitimately co-operate with and even exercise himself. So a German opponent of Hitler's war who did not have the legal option of conscientious objection but went into underground opposition might nonetheless have been entitled to join in defensive artillery attacks upon Allied planes attacking Dresden.

The Inscrutability of Conscience

In a different article, Broad raises another important issue when he questions the belief that it is possible to determine whether an objection is conscientious.[27] This is clearly central to the operation of tribunals charged with precisely such determinations, but Broad's critique also raises the spectre that even the objectors cannot establish this to their own satisfaction. Broad's basic idea is that there are two elements that must be present in a conscientious objection: one is the belief that the war is unjust (or that all wars are unjust), and the other is the actual influence upon the decision not to serve exerted by that belief. It is basically this second element that Broad concentrates upon. He distinguishes two categories of conscientious action: fully conscientious and semi-conscientious.[28] An act is fully conscientious if and only if it is either purely conscientious or predominantly conscientious. A purely conscientious action is one in which the agent both believes that the proposed action is right (or the most right of the alternatives available) and desires to do what is right, and in which this is the agent's only motive for so acting. A predominantly conscientious action is one in which the same belief/desire complex is present along with other beliefs/desires pertinent to the action, but the conscientious complex is necessary and sufficient for the performance of the action.[29] A semi-conscientious action is one in which the conscientious component (the belief/desire complex) is either sufficient but superfluous or indispensable but inadequate. This needs a bit of explanation, and is worth pursuing in any case because it raises intrinsically interesting questions about motivation.

---

[27] C. D. Broad, "Conscience and Conscientious Action," in Broad's *Critical Essays in Moral Philosophy*, ed. David R. Cheney (London: George Allen & Unwin, 1971), pp. 136–155.

[28] See ibid., pp. 150–153. There is a third category discussed briefly by Broad, namely, contra-conscientious action, but this need not concern us here.

[29] Broad's definition is slightly more complex, but that will not affect our discussion here.

Consider the case in which agents are convinced after due deliberation and access to information that a particular war is unjust and conclude that they should not serve in it, but are also aware that their fear of the dangers of death and injury in the war gives them a powerful nonconscientious motive to avoid service. Broad imagines two scenarios: one in which the conscientious motive is sufficient to produce the refusal but not necessary (since, in its absence, the agent would act to the same effect on the fear of death and injury), and another in which the conscientious motive is necessary but not sufficient (since, without the reinforcement of the fear, the agent would not act on the conscientious motive, though, equally, the agent would not act merely from fear). If we think of conscientious action as requiring a sufficient conscientious motive, we will treat the first case as conscientious and the second as not; whereas if we think that it requires indispensability, we will treat the second case as conscientious and the first as not. The tendency to vacillate here prompts Broad to call both types semi-conscientious. Broad claims that "it is hardly credible" that a conscientious objector's decision could be a purely conscientious act because "everyone fears death and wounds" and so the objector will have at least one other motive for refusing service. Consequently, the action will be predominantly conscientious or semi-conscientious. In either case, he asks, how can the subject be justified in thinking that his action flows from his conscientious motive rather than from the nonconscientious motive? Broad's thought here seems to be that with either predominantly conscientious or semi-conscientious actions, the agent must be able to say how he would have acted in the counterfactual situation of the nonconscientious factor being absent or in the counterfactual situation of the conscientious factor being absent, but how can he confidently answer such questions? More urgently, how can a tribunal answer the third-person versions of such questions?

Ingenious as this line of argument appears, it is hard to believe that its conclusion follows. For one thing, as Broad admits, it applies just as much to the decision to fight as to the decision to object, since most fighters will have motives other than patriotic duty for their actions, for example, fear of being thought cowardly or love of adventure. Yet there surely are many people who do "answer their country's call" out of patriotic duty, and it is hard to believe that neither they nor we can ever know that this is so. Moreover, Broad's worry applies well beyond the subject of this chapter, since it is notorious that we have "mixed motives" for most of our actions. Broad's picture relies upon what is nowadays called a causal theory of mind – in particular, a causal theory of motivation – and this, though fashionable, is not uncontroversial. It is merely worth noting that the vacillation about the role of necessity and sufficiency of factors reflects puzzles within metaphysics about how to understand causation, and it is significant that theories of this type have difficulty dealing with cases of causal overdetermination and preemption. Nonetheless, I do not think it necessary to challenge the theory of mind at work here nor to delve into the philosophical problem of causation, because Broad's problem can be dealt with at a different level.

Whatever the correct philosophical analysis or theory of causation, we can know that x causes y without first knowing or being able to apply the analysis in question. If, for example, the analysis required that there must be some covering law, L, relating x and y appropriately, we could still know that x caused y without knowing that there was any such requirement and without knowing what L was. Without knowing or applying any relevant covering law, I can know that the falling coconut caused Jones to be unconscious, that my headache is making me irritable, or that (if some reasons are causes) I am punching Smith because he insulted my wife. Similarly for the "possible worlds" story, whatever it might be. One can know what one's actual motives, in the sense of reasons for acting, are in some situation in which one actually has several different reasons for so acting without first determining what one would do in some hypothetical situation in which one lacks some of those reasons. We are not of course infallible about any of this, but our access to the reasons we act upon is at least as secure as our recognition of physical causation. Conscientious objectors are not speculating; they are reasoning and acting here and now, and these exercises in practical reasoning proceed (as Aristotle claimed) from premises and principles to conclusions in action. Whether I would have come to the same or different conclusions from other premises that, in some sense, I also have is hardly to the point for me. Nor should it be much to the point for the tribunals. They are to decide whether this reasoning is serious moral deliberation on my part, issuing in this decision. This is no doubt difficult enough, but there is no point in making it seem totally mysterious.[30]

We can demystify matters in another way if we shift perspective and think of the tribunal as concentrating upon whether forcing these persons to go to war would violate their deep moral convictions. Evidence of this might be drawn from the way they discuss and support these convictions before the tribunal, and from the ways they have expressed themselves and behaved in the past with respect to the reasoning and convictions they now espouse. As mentioned earlier, religious affiliations and activities may be seen as relevant here in providing solid evidence of the existence and role of these convictions, though there is no reason to believe that this is the only sort of evidence available.

There remain further questions about what precisely are moral convictions. I have put the matter in a context of reasoning, and I think that this is vital, but before I am accused of a typical philosopher's obsession with reason, let me say that the idea of conscience needs more investigation, and

---

[30] A parallel not involving motives: a tribunal can readily determine that Brown shot Smith even when Jones, waiting in the wings, would have shot him if Brown hadn't, and it can determine that Brown shot Smith even if Jones did so at the same time.

that although such investigation must involve attention to a kind of practical reasoning, it must also explore springs of moral insight and understanding that may not involve highly articulate tracts of theorising. In saying this much I do not, however, mean to endorse that tradition which regards the modern idea of conscience (and perhaps especially the idea of conscientious objection) as a specifically Protestant and individualist, even subjective, concept. In discussing conscientious objection, Michael Walzer, and before him John Dewey, have given prominence to this picture (though Walzer recognises that it departs in certain ways from earlier understandings).[31] I cannot now provide a full theory of conscience, but although the idea of conscience that Walzer and Dewey use to gain an understanding of conscientious objection has certainly had currency, it is only one conception of conscience, and it seems to me a defective one. It is certainly inadequate for grasping the legitimate role that the concept of conscience can play, and has played, in our understanding of moral thinking generally, and the role it should play when we discuss the significance of selective conscientious objection.[32]

[31] Walzer, *Obligations*, p. 121ff.; and John Dewey, "Conscience and Compulsion," in John Dewey, *The Political Writings*, ed. Debra Morris and Ian Shapiro (Indianapolis: Hackett, 1993), p. 194.
[32] For a good beginning to a discussion of the complexities of conscience, see Eric Darcy, *Conscience and Its Right to Freedom* (New York: Sheed and Ward, 1961).

12

Weapons of Mass Destruction

Thro cells of madness, haunts of horror and fear
Tennyson, "Maud"

The problems posed by what are called weapons of mass destruction (WMD) loom large in contemporary international politics. Their alleged presence in Iraq was the principal public reason for the Iraq war, and their actual absence an embarrassment, if not a political and moral disaster, for the invaders and their supporters. Iran's alleged pursuit of them is the focus of another international crisis, so clarification of the nature of such weapons and the distinctive dangers they pose, or even are believed to pose, calls for specific treatment here, even though some of the problems raised by WMD will require revisiting some matters that have been dealt with in earlier chapters.

Since there is usually a tremendous amount of destruction in war, whatever weapons are used, it may seem that the concentration on specific weapons as "weapons of mass destruction" is peculiar. Is the machine gun a weapon of mass destruction because its use has enabled the efficient and rapid killing and injuring of vastly more people than previous weapons? Is the aeroplane, especially the bomber? These are not normally viewed with the disapproval reserved to WMD. Why not? There seem to be two reasons. First, these weapons are not in themselves geared to the idea of mass destruction, though that has indeed proved to be a common employment. The machine gun could be used in certain circumstances simply to accomplish the death of a small number of people more certainly than weapons that fired less rapidly. Second, and more importantly, one crucial problem about WMD primarily concerns not the number but rather the type of people killed. One thing morally problematic about what are usually classed as WMD is that they either inherently fail to discriminate between legitimate and nonlegitimate targets or are believed to have this defect. They are (or are believed to be) such that their normal use will rain death and destruction

249

upon the just and unjust, upon civilians and troops, upon hospitals and military installations alike. Nuclear weapons fit into this category, as do certain chemical and biological agents.

The point about employment serves to highlight both connections and disconnections between WMD and conventional weapons. Both types of weapon can be immoral in the same way, namely, by violating the principle of discrimination. The firebombing of Tokyo and the destruction of Dresden are good examples of conventional attacks that are open to the same kind of moral condemnation as the use of nuclear weapons. Indeed, in their immediate effects these were comparable to the nuclear bombings of Hiroshima and Nagasaki. But conventional bombing need not be quite as morally undiscriminating as this, whereas it seems inherent in the idea of WMD that they are geared to violation of the principle of discrimination. Of course, there are rare circumstances in which a case can be made for the standard WMD being used ethically – a low radiation–yielding nuclear bomb used against an armed enemy fleet in a remote ocean location, or a poisonous chemical agent used against an individual like Hitler who is in charge of waging an unjust war. It may even be that some weapons standardly classed as WMD, though they can be used to violate the principle of discrimination, do not have an inherent tendency to do so. To this I shall return.

Much anxiety is directed to the threat posed by access to chemical and biological weapons on the part of individuals and small groups, and certainly any such use, were it to be effective, would constitute a dangerous form of terrorism. Nonetheless, the fear of WMD terrorism can obscure the fact that the use of these weapons by nonstate actors has so far been very rare (and not very successful). By far the greatest damage done by way of mass destruction of civilian (and military) populations has been done by states: witness the use of poison gas in World War I, the nuclear devastation of Hiroshima and Nagasaki by the United States, and the gassing of Iranians by Iraqi forces in the Iran-Iraq war. (It should be remarked that the Iraqi weapons of mass destruction are estimated to have killed only 6,000 as against the U.S. slaughter of around 200,000 (mostly civilian) Japanese in the atomic raids of World War II.)[1] Moreover, conventional weapons such as bombs, rockets, and mines have been used by powerful states in precisely the same way as WMD, namely, to kill and maim large numbers of civilians.

It is true that states are not entirely excluded from the current discussion, since there is a great deal of anxiety about WMD proliferation. But this

---

[1] Estimates vary, ranging from the more conservative figures of 66,000 killed in the Hiroshima bombing and 39,000 at Nagasaki, to 200,000 at Hiroshima and 150,000 at Nagasaki. For a sample of estimates see the following website: <www.news.bbc.co.uk/1/hi/world/asia-pacific>.

anxiety is principally directed at so-called rogue states who have not yet been accepted into the club of the righteous possessors of the implements of mass destruction. Many of the "rogue" states are indeed dictatorial and oppressive, yet Western powers have supported them politically and supplied them with arms and armament technology in the past (witness Iraq and Pakistan) and have devoutly supported, or averted their gaze from, the nuclear arming of Israel. Furthermore, by a number of criteria there is much that is "roguish" about the behaviour of the major Western states. If ethics is our concern, then this partiality about illegitimate use of weapons needs to be dispelled.

It has been argued that the "taboo" against chemical weapons, in particular, has a large element of irrationality in it, since some chemical weapons need not be indiscriminate and are less devastating in their effects than many conventional weapons. It is true that the use of poison gas in World War I was heavily concentrated upon attacking troops, not civilians, and that various proposals to use gas against civilian populations came to nothing. Even so, it is estimated that at least 5,000 civilians suffered from the effects of the military use of poison gas, and over a hundred were killed.[2] This "inevitable spillover" (as one authority called it) may nevertheless be within the acceptable limits of unintended "collateral damage" given the massive damage to troops that was its primary objective.[3]

I do not intend to adjudicate here the claim that some common candidates for WMD status do not violate the discrimination principle. But the possibility that this is so leads to other reasons for concern about WMD. One of these harks back to Hobbes's prohibition on unnecessary cruelty. There is the idea that some weapons are morally obnoxious whether they violate discrimination or not. This certainly responds to reactions that people have often had to the development of new weapons, especially when they involve any element of dramatic suffering. But it may be responded that this "gut feeling" is misleading and even sentimental. Most deaths and injuries in war are ghastly and involve cruel suffering, even when they are inflicted "conventionally," for example, by rifle, bayonet, mortar, cannon, or bomb. It may be replied that such weapons are not intended to create extreme suffering, though that is sometimes their effect, but even if this is so, it seems less adequate as a response to the use of napalm and flamethrowers.

One thing the issue of cruelty opens up is the relevance of another condition of the just war tradition concerning the JIB, and that is proportionality. Whether some weapon is cruel depends in part upon whether its use is really necessary to achieve an objective commensurate with the suffering caused.

---

[2] Richard M. Price, *The Chemical Weapons Taboo* (Ithaca, NY: Cornell University Press, 1997), p. 62.

[3] Ibid.

On behalf of flamethrowers, for instance, it might be argued that they *can* be used legitimately when enemy troops cannot be removed in other ways from bunkers, caves, or dugouts without great loss of life to your own troops or without damage to other significant strategic objectives. This is on the assumption that there are serious military reasons for removing them. In other circumstances, their use, even against combatants, is immoral because disproportionate.[4]

The idea of proportionality comes into play not only in explication of cruelty but also with regard to mass destruction itself. I have argued that a primary reason for concern about WMD is their propensity to kill the wrong people rather than their tendency to kill large numbers. But it remains true that weapons whose purpose, or most likely use, is to kill very large numbers of people immediately raise an issue of proportionality, even if the people killed are otherwise legitimate targets. Most of the killing in World War I was that of soldiers in battle, so noncombatant immunity was not as great an issue as it later became; nonetheless, the sheer numbers killed posed an acute problem, only fully appreciated after the war, because it raised the question of whether the war goals, and the means of pursuing them, could possibly justify such losses. It also pointed to the often-neglected issue of the consequences of such loss of life for the civilian population and for the future of the warring societies. If there were weapons (like nuclear and certain biological weapons) that guaranteed such outcomes, even when used solely against armies, this would also pose a challenge to their use.

There is an important issue involving both discrimination and proportionality that is pretty much neglected in the just war tradition, though I think it has the resources to deal with it, and it has received (as noted in Chapter 9) some attention in the Geneva Protocols. This is the matter of war and the environment. If one thinks that morality requires a concern for the natural environment and for at least some animal life that is independent of other human interests, then one will regard environmental destruction by bombing or poisoning as raising an acute moral issue of wrongful targeting. But even if one's valuation of the environment is more instrumentally concerned with human welfare, a powerful case can be made against the various forms of devastation that much modern weaponry visits upon the natural world. The consequences of such destruction for future human beings, in no sense guilty of the wrongs that licensed the war in the first place, are often horrendous in terms of death, maiming, disease, damage to food supplies, and so on. Furthermore, the point about the environment can be extended (as mentioned in Chapter 9) to the destruction of the cultural environment of architecture and artistic creation.

---

4 See my earlier discussion of the difficulties in the idea of proportionality in Chapter 5, and the references there. While the points made here stand on the evident intuitive sense that the idea makes, they are consistent with the theoretical expansion of it in Chapter 5.

WMD Deterrence

An important political use for WMD is that of deterrence. The moral and technical problems associated with this use are mostly familiar from the debate about nuclear deterrence, and can be regarded as generalisations from it. There is first the complex factual question about the effectiveness of such weapons as deterrents. This is a much muddier issue than often supposed, since the possession of WMD sometimes seems to inhibit attack and sometimes doesn't. Indeed, it can increase the tensions and misunderstandings that all too often lead to war. In other contexts, the enormity of the threatened outcome tends to render the deterrent useless, as was the case for much of the Cold War when both the Soviets and the United States knew that the use of WMD would be irrational to prevent such wrongs as the Soviet invasion of Afghanistan or the U.S. war in Vietnam. As to the ethical questions around deterrence, the nuclear debate has familiarised us with a nest of problems here. Some of these concern the *consequences* of such policies and include the great risks of deterrence failure as well as the risks of escalation from conventional to nuclear war that are inherent in the possession of nuclear weapons.

Aside from consequences, however, there are two other sources of concern about deterrence that arise from its very nature. The first is a matter of the relation between the outcome of the deterrence and the attitude that is required to sustain it. I will be brief about this because I have written extensively about it elsewhere.[5] The nuclear deterrent is still the primary case, and it has been sustained by a (conditional) determination to violate massively the principle of discrimination. This staunch intention has been shared by Western and non-Western powers. It is a profoundly immoral commitment that has, I believe, had a corrupting effect upon much political life in the last sixty-odd years. Its immorality is related to what Gregory Kavka has called "the wrongful intentions principle" (WIP), which declares that if it is morally wrong to do X, then it is morally wrong to intend to do it. This principle is strongly entrenched in many religious traditions and in much common morality and law, but it has come under question or challenge by some philosophers, notably Bernard Williams, Kavka himself, David Lewis, and Jeff McMahan. I have defended the principle (and the corruption claim) against these objections elsewhere and will not repeat the defence at length here.[6] Some brief comments, however, are necessary.

The immorality of the nuclear threat is sometimes concealed by the idea that it is all somehow a bluff (at least by "us") so that there is really no

---

[5] See especially C. A. J. Coady, "Escaping from the Bomb," in Henry Shue (ed.), *Nuclear Deterrence and Moral Restraint: Critical Choices for American Strategy* (Cambridge and New York: Cambridge University Press, 1989), pp. 163–225; and C. A. J. Coady, "Deterrent Intentions Revisited," *Ethics* 99, no. 1 (1988), pp. 98–108.

[6] Coady, "Deterrent Intentions Revisited."

intention to use the weapons, but I consider this a self-comforting delusion. It is conceivable that the political leader may like to think it a bluff, and may even be determined him- or herself never to give the order to use, whatever the circumstances, but, in order for the deterrent to work, there must be no wider knowledge of this determination in government and military circles. Hence, any decision the leader takes must go against the whole orientation of the senior echelons of government and the military, as well as his or her own record of public declaration on the matter. There is therefore a huge likelihood that the decision will be disregarded as aberrational or worse, leading to replacement of the leader with someone more resolute. In fact, we have no reason to believe that the actual leaders of WMD states are in any way insincere in their deterrent intentions.

David Lewis, in an important and ingenious defence of limited nuclear deterrence, has provided an argument that makes it seem that the wrongful intentions criticism misses the point because the deterrent works by the very existence of the weapons: no intentions to use are needed, since what he calls, following McGeorge Bundy, "existential deterrence" is enough.[7] Even detailed plans for massive destruction drawn up by the deterring power are no token of intention to destroy; they are the sort of things that military people are required to project and give no indication of actual intention. Moreover, a nuclear strike by one side, even of the "surgical" kind, would produce an extraordinary degree of confusion and uncertainty that, in turn, would make a response to it highly unpredictable and uncertain. Deterrence has no need of conditional intentions in order to do its protective work.

It is certainly true that mere information about the quantity and capacity of weapons plus uncertainty about an opponent's intentions can be a deterrent, but this is because those deterred have some reason to fear that the weapons may be used against them in some circumstances. We cannot discount altogether the way this fear has been supported in the past by the frequently reiterated declarations of intention to use WMD and by public governmental policy and planning. In the climate of the Cold War, what uncertainties existed were not about whether we (or they) would respond at all, but about just *how* monstrous the retaliation would be. Moreover, even if nuclear or WMD deterrence did not embody the explicit intention to do evil, it would involve states of mind that are equally to be condemned, such as the readiness to form such an intention in certain eventualities, or an attitude of compliance with or supervision of a situation in which nuclear or biological devastation is one of the options available. What, for instance,

---

[7] Lewis's defence is conducted in two places, in both of which he makes use of the notion of "existential deterrence." See David Lewis, "Devils Bargains and the Real Worlds," in Douglas MacLean (ed.), *The Security Gamble: Deterrence Dilemmas in the Nuclear Age* (Totowa, NJ : Rowman & Allanheld, 1984), pp. 148–151; and David Lewis, "Finite Counterforce," in Shue (ed.), *Nuclear Deterrence and Moral Restraint*, pp. 65–73.

do we think of the moral standing of a person who, as a means of deterrence, sets up a device that, when triggered by an intruder, will either kill the intruder, play a Mozart concerto, kill the intruder's innocent relatives, or kill huge numbers of innocent people in the neighbourhood where the intruder lives? The device, even if successful as a deterrent, involves shocking moral irresponsibility, and the situation would hardly be morally improved if the outcome were left not to chance but to an Ultimate Decider who had the moral outlook of Richard Nixon or Chairman Mao.

It is sometimes thought that the conditional intention is harmless because its effects on the enemy render it certain that the condition will never be realised and hence that the intention will never have to be acted on. Such certainty is, of course, not to be had, but some philosophers have used the idea of it to claim that the argument for the immorality of the conditional intention is flawed. The objection is that even if the preventive effect were certain, the argument from the WIP would still have to hold that the intention was immoral, and indeed as immoral as if the conditional outcome was merely possible or likely. Indeed, proponents of the argument from WIP seem to hold that any such conditional intention is just as immoral as a direct intention to slaughter the innocent. Bernard Williams has urged this objection forcefully, and he has been followed by Jeff McMahan. Here is Williams:

If it were *certain* that threatening some dreadful thing would prevent some great crime or suffering, would that really leave the threat as morally no better than the dreadful deed that I wouldn't need to perform? I am not suggesting that such certainty exists in the case of nuclear deterrence. The point is simply whether the argument works in the abstract.[8]

The primary response to this problem is simply to deny that a proponent of the WIP needs to hold the "morally no better" thesis. The WIP argument concludes that deterrence is immoral because it incorporates a seriously immoral intention, but it need not insist that this conditional intention is as bad as various other conditional intentions or other categorical intentions. Nor does it imply that the agent is as great a scoundrel as certain other agents who have less attachment to the good than one who implements a deterrent policy may have. It seems that something can be very seriously wrong without being as wrong as certain other serious wrongs. Deceitfully causing grave harm to someone's reputation is not as wrong as torturing him slowly to death, but nonetheless it is seriously immoral. Two acts or states may both be above the threshold of the seriously immoral, yet one may still be, in the nature of things, worse than the other.

---

[8] Bernard Williams, "How to Think Sceptically about the Bomb," *New Society* 62 (November 18, 1982), p. 289.

A further problem with the certainty scenario (which Williams admits does not actually apply to the nuclear example) is that there is a conceptual mystery about how someone could have an intention to do X if and only if Y where she is certain that Y will never occur. Admittedly her knowledge that Y will not occur is based on her knowledge that the enemy believes that if it does Y, she will do X, and believes this because she has announced her conditional intention to do X. There is no barrier to an announcement, but announcing an intention is not having it. If announcing is not enough, and only actual possession of the intention will produce the enemy's belief and the knowledge of it, then paradox appears to result. Intentions are not just dispositional states one causes oneself to have in any way at all. They are essentially related to the possibilities of practical reasoning, which are themselves epistemic rather than logical or metaphysical. If you consider the nonoccurrence of A to be certain, you are thereby excluding the occurrence of A from your practical deliberations, and thus also excluding any question of what you intend to do if A occurs. Hence your certainty removes the possibility of your forming the intention that is supposed to create the certainty.

Earlier, I referred to a second source of concern about deterrence. This consists in the fact that deterrence is a strategy of fear creation. Sometimes, of course, one needs to arouse fear for purposes of protection against those bent upon damage, but, as pacifists rightly point out, the generation of fear is a profoundly ambiguous exercise. This is true for several reasons. One is that the purposes for which the fear is created are inherently open to different interpretations; the deterrer is given to thinking that his purposes are benign, but it would be naïve to think that this is how others must interpret his threats and armed displays. The more powerful, and the more indiscriminate, the displays and threats, the more likely their targets are to think them aggressive rather than defensive, and to take steps to protect themselves. This is one of the causes of escalation and proliferation, but even if the targets do not respond in kind, the deterrent stance, especially when it becomes a permanent posture, tends to have a poisonous effect upon political relations. The deterrer finds increasing dangers abroad that require the expansion of military might and the strengthening of an overkill deterrent capacity. Fear itself fuels the creation of further fear.

It would be utopian to deny any role to fear in international relations or politics more generally, but it is a motivation that needs careful controlling. Machiavelli argued that fear is an essential element in politics in that a ruler should try to be both feared and loved by his subjects, but should prefer fear to love if a choice between the two has to be made. Even so, Machiavelli realised that fear could turn into a destabilising hatred, and he cautioned against this risk.[9] It could be argued that Machiavelli underestimated this

9 Niccolo Machiavelli, *The Prince*, ed. Peter Bondanella, trans. Peter Bondanella and Mark Musa (Oxford: Oxford University Press, 1984), Chapter 17, pp. 55–58.

risk within civil society, but there is an even greater risk of fear generating hatred in an international order governed by the fear of deterrence. Such an order of fear inherits some of the problems of a domestic government of fear. In particular, the climate of dominating fear is not a long-term recipe for the creation of genuine peace. For peace, if less than divine harmony, is more than mere stability. As will be argued in Chapter 13, it requires a certain level of amicable dispositions which are dissipated by a sustained atmosphere of fear. Peace is an ideal that has always played a role in just war thinking, though its significance has sometimes been submerged by the more legalistic conditions, and sometimes by the bellicose subject matter, of the tradition. Not only is peace broadly preferable to war (so that war must be a "last resort," as one of the conditions of the JAB puts it), but the point of waging a just war, as Augustine insisted, is to establish peace.[10]

Finally, it is worth noting that the rise, or reemergence, of substate terrorism in recent decades has reduced the capacity of states to deter some of their enemies with WMD. When the opponent is not another state, but organised citizens of one's own state, or a loose-knit international assembly like al Qaeda, then the threat to devastate a city or enemy populations more broadly does not make much sense. This is one reason why powerful states are anxious to find other states that they can identify with the terrorists. Talk of "harbouring," "encouraging," "supporting" serves the function of identifying a state against which pressure, including deterrent pressure, can be brought. Often, as with Iraq before the invasion of 2003, the link is tenuous or merely fanciful; sometimes it has more reality, but hardly enough to make the threat particularly plausible.

The Problems of Proliferation

Opposition to proliferation of WMD has an air of paradox about it because those most concerned to denounce the prospect of the spread of ownership of these weapons are often those who already have them in some form and are prepared to use them *in extremis*. The paradox arises from the fact that if there are good arguments for the United States, for instance, to have nuclear weapons for deterrence or even for use, why aren't these also good arguments for any nation with defence needs? If nuclear deterrence is so good for world stability, why shouldn't its benefits be spread around, as the neo-realist Kenneth Waltz once notoriously argued.[11]

The paradox can be resolved by pointing out that "we" are somehow special, because we are either especially imperilled or exceptionally good.

---

[10] For a discussion of Augustine's account of peace, see Chapter 13 of this volume and C. A. J. Coady and Jeff Ross, "St. Augustine and the Ideal of Peace," *American Catholic Philosophical Quarterly* 74, no. 1 (Winter 2000), pp. 153–161.

[11] Kenneth N. Waltz, *The Spread of Nuclear Weapons: More May Be Better* (London: International Institute for Strategic Studies, 1981).

The former is hardly plausible, since many states can persuasively argue that they face more serious dangers from other states than France or the United States or Russia does (whatever problems they have with terrorism). As for the latter, our conviction that we are "holier than them" is likely to be viewed differently by them. Indeed, in the case of the United States the argument is particularly hard to run, since it is one the few nations that have actually used WMD to devastating effect. Many Americans are so convinced of their nation's unique moral status that they find the failure of the rest of the world to accord it moral superiority baffling. This was the burden of many comments by the U.S. leadership in the wake of the dreadful terrorist attacks of September 11. President Bush expressed amazement at the mis-understanding that led people to hate America: "Like most Americans," he said, "I just can't believe it because I know how good we are."[12] This was reflected in much of the quasi-religious political rhetoric evoked in Wash-ington by the attack: "good versus evil," "coalitions of the good," "crusade," "operation infinite justice," and so on. Those beyond American shores (and many within) are right to view this picture with incredulity, since good and evil, and much in between, are more evenly distributed amongst people and nations than this rhetoric suggests.

Pointing this out is liable to provoke the accusation that one is committed to the dreaded "moral equality" thesis, whereby all states must be treated as equally good. But this is a red herring. The point is not that all nations weigh equally in the moral scales, but that none are immune from moral and intellectual faults. One of the good things stressed by realist thinkers is precisely that moralistic stances in foreign affairs are invariably directed outward and often serve to blind nations to their own sins. In the context of proliferation, this makes the provision of moral and legal exemptions to oneself an impediment to dealing with it.[13]

But in spite of this, contrary to Waltz, WMD proliferation is a bad thing. The more states that engage in the deterrence game with these weapons, the greater the risk that they will be used, with consequences that are likely to be not only immoral but disastrously so. No doubt the existing WMD states are acting in bad faith when they denounce proliferation while keeping many of their WMD, but this does not mean that the spread of such weapons and deterrence strategies is thereby made more acceptable. In some ways, the problem is like that of global pollution. The wealthy polluters are in no position to point the finger at the poorer countries that increase pollution as they drive toward development, but increased pollution is still a bad idea.

---

[12] Quoted in Liam Kennedy and Scott Lucas, "Enduring Freedom: Public Diplomacy and U.S. Foreign Policy," *American Quarterly* 57, no. 2 (2005), p. 309.

[13] For a discussion of moralism and realism, see my "The Moral Reality in Realism," in C. A. J. Coady (ed.), *What's Wrong with Moralism?* (Oxford: Blackwell, 2006), and in *Journal of Applied Philosophy* 22, no. 2 (2005), pp. 121–136.

In the case of proliferation, a serious contribution to stemming it would be for the existing WMD powers to abandon these weapons. To their credit, some steps along this path have been taken, but they are both ambiguous and inadequate. This brings us to the topic of WMD disarmament.

The Prospect for Disarmament

On my interpretation of the just war tradition, the right to wage war represents a certain concession to the vagaries of the human condition and the uncertainties of the international order. The tradition emphasises the priority of peace and places strong restrictions on resort to war. Hence, it favours efforts to remove the likelihood of war, and implies that where disarmament measures would help that removal, they should be supported. It seems very plausible that universal WMD disarmament and renunciation fit this bill.

One intellectual obstacle to this development is the possibility discussed earlier that some weapons usually classed as WMD need not violate nor inherently tend to violate the JIB. A reasonable response to this worry is to insist that it makes more prudential sense to ban classes of weapon than to pick and choose amongst them. There is a familiar insight here that lies behind many legal prohibitions (and indeed provides much of the impulse towards such moral theories as rule utilitarianism). An illustration used in an earlier chapter to different effect is equally relevant here. When there are heat waves in Australian states, authorities will often declare "a day of total fire-ban" prohibiting the lighting of any fires in the open. This applies to every class of person and to every fire, even though very experienced country folk may be perfectly capable of keeping a small fire under control. The danger of allowing exemptions is too great. Similarly with the WMD ban: given the awful prospects of many of these weapons for violating the principle of discrimination and encouraging further technological development in the same direction, it makes sense to put a stop to the whole class, even if some claims to membership in the class are more a matter of appearance than reality. This is especially so when there already exists a degree of international respect for such a ban, and when we may anticipate reasonable prospects of enforcing it.

Another objection to WMD disarmament is that it may distract attention from the need for more general disarmament, just as a concern for the horror of WMD damage may obscure the terrible effects of conventional war. This point is characteristically made by pacifists and is urged by Robert Holmes in his introduction to *On War and Morality*.[14] I am sympathetic to the

---

[14] Robert Holmes, *On War and Morality* (Princeton, NJ: Princeton University Press, 1989), p. 4; and Robert Holmes, "Pacifism and Weapons of Mass Destruction," in Sohail H. Hashmi and Steven P. Lee (eds.), *Ethics and Weapons of Mass Destruction: Religious and Secular Perspectives* (Cambridge and New York: Cambridge University Press, 2004), p. 466.

concern, but the risk is surely worth taking. Moreover, there is the contrary prospect that reduction in WMD armaments will produce a momentum in favour of more general disarmament proposals and antiwar attitudes. There is a tendency in pacifist thinking to advocate all-or-nothing solutions, but incremental measures are often more realistic and may encourage a developing pace in disarmament.

Similar considerations apply to the stark opposition between proponents of multilateral and unilateral disarmament. The debate is largely a product of the Cold War and reflects some of the gross simplifications of that conflict. The options are not really between the totally multinational and the totally unilateral, but between judicious resorts to various combinations of the two. Some unilateral measures that may prompt more multilateral ones can safely be adopted, and agreements between some powers can precede general acceptance by all nations. Similar points could be made about inspection regimes. No agreement will be perfect, but this should not impede commitment to steps along the road to a more peaceful world.

A major problem with disarmament measures is the disproportion of military and political power in the international order. It is not surprising that weak, unstable states that have, or think they have, good reason to fear their neighbours or remote but influential powers are anxious to obtain or keep weapons that are thought to give them some kind of military leverage. This is one of the things that promotes proliferation. Another is the "status symbol" effect of possessing what are regarded as super-weapons. Add to these problems the unwillingness of the powerful states to abandon nuclear weapons and their tendency to drag their heels over chemical and biological weapons, and you have a potent recipe for deadlock.

Two Scenarios for Progress

Against this background, there are two scenarios for future action on WMD that need to be considered. The first is one that has recently gained favour in many quarters in the West, especially the United States. This is basically the strategy of reviving imperialism, or, as some put it, "Pax Americana." The idea is that the United States (with or without its allies) should more overtly embrace a hegemonic role in the world and should use military might to invade "rogue states" and either replace them with client regimes or run them as colonies, no doubt with some form of pliant democracy as a long-term goal. A scenario of this sort emerged at the top levels of U.S. policy formation in the wake of the terrorist attacks on the World Trade Center and the Pentagon and the U.S. counterattack upon Afghanistan.[15] It is no

---

[15] A striking expression of this mind-set is to be found in the writings of Max Boot, sometime opinion page editor of *The Wall Street Journal.* See his article "Colonise Wayward Nations" in *The Australian,* October 15, 2001, p. 13.

accident that the role of the nonexistent WMD in Saddam Hussein's Iraq was given as the principal public reason for the 2003 invasion of Iraq.

Not only has the implementation of this approach proved disastrous in the particular case of Iraq, but the general strategy is likely to compound the international imbalance that feeds the drive to procure and keep WMD. It is also likely to provide more motivation for international terrorist attacks (with or without WMD) and to recruit more people to terrorist ranks. The reactions to such U.S. domination by the substantial powers that lie outside the new Raj (such as Russia, China, and India) are also unlikely to be positive, despite attempts to placate them like President Bush's nuclear overtures to India. (The latter, of course, is a paradoxical version of the Pax Americana strategy in that it is likely to encourage proliferation by its contempt for the Nuclear Proliferation Treaty and its benign attitude towards escalation by one member of the nuclear club, but such disregard for the treaty and international consensus is fully in the spirit of the new hegemonism.) The strategy is also likely to inherit all the follies and crimes that went with old-fashioned imperialism. The fact that U.S. meddling in the affairs of Central and South America throughout the twentieth century was almost uniformly disastrous for the peoples and politics of those regions should give grounds for suspicion of the new strategy. Nor is one's confidence in any such policy increased by the absurd perceptions (mentioned earlier) that U.S. political leaders and even many intellectuals entertain of themselves and their state as paragons of goodness. Robert Kagan's recent justification for U.S. hegemonic disregard for international laws and rules that the U.S. expects others to keep rests in part (where it doesn't rest on the dictum "might is right") on a ludicrous picture of the unfailing nobility of American motives in foreign policy.[16] Reprising some version of Kipling's "white man's burden" is hardly an appetising prospect for the new century, though Kipling's description of those under hegemonic protection as "new-caught, sullen peoples, half-devil and half-child" must have a sad resonance for Western liberators anchored with their burden in Iraq.

The second scenario is the internationalist one aimed at cooperation and at resort to law rather than mayhem. There is certainly a leadership role here for the United States, but it is mostly one of moral and political initiative rather than crushing power. Here the one superpower has an ambiguous record. On the positive side, the U.S. government or its citizens have often sponsored moves aimed at gaining international cooperation via legal instruments to achieve a more secure, peaceful, and fair international order. But, on the negative side, the U.S. government has then often failed to ratify or endorse the collaborative outcomes of these initiatives. The record of successive U.S. governments on the ratification of international treaties

---

[16] Robert Kagan, *Of Paradise and Power: America and Europe in the New World Order* (New York: Knopf, 2003).

and conventions is poor, to put it mildly. The United States remains one of only two states to refuse ratification of the Convention on the Rights of the Child (the other is Somalia, which basically doesn't have a government). Although it ratified the Biological Weapons Convention of 1972, it has rejected the International Criminal Court, the establishment of which it originally supported and which could be a significant factor in dealing with terrorists and perpetrators of atrocities in war. This rejection has been accompanied by positive efforts to undermine the court's jurisdiction, such as bilateral immunity agreements by which nations are pressured to agree not to abide by the ICC's jurisdiction with regard to U.S. soldiers.[17] It has also refused to renew its adherence to the International Nuclear Test Ban Treaty. There are indeed flaws in all of these agreements and in the many others that the United States has rejected, but all efforts at international cooperation involve compromise, and the official American position too often amounts to the demand for cooperation only on U.S. terms. The criminal court rejection, for example, is based on the idea that the court should have jurisdiction over other nationalities but that it is unacceptable for the court to have jurisdiction over Americans. As one senior U.S. army official explained to me: "We're the good guys!" This rejection of universality is perverse to the point of arrogance.

There is no certainty that the second scenario will be successful in reducing or eliminating the dependency on WMD, but, for the most part, we do not live in a world of certainties. It is probable that the cooperative path offers more hope for the future, since it is all too likely that the domination scenario will create animosities, fears, and countermeasures that are likely to negate its short-term achievements. This is not to deny that U.S. military power may on occasion be appropriate in dealing with the problem of WMD. Rather, it is to emphasise the primacy of the second scenario and to locate such uses within that framework.

[17] For further discussion of the United States' undermining of the ICC, see Dominic McGoldrick, "Political and Legal Responses to the ICC," in Dominic McGoldrick, Peter Rowe, and Eric Donnelly (eds.), *The Permanent International Criminal Court: Legal and Policy Issues* (Oxford: Hart Publishing, 2004), pp. 423–437.

13

The Ideal of Peace

Prepare for war with peace in thy soul.

The *Bhagavad Gita*, 2.38

There can be no doubt that the value of peace has served as a significant inspiration for theorists and activists over the centuries. Thomas Hobbes made the pursuit of peace a foundation stone of his laws of nature and a reiterated theme in his discussion and elaboration of them, and they, in turn, supported his whole ethic and political philosophy. His first "and fundamental" law of nature is "to seek Peace and follow it."[1] Pacifists, of course, are devoted to peace, but many nonpacifists claim an equal dedication, even if it lacks the same consequences. As mentioned in Chapter 1, the United States Strategic Air Command, whose constant task was to maintain the credibility of nuclear devastation, even had as its motto "Peace is our profession," without any apparent awareness of the delightful ambiguity contained in the word "profession." Hugo Grotius called his famous treatise on the law of war *The Rights of War and Peace (De Jure Belli Ac Pacis)*, and declared "the unabated desire and invariable prospect of peace" to be "the only end for which hostilities can be lawfully begun."[2] The Lieber Code says of many nations and great governments related to one another in close intercourse in "modern times": "Peace is their normal condition; war is the exception. The ultimate object of all modern war is a renewed state of peace."[3]

It is clear, then, that the value of peace has traditionally had a place in just war theory, though it has sometimes been positioned so far in the

---

[1] Thomas Hobbes, *Leviathan*, ed. C. B. Macpherson (Harmondsworth: Penguin, 1968), Chapter 14, p. 190.

[2] Hugo Grotius, *The Rights of War and Peace (De Jure Belli Ac Pacis)*, trans. A. C. Campbell (Pontefract: Printed by B. Boothroyd, 1814), Book III, Chapter 25, pp. 417–418.

[3] The Lieber Code: Instructions for the Government of Armies of the United States in the Field, Article 29, accessed January 27, 2005, at <http://www.geocities.com/CapitolHill/Senate/3616/lieber_code.html>.

background as to obscure its real significance. Since St. Augustine is more explicit than most about what is meant by the reference to peace, let us begin with his account. Standing at the source of just war theorising, Augustine gives peace a pivotal role in his thinking about both war and politics, and his complex legacy needs more unpacking than it seems so far to have received. I will argue that Augustine operates with three conceptions of peace, connected under the concept of order, and that only one of these can be helpful in developing an ideal of peace that could feasibly help with discussions of the morality of war.

Augustine's emphasis upon the role of peace goes so far as to affirm the ubiquitous nature of the devotion to peace. He sees the desire for peace as an essential ingredient of human nature, much like the desire for enjoyment. In his discussions of war, Augustine argues that even war making is essentially oriented to peace; it is not only that rulers and warriors ought to be concerned with peace, but that they inevitably are:

Indeed, even when men choose war, their only wish is for victory; which shows that their desire in fighting is for peace with glory. For what is victory but the conquest of the opposing side? And when this is achieved, there will be peace. Even wars, then, are waged with peace as their object, even when they are waged by those who are concerned to exercise their warlike prowess, either in command or in the actual fighting. Hence it is an established fact that peace is the desired end of war. For every man is in quest of peace, even in waging war, whereas no one is in quest of war when making peace.[4]

Augustine's Peace – Thin and Thick

Augustine's position is a very significant one, especially in a writer who has some claim to be a founder of the just war tradition. Its first significance lies in the important insight that war is primarily instrumental, so that even the most bloodthirsty warriors and rulers resort to war in order to further some other, broadly political purposes. (As we saw in Chapter 1, this is an insight anticipated by Aristotle, who says: "no-one desires to be at war for the sake of being at war, nor deliberately takes steps to cause a war: a man would be thought an utterly bloodthirsty character if he declared war on a friendly state for the sake of causing battles and massacres.")[5] But the instrumentality thesis is distinct from the ubiquity-of-peace-seeking thesis. It is only by adopting an extremely attenuated conception of peace that Augustine achieves the ubiquity conclusion. This "thin" understanding of peace as basically whatever order is established by the cessation or absence

4 St. Augustine, *The City of God*, ed. Henry Bettenson (New York: Penguin, 1972), Book XIX, Chapter 12, p. 866.
5 Aristotle, *Nicomachean Ethics*, trans. H. A. Rackham (London: William Heinemann, 1962), Book 10, Chapter 7, p. 615.

of war has the virtue of establishing some sort of universality in the desire for peace, and it also has the merit of implying a reasonably neutral, empirical way of determining when peace has occurred and giving us a palpable goal to seek. But it has certain major disadvantages, the principal one being that it fails to make for an ideal of peace that is sufficiently benign. In the Sermon on the Mount, Christ did not mean to reassure warmongers like Genghis Khan when he said, "Blessed are the peacemakers." The enslaved survivors of a brutal conquest of arms may be able to gain some consolation from the thought that the worst is over, but they can hardly rejoice in the achievement of peace. The remark of Tacitus, "They make a wilderness and call it peace," draws scornful attention to the deficiencies attendant upon uses of the thin notion of peace.

Augustine's discussion of peace is complex and full of tensions, and has targets beyond the issue of war. As with much of his examination of social and political ethics, he shows a certain ambivalence toward, and even impatience with, the values of the earthly city, and exhibits an inclination to put a gulf between the goods of the political order and the spiritual goods that can be enjoyed only in fellowship with God.[6] Often, the crucial fact about life here below consists in whether it is orderly enough to allow the Christian to get on with his or her spiritual quest in relative safety and freedom. Hence the importance of any sort of peace and the close link between peace and order. We see this at work in Chapter 17 of Book XIX of *The City of God*, where he professes indifference to the exact nature of the laws and customs that sustain any given peace so long as it does not impede the seeking after salvation in the true religion: "She [the heavenly city] takes no account of any difference in customs, laws, and institutions, by which earthly peace is achieved and preserved – not that she annuls or abolishes any of those, rather, she maintains them and follows them . . . provided that no hindrance is presented thereby to the religion which teaches that the one supreme and true God is to be worshipped."[7] This attitude opens the way to a certain indifference to the morality of the means by which peace is sustained in earthly kingdoms and human associations more generally. In his discussion of the violent robber who is a possible counterexample to the Augustinian thesis that everyone seeks peace, Augustine points out that such a person is anxious to establish peace amongst his criminal associates and in his own domestic circumstances. In the latter case, "he scolds and punishes; and, if need be, he employs savage measures to impose on his household a peace which, he feels, cannot exist unless all the other elements in the same domestic society are subject to one head; and this head, in his own home,

---

[6] For a nice discussion of the ambiguities in Augustine's attitude to earthly ethics and politics, see John Langan, "The Elements of St. Augustine's Just War Theory," *The Journal of Religious Ethics* 12 (1984), pp. 19–38.

[7] St. Augustine, *City of God*, Book XIX, Chapter 17, p. 878.

is himself."[8] The brutality and oppression by which this peace is established and, presumably, maintained does not count against its being a peace. This is the thin conception at work.

Yet Augustine recognizes that some versions of peace are more valuable than others, and he also acknowledges the temptation to employ a richer concept of peace in place of the thin one. So he says:

> For no creature's perversion is so contrary to nature as to destroy the very last vestiges of its nature. It comes to this, then; a man who has learnt to prefer right to wrong and the rightly ordered to the perverted, sees that the peace of the unjust, compared with the peace of the just, is not worthy even of the name of peace. Yet even what is perverted must of necessity be in, or derived from, or associated with – that is, in a sense, at peace with – some part of the order of things among which it has its being or of which it consists. Otherwise it would not exist at all.[9]

Here Augustine envisages the possibility of a richer notion of peace, "the peace of the just," but insists that the iniquitous imposition of order still counts as a sort of peace. Indeed, so strong are the metaphysical links connecting existence, order, and peace here and in the passages surrounding this quotation that they would seem to commit Augustine to the view that war itself is a sort of peace, since it exists. Here the understanding of peace is at its very thinnest and most metaphysical, and, from the point of view of any study of war, at its least useful. Let us set this bare metaphysical conception aside, and take the thin conception, more practically, to be that which treats peace as the state of societies that are not at war.[10] This connects more sensibly with political realities and still provides a contrast with richer conceptions of peace, such as the peace of the just, since nations may coexist without violent hostilities between them even where the settlement or arrangement that has brought this condition about is far from just. The thin conception is descriptively adequate for characterising empirical realities and some human goals, but, as we saw in discussing Augustine's ubiquity thesis, it is seriously deficient if we are interested in an ideal of peace as something to be striven for in a context of international dispute and diplomacy. No doubt the absence of war brought about by the success of a vicious, unjust conquest has something to be said for it – namely, the carnage has stopped. But this seems too minimal to count as the object of "peace-making" or explain the attraction of the ideal of peace. What, then, of the rich conception? My contention is that rich conceptions of peace

---

[8] Ibid., Chapter 12, p. 867.

[9] Ibid., p. 869.

[10] Since, as we have seen, Augustine often moves freely between considerations about households and other small groupings to reflections on larger political societies, such as states and empires, the contrast between peace and war may also apply to violent episodes or practices within these smaller societies. But my chief concern here will be with war in its more common, large-scale meaning.

tend to exhibit the opposite fault of being too morally loaded. To see this, let us look first at a very rich account of peace to be found in Augustine.

The most striking contrast with the thin conception is the rich conception of peace employed by Augustine when he discusses the life and inner dynamic of the heavenly city. "We see then," he says, "that the Supreme Good of the City of God is everlasting and perfect peace, which is not the peace through which men pass in their mortality, in their journey from birth to death, but that peace in which they remain in their immortal state, experiencing no adversity at all."[11] This thick conception is thus implicated with the joys of salvation (for those who are saved) and with ultimate justice: it is "the perfectly ordered and completely harmonious fellowship in the enjoyment of God, and of each other in God."[12] The conceptual distance of this heavenly peace from earthly peace is such that Augustine, at one point, thinks it better not to use the term "peace" to describe the fulfilment of the life of the heavenly city. So he says: "But the word 'peace' is freely used in application to the events of this mortal state, where there is certainly no eternal life; and so I have preferred to use the term 'eternal life' instead of 'peace' in describing the end of this City.... "[13] But this is not a preference that Augustine adheres to later in the work. In any case, heavenly peace is plainly too rich and demanding a notion to be useful for debates about the role of ideals here on earth, and, as we have seen, Augustine himself explicitly contrasts it with the peace of the earthly life; nonetheless, it is helpful in suggesting the need for something less rich that I shall call the medium conception.

But before developing this idea, we must ask whether the rich conception mentioned earlier, namely, "the peace of the just," is, as I claimed, too morally loaded for our purposes. The answer to this question depends to a degree upon what is meant by "the peace of the just."

The "Medium" Conception of Peace

The path to a more practically relevant construal of peace (the medium conception) may, however, be built from Augustine's explicit definitions of peace. One definition, offered in Book XIX, is: "...peace is ordered harmony; and the basis of this order is the observance of two rules: first, to do no harm to anyone, and, secondly, to help everyone whenever possible."[14] Augustine then elaborates on his conception of peace as ordered harmony in relation to "earthly peace" by saying: "So also the earthly city, whose life is not based on faith, aims at an earthly peace, and it limits the

---

[11] St. Augustine, *City of God*, Book XIX, Chapter 20, p. 881.
[12] Ibid., Chapter 17, p. 878.
[13] Ibid., Chapter 11, p. 865.
[14] Ibid., Chapter 14, p. 873.

harmonious agreement of citizens concerning the giving and obeying of orders to the establishment of a kind of compromise between human wills about the things relevant to mortal life."[15] The idea of compromise associated here with peace as ordered harmony suggests a situation in which at least some of the interests of the parties involved have been honoured. This comports with Augustine's characterization of the way in which just men rule in the household: "they do not give orders because of a lust for domination but from a dutiful concern for the interest of others, not with pride in taking precedence over others, but with compassion in taking care of others."[16] Inasmuch as Augustine recommends that households be run in the manner of the city, it appears that the ruler of a city should in some analogous way be attentive to the interests of citizens.[17] Moreover, this attentiveness seems to be an integral part of peace as ordered harmony (Augustine's Latin is *ordinata concordia*), and it involves the "compromise between human wills" eschewing "lust for domination" that sets it apart from the thin conception of peace embodied in the brutal robber paterfamilias mentioned earlier, and from the condition of a crushed and humiliated, but no longer resisting, people lorded over by a triumphant conqueror. This medium interpretation of peace extracted from Augustine's definition in terms of ordered harmony is reinforced by the consideration of another definition he gives later, when he says: "The peace of all things is the tranquillity of order."[18] The reference to tranquillity points to states of mind that accompany the order that is peace, and these states of mind seem plainly inconsistent with any merely dominational model of peace.

Our discussion indicates that what may be needed in an ideal of peace to supplement the theory of just warfare is a conception of peace that develops the insights of Augustine contained in what I have called his medium conception of peace. This requires something more robust than a mere cessation of war or violent conflict, though not something so robust as to absorb the ideal of peace into that of justice or liberty. (Such an absorption tends to afflict those who are too impressed by the rich conception.) We need to leave room for the phrase "just peace" to be more than a pleonasm, and for a legitimate space between "unjust peace" and "not a peace at all." Here Hobbes may be a useful guide, since he makes a parallel point about war when he says:

For Warre consisteth not in Battell onely, or the act of fighting; but in a tract of time, wherein the Will to contend by Battell is sufficiently known: and therefore the

[15] Ibid., Chapter 17, p. 877.

[16] Ibid., Chapter 14, p. 874.

[17] "Consequently it is fitting that the father of a household should take his rules from the law of the city, and govern his household in such a way that it fits in with the peace of the city." St. Augustine, *City of God*, Book XIX, Chapter 16, p. 876.

[18] Ibid., Chapter 13, p. 870.

notion of Time, is to be considered in the nature of Warre; as it is in the nature of Weather. For as the nature of Foule weather, lyeth not in a showre or two of rain; but in an inclination thereto of many days together: So the nature of War, consisteth not in actuall fighting; but in the known disposition thereto, during all the time there is no assurance to the contrary. All other time is PEACE.[19]

A peace must have something in it that at least quiets the dispositions to violence, hostility, and aggression that are typical of war, even if it does not eliminate them entirely. The defeated or disadvantaged parties to the peace may have legitimate grievances remaining, but in a genuine peace there is a settling of dispositions into a certain tranquillity so that the recurrence of violent conflict is not imminent and the maintenance of order does not require inordinate violence. The "ordered harmony" of earthly peace demands some degree of coordination of interests amongst previously warring or violently disposed hostile parties that, like all compromise, involves losses and gains. Yet in its offering a serious measure of respect to the interests of those who are defeated, or to those who are disadvantaged by the cessation of hostilities, it helps ensure the endurance of calm rather than foul weather. Some condition like this seemed to be in Marshal Foch's mind when he said, with deliberate hyperbole, of the peace of Versailles, "This is not a peace treaty, it is an armistice for twenty years."

In terms of an ideal, then, the pursuit of peace can be distinguished from the goal of the mere cessation of hostilities on any terms. There has to be something involved in the cessation or absence of hostilities that has an inherent stability about it that can be enjoyed. It may not be what either party to the conflict originally sought when they took up arms, but it cannot be so totally crushing as to keep alive and potent the dispositions to war that preceded it. The victory/defeat itself may have been crushing, in the sense of overwhelming and devastating, but the settlement must offer something hopeful to the conquered if it is to count as peace. Again, it must be stressed that what it offers may be less than full justice.

If peace is understood in this way, what attractions would it have as an ideal? Well, one attraction is that a world or a geographical region that is at peace is a world or region that lacks various conspicuous evils associated with warfare and similar forms of violence. These are often calamitous evils, even though they are not the only evils in the world. Moreover, they are evils that human beings are prone to inflict on one another, so that the likelihood of their occurrence is alarmingly high, and yet they are within human control and, in principle at least, subject to human prevention.

In the light of this, an ideal of peace should stimulate efforts to maintain peace in the face of threats to it, and to reestablish peace when it has been destroyed by war. Central to the pursuit of such an ideal of peace is an ability

---

[19] Hobbes, *Leviathan*, Chapter 13, pp. 185–186.

to negotiate some kind of "compromise between human wills about the things relevant to mortal life."[20] It was such an ability that Augustine praised a year before he died in what was his last letter on the subject of peace, written to the soldier Darius, who had just concluded peace negotiations with the Vandals. After praising warriors who, bravely defending the state and its interests, achieve peace by force of arms, Augustine says:

But it is a higher glory still to slay war itself with the word, than men with the sword, and to procure or maintain peace by peace, not by war. For those who fight, if they are good men, doubtless seek for peace; nevertheless it is through blood. Your mission, however, is to prevent the shedding of blood. Yours, therefore, is the privilege of averting that calamity which others are under the necessity of producing.[21]

This comment exhibits the way in which Augustine thinks of the ideal of peace as showing that peaceful means of settling political disputes are superior to violent solutions (in line with the "last resort" condition of the JAB). He thereby places the ideal of peace as a governing, indeed inhibiting, factor in the thinking that considers the resort to war for solving political problems. As such, it figures as a significant background to the conditions of the JAB. Augustine's comment also suggests two other things. The first is the role of the ideal in guiding our attitudes towards the ending of violent conflicts, even on the part of the justified side (if there is one), and the second is the relation of the ideal to the outlook of pacifism. Let us consider these in turn.

A Just Ending of War

First, the ending of conflict. It is a curiosity of the just war tradition that far more attention is paid to the ethical (including prudential) considerations having to do with beginning and conducting war than with those related to ending it. The very names *jus ad bellum* and *jus in bello* testify to this emphasis. Yet a just ending to warfare, *jus post bellum*, calls for more than cursory attention, both because the closing stages of war can be the occasion for tremendous but possibly avoidable suffering and because the way in which a war is ended can determine much about the subsequent peace.[22] The first point is dramatically illustrated by the last few months of the European

---

[20] St. Augustine, *City of God*, Book XIX, Chapter 17, p. 877.

[21] *Ep. Ad Darium*, 229. Quoted in John Eppstein, *The Catholic Tradition of the Law of Nations* (Washington, DC: Catholic Association for International Peace, 1935), p. 79. Notice that the qualification "if they are good men" appears to modify the earlier emphasis in the *City of God* on the idea that *everyone* who fights seeks peace, and so marks a shift from the thin to the medium conception of peace.

[22] Michael Walzer does give some attention to the matter. See his *Just and Unjust Wars: A Moral Argument with Historical Illustrations*, third edition (New York: Basic Books, 2000), Chapter 7.

theatre of World War II and the devastation wrought by the Soviet army in its push through eastern Germany to Berlin. The vindictive brutality of the Soviet troops against civilians and prisoners can be partly explained, though not excused, by its being revenge for the ruthless slaughter that German troops had earlier inflicted upon the Soviet population in their drive into Russia. Whatever the explanation may be, rape, pillage, and casual murder by Soviet troops were commonplace. It is estimated that at least two million German women were raped by Soviet soldiers during the invasion, and that perhaps as many as 10 percent of these later died, mostly by their own hands. A high percentage of those raped, possibly a majority, were victims of multiple rape.[23] And this is not to take into account the massive loss of life amongst German soldiers fighting hopeless battles awaiting a surrender that would never come, or the Soviet troops who also died or were maimed fighting beyond a point at which the hostilities might have been sensibly ended. This is not to say that the realities actually allowed for an earlier cessation of the war in the East, but merely to indicate some of the awful costs involved in not achieving an earlier end. What is also true is that there was little or no will amongst the opposing leaderships to seek an earlier end to the carnage. We shall explore some of the reasons for that later, but my point is that efforts to bring an end to the war that would have avoided many of the horrors of the last months are dictated by an adequate understanding of the just war tradition.

The second point recalls the debate about the role played in preparing the ground for World War II by the punitive reparation provisions in the Treaty of Versailles that ended World War I. I do not want to enter that debate here, but its very existence shows the potential for future mischief that provisions for ending a war can have. Nor is it irrelevant that the Allied agreement on a demand for unconditional surrender in World War II helped provide Stalin with the opportunity to subject Eastern Europe to totalitarian misery for more than forty years. This outcome was also assisted, at least in the case of the occupation of Germany, by the reluctance of the Allied military forces to press on to Berlin. Eisenhower thought that political considerations about the future of Europe after the war should have no place in military decisions about how to proceed with the war. As he put it: "future division of Germany did not influence our military plans for the final conquest of the country."[24] But this of course ignores some of the moral considerations having to do with the right way to end a war, even if it did show a proper concern for the safety of his own troops. The military leaders may have thought differently about the matter had they realised the degree to which large sections of the

[23] A brilliant account of these and other atrocities can be found in Antony Beevor, *Berlin: The Downfall, 1945* (London: Viking, 2002). The estimates about rape are on p. 410.
[24] Ibid., p. 203.

German army were anxious to surrender to the Western forces rather than fall into the hands of the Russians.[25] This failure to realise was in turn influenced by their misunderstanding of the barbaric nature of Stalin's regime and the degree to which this affected the behaviour of the Soviet army.

As already mentioned, one crucial element in achieving a just end to hostilities is negotiation, especially negotiation on terms of surrender or settlement. But there is much in modern war that militates against negotiation. Because so many modern wars have been passionately ideological (as indeed have quite a few in the past), the very idea of negotiating with enemies prior to crushing them can seem preposterous or even immoral. Something like this seems to have been behind the appeal of "unconditional surrender" in World War II. The brutality and evil that marked the Nazi and Japanese regimes were thought to be such that no negotiated cessation to the hostilities could be considered. In the end, certain implicit understandings regarding the continuing role of the emperor were part of the settlement of the Pacific war. But in the case of Nazi Germany, it was understandably believed that Nazism had to be eliminated (as much as possible) from German government and its structures, and there seemed to be no way of doing this without inflicting a crushing defeat and total occupation. So Michael Walzer has argued that unconditional surrender was an appropriate war aim in the case of the 1939–45 war against Germany, but only because of the evil of the Nazi regime, which "rightly places Nazism outside the (moral) world of bargaining and accommodation" (p. 113). But he thinks of this as a limiting case, and specifically rejects the case for unconditional surrender in the war against Japan. Yet none of this explains the contemptuous attitude taken by Churchill and his government towards even the possibility of working out some terms for negotiated surrender with the underground opposition to Hitler within Germany. Of course, it is entirely speculative whether greater efforts to end the war by negotiation would have been successful, especially when success must also be measured in terms that required eliminating Nazism and establishing conditions to secure enduring peace. Nor can the significance of Hitler's unbalanced intransigence, especially for those Germans who dissented from it, be underestimated. Nonetheless, there were significant groups within Germany who wanted to negotiate a peace settlement, some as early as May 1941, when the group associated with Carl Gördeler, a former mayor of Leipzig, forwarded a proposal to London through neutral channels.[26] Later, of course, widespread opposition to the war amongst German elites led to the ill-fated attempt on

---

[25] Ibid.

[26] The role of this group and other oppositional elements is explored in Paul Kecskemeti's excellent book, *Strategic Surrender: The Politics of Victory and Defeat* (Stanford, CA: Stanford University Press, 1958). Kecskemeti is a strong critic of the difficulties inherent in the doctrine of "unconditional surrender," and some of his arguments are echoed in the text.

Hitler's life in July 20, 1944. No doubt there were all sorts of difficulties with the various peace "feelers," including, most notably, the difficulty of removing Hitler and his henchmen, and I do not suggest that they should simply have been accepted. What is instructive, however, is that they were comprehensively ignored. Many different factors lie behind this disregard, but one surely is the idea that only total military and political defeat of the enemy could provide a suitable end to the war. This conviction underpinned the declared policy of "unconditional surrender." There was certainly room for discussion with oppositional elements in Germany with a view to ending the war on terms that would have meant both less death and damage and the prospect of a reconstructed German polity that posed no further threat of war or genocide. This may not have proved feasible, but the rejection of its possibility suggests a failure to keep the ideal of peace operative. Moreover, a clear statement of stringent terms short of unconditional surrender might have helped speed a German capitulation in spite of the insane delusions of the Nazi leadership.

The impediments placed by the policy of "unconditional surrender" to the just settlement of war are vividly illustrated by the bungling that accompanied the surrender of Italy during World War II. The Italians saw the writing on the wall with the Allied successes in North Africa, and in July 1943 the king dismissed Mussolini and appointed Marshal Badoglio to head a new government. Badoglio was eager to negotiate a surrender with the Allies but was justifiably anxious about the German reaction, given the strength of their armed forces in Italy. This situation created plenty of opportunities for misunderstanding and ambiguity, so the process was bound to be difficult. But the difficulties were compounded by the doctrine of unconditional surrender and by a certain moralising attitude towards dealing with anyone who had fully co-operated (like Badoglio and King Victor Emmanuel) with the Fascist leadership. Whatever argument there was for a policy of "unconditional surrender" towards Nazi Germany had little force in the case of Fascist Italy, but the Allies demanded that it apply across the board. Consequently, opportunities to enlist the Italians as "co-belligerents" against the Germans were missed and, as Paul Kecskemeti concludes: "The Allies' refusal to pay any political price for surrender merely made the job of extricating Italy from the German clutches a more expensive one."[27]

The objection to negotiation with Badoglio because of his association with Mussolini's regime is understandable but eventually self-defeating. It involves both an unrealistic desire to negotiate only with the morally pure, and an unrealistic assessment of what past impurities may mean for present negotiating prospects. Negotiation does not require that one's negotiating partners be morally or politically respectable (though that might help in

---

[27] Ibid., p. 118. For Kecskemeti's comprehensive discussion of the circumstances surrounding the Italian capitulation, see his Chapter 4.

certain circumstances), but rather that their motivations are such that they can recognise opportunities for advantage, and that they will be so constrained by circumstances as to be truthful and faithful enough to promote the desired outcome. What is required of a negotiating partner, especially in the context of seeking to end armed hostilities, is not a highly moral version of "good faith" but a minimally rational one. Good faith and character would be better, but where it isn't available, lesser coinage may have to do. So we do not need to have or express a high opinion of our partner's moral standing. Negotiating does not per se amount to condoning. And there are ways of avoiding its having the effect of condoning or excusing past conduct.

Here a word is in order about demonisation. The tendency to portray one's enemy as so evil as to be demonic has several bad effects. One is that of treating the whole enemy population – or, less drastically, the whole of the enemy civil and political apparatus – as tainted with the same satanic brush as the leadership itself. But no matter how evil a particular leader or the group immediately associated with direct power may be, it is usually a mistake to imagine this evil as pervasive of the whole enemy society. It is even a mistake to think of all the associates or ruling party members in the same way. There were "good Nazis," for example, who risked their lives to help Jews escape from persecution in Eastern Europe; and one of the most remarkable examples of this phenomenon occurred in China. John Rabe was a businessman and convinced Nazi, indeed the acknowledged leader of the Nazi Party in Nanjing (or Nanking, as it was then more commonly called) during the brutal Japanese attack upon and occupation of the city in 1937. Rabe, along with other foreigners, established a safety zone for Chinese fleeing Japanese butchery and took extraordinary risks to save Chinese lives. Although hundreds of thousands of Chinese civilians were murdered and tortured, Rabe and his companions are said to have saved hundreds of thousands more by their unarmed courage. The story of this remarkable man is told by Iris Chang in her book, *The Rape of Nanking*.[28]

Another bad effect of demonisation is its tendency to reduce the demonised figure to a malevolent force with no other motivation than the promotion of pure evil. Vile leaders like Hitler and Stalin come close to fitting this caricature, but even they had more intelligible and human motives for some of their misdeeds than this picture suggests. Opponents of demonisation sometimes think that their opposition to it commits them to the view that the idea of evil cannot be applied at all, and, in particular, that there are no evil people in the world. This is not my position. I think that evil is real and that there are plenty of evil people fairly evenly distributed throughout the earth. The problem with demonisation is more a matter of focus.

---

[28] Iris Chang, *The Rape of Nanking: The Forgotten Holocaust of World War II* (Harmondsworth: Penguin, 1997).

It localises the evil and sees nothing but evil in that location, and usually nothing but good in other locations, notably in the vicinity of home. This makes for deficient understanding of the enemy and of oneself.

In the context of concluding hostilities, the demonisation of the enemy can clearly work as a factor that removes negotiation from consideration. Another factor is the effect of existing losses. There comes a point in a campaign or war where the expenditure of the lives of one's own troops has been so great that anything short of total crushing of the enemy can seem a betrayal of those who have already died. If we add to this the enemy record (real or imagined) of perpetrating war crimes against your civilian population, then anything like negotiation or compromise on terms of surrender will seem repugnant. Though this is humanly understandable, it is surely irrational. It is, in some respects, a grim relative of the phenomenon that economists refer to as "escalation commitment" in the presence of "sunk costs," whereby, having made an investment that has failed to deliver, the investor refuses to consider the costs as past and irretrievable and increases commitment to the path that has proved unprofitable.[29] Loyalty to those who have sacrificed their lives in the past need not require the continuance of such suffering. The meaning of their deaths can be sustained in other ways, including a just end to the conflict. The slogan "no negotiation with terrorists" captures both the emotional appeal and the irrationality of the "sunk costs" thinking, though it also has roots in the demonisation process. Those most loud in their use of the slogan often end up swallowing their words, but usually after more years of unnecessary carnage.

I have put considerable emphasis on the possibilities of negotiation, but I do not mean to imply that the ideal of peace requires a rush to the negotiating table or that *any* settlement that ends a war is thereby a morally welcome outcome. Just as the need to negotiate the selling of a house does not entail the acceptance of any offer at all, so negotiating an end to warfare will be constrained by ideas of desirable outcomes. These will include the governing concerns related to legitimate war aims, the respective strengths of the parties at the time, reasonable predictions of the trend of the conflict, and the likely role of negotiations (with these people, at this time, in these circumstances) in establishing the sort of peace sketched earlier in the discussion of a "medium" notion of peace, namely, one that is likely to embody an enduring concord between the former enemies and within the defeated nation. This may mean that it is sometimes important to fight on

---

[29] As one author puts it: "Research findings imply that individuals are prone to a particular bias in sequential decisions, namely, a tendency to escalate commitments. Decision-makers improperly consider sunk costs, which is part of a general behavioural trait carrying various titles such as 'escalation commitment', 'sunk cost phenomenon', and 'sunk cost problem.'" Dipankar Ghosh, "Sunk Costs," in Rashad Abdel-Khalik (ed.), *The Blackwell Encyclopaedia of Management*, vol. 1 (Cambridge, MA: Blackwell, 1997), p. 272.

when there is a realistic chance of ultimately gaining a better negotiating position.

A central aim in the ending of a war for those who are fighting a just war should be that of leaving the population of the surrendering enemy nation in a position to contribute to an independent political life for themselves after the war. Such a political life may have to be very different from that which they experienced before and during the war, especially where its forms contributed to the waging of the unjust war. There will be many ways of achieving such a fresh political existence depending upon such matters as how much the current leaders of the enemy nation or group have contributed to war crimes or been driven by ideologies the persistence of which is likely to seriously inhibit prospects for enduring peace. But legitimate war aims should not include an occupation or domination of the defeated enemy that would amount to ongoing colonisation. This in turn means that what Kekskemeti calls a "vacuum" policy must be highly dubious.[30] This is the policy that accompanied the unconditional surrender doctrine in World War II and involved the refusal of any recognition of even temporary political authority on the losing side, even if it were allowed to reside in those who were opposed to the existing war leadership. Nothing can guarantee that leaving indigenous leaders in place will not be risky, but even the total occupation of an enemy nation and political colonisation for a time must face similar risks while the "reconstruction" of the losing country is under way (witness the large number of Nazi officials who reemerged in positions of power after democratisation and de-Nazification), and it faces the additional burden of having to handle the chaos, suffering, and devastation that a vacuum policy and a military occupation commonly create. In addition to the merit in preserving some indigenous political authority and structures, it is also important to try to preserve elementary civilian infrastructures in the defeated enemy territory. Destruction of communications facilities, electricity grids, and other sources of power is likely to make the transition to a peaceful world more difficult. (It may well involve in addition, as we saw in Chapter 7, violation of certain principles of the JIB.)

There are of course several different scenarios for negotiated settlements that complicate how we should think of them in moral terms. Let us consider abstracted versions of some of them. One scenario is that of a side that (for the most part) is engaged justly in the fighting of a war and has achieved sufficient dominance to make negotiations feasible on terms that respect its legitimate cause and the associated war aims. This is basically the scenario I have most commonly had in view in the comments made so far. Here, the negotiations of the superior power are informed by both principled and prudential considerations of the sort mentioned earlier. As for its enemy, its war aims are illegitimate and should play no part in the outcome of the settlement. Given this scenario, they are unlikely to do so. But there will

---

[30] Kecskemeti, *Strategic Surrender*, p. 219.

be other prudential and political considerations that will inevitably be in play, such as ensuring the continuation of the enemy's nation-state, or of some of its significant structures and economic resources, and so on. Here, the resolution of these issues is largely a matter of bargaining, though an outcome that, for instance, proposed slavery or destitution for the enemy populace would clearly be immoral. An opposite scenario is that in which the unjust side in the war has become dominant to the point where the just side cannot achieve its legitimate war aims, but may do better by negotiating for much less than by awaiting total defeat. Sometimes a policy of "fight to the death" may be morally and rationally defensible, as when the alternative is slaughter or brutal enslavement, but the odds are not always stacked that way. The case of France's surrender to the Nazis in World War II is an interesting one. Marshall Petain's government thought they could negotiate a good deal, and, given the desperate military situation of the French forces, in certain respects they did. The Vichy government became subservient to German interests but retained a degree of French control over part of the country and some of the overseas colonies, and many French lives, both military and civilian, were spared. The subservience became greater and French control much diminished as the war progressed, partly because the war expanded and continued much longer than either Hitler or the Petain group had expected. And the Nazis proved to be no ordinary conquerors: their program of extermination and genocide was not on the table until later, but any bargain that requires surrendering citizens to torture and death is a bad deal.

Can we draw some principles relating to the justice of ending armed conflict from this discussion? In the nature of the case, they will have to have the sort of generality and openness to interpretation associated with the rules of the JAB. There should also be a continuity between the dictates of the JAB, the JIB, and *jus post bellum*: the just aims of the war should dictate the limits of what can be done to the defeated enemy, just as the rationale for the principle of discrimination will dictate respect for enemy noncombatants after war's end. Moreover, it would be good to frame the rules so that they not only reflected the appropriate advice and constraints on victorious just warriors, but also had force with unjust conquerors. Here there is an echo of the dichotomy we noted in Chapters 3 and 6 between the basic moral orientation of the JAB and the JIB in addressing justified war, and the legal/political imperatives of what Vattel called "regular war." In other words, the principles should apply not only to just warriors but also to unjust warriors who regard their cause as just and are thereby under some pressure to abide by the restraints of the JIB and the legal rules it supports. Here are some suggestions:

1. War aims should never be framed in such a way that they leave no room for negotiated surrender on terms short of a total capitulation that leaves a population at the mercy of the conqueror.

2. Terms of surrender or settlement should seek the establishment of peace in the "medium" sense we extracted from the discussion of Augustine.

3. Punishment for enemy war crimes should be referred to the International Criminal Court, to which allegations of victor crimes should also be referred.

4. The conduct of war should look to the optimal conditions for postwar peace. The destruction of enemy infrastructure and civilian capacity should be kept to a minimum, even where it is not directly forbidden by the JIB.

Pacifism

This brings us to the issue of pacifism. Philosophers who discuss issues having to do with war have, on the whole, been very unsympathetic to pacifism. Jan Narveson's well-known essay, which alleges that pacifism is incoherent, is the most dismissive and, I think, the least philosophically plausible, but Elizabeth Anscombe speaks for many philosophers when she says that pacifism is "an illusion" that has "corrupted enormous numbers of people."[31] These comments are made in spite of Anscombe's belief that wars "have mostly been mere wickedness on both sides."[32]

Narveson's muddled argument for some kind of logical self-contradiction in pacifism has been successfully dismantled by others, so all I shall say here is that it relies crucially upon the premise that if one has a right, it then follows logically that one has a further right to do "whatever may be necessary to prevent infringements" of the original right.[33] In the case of pacifism, the application of this idea is that if you have a right not to have violence done to you, then you may do "whatever is necessary" to prevent violence being done to you. But surely it is sometimes necessary to deploy violence to prevent violence being done, and hence the pacifist is allegedly involved in absurdity in holding both that you have the right not to have violence done to you, and that it is impermissible to use violence to prevent infringement of your right. But the absurdity is in Narveson's premise. What you can morally do to prevent violations of your rights is never determined by mere efficacy of means. If someone is about to violate your property rights by stealing a jam tart from your open motor car and the only way you can prevent him is by shooting him, then the efficacy of the means is at odds with its morality.

---

[31] G. E. M. Anscombe, "War and Murder," in Richard A. Wasserstrom (ed.), *War and Morality* (Belmont, CA: Wadsworth, 1970), pp. 42 and 49.

[32] Ibid., p. 44.

[33] Jan Narveson, "Pacifism: A Philosophical Analysis," in Wasserstrom (ed.), *War and Morality*, p. 72. The most thorough critique of Narveson is contained in Jenny Teichman's "On Pacifism," *Philosophical Investigations* 5 (1982), pp. 72–83. See also her *Pacifism and the Just War: A Study in Applied Philosophy* (Oxford: Basil Blackwell, 1986).

And this is true of more substantial rights. Consider the idea that we are entitled to engage in rape if it is necessary to prevent rape. As we saw earlier, if the most effective (or even only) way of defeating an enemy is by attacking innocent people, then it is at least not obvious that this is morally allowable. Certainly, its permissibility is not entailed by what it means to have a right.

There is another feature of Narveson's critique that is more important for our present purposes, and that is his narrow definition of pacifism. Like many others, he treats pacifism as a personal doctrine about the use of any form of violence. No doubt some pacifists have held that it is always wrong to use violence, and others that it is always wrong to use extreme or lethal violence, but pacifism is (as many writers, including some philosophers, are increasingly insisting) primarily advancing a thesis about war. In its simplest terms, the thesis is that war is a very bad thing and that we should do our utmost to avoid it. These terms might be thought far too simple since surely this idea is broadly shared well beyond pacifist circles. But this is not so clear. For one thing, as our discussion of militarism and the romantic attitude towards war in Chapters 1 and 3 showed, there are many people who do not have this negative response to the prospect of war. For another thing, many of those who do hold the thesis are attached to it in a superficial way and do not bring with their assent the characteristic pacifist determination that avoidance of war is a primary moral and political commitment.

To explore the nature of this commitment further, we should distinguish different ways in which it may figure in the outlooks of individuals and of movements. First, let us set aside what might be called private pacifism, namely, the principled determination not to be involved in war oneself without any implication that this a universal obligation. How can this be "principled" without such universality? Well, it might be a moral or religious response to a particular calling with the implication that others who are similarly called (if there be any) have a similar obligation. Some religious pacifists are like this. There are various versions of private pacifism, but my concern is elsewhere, so I will not pursue its complexities further. But public pacifism can also take many forms. One form is that of unqualified opposition to any war at all. This is what is usually thought of as principled pacifism. It will indeed be entailed by a principled and unqualified opposition to *any* use of violence in any circumstances, but this entailment is only one way of supporting principled pacifism. More plausible support is surely provided by an examination of the nature and usual consequences of war itself. And there are many pacifists who are not opposed to the use of violence by police (within legal and moral limits) or, for that matter, in certain sports, but who are vehemently opposed to war.

We must distinguish further because there is another form of public pacifism that is often obscured by that examined already. This is a rejection of war as a normal and systematic element in international relations. Here, the idea is that war as a settled institution for dealing with international problems should be abolished and that peaceful institutions should take its place. Kant's essay on "Perpetual Peace" as well as Erasmus's many writings on the evils of war can be seen as reflecting this outlook.[34] Following Andrew Alexandra, we might call this institutional pacifism.[35] It does not entail unqualified opposition to particular wars here and now, for it may be that the transition from the war system to a peace system will require an occasional resort to war in the transitional phase. Had the Nazis and Japanese not been defeated by arms, it might be argued, war as an dominant element in international relations might have been solidified to an even greater degree than is now the case. To this extent, then, the idea of a just war may be compatible with that of institutional pacifism. Institutional pacifists will maintain a high degree of scepticism about the moral and political legitimacy of resort to war during what they view as a transitional period, but they might allow that just war is sometimes permissible during that period. This seems to have been the position of both Erasmus and Kant.[36] Whether such thinkers do give limited endorsement to just war will depend in part on certain strategic judgements. These will be concerned with whether the limited endorsement makes the transition to a peace system more or less likely. Institutional pacifists who take an unqualified stance of opposition to any war are relying on the judgement that any war at all will set back progress toward what Kant called "perpetual peace." And here their position will coincide with that of the principled public pacifists who oppose war unconditionally. But for the former at least, this is a prudential judgement that can be open to dispute.

Those who contest this judgement might appeal to "transitional morality," an idea that is akin to what I have elsewhere called "extrication morality." There are many moral situations in which we must suffer and even condone what is less than ideal in order to move beyond a morally bad situation while still preserving a commitment to the ideal. Someone who believes passionately that child labour is a thoroughly bad thing may nonetheless have to tolerate some degree of it in certain situations in order to move things forward to a position where it is wholly a thing of the past. This was indeed the situation of people who were combating child labour in the West in the past and of those who are still concerned with it in other parts

34 Immanuel Kant, "Perpetual Peace," in his *On History*, ed. Lewis White Beck (Indianapolis and New York: Bobbs-Merrill, 1963), pp. 85–135; Desiderius Erasmus, *The Complaint of Peace* (Boston: Charles Williams, 1813) (original 1517).

35 Andrew Alexandra, "Political Pacifism," *Social Theory and Practice* 29, no. 4 (2003), pp. 289–606.

36 For a good discussion of the tradition of "perpetual peace," exemplified by Kant and Erasmus, see Sissela Bok, *Common Values* (Columbia: University of Missouri Press, 1995), Chapter 4, pp. 82–103. Where I view this tradition as a form of pacifism, Bok treats it as a tradition separate from both just war thinking and pacifism. Nothing important, I think, turns on this difference of classification.

of the world today. Someone working for total abolition might nonetheless, depending on the economic and political climate, count it a moral victory to establish a law restricting child labour to those over twelve. Then they might move to fourteen, and so on until abolition. An example, in a grim context, is provided by the International Convention on the Rights of the Child, which originally determined that no child should be eligible for military service until age fifteen, even though all its other provisions of rights and protection worked with age eighteen. This was clearly a compromise intended to take into account various countries that relied heavily on child soldiers, and for many of these the restriction to children fifteen and older represented a genuine challenge. This was, indeed, a challenge that many ignored, but at least there were forms of pressure that could be brought to bear. Having worked with fifteen for eleven years, in 2000 the UN managed to have passed an optional Protocol to the Convention raising the age at which soldiers could be recruited for combat to eighteen and also fixed eighteen as the minimum age at which conscription for the armed forces (in any capacity) could apply. This has been widely endorsed, though it was initially opposed by Great Britain, which recruited sixteen-year-olds for active service, and the United States, which regularly enlisted seventeen-year-olds, though not, in practice, for combat duty. The Protocol originally aimed to ban military recruitment of anyone under age eighteen, but pressure, principally from the United States, produced a compromise so that it is still possible to recruit for noncombat duties at seventeen but only with strong conditions regarding parental or guardian consent. This compromise has resulted in the U.S. Senate voting to ratify the Protocol, with some qualifications, even though, as noted in an earlier chapter, it remains one of only two nations (the other is Somalia) not to have ratified the Convention itself. At the start of 2003, there were 111 signatories to and 45 ratifications of the Protocol. This clearly represents a step forward, even though it does not satisfy the ideal agenda of those various groups working for a total end to child soldiering. They think it is worth tolerating the continued recruitment of seventeen-year-olds to the U.S. armed services (with stringent precautions) because the U.S. commitment to the new Protocol strengthens the campaign against the grosser employments of child warriors in other parts of the world. This campaign has much stronger objectives than the improvements contained in the Protocol, but these improvements, with all their inadequacies, constitute a way forward.

So it may be with progress toward the elimination of war. If it is, some of the steps forward must be, or must involve, institutional reforms. These cannot be predicted in detail, but they should involve movement towards an increase in the authority of international institutions so that the need for individual state military solutions to interstate or global political problems gives way to either diplomatic or policing solutions. The further development of regulatory and reformatory international institutions represents a way of moving beyond the state of nature picture of international relations that has understandably dominated a great deal of thinking about the international order and influenced the shape of just war theorizing, especially in its implementation dimension.[37] We are a long way from a dramatic transformation of our present arrangements, but there are some hopeful signs. With all its faults, the United Nations has survived sixty years, where the League of Nations lasted only twenty-seven (1919–46). Nor has this endurance been without remarkable successes, notably in providing checks to political violence. It is understandable that the UN's signal failures, such as Rwanda, should attract attention, but a recent report shows that there has been a great reduction in the number of wars and their intensity since 1992, a great deal of which is attributable to the efforts of the UN. According to the *Human Security Report 2005*, UN conflict-prevention and peace-building efforts have had a major role in reducing armed conflict by about 40 percent since 1992.[38] There is some room for dispute about some of the details of the report, but it seems clear that the UN has been far more effective in the striving for peace than its critics usually allow. The organization still commands a great deal of respect throughout the world, an attitude that contrasts with a negative stance towards it in some powerful quarters, notably the political right in the United States. Like all institutions, it stands in need of scrutiny and indeed reform, but its survival as a focus for international authority is vital for the enterprise of limiting, and perhaps eventually of abolishing, resort to war.

[37] Allen Buchanan rightly stresses the way in which moral judgements can be shaped by institutional realities, and this is, as he argues, as true of just war thinking as of other areas. As mentioned in Chapter 5, I am less persuaded of the direction and claimed significance of his specific proposals for institutional change.

[38] *Human Security Report 2005* (Oxford: Oxford University Press, 2005).

14

The Issue of Stringency

> The art of our necessities is strange,
> That can make vile things precious.
> Shakespeare, *King Lear*

The requirements, prohibitions, and permissions of just war theory that have been discussed throughout this book may be interpreted in more or less stringent ways. To some extent, this mirrors what happens in morality more generally, for there are degrees of importance and even of force that attach to different forms of moral judgement. An obvious one is the difference between strict obligation and the pull of supererogation: between, that is, what we must do or avoid doing and what it would be admirable or even saintly, but not strictly binding, to do.[1] Others have distinguished what is morally obligatory from what would merely be morally decent.[2] Then again, the distinction between obligations and ideals is sometimes elucidated (at least in part) in terms of a difference in stringency of requirement.[3] These contrasts raise many problems and need more discussion than they will receive here, but what intuitive plausibility they have can serve to introduce a pressing issue about the force of the prohibitions of just war theory, especially those of the JIB.

---

[1] There is a philosophical debate about whether the category of supererogation makes sense, but here I shall take it at face value for the purposes of our discussion. See Marcia Baron, "Kantian Ethics and Supererogation," *Journal of Philosophy* 84, no. 5 (1987), pp. 237–262; and J. O. Urmson, "Saints and Heroes," in A. I. Melden (ed.), *Essays in Moral Philosophy* (Seattle: University of Washington Press, 1958).

[2] As does Judith Jarvis Thomson in her influential article "A Defense of Abortion," *Philosophy and Public Affairs* 1, no. 1 (1971), pp. 47–66.

[3] I have attempted a more detailed account of what is distinctive of moral ideals in "Concerning Ideals" (Uehiro Lectures in Practical Ethics, Oxford University, May 2005). This will be published by Oxford University Press as part of a book provisionally entitled *Morality and Feasibility*.

All of these prohibitions and requirements, of course, are subject to the necessity for interpretation in concrete circumstances, as we saw clearly in the discussion of proportionality and the debates about the grey areas of noncombatant status. Here, as elsewhere in morality, there will be plenty of room for the exercise of practical reason and judgement in the interpretation and implementation of moral principles. Rather than examine all the just war moral principles, injunctions, rules, and so on, however, I want to concentrate on the stringency of one central prohibition about which debate has arisen in the philosophical literature and beyond: this is what I have argued to be the profound moral prohibition on the intentional killing of noncombatants inherent in the principle of discrimination. My focus is on the differences between those who see this JIB constraint as important but defeasible in certain extreme conditions and those who hold that it can never be overridden. One's position on this is not only of the first importance for determining the decisions that may legitimately be made during the conduct of interstate warfare, but also for the moral evaluation of terrorism, as was explained in Chapter 8. I argued there that terrorism is best understood as the tactic of directing violent attacks upon noncombatants for political purposes, and hence as a violation of what is involved in the just war principle of discrimination. So the idea that the principle admits of exceptions seems itself to allow that terrorism may sometimes be justified.

Let us look more carefully at this. The idea of exemptions from profound moral constraints is not restricted to the issue of deliberate killing of the innocent, and it has taken many different forms in contemporary moral philosophy. Some of these are closely associated with the philosophy of utilitarianism. In its simplest form, act utilitarianism, and certain allied forms of thought, hold that all moral constraints are simply "rules of thumb" that can and should be overruled if calculations of the overall outcomes of so doing show that it is productive of more general happiness than sorrow. This seems to me a deeply misguided view of ethics, but I cannot offer a full-scale rebuttal here. Its principal defect in the present circumstances is that, in essence, it doesn't allow that the profound moral constraints against killing the innocent are really profound at all. That is why it calls them "rules of thumb" along with all sorts of other shorthand adages in the moral life. Even more complex rule-utilitarian approaches, like that of Brandt mentioned earlier, make the rationale for the prohibition far too extrinsic to what is done and far too superficial and contingent. This shows itself even in the prose in which they try to express their position. Consider the following from Brandt, which possibly expresses, he thinks, a "proper (not ideally precise) rule" for allowing the massacre of civilians in suitable circumstances: "substantial destruction of lives and property of enemy civilians is permissible only when there is good evidence that it will significantly enhance the prospect of victory."[4] In case the reader finds this a trifle glib, Brandt elaborates. More precisely, he thinks that this rule needs to be interpreted in the light of the following general principle:

[A] military action (e.g., a bombing raid) is permissible only if the utility (broadly conceived, so that the maintenance of treaty obligations of international law could count as a utility) of victory to all concerned, multiplied by the increase in its probability if the action is executed, on the evidence (when the evidence is reasonably solid, considering the stakes) is greater than the possible disutility of the action to both sides multiplied by its probability.[5]

Knowing what we do of human fallibility, our capacity for self-deception, and the fragility of our assessments of importance, probability, and "stakes," especially during the "fog" of battle, the likely consequences of this sort of abstract thinking are terrifying. Imagine yourself and your family on the receiving end of this calculus by an enemy! Dedicated utilitarians should (on their own principles) take the consequences of licensing this sort of thinking into account when engaging in their often-bizarre calculations. Some, in recognition of Sidgwick's cautionary note on the matter, at least gesture at doing so, and hold that it would be a bad thing were people generally to govern their conduct by recourse to utilitarian principles rather than respect for ordinary moral rules and prohibitions. There is room for debate about what this concession does to the status of utilitarianism as a moral outlook, but it represents a retreat from the insouciance of Brandt's recommendation.[6] Nonetheless, in practice the majority of utilitarian thinkers cheerfully issue formulas and prescriptions as chilling as Brandt's in their implications.

The more interesting exemption questions are posed by professed non-utilitarians like Michael Walzer, who *do* think the immunity of the non-combatant restriction profound, and worry about any permission to breach it. Such people don't believe that ordinary calculations of utility, such as Brandt's, can possibly override these sorts of constraints. Nonetheless, they think that certain circumstances can allow the regrettable but morally painful choice to violate such deep norms.

Here it seems possible to distinguish two positions, though they have a tendency to merge. The first is that associated with many forms of modern

---

[4] R. B. Brandt, "Utilitarianism and the Rules of War," in Marshall Cohen, Thomas Nagel, and Thomas Scanlon (eds.), *War and Moral Responsibility* (Princeton, NJ: Princeton University Press, 1974), p. 36.

[5] Ibid., p. 37.

[6] I have had my say on the Sidgwickian defusing manoeuvre in my "Henry Sidgwick," in C. L. Ten (ed.), *The Routledge History of Philosophy, Vol. VII: The Nineteenth Century* (London: Routledge, 1994), pp. 122–147.

intuitionism, as classically expressed, for instance, by W. D. Ross.[7] We might call this "balanced exceptionalism." The second position is that of "supreme emergency," one associated most commonly with the name of Michael Walzer and the tradition of "dirty hands."[8] It will be the principal focus of my attention later. But first, balanced exceptionalism. The basic outlook indicated by this phrase is much more widespread amongst theorists than the intuitionist philosophy itself, but I shall use the intuitionist framework to spell it out. Here, there are various moral principles that are revealed to reflective thought, and they give rise to "prima facie obligations" or "prima facie duties." The force of these is generally independent of the calculation of consequences, but whether something is *actually* obligatory will depend upon whether there are other prima facie obligations that outweigh it, and some of these may involve the calculation of consequences, as in the case of a duty of beneficence. So the obligation not intentionally to kill the innocent, being, like all the rest, prima facie, may be overruled by (say) the obligation to advance the good of one's community. In this outlook, no initial prohibition can be presumed absolute, and the final binding prohibition or obligation determines one's duty with finality and, as it were, without loss. There may be a sense of regret that one cannot avoid doing something that is prima facie wrong – it would be more comfortable if one's prima facie duties did not conflict and therefore need resolution – but no wrong can be attributed to you if you have done the balancing conscientiously.[9] The balanced exceptionist can of course acknowledge that some prima facie duties are stronger than others, and hence that some presumptive wrongs carry more heft than others. Indeed, the balancing story commits the outlook to this acknowledgement, since there would be no point to the talk of balancing as a procedure for decision making unless there were such differences of weight. But the fact remains that the granting of exemption from the prohibition on intentionally killing the innocent is part of a normal, even

[7] W. D. Ross, *The Right and the Good* (Oxford: Clarendon Press, 1930).

[8] This is not the place for a full discussion of this complex tradition, but I have discussed it elsewhere. See C. A. J. Coady, "Messy Morality and the Art of the Possible," *Proceedings of the Aristotelian Society*, supp. vol. 64 (1990), pp. 259–279; "Politics and the Problem of Dirty Hands," in Peter Singer (ed.), *A Companion to Ethics* (Oxford: Blackwell, 1993), pp. 373–383; "Dirty Hands," in Robert Goodin and Philip Pettit (eds.), *A Companion to Contemporary Political Philosophy* (Oxford: Blackwell, 1993), pp. 422–443; and "Dirty Hands," in Laurence and Charlotte Becker (eds.), *The Encyclopaedia of Ethics*, second edition (London: Routledge, 2001), pp. 407–441. For Walzer's influential statement of the position, see "Political Action: The Problem of Dirty Hands," *Philosophy and Public Affairs* 2, no. 2 (Winter 1973), pp. 160–180.

[9] Ross does indeed recognise that there can be a sort of residue effect of the fact that a prima facie duty has been overruled. Since we still recognise the prima facie duty as such, then we may feel "compunction" at not being able to fulfil it but "not indeed shame or repentance." And, in some cases, we may have some further duty to make up "somehow" for the right decision not to heed the prima facie duty. Ross, *The Right and the Good*, p. 28.

routine, business of balancing presumptive obligations in order to find what is finally obligatory or prohibited. If the scales tell you that it is morally permitted or even morally obligatory intentionally to kill the innocent, then in these circumstances it cannot be wrong to do so.[10]

The Dirty Hands Tradition and Supreme Emergency

The second exemption position emerges from the discussion of what has been called "dirty hands." This tradition can be traced back at least to Machiavelli, is glimpsed in Max Weber, and has found eloquent modern expression in Michael Walzer.[11] Although it has some affinities with balanced exceptionalism, it seems to be distinguishable from that outlook by three things. The first is its emphasis on the political realm as the principal focus for the making of exceptions to what seem to be powerful moral prohibitions; the second is its common emphasis upon the extreme nature of the situations in which the powerful moral rule must be disregarded; and the third, and perhaps most important, is its stress upon the abiding wrongness that is done by the necessary violation of the moral prohibition. Together, these provide a distinct contrast to the intuitionist tradition and balanced exceptionalism. In particular, the dirty hands theorists seem to want to treat such moral prohibitions as that upon intentionally killing the innocent as far more than "prima facie" or presumptive. They think them profound. Theorists like Walzer believe that ordinary calculations of utility cannot override these sorts of constraints, but they also hold that such constraints cannot yield at all comfortably to standard countervailing duties and obligations. This second point tends to be implicit in the dirty hands literature, whereas the anti-utilitarian point is overt.[12] Nonetheless, despite the contrast, there comes a point where the gravity of the consequences or the gravity of the conflicting duty can demand the regrettable but morally painful choice to violate such deep norms.

The basic idea, we may here take from the tradition, plausibly traceable to Machiavelli, is that certain necessities of life may require the overriding of profound and otherwise "absolute" moral prohibitions in extreme

---

[10] Thomas Nagel discusses something quite close to this sort of "balanced exceptionalism" in his paper "War and Massacre," in Thomas Nagel, *Mortal Questions* (Cambridge: Cambridge University Press, 1979), p. 62. He calls his version "threshold deontology" and contrasts it with both utilitarianism and absolutism.

[11] Niccolò Machiavelli, *The Prince*, ed. Peter Bondanella (Oxford: Oxford University Press, 1984); Max Weber, "Politics as a Vocation," in H. H. Gerth and C. Wright Mills (eds.), *From Max Weber: Essays in Sociology* (London: Routledge & Kegan Paul, 1948), pp. 117–128; and Walzer, "Political Action."

[12] Walzer's discussions of dirty hands problems (in both "Political Action" and *Just and Unjust Wars*) emphasise the contrast with plain utilitarianism, but it is clear that there can be a related contrast with balanced exceptionalism.

situations. Walzer's defence of the terror bombing of German cities in World War II in terms of "supreme emergency" is clearly in the tradition. Indeed, although he does not use the term "dirty hands" in his initial exploration of supreme emergency in his book *Just and Unjust Wars*, he makes it clear in a later essay that supreme emergency is a case, indeed the exemplary case, of dirty hands.[13] Walzer does not defend the bombing unequivocally. He thinks that, though it was morally wrong as a violation of the principle of discrimination, it was justified by the plea of supreme emergency in the early stages of the war. In the later stages, however, it was just plain morally criminal, since an Allied victory could reasonably be foreseen on the basis of morally legitimate targeting and fighting. The bombing of Dresden was therefore an outright atrocity, though the bombing of other German cities up to 1942 was not. He is clear that the bombing in this earlier phase was a violation of the principle of discrimination and interestingly (from the point of view of our discussion of terrorism in Chapter 8) refers to it at one point as "terrorism."[14] It was morally wrong, and implies guilt, but it had to be done.

Walzer's use of the category supreme emergency here is based on the idea that the need to defeat Nazi Germany was no ordinary necessity. Hitler's victory would have been a dire blow to civilisation. The enormity of his regime and its practices was such that his extended empire would have been a disaster for most of the people living under its sway. In addition, the threat of Hitler's victory was present and urgent, and the bombing of German cities aimed directly at the civilian populations was the only offensive weapon the British had.

Now, two things are worth noting about this characterisation. The first is that some of the matters that Walzer seems to factor into this dire judgement on Germany's war efforts were not factors that were known to Churchill and his advisers or that influenced the decision to use strategic bombing. Hitler was known to be anti-Semitic and to have persecuted Jews and political opponents, but not to have a program of genocide in hand. He was perceived as a very dangerous warmonger rather than a genocidal maniac. So part of the legitimation deployed by Walzer is largely ex post facto. Second, Walzer makes the issue of Germany's possible victory, but not Japan's, a matter of supreme emergency. Japan's war, he claims, was "a more ordinary sort of military expansion, and all that was morally required was that they be defeated, not that they be conquered and totally overthrown."[15] This is part of his argument against the atomic bombing of Hiroshima and Nagasaki.

[13] Michael Walzer, "Emergency Ethics," Chapter 3 in Michael Walzer, *Arguing About War* (New Haven, CT and London: Yale University Press, 2004), see especially pp. 45–46.
[14] Michael Walzer, *Just and Unjust Wars: A Moral Argument with Historical Illustrations*, third edition (New York: Basic Books, 2000), p. 260.
[15] Ibid., pp. 267–268.

He denies that this was required by supreme emergency, in part because Japan was no longer in a position to win the war, so the threat was no longer imminent, and in part because the Japanese did not represent the same danger to civilisation as their Nazi allies. He thinks it mere utilitarianism that the atomic bombs were (allegedly) needed to end the war more quickly with less loss of life, and argues that an ordinary (rather than an unconditional) surrender would have been the morally licit path to ending the war.

As indicated in the previous chapter, I have no enthusiasm for the doctrine of unconditional surrender, but Walzer's relatively benign view of Japanese aggression is hard to take seriously. I feel inclined to say: "Tell that to the Chinese." In the Japanese invasion of China in the 1930s it is soberly estimated that more than 300,000 Chinese civilians were massacred in Nanjing alone in a racist rampage of raping, beheading, and bayoneting that lasted six weeks.[16] Nor was the racist and brutal behaviour of so many Japanese warriors much better in the rest of Southeast Asia during the war. Those directly threatened with a Japanese victory in Asia and the Pacific would clearly have had a much sounder case for talking of supreme emergency than Walzer allows. Had they the capacity at the time to terrorise Japanese cities (as the Americans later did), then it would seem that supreme emergency would have licensed their attacking the innocent. But if this is so, then it is hard to resist the suspicion that supreme emergency is too elastic to do the job required; so elastic, indeed, that whenever you are engaged in legitimate self-defence and seem to be losing, you will be able to produce plausible reasons of supreme emergency for attacking the innocent. This is a matter to which I will return.

A further curiosity of Walzer's argument is that it is presented in *Just and Unjust Wars* primarily as an argument available to states and their representatives. This is not exclusively true of the tradition of the dirty hands debate (it is less true of Weber, for instance), but it is a pronounced emphasis of Walzer's treatment.[17] True, his primary focus is on the political community, but it is those political communities that project themselves as states that bear the burden of his argument. Yet if we think only of the connotations of supreme emergency, it is not at all obvious that the issue can be so restricted. Palestinian resistance groups, for example, can mount a powerful case that they face a hostile power bent upon their subordination and dispossession to a degree that threatens not only their lives but their way of life. Chechnians and many other victims of unrelenting state oppression and terrorism also

---

[16] See, for instance Iris Chang, *The Rape of Nanking: The Forgotten Holocaust of World War II* (Melbourne: Penguin, 1997), pp. 4–6.

[17] This is particularly surprising given that Walzer derives the term "dirty hands" from Sartre's play of the same name, which is concerned with the supposed necessity for revolutionaries to violate morality in pursuit of their cause. See Jean-Paul Sartre, *No Exit and Three Other Plays* (New York: Vintage, 1955).

have a solid case. Even the various groups around Osama bin Laden may well see themselves as qualifying for this exemption. No doubt it can be argued that there are various delusions and mistakes implicit in their outlooks, but the history of warfare is replete with similar delusions and mistakes.

The Pro-State Bias

In his discussion of supreme emergency, Walzer makes explicit his pro-state bias. "Can soldiers and statesmen override the rights of innocent people for the sake of their own political communities? I am inclined to answer the question affirmatively, though not without hesitation and worry."[18] And he goes on to speak of nations in a way that identifies political communities and nations. Of course, even Walzer's language here leaves logical space for the idea that nations or political communities can be driven by necessity even when they do not possess a state or have been deprived of one. Yet it is clear that recourse by such people or their real or imagined leaders to supreme emergency is far from his mind. Indeed, in another place, the original publication of the article "Terrrorism: A Critique of Excuses," where he is explicitly concerned with substate agents employing terrorism, Walzer argues that such terrorism can *never* be justified or excused. Although he doesn't define terrorism very clearly, it is obvious that he is operating with a version of the tactical definition, saying such things as "[terrorism] is indefensible now that it has been recognized, like rape and murder, as an attack upon the innocent."[19] He makes his total condemnation explicit: "I take the principle for granted: that every act of terrorism is a wrongful act."[20] Although even this leaves theoretical room for a "dirty hands" move to claim the wrongful act as necessary, it is clear that Walzer does not envisage such room being available for substate terrorists. In fact, his article is devoted to examining excuses for terrorism, since he takes it as axiomatic that there can be no justifications of any sort. But he reaches the same conclusion about excuses, even though some of the excuses that he examines are formally very similar to the necessity arguments he endorses as justifications under the rubric of supreme emergency in the case of the terror bombing in World War II. Most notably, he holds that the argument that no other strategy is available is never a valid reason for terrorist acts, even though it figures

---

[18] Walzer, *Just and Unjust Wars*, p. 254.
[19] Walzer, "Terrorism: A Critique of Excuses," in Steven Luper-Foy (ed.), *Problems of International Justice* (Boulder, CO: Westview Press, 1988), p. 238. Actually, Walzer's understanding of terrorism as an attack upon the innocent also includes the idea that the attack is intended to spread fear amongst other members of the group attacked. This would clearly include acts and policies of state terrorism such as the British bombing of German cities as well as attacks by substate groups.
[20] Ibid.

prominently in his case for the necessity of the Allied terror bombing.[21] He seems to have forgotten his description of that bombing as "terrorism."

Why should states, or the political communities they represent, enjoy the supreme emergency licence when other groups do not? This is particularly pertinent when we admit, as Walzer earlier did, that states can employ terrorism (in the tactical sense). The primacy of the political community that Walzer sees as validating the special role of (most) states is highly suspect. Walzer admits of individuals that they can never attack innocent people to aid their self-defence.[22] He then adds: "But communities, in emergencies, seem to have different and larger prerogatives. I am not sure that I can account for the difference, without ascribing to communal life a kind of transcendence that I don't believe it to have."[23] Walzer goes on to try to locate the "difference" in the supposed fact that "the survival and freedom of political communities . . . are the highest values of international society."[24] Perhaps these are the highest values of international society, but this is hardly surprising if one construes international society as a society of political communities, namely, recognised states. What is needed, at the very least, is an argument that locates the survival and freedom of states as the highest *human* value, one that is capable of justifying the overriding that supreme emergency requires. I doubt that any such argument exists. We should certainly avoid the temptation to identify the survival of a state with the survival of the regime that runs it. But neither should we identify the survival of the state with the survival of its subjects. Some states may deserve to perish, and their former subjects may be better for their demise. And even where threatened states do not deserve to perish, their disappearance is not equivalent to the massacre of their subjects or citizens. Nor is it enough to point to the undoubted value of political life, for there are many other values, such as family relationships, friendship, and moral integrity, that are equally if not more significant. And even if some argument could show the preeminent value of political community and the life it allows, this would still leave a gap between political community and state, a gap that Walzer's argument here obscures. (I stress "here" because in later publications Walzer is more explicit about the gap and qualifies his position on terrorism. This is something I shall attend to later.) Some revolutionary or dissenting groups can

---

[21] Ibid., p. 239. In *Just and Unjust Wars*, Walzer accepts as part of a valid "dirty hands" justification that the bombing was the only offensive weapon the British had – "the bombers alone provide the means of victory," as he quotes Churchill as saying in September 1940. See ibid., p. 259.

[22] Ibid., p. 254. At least this seems to be what he is saying. The issue is confused by his tendency here and elsewhere to put the point as though he were reporting common opinion: ". . . it is not usually said of individuals in domestic society that they necessarily will or that they morally can strike out at innocent people, even in the supreme emergency of self-defence. They can only attack their attackers."

[23] Ibid.

[24] Ibid.

plausibly claim to be or to represent political communities and to deploy violence in defence of a threatened political life. If so, the value that is supposed by Walzer to legitimate resort to supreme emergency should be available to them as well.

Yet this is precisely what Walzer seems at pains to deny. The contrast in treatment is starkly reflected in what Walzer says of the terrorist excuse that attacking the innocent is the only option they have. Walzer's objection is that other strategies are available if you are opposing liberal and democratic states and that terrorism never works against totalitarian states.[25] In discussing what he treats as a further excuse, that "terrorism works (and nothing else does)"[26] he adds that this efficiency excuse depends for its success on that of "the only option" excuse or that of the structurally similar "last resort" excuse. Indeed, these three excuses are closely related, and Walzer admits of the efficiency test that it goes beyond an excuse and aims to constitute a justification in consequentialist terms. If so, the question of a dirty hands justification surely arises, and Walzer even mentions the dirty hands of the terrorists, but he doesn't invoke any form of supreme emergency on their behalf. This must be, at least in part, because he thinks that the consequentialist considerations are defective on their own terms. As he argues: "I doubt that terrorism has ever achieved national liberation – no nation that I know of owes its freedom to a campaign of random murder – although terrorism undoubtedly increases the power of the terrorists within the national liberation movement."[27]

These arguments are hardly decisive as they stand, and they become still less persuasive when set against what Walzer says of the World War II bombing. As to the arguments themselves, the claim that terrorism will work (and nothing else will) need not mean that terrorism must work all by itself, as Walzer's comment about failure to achieve national liberation might suggest. The "nothing else" claim need only mean that nothing else will fulfil the role that has been assigned to terrorism. Hence the terrorist is not committed to the view that national liberation can be achieved by terrorism alone. So understood, the question is whether terrorism has ever made a crucial, irreplaceable contribution to national liberation (or the achieving of the significant revolutionary goals, whatever they are). To say the least, this is a very difficult matter to decide. Did the terrorism of groups like the Stern gang play such a part in establishing the state of Israel? But, in any case, the question is structurally very similar to the one Walzer poses for the legitimacy of the British bombing.

As we saw earlier, Walzer is sympathetic to the "only option" story for the early stages of the World War II terror bombing even while admitting that serious studies have subsequently found the campaign to have been futile

---

[25] Walzer, "Terrorism: A Critique of Excuses," pp. 239–240.
[26] Ibid.
[27] Ibid.

on its own terms. He thinks Churchill had to gamble because the stakes were so very high and the danger imminent. Walzer doesn't, of course, think that this means that probability has no relevance to the gamble, but just that the estimated probability doesn't have to be set so high. It can also be pretty vague. As Walzer says of the bombing, "It makes no sense at this point to quantify the probabilities. I have no clear notion what they actually were or even how they might be calculated given our present knowledge, nor am I sure how different figures, unless they were very different, would affect the moral argument."[28] This is strikingly at odds with what he says about nonstate terrorists who argue that attacking noncombatants is the only option they have. They have no such latitude with probabilities, no matter how imminent and awful the threat. It seems that threats to their political community can never be great enough to constitute the sort of "immeasurable evil" that Walzer sees in the Nazi threat.[29] I am at a loss (inevitably) in trying to gauge "immeasurable" evils, but it would not seem impossible that various struggles against brutal, murderous, tyrannical regimes could sometimes reasonably be viewed as confronting supreme emergency. Of course, they cannot hope to succeed against a totalitarian state, according to Walzer, because terrorism can never succeed against a totalitarian state. Yet the terrorism of the World War II bombers was itself directed against a totalitarian state and was posited on the subjects of that state being able to influence the state's policy and workings.

We should conclude that the attempt to restrict the supreme emergency exemption to states is unpersuasive. Either it applies more generally or it does not apply at all. More recently, Walzer himself seems to have come close to this conclusion, much as it goes against the grain of his discussion in the original version of "Terrorism: A Critique of Excuses." In his reprinting of this essay in his new book, *Arguing about War*, he has added a bracketed paragraph that partially acknowledges the problems posed by an asymmetry between states and substate political groups. He now says that considerations of supreme emergency may also apply to (substate) terrorists, "but only if the oppression to which the terrorists claimed to be responding was genocidal in character," and he construes this as involving "an imminent threat of political and physical extinction."[30] He then claims that this has not been true of any recent terrorist cause.

The Second Difficulty

This brings me to my second difficulty with the category of supreme emergency. If we reject Walzer's attempt to restrict the supreme emergency

---

[28] Walzer, *Just and Unjust Wars*, p. 259.
[29] Ibid.
[30] Michael Walzer, *Arguing About War* (New Haven, CT and London: Yale University Press, 2004), Chapter 4, "A Critique of Excuses," p. 54.

exemption to states, the question arises whether the broadening of the potential application of supreme emergency considerations provides a reason for scepticism about the category itself. Those in the dirty hands tradition who restrict its application to the sphere of state politics are partly moved by a certain romanticism about the superiority of the values served by states and by politics more generally. But they are also concerned to preserve the rarity value of the dirty hands exemption. As the name suggests, the supreme emergency story, as a version of the dirty hands tradition, gets its persuasiveness from the idea that its disruptive power to override profound moral prohibitions is available only in the rarest of circumstances. Any broadening of the reach of those circumstances tends to reduce the rarity value of the exemption, and hence to increase the oddity of the idea that it can be right to do what is morally wrong. Walzer's latest treatment of the issue is even more explicit about this than either his original explanation of dirty hands or his first treatment of supreme emergency. He stresses that "... dirty hands aren't permissible (or necessary) when anything less than the ongoingness of the community is at stake, or when the danger we face is anything less than communal death."[31] It is natural to take the disjunction here as explanatory rather than as providing another option: the danger of communal death explains what is meant by "when ongoingness is at stake." Walzer has, I think, moved a considerable distance towards narrowing the appeal to dirty hands since his original article on the subject, where the exemption was available for a politician running for office who "must" have immoral dealings with a corrupt ward boss in order to get his support.[32] But if my objections are correct, then the form of the supreme emergency category is dubiously consistent with the restricted content that Walzer now assigns to it.

Indeed, if we reject the primacy of the state, or even of the political community, the way is open to allow that the exemption can apply to huge corporations, the existence of which is central to the lives and livelihoods of so many. Or, contrary to Walzer's declared position, it might apply to individuals when they are really up against the wall and their survival, or that of close dependants, is at stake. Yet the more we move in this direction, the more the currency of supreme emergency seems devalued.

These considerations suggest that the category of supreme emergency, in spite of its surface clarity, is conceptually opaque. This opacity is alarming enough in itself, since it means that those using the concept may not be making clear sense, even to themselves. Yet, in the context of public discourse about war and terrorism, we should be particularly worried about allowing exemptions from profound moral and legal constraints under categories that are, at the very least, so open to divergent interpretations. Both

[31] Ibid., p. 46.
[32] See Walzer, "Political Action," pp. 165–166.

the morality and legality of political violence must be concerned with the dangerous consequences of allowing justifications or exemptions that are likely to be exploited by any side to a conflict. On Walzer's own account, the "legitimate" resort to terror in the early stages of World War II led rapidly to its illegitimate use thereafter, with disastrous human consequences for hundreds of thousands of German and Japanese civilians. Moreover, one party's resort to supreme emergency is likely to encourage other parties (including the current enemy) to tread the path of exemption; they are unlikely to cede the point that the original violator's resort to exemption is legitimate where their own is not. Even in Walzer's own exposition, the ambiguities of notions like "ongoingness of the community" and "communal death" open vistas of exploitation and conflicting interpretation. Sometimes he seems to include physical extinction along with the elimination of the values of a political community, but most of the stress of his exposition, especially in his most recent writing, is on the latter. So he talks of "political and physical extinction" but also in recent writing stresses the communitarian basis of his argument.[33] He explains the extinction of a political community (actually talking of its "replacement") as requiring "either the elimination of the people or the coercive transformation of their way of life."[34] This disjunction is not merely explanatory and indicates that, absent widespread massacre of the people, the realistic threat of coercive transformation of their way of life is sufficient to allow for the preventive slaughter of innocents. Since virtually any armed conquest could plausibly be held to involve such a transformation, the phrase opens the way, despite Walzer's concern to avoid it, to widespread resort to supreme emergency. And this prospect should be apparent to anyone considering the validity of allowing the exemption.[35] In the context of the counterterrorism atmosphere sustaining so much international politics at present and arousing so much fear of threats to ways of life, the promulgation of a doctrine of supreme emergency is fraught with danger.

It may be objected that these are mere practical problems about the promulgation of what may nonetheless be a "true" moral thesis. Perhaps the supreme emergency exemption states a moral truth that it would be morally disastrous to publicise. Even to concede this would be to rob the exemption of much of its point, since it is supposed to form part of the publicly accessible wisdom about the waging of war and other forms of political violence. But the objection's distinction between the truth of a moral thesis and the value or disvalue of its promulgation is, in any case, debatable as a

---

[33] Walzer, *Arguing About War*, pp. 42–45 and 49–50.
[34] Ibid., p. 49.
[35] It is true that the objection involves attention to tendencies or likely consequences, but like many other considerations to do with likely or possible consequences, it is open to use by non-consequentialists.

universally applicable distinction. Even those of us who think that truth, in some substantial sense, does apply to moral discourse need to acknowledge that moral truths are supported by practical reason and are dependent in complex ways on issues of practicality. This is particularly pertinent to matters of political morality, where the need for public accessibility and the real possibility of rational public endorsement are rightly prominent.[36]

In reply, it might be urged that the problem for supreme emergency also arises with other categories within the public writ of just war thinking, and yet we don't reject them as "conceptually opaque." Consider "just cause" itself. This forms an integral part of the JAB, yet, like supreme emergency, it is open to a variety of interpretations, and it is common enough for both sides to claim their cause as just. True enough, but there are several differences between the categories of just cause and supreme emergency. One is that categories like just cause do not function as escape clauses or exemption conditions from otherwise demanding prohibitions. They have initial moral plausibility as part of acceptable public reasoning about war, given only that the resort to war can be morally justified at all. Hence they provide material for debate, discussion, and codification in such arenas as international law where the primacy of self-defence as instantiating just cause is explored and extensions and possible additions to it are interrogated. So there are complex debates and adjudications about preemptive defence, the legitimacy of invited interventions in civil wars or military aid to governments suppressing civil unrest, and so on.[37] To my knowledge, there have been no such attempts at legal discussion or codifying of supreme emergency. This is not surprising. To adopt a device favoured by many political philosophers, we may imagine a state-of-nature discussion about self-defence as just cause for war, on the one hand, and supreme emergency as a reason for abandoning the immunity of the innocent, on the other. I think it plausible, to say the least, that agreement on self-defence as just cause might be reached, whereas the supreme emergency exemption would have a much harder time of it, simply because, under the veil of ignorance about one's status as combatant/noncombatant, member of whichever side, and so on,

---

[36] There are connections here with Kant's principle of publicity and Rawls's related, though rather different, appeal to publicity in his elaboration of an idea of public reason, but this is not the place to explore the matter further. See Immanuel Kant, *Perpetual Peace: Appendix II*, in Kant, *On History*, ed. Lewis White Beck (Indianapolis: Bobbs-Merrill, 1963), especially pp. 129–30; and John Rawls, "The Idea of Public Reason Revisited," in John Rawls, *The Law of Peoples* (Cambridge, MA: Harvard University Press, 1999).

[37] For a clear discussion of these issues and many others to do with the international law of war and peace, see Oscar Schachter, "The Role of International Law in Maintaining Peace," in W. Scott Thompson and Kenneth M. Jensen, with Richard N. Smith and Kimber M. Schraub (eds.), *Approaches to Peace: An Intellectual Map* (Washington, DC: United States Institute of Peace, 1992), pp. 67–127.

any participant is likely to see the risks of allowing the exemption as too great.[38]

My own view is that the supreme emergency story suffers from grave defects whether it is offered as an exemption on behalf of a state or by some less established political community, or a group claiming to represent either. Apart from the problems already discussed, it also involves an undervaluation of the depth and centrality of the prohibition on intentionally killing the innocent. In spite of Walzer's agonising about the need to acknowledge that we have violated an important moral restraint by our bombing or other terror tactic, he locates the prohibition of attacking noncombatants within what he calls "the war convention." Although there is some unclarity about what he means by this, the terminology suggests that the prohibition is itself somehow merely conventional, though I doubt that this could be Walzer's considered position. On the contrary, it is, as I have argued, basic to what makes it legitimate to wage a just war at all. More generally, the prohibition on intentionally killing innocent people functions in our moral thinking as a sort of touchstone of moral and intellectual health.[39] To suspend this, for reasons of necessity or supreme emergency, is to bring about an upheaval in the moral perspective. The situation is, I think, something like that supposed by the philosopher Quine to operate with empirical and scientific knowledge. Quine thinks that no propositions, even those of logic, are beyond revision or abandonment, but that some are more deeply entrenched in our way of thinking and responding to the world than others and so less revisable. Some, indeed, may be so deeply entrenched that we cannot imagine what it would be like to have to give them up. Wittgenstein makes some similar suggestions in his book *On Certainty*, but explicitly includes many ordinary empirical propositions in the central core.[40] My suggestion is that some of our moral beliefs have an analogous position in the framework of our moral thinking. Rejection of them leads to an imbalance and incoherence in moral thought and practice parallel to (though very different in kind from) the rejection of entrenched propositions in empirical and theoretical thinking. Such rejection does not have the same implication of immediate absurdity

---

[38] I have no great confidence in state of nature/veil of ignorance arguments as foundational for morality or even for justice, but they can serve a useful purpose in firming up moral intuitions and exhibiting the ways in which partiality in moral thinking may be corrected.

[39] I do not mean to take a stand here against all cases of assisted suicide or mercy killing, since many of these involve the consent or request of the person killed, or, at the very least, are done for his or her good and in the belief that this end is what they wish for. The central application of the principle of discrimination is concerned with people who are to be killed against their will and for the good of others.

[40] Ludwig Wittgenstein, *On Certainty*, ed. G. E. M. Anscombe and G. H. Wright, trans. D. Paul and G. E. M Anscombe (Oxford: Basil Blackwell, 1969); and Willard Van Orman Quine, "Two Dogmas of Empiricism," *The Philosophical Review* 60 (1951), pp. 20–43.

that attaches, for instance, to the belief of someone who really thinks that his head is a pumpkin (to echo Descartes' example), but there can be a sort of incomprehension involved in facing some disturbing beliefs and decisions of practical life. Consider, for example, the brutal butcheries practiced as a matter of course in the judicial punishments of yesteryear. Don't we now find ourselves at a somewhat baffled and disoriented distance from the practice embedded in the sentence "to be hung, drawn and quartered"? True, many of our ancestors viewed this as appropriate and normal, and there are moral and legal criminals who would practice such cruelties even today (though seldom in the context of judicial punishment). Nonetheless, there is something in our practical intellect as it has developed that finds the mind-set of such people not only repellent but beyond comprehension. Of course, we can understand the cultural background and relevant beliefs to a considerable extent (it is the task of historians to help with this), but there is still something that blocks full comprehension of those who perpetrated and those who enjoyed witnessing these acts. Much the same could be said of our reactions to ritual human sacrifice and many other morally horrific acts that have been prevalent in the past. To many of us, the revival of torture as a defensible method of interrogation or punishment creates a similar reaction.

These considerations will not be compelling to every reader, partly because there is an understandable reluctance amongst contemporary Western intellectuals to treat *any* moral rule or prohibition as beyond exemption. We are wary of "absolutes" in all areas of thought. To this extent, there is something futile about trying to engage in a debate about exemptions to the principle of discrimination. Those who reject the idea of exemptions from this profound moral imperative are arguing with people who take it as a basic fact that there will always be exemptions to any moral prohibition. It is hard to see how either side can have a compelling case in such a situation. Nonetheless, it is worth pointing out that even utilitarianism accepts absolutes insofar as it treats its basic injunction to act so as to produce the greatest good of the greatest number as beyond exemption. And much the same is true of various forms of consequentialism. Indeed, it is plausible that something similar will be true of all moral theories, so I suspect that the debate is not really about whether there are moral absolutes, but rather about how many there are, and at what level of thinking they may be found.[41]

Of course, any absolute commitment will face problems when the commitment confronts messy realities that challenge the very basis of the commitment. The category of "moral dilemma" itself speaks to the alarming prospect that our deepest moral imperatives may not always cohere. We saw

---

[41] Considerations rather like these have led Shelly Kagan, himself a consequentialist, to conclude: "Talk of absolutism reveals little if anything about a person's normative theory." Shelly Kagan, *Normative Ethics* (Boulder, CO: Westview Press, 1998), p. 94.

some of the force of this in the discussion in Chapter 7 of innocent shields. It seems likely that faced with certain ghastly concrete choices such as Sophie's choice, discussed there, the resources of even the richest morality run out. And other contexts of extreme malice and danger, such as life in the Nazi death camps or the Soviet Gulag, may pose similar choices.[42] But, if so, I think we do violence to our situation by proclaiming in advance general conditions or circumstances in which exemption must be given to our deepest moral prohibitions. It is pertinent here that moral dilemmas must be distinguished from dirty hands. In the former category, there is no ordained right answer to the problem, whereas in dirty hands scenarios it is supposed to be obvious that one should choose the "necessary" course over the moral one. Consider the parallel with rape. According to supreme emergency or even what I have earlier called "balanced exceptionalism," we cannot exclude the possibility that rape may be *required* to preserve some great value, such as community continuity. But anyone who goes about seriously contemplating conditions under which rape may be obligatory (though still immoral, as insisted by advocates of the dirty hands category) is tempting fate. Certainly, we need to be careful about cultivating any attitude that undermines the resolute commitment to virtuous action. The path of exemptions in either of its forms does just this. I do not want to say, in the spirit of Elizabeth Anscombe, that an advocate of dirty hands or balanced exceptionalism should not be spoken to because "he shows a corrupt mind."[43] Discussion should always proceed with people who show good will, but any such discussion should be open about the dangers attendant upon attitudes adopted. Two things are important in doing moral philosophy: one is intellectual openness to a range of views, including confronting ones, and another is an awareness that intellectual exercises in this area can have profound implications for life.

For our purposes, the issue may be focussed in practical terms by considering the case of terrorism and supreme emergency, since this clearly presents us with two options. Either we insist that major terrorism (as characterised by the tactical definition) is always morally wrong and never to be allowed, or we accept that there can be circumstances in which the values served by terrorist acts are so important that it is right to do them.[44] If the latter, then

---

[42] Rab Bennett describes the agony of prisoner doctors in Nazi camps who felt driven to poison newborn babies because every prisoner woman with a child was marked by the Nazis for death. Bennett, *Under the Shadow of the Swastika* (London: Macmillan, 1999), pp. 290–291.

[43] G. E. M. Anscombe, "Modern Moral Philosophy," *Philosophy* 33 (1958), p. 17.

[44] I am here ignoring those cases of terrorism that involve only destruction of the property of innocent people. As mentioned in Chapter 8, there may be cases of that kind which concern only minor damage, not itself deeply threatening to the well-being of the noncombatants themselves, that will merit lesser condemnation, and may even be justified, though regrettable. So justified revolutionaries, with their backs to the wall, may argue plausibly
(*cont.*)

this exemption, for supreme emergency or otherwise, cannot be allowed only to states. Its legitimacy must in principle be more widely available, and decided on a case-by-case basis. My own conviction is that we surely do better to condemn the resort to terrorism outright with no leeway for exemptions, be they for states, revolutionaries, or religious and ideological zealots of any persuasion.

(*footnote 44 cont.*)
that they can destroy some nonessential noncombatant property in order to escape an attack. Even here, issues of restitution or restoration may arise. The point is similar to that made by Joel Feinberg about a case not involving political violence. See Joel Feinberg, "Voluntary Euthanasia and the Inalienable Right to Life," *Philosophy and Public Affairs* 7 (1978), pp. 93–123.

Bibliography

Alexandra, Andrew. "Militarism." *Social Theory and Practice* 19, no. 2 (Summer 1993), pp. 205–224.

Alexandra, Andrew. "Political Pacifism." *Social Theory and Practice* 29, no. 4 (2003), pp. 589–606.

Anglin, Mary K. "Feminist Perspectives on Structural Violence." *Identities* 5, no. 2 (1998), pp. 145–151.

Anscombe, G. E. M. "War and Murder." In Richard A. Wasserstrom (ed.), *War and Morality*. Belmont, CA: Wadsworth, 1970, pp. 42–53.

Aquinas, Thomas. *The "Summa Theologica" of St. Thomas Aquinas.* London: Burns Oates & Washbourne Ltd., 1916.

Ardrey, Robert. *The Territorial Imperative: A Personal Inquiry into the Animal Origins of Property and Nations.* New York: Atheneum, 1966.

Arendt, Hannah. *On Violence.* London: Allen Lane, The Penguin Press, 1970.

Aristotle. *Nicomachean Ethics*, trans. H. A. Rackham. London: William Heinemann Ltd., 1962.

Aristotle. *Nicomachean Ethics*, trans. David Ross. Oxford: Oxford University Press, 1998.

Aristotle. *The Basic Works of Aristotle*, ed. Richard McKeon. New York: Random House, 1941.

Aron, Raymond. *Peace and War: A Theory of International Relations*, trans. Richard Howard and Annette Baker Fox. Garden City, NY: Doubleday, 1966.

Ashcroft, Richard E. "Ethics Committees and Countries in Transition: A Figleaf for Structural Violence?" *British Medical Journal* 331 (2005), pp. 229–230.

Augustine, St. *The City of God*, ed. Henry Bettenson. New York: Penguin, 1972.

Austin, J. L. "A Plea for Excuses." In J. L. Austin, *Philosophical Papers*. Oxford: Oxford University Press, 1961, pp. 123–152.

Bacevich, Andrew J. Review of Russell W. Glenn, *Reading Athena's Dance Card: Men against Fire in Vietnam* (Annapolis, MD: Naval Institute Press, 2000). *Journal of Cold War Studies* 4, no. 2 (2002), pp. 135–137.

Barnes, Jonathan. "The Just War." In *The Cambridge History of Later Medieval Philosophy*, ed. Norman Kretzman, Anthony Kenny, and Jan Pinborg. Cambridge: Cambridge University Press, 1982, pp. 771–784.

Baron, Marcia. "Kantian Ethics and Supererogation." *Journal of Philosophy* 84, no. 5 (1987), pp. 237–262.

Beckerleg, Susan, and Gillian Lewando Hundt. "Women Heroin Users: Exploring the Limitations of the Structural Violence Approach." *International Journal of Drug Policy* 16 (2005), pp. 183–190.

Beevor, Antony. *Berlin: The Downfall, 1945*. London: Viking, 2002.

Beitz, Charles R. "Bounded Morality: Justice and the State in World Politics." *International Organization* 33 (1979), pp. 405–424.

Bennett, Rab. *Under the Shadow of the Swastika: The Moral Dilemmas of Resistance and Collaboration in Hitler's Europe*. London: MacMillan, 1999.

Bettelheim, Bruno. *The Informed Heart*. Glencoe, IL: Free Press, 1960.

Bok, Sissela. *A Strategy for Peace*. New York: Pantheon, 1989.

Bok, Sissela. *Common Values*. Columbia: University of Missouri Press, 1995.

Bory, Francoise. *Origin and Development of International Humanitarian Law*. Geneva: International Committee of the Red Cross, 1982.

Boulton, David. *Objection Overruled*. London: MacGibbon & Kee, 1967.

Brandt, R. B. "Utilitarianism and the Rules of War." In Marshall Cohen, Thomas Nagel, and Thomas Scanlon (eds.), *War and Moral Responsibility*. Princeton, NJ: Princeton University Press, 1974, pp. 25–45.

Broad, C. D. "Conscience and Conscientious action." In C. D. Broad, *Critical Essays in Moral Philosophy*, ed. David R. Cheney. London: George Allen & Unwin, 1971, pp. 136–55.

Broad, C. D. "Ought We to Fight for Our Country in the Next War?" In C. D. Broad, *Ethics and the History of Philosophy: Selected Essays*. London: Routledge & Kegan Paul, 1952, pp. 232–243.

Buchanan, Allen. "Institutionalizing the Just War." *Philosophy and Public Affairs* 34, no. 1 (2006), pp. 2–38.

Burchett, Wilfred, and Derek Roebuck. *The Whores of War: Mercenaries Today*. Harmondworth: Penguin, 1977.

Burmester, H. C. "The Recruitment and Use of Mercenaries in Armed Conflict." *American Journal of International Law* 72 (1978), pp. 37–56.

Buzan, Barry. "Who May We Bomb." In Ken Booth and Tim Dunne (eds.), *Worlds in Collision: Terror and the Future of Global Order*. New York: Palgrave, 2002, pp. 85–94.

Carr, E. H. *The Twenty Years' Crisis, 1919–1939: An Introduction to the Study of International Relations*. London: Macmillan, 1956.

Ceadel, Martin. *Thinking about Peace and War*. Oxford: Oxford University Press, 1987.

Chalfont, Alun. *Montgomery of Alamein*. New York: Atheneum, 1976.

Chambers, James. *Palmerston: The People's Darling*. London: John Murray, 2004.

Chang, Iris. *The Rape of Nanking: The Forgotten Holocaust of World War II*. Harmondsworth: Penguin, 1997.

Chapman, Guy. *A Passionate Prodigality*. London: MacGibbon & Kee, 1965.

Chomsky, Noam. "An Exception to the Rules" (review of *Just and Unjust Wars* by M. Walzer). *Australian Outlook* 32, no. 3 (December 1978), p. 363. Originally printed in *Inquiry*, April 17, 1978, pp. 23–27.

Christopher, Paul. *The Ethics of War and Peace: An Introduction to Legal and Moral Issues*. Englewood Cliffs, NJ: Prentice-Hall, 1994.

Clausewitz, Carl von. *On War*, ed. and trans. Michael Howard and Peter Paret. Princeton, NJ: Princeton University Press, 1976.

Coady, C. A. J. "Defining Terrorism." In Igor Primoratz (ed.), *Terrorism: The Philosophical Issues*. Hampshire and New York: Palgrave, 2004, pp. 3–14.

Coady, C. A. J. "Deterrent Intentions Revisited." *Ethics* 99, no. 1 (1988), pp. 98–108.

Coady, C. A. J. "Dirty Hands." In Laurence and Charlotte Becker (eds.), *The Encyclopaedia of Ethics*, second edition. New York: Routledge, 2001, pp. 407–410.

Coady, C. A. J. "Dirty Hands." In Robert E. Goodin and Philip Pettit (eds.), *A Companion to Contemporary Political Philosophy*. Cambridge, MA: Blackwell, 1993, pp. 422–430.

Coady, C. A. J. "Escaping from the Bomb." In Henry Shue (ed.), *Nuclear Deterrence and Moral Restraint: Critical Choices for American Strategy*. Cambridge and New York: Cambridge University Press, 1989, pp. 163–225.

Coady, C. A. J. "Henry Sidgwick." In C. L. Ten (ed.), *The Routledge History of Philosophy, Vol. VII: The Nineteenth Century*. London: Routledge, 1994, pp. 122–147.

Coady, C. A. J. "Hobbes and the Beautiful Axiom." *Philosophy* 65 (1990), pp. 5–17.

Coady, C. A. J. "How New Is the 'New Terror'?" *Iyyun: The Jerusalem Philosophical Quarterly* 55, no. 1 (January 2006), pp. 49–65.

Coady, C. A. J. "Mercenary Morality." In A. G. D. Bradney (ed.), *International Law and Armed Conflict*. Stuttgart: Franz Steiner Verlag, 1992, pp. 55–69.

Coady, C. A. J. "Messy Morality and the Art of the Possible." *Proceedings of the Aristotelian Society*, supp. vol. 64 (1990), pp. 259–279.

Coady C. A. J. "Natural Law and Weapons of Mass Destruction." In Sohail H. Hashmi and Steven P. Lee (eds.), *Ethics and Weapons of Mass Destruction: Religious and Secular Perspectives*. Cambridge: Cambridge University Press, 2004, pp. 111–131.

Coady, C. A. J. "Politics and the Problem of Dirty Hands." In Peter Singer (ed.), *A Companion to Ethics*. Oxford: Blackwell, 1993, pp. 373–83.

Coady, C. A. J., and Jeff Ross. "St. Augustine and the Ideal of Peace." *American Catholic Philosophical Quarterly* 74, no. 1 (Winter 2000), pp. 153–161.

Coady, C. A. J. "Terrorism and Innocence." *Journal of Ethics* 8, no. 1 (2004), pp. 37–58.

Coady, C. A. J. *The Ethics of Humanitarian Intervention* (Peaceworks 45). Washington, DC: United States Institute of Peace, 2002.

Coady, C. A. J. "The Leaders and the Led: Problems of Just War Theory." *Inquiry* 23 (1980), pp. 275–291.

Coady, C. A. J. "The Moral Reality in Realism." In C. A. J. Coady (ed.), *What's Wrong with Moralism?* Oxford: Blackwell, 2006, pp. 121–136.

Coady, C. A. J. "The Moral Reality in Realism." *Journal of Applied Philosophy* 22, no. 2 (2005), pp. 121–136.

Coady, C. A. J. "War for Humanity: A Critique." In Deen K. Chatterjee and Don Scheid (eds.), *Ethics and Foreign Intervention*. Cambridge and New York: Cambridge University Press, 2003, pp. 274–295.

Coates, A. J. *The Ethics of War*. Manchester and New York: Manchester University Press, 1997.

Cohen, Sheldon M. *Arms and Judgement: Law, Morality and the Conduct of War in the Twentieth Century*. Boulder, CO: Westview Press, 1989.

Collins, Tim. *Rules of Engagement: A Life in Conflict.* London: Headline Book Publishing, 2005.

Commager, Henry Steele. "Ethics, Virtue, and Foreign Policy." In Kenneth W. Thompson (ed.), *Ethics and International Relations,* vol. 2. New Brunswick, NJ: Transaction Books, 1985, pp. 127–137.

Constant, Benjamin. *Political Writings,* ed. and trans. Biancamaria Fontana. Cambridge: Cambridge University Press, 1988.

Crenshaw, Martha. "The Causes of Terrorism." *Comparative Politics* 13 (1981), pp. 379–399.

Dallaire, Romeo. *Shake Hands with the Devil: The Failure of Humanity in Rwanda.* New York: Carroll and Graf, 2003.

Darcy, Eric. *Conscience and Its Right to Freedom.* New York: Sheed and Ward, 1961.

Debray, Régis. *Revolution in the Revolution?,* trans. Bobbye Ortiz. London: Monthly Review Press, 1967.

Dewey, John. "Conscience and Compulsion." In John Dewey, *The Political Writings,* ed. Debra Morris and Ian Shapiro. Indianapolis: Hackett, 1993, pp. 192–194.

Dinstein, Yoram. "The New Geneva Protocols: A Step Forward or Backward?" *The Year Book Of World Affairs* 33 (1979), pp. 265–283.

Dixon, Norman. *On the Psychology of Military Incompetence.* New York: Basic Books, 1976.

Doppelt, Gerald. "Walzer's Theory of Morality in International Relationships." *Philosophy and Public Affairs* 8 (1978), pp. 3–26.

Doyle, Michael W. *Ways of War and Peace: Realism, Liberalism and Socialism.* New York and London: Norton, 1997.

Dubner, Barry H. *The Law of International Sea Piracy.* The Hague: Martinus Nijhoff, 1980.

Dworkin, Ronald. *Taking Rights Seriously.* London: Duckworth, 1978.

Ehrenreich, Barbara. *Blood Rites: Origins and History of the Passions of War.* London: Virago, 1997.

Eppstein, John. *The Catholic Tradition of the Law of Nations.* Washington, DC: Catholic Association for International Peace, 1935.

Erasmus, Desiderius. "A Tract of the Society for the Promotion of Permanent and Universal Peace." In Desiderius Erasmus, *Extracts from the Writings of Erasmus on the Subject of War.* London: Thomas Ward & Co., 1838.

Erasmus, Desiderius. *The Complaint of Peace.* Boston: Charles Williams, 1813.

Fanon, Frantz. *The Wretched of the Earth,* trans. Constance Farrington. New York: Grove Press, 1963.

Feinberg, Joel. "Voluntary Euthanasia and the Inalienable Right to Life." *Philosophy and Public Affairs* 7 (1978), pp. 93–123.

Fotion, Nicholas, and Gerard Elfstrom. *Military Ethics: Guidelines for Peace and War.* London: Routledge & Kegan Paul, 1986.

Franck, Thomas M. "A Holistic Approach to Building Peace." In Olara A. Otunnu and Michael W. Doyle (eds.), *Peacemaking and Peacekeeping for the New Century.* Lanham, MD: Rowman and Littlefield, 1998, pp. 275–296.

Frankland, Noble, and Charles Websater. *The Strategic Air Offensive against Germany 1939–1945,* vol. 3. London: Her Majesty's Stationary Office, 1961.

Fuller, J. F. C. *The Conduct of War: 1789–1961.* London: Eyre Methuen, 1972.

Fullinwider, Robert K. "War and Innocence." In Charles R. Beitz, Marshall Cohen, Thomas Scanlon, and A. John Simmons (eds.), *International Ethics: A Philosophy and Public Affairs Reader.* Princeton, NJ: Princeton University Press, 1985, pp. 90–97.

Galbraith, John Kenneth. *The Culture of Contentment.* New York: Houghton Mifflin, 1992.

Galtung, Johan. "Violence, Peace and Peace Research." *The Journal of Peace Research* 6 (1969), pp. 167–191.

Garrett, Stephen A. "Political Leadership and Dirty Hands: Winston Churchill and the City Bombing of Germany." In Cathal J. Nolan (ed.), *Ethics and Statecraft: The Moral Dimension of International Affairs.* Westport, CT: Greenwood Press, 1995, pp. 75–91.

Garver, Newton. "What Violence Is." *The Nation* 209 (1968), reprinted In James Rachels and Frank A. Tillman (eds.), *Philosophical Issues: A Contemporary Introduction.* New York: Harper Collins, 1972, pp. 223–228.

George, Alexander L. *Forceful Persuasion: Coercive Diplomacy as an Alternative to War.* Washington, DC: United States Institute of Peace Press, 1991.

Ghosh, Dipankar. "Sunk Costs." In Rashad Abdel-Khalik (ed.), *The Blackwell Encyclopaedia of Management*, vol. 1. Cambridge, MA: Blackwell, 1997, pp. 272–274.

Glover, Jonathan. *Causing Death and Saving Lives.* Harmondsworth: Penguin, 1977.

Goodin, Robert. *What's Wrong with Terrorism.* Cambridge: Polity, 2006.

Gordon, Joy. "Cool War: Economic Sanctions as a Weapon of Mass Destruction." *Harper's Magazine*, November 2002, pp. 43–49.

Gray, J. Glenn. *The Warriors: Reflections on Men in Battle.* New York: Harper and Row, 1970.

Green, Karen. "Prostitution, Exploitation and Taboo." *Philosophy* 64 (1989), pp. 525–534.

Grossman, Lieutenant Colonel Dave. *On Killing: The Psychological Cost of Learning to Kill in War and Society.* Boston: Little, Brown, 1995.

Grotius, Hugo. *The Rights of War and Peace (De Jure Belli ac Pacis)*, vol. 2, trans. Francis W. Kelsey. Oxford: Clarendon Press, 1925.

Grotius, Hugo. *The Rights of War and Peace (De Jure Belli ac Pacis)*, trans. A. C. Campbell. Pontefract: Printed by B. Boothroyd, 1814. (A recent edition is *The Rights of War and Peace*, ed. Richard Tuck, 3 vols. Indianapolis: Liberty Fund, 2005.)

Grundy, Kenneth W., and Michael A. Weinstein. *The Ideologies of Violence.* Columbus, OH: Merrill, 1974.

Guevara, Che. *Bolivian Diary*, trans. Carlos P. Hansen and Andrew Sinclair. London: Jonathan Cape/Lorrimer, 1968.

Harris, John. *Violence and Responsibility.* London: Routledge & Kegan Paul, 1980.

Hegel, Georg Wilhelm Friedrich. *The Philosophy of Right*, trans. T. M. Knox. Oxford: Clarendon Press, 1952.

Hehir, J. Bryan. "Intervention: From Theories to Cases." *Ethics and International Affairs* 9 (1995), pp. 1–13.

Hobbes, Thomas. *Leviathan*, ed. C. B. Macpherson. Harmondsworth: Penguin, 1968.

Hobbes, Thomas. *Leviathan*, ed. Michael Oakeshott. Oxford: Basil Blackwell, 1962.

Hobbes, Thomas. *The Elements of Law: Natural and Politic*, ed. Ferdinand Tonnies. Cambridge: Cambridge University Press, 1928.

Hoffmann, Stanley. *World Disorders: Troubled Peace in the Post-Cold War Era*. Lanham, MD: Rowman & Littlefield, 1998.

Holmes, Robert L. *On War and Morality*. Princeton, NJ: Princeton University Press, 1989.

Holmes, Robert, L. "Pacifism and Weapons of Mass Destruction." In Sohail H. Hashmi and Steven P. Lee (eds.), *Ethics and Weapons of Mass Destruction: Religious and Secular Perspectives*. Cambridge and New York: Cambridge University Press, 2004, pp. 451–469.

Honderich, Ted. *Violence for Equality: Inquiries in Political Philosophy*. Harmondsworth: Penguin, 1980.

Hughes, Martin. "Terrorism and National Security." *Philosophy* 57 (January 1982), pp. 5–25.

Humboldt, Wilhelm von. *The Limits of State Action*, ed. and trans. J. W. Burrow. Indianapolis: Liberty Fund, 1993.

Hurka, Thomas. "Proportionality in the Morality of War." *Philosophy and Public Affairs* 33, no. 1 (2005), pp. 34–66.

James, William. "The Moral Equivalent of War." In William James, *Essays in Religion and Morality*. Cambridge, MA: Harvard University Press, 1982, pp. 162–173.

Jinks, Derek. "The Declining Significance of POW Status." *Harvard International Law Journal* 45, no. 2 (2004), pp. 367–442.

Johnson, James Turner. *Ideology, Reason and the Limitation of War*. Princeton, NJ: Princeton University Press, 1975.

Johnson, James Turner. *Just War Tradition and the Restraint of War: A Moral and Historical Inquiry*. Princeton, NJ: Princeton University Press, 1981.

Johnson, James Turner. *The Quest for Peace: Three Moral Traditions in Western Cultural History*. Princeton, NJ: Princeton University Press, 1987.

Kagan, Robert. *Of Paradise and Power: America and Europe in the New World Order*. New York: Knopf, 2003.

Kagan, Shelly. *Normative Ethics*. Boulder, CO: Westview Press, 1998.

Kahn, Paul W. "From Nuremberg to The Hague: The United States Position in *Nicaragua v. United States* and the Development of International Law." *The Yale Journal of International Law* 12, no. 1 (1987), pp. 1–62.

Kahn, Paul. "The Paradox of Riskless Warfare." *Philosophy and Public Policy Quarterly* 22, no. 3 (2002), pp. 2–8.

Kahn, Paul. "War and Sacrifice in Kosovo." *Philosophy and Public Policy Quarterly* 20, no. 3 (1999), pp. 1–6.

Kamm, Frances. "The Doctrine of Triple Effect and Why a Rational Agent Need Not Intend the Means to His End." *Proceedings of the Aristotelian Society*, supp. vol. 74 (2000), pp. 41–57.

Kant, Immanuel. *On History*, ed. Lewis White Beck. Indianapolis and New York: Bobbs-Merrill, 1963.

Kant, Immanuel. *The Critique of Judgement*, trans. J. C. Meredith. Oxford: Clarendon Press, 1928.

Kavka, Gregory S. *Moral Paradoxes of Nuclear Deterrence*. Cambridge: Cambridge University Press, 1987.

Kecskemeti, Paul. *Strategic Surrender: The Politics of Victory and Defeat.* Stanford, CA: Stanford University Press, 1958.

Keegan, John, and Richard Holmes. *Soldiers: A History of Men in Battle.* London: Hamish Hamilton, 1985.

Kennedy, Liam, and Scott Lucas. "Enduring Freedom: Public Diplomacy and U.S. Foreign Policy." *American Quarterly* 57, no. 2 (2005), pp. 307–333.

Klare, Michael. *Rogue States and Nuclear Outlaws: America's Search for a New Foreign Policy.* New York: Hill and Wang, 1995.

Kuflik, Arthur. "A Defense of Common-Sense Morality." *Ethics* 96 (1986), pp. 784–803.

Lacy, James L. "Alternative Service: The Significance of the Challenge." In Michael F. Noone, Jr. (ed.), *Selective Conscientious Objection: Accommodating Conscience and Security.* Boulder, CO: Westview Press, 1989, pp. 107–115.

Langan, John. "The Elements of St. Augustine's Just War Theory." *The Journal of Religious Ethics* 12 (1984), pp. 19–38.

Langan, John. "The Good of Selective Conscientious Objection." In Michael F. Noone, Jr. (ed.), *Selective Conscientious Objection: Accommodating Conscience and Security.* Boulder, CO: Westview Press, 1989, pp. 89–106.

Langguth, A. J. *Hidden Terrors.* New York: Pantheon Books, 1978.

Laqueur, Walter. "Reflections on Terrorism." *Foreign Affairs* 65, no. 1 (1986), pp. 86–100.

Laqueur, Walter. *Terrorism.* London: Weidenfeld & Nicolson, 1977.

Laqueur, Walter. *The Age Of Terrorism.* Boston: Little, Brown, 1987.

Lee, Steven. "Is Poverty Violence?" In Deanne Curtin and Robert Litke (eds.), *Institutional Violence.* Amsterdam and Atlanta: Rodopi, 1999, pp. 5–12.

Lefever, Ernest W. "Moralism and US Foreign Policy." Washington, DC: The Brookings Institute, 1973

Levi, Primo. *The Drowned and the Saved,* trans. Raymond Rosenthal. New York: Vintage, 1989.

Lewis, David. "Devils Bargains and the Real Worlds." In Douglas MacLean (ed.), *The Security Gamble: Deterrence Dilemmas in the Nuclear Age.* Totowa, NJ: Rowman & Allanheld, 1984, pp. 141–154.

Lewis, David. "Finite Counterforce." In Henry Shue (ed.), *Nuclear Deterrence and Moral Restraint.* New York and Cambridge: Cambridge University Press, 1989, pp. 51–114.

Liddell Hart, B. H. *The Memoirs of Captain Liddell Hart,* vol. 1. London: Cassell & Co., 1965.

Lineberry, R. C. *The Struggle against Terrorism.* New York: Wilson, 1977.

Litwak, Robert. *Rogue States and U.S. Foreign Policy: Containment after the Cold War.* Washington, DC: Woodrow Wilson Center Press; Baltimore: Johns Hopkins University Press, 1999.

Lorenz, Konrad. *On Aggression.* New York: Harcourt Brace and World, 1966.

Luban, David. "Intervention and Civilization: Some Unhappy Lessons of the Kosovo War." In Pablo de Greiff and Ciaran Cronin (eds.), *Global Justice and Transnational Politics: Essays on the Moral and Political Challenges of Globalisation.* Cambridge, MA and London: MIT Press, 2002, pp. 79–115.

Luban, David. "Just War and Human Rights." *Philosophy and Public Affairs* 9 (1980), pp. 160–181.

Luban, David. "Preventive War." *Philosophy and Public Affairs* 32, no. 3 (2004), pp. 207–248.

Luban, David. "The Romance of the Nation-State." *Philosophy and Public Affairs* 9 (1980), pp. 392–397.

Machiavelli, Niccolò. *The Discourses*, vol. 1, ed. and trans. Lesley J. Walker. London: Routledge, 1950.

Machiavelli, Niccolò. *The Prince*, ed. Peter Bondanella, trans. Peter Bondanella and Mark Musa. Oxford: Oxford University Press, 1984.

Mallett, Michael. *Mercenaries and Their Masters*. London: Bodley Head, 1974.

Manning, Frederick. *The Middle Parts of Fortune*. London: Granada, 1977.

Marighela, Carlos. *Handbook of Urban Guerrilla Warfare*. In Carlos Marighela, *For the Liberation of Brazil*, trans. John Butt and Rosemary Sheed. Harmondsworth: Penguin, 1971, pp. 61–97.

Marinetti, Filippo Tommaso. "The Futurist Manifesto." *Le Figaro*, February 20, 1909.

Martin, Michel L. "France: A Statute but No Objectors." In Charles C. Moskos and John Whiteclay Chambers II (eds.), *The New Conscientious Objection: From Sacred to Secular Resistance*. Oxford: Oxford University Press, 1993, pp. 80–97.

Martin, Susan Taylor. "'No-Fly' Zone Perils Were for Iraqis, Not Allied Pilots." *The St. Petersburg Times*, October 29, 2004, online at <www.sptimes.com/2004/10/29/columns/_No_fly_zone_perils_.shtml>.

McGoldrick, Dominic. "Political and Legal Responses to the ICC." In Dominic McGoldrick, Peter Rowe, and Eric Donnelly (eds.), *The Permanent International Criminal Court: Legal and Policy Issues*. Oxford: Hart Publishing, 2004, pp. 389–449.

McIntyre, Alison. "Doing Away with Double-Effect." *Ethics* 111 (2001), pp. 219–225.

McMahan, Jeff. "The Ethics of International Intervention." In Kenneth Kipnis and Diana T. Meyers (eds.), *Political Realism and International Morality: Ethics in the Nuclear Age*. Boulder, CO: Westview Press, 1987, pp. 75–101.

McMahan, Jeff, and Robert McKim. "The Just War and the Gulf War." *Canadian Journal of Philosophy* 23 (1993), pp. 501–541.

McNamara, Robert S., with Brian VanDeMark. *In Retrospect: The Tragedy and Lessons of Vietnam*. New York: Times Books, 1995.

Mill, John Stuart. "A Few Words on Non-Intervention." In *Collected Works, Vol. XXI: Essays on Equality, Law and Education*, ed. John M. Robson. Toronto and Buffalo: University of Toronto Press, 1984, pp. 109–124.

Miller, Ronald B. "Violence, Force and Coercion." In Jerome A. Shaffer (ed.), *Violence*. New York: McKay, 1971, pp. 11–44.

More, Thomas. *Utopia*. Harmondsworth: Penguin, 1974.

Morgenthau, Hans. *Politics among Nations: The Struggle for Power and Peace*, fifth edition. New York: Knopf, 1973.

Moskos, C., and John Whiteclay Chambers II (eds.). *The New Conscientious Objection: From Sacred to Secular Resistance*. Oxford: Oxford University Press, 1993.

Mosley, Nicholas. *Julian Grenfel: His Life and the Times of His Death*. London: Weidenfeld and Nicolson, 1976.

Musto, Ronald G. *The Catholic Peace Tradition*. Maryknoll, NY: Orbis Books, 1986.

Nagel, Thomas. *Mortal Questions*. Cambridge: Cambridge University Press, 1979.

Nagel, Thomas. "War and Massacre." In Marshall Cohen, Thomas Nagel, and Thomas Scanlon (eds.), *War and Moral Responsibility*. Princeton, NJ: Princeton University Press, 1974, pp. 3–24.

Narveson, Jan. "Pacifism: A Philosophical Analysis." In Richard A. Wasserstrom (ed.), *War and Morality*. Belmont, CA: Wadsworth, 1970, pp. 63–77.

Norman, Richard. *Ethics, Killing and War*. Cambridge: Cambridge University Press, 1995.

Nozick, Robert. "Coercion." In Sidney Morgenbesser, Patrick Suppes, and Morton White (eds.), *Philosophy, Science and Method*. New York: St. Martin's Press, 1969, pp. 440–472.

Parfit, Derek. *Reasons and Persons*. Oxford: Clarendon Press, 1984.

Paskins, Barry, and Michael Dockrill. *The Ethics of War*. London: Duckworth, 1979.

Plato. *The Gorgias*, trans. Walter Hamilton. Harmondsworth: Penguin, 1960.

Post, Jerrold M. "Terrorist Psycho-Logic: Terrorist Behaviour as a Product of Psychological Forces." In Walter Reich (ed.), *Origins of Terrorism: Psychologies, Ideologies, Theologies, States of Mind*. Washington, DC: Woodrow Wilson Center Press and Cambridge: Cambridge University Press, 1990, pp. 22–40.

Price, Richard M. *The Chemical Weapons Taboo*. Ithaca, NY: Cornell University Press, 1997.

Primoratz, Igor. "Michael Walzer's Just War Theory: Some Issues of Responsibility." *Ethical Theory and Moral Practice* 5 (2002), pp. 221–244.

Quine, Willard Van Orman. "Two Dogmas of Empiricism." *The Philosophical Review* 60 (1951), pp. 20–43.

Ramsey, Paul. *The Just War: Force and Political Responsibility*. Lanham, MD: University Press of America, 1983.

Rawls, John. *A Theory of Justice*. Oxford: Oxford University Press, 1972.

Rawls, John. "Fifty Years after Hiroshima." In Kai Bird and Lawrence Lifschultz (eds.), *Hiroshima's Shadow: Writings on the Denial of History and the Smithsonian Controversy*. Stony Creek, CT: The Pamphleteer's Press, 1998, pp. 474–479. Originally published in *Dissent* 42, no. 3 (1995), pp. 321–331.

Rawls, John. "The Idea of Public Reason Revisited." In John Rawls, *The Law of Peoples and the Idea of Public Reason Revisited*. Cambridge, MA: Harvard University Press, 1999.

Rawls, John. "The Law of Peoples." *Critical Inquiry* 20, no. 1 (Autumn 1993), pp. 36–68 (reprinted in his *The Law of Peoples and the Idea of Public Reason Revisited*).

Reichberg, Gregory. "Just War and Regular War: Competing Paradigms." In David Rodin and Henry Shue (eds.), *Just and Unjust Warriors*. Forthcoming, Oxford University Press.

Ritchie, Robert C. *Pirates: Myths and Realities*. Minneapolis: University of Minnesota Press, 1986.

Roberts, Adam, and Richard Guelff (eds.). *Documents on the Laws of War*. Oxford: Clarendon Press, 2000.

Rodin, David. *War and Self-Defense*. Oxford: Clarendon Press, 2002.

Ross, W. D. *The Right and the Good*. Oxford: Clarendon Press, 1930.

Russell, Frederick H. *The Just War in the Middle Ages*. Cambridge: Cambridge University Press, 1975.

Santayana, Georges. *Soliloquies in England and Later Soliloquies*. Ann Arbor: University of Michigan Press, 1967.

Sartre, Jean-Paul. *No Exit and Three Other Plays*. New York: Vintage Books, 1955.

Sassoon, Siegfried. *Collected Poems 1908–1956*. London: Faber and Faber, 1961.

Sassoon, Siegfried. *Memoirs of an Infantry Officer*. London: Faber and Faber, 1965.

Scahill, Jeremy. "No-Fly Zones over Iraq: Washington's Undeclared War on 'Saddam's Victims'" at www.IraqJournal.org.

Schachter, Oscar. "The Role of International Law in Maintaining Peace." In W. Scott Thompson and Kenneth M. Jensen, with Richard N. Smith and Kimber M. Schraub (eds.), *Approaches to Peace: An Intellectual Map*. Washington, DC: United States Institute of Peace, 1992, pp. 65–127.

Schlesinger, Arthur, Jr. "The Necessary Amorality of Foreign Affairs." *Harper's Magazine*, August 1971, pp. 72–77.

Schmid, Alex Peter. *Political Terrorism: A Research Guide to Concepts, Theories, Data Bases and Literature*. Amsterdam: Transaction Books, 1983.

Schreiber, Jan. *The Ultimate Weapon: Terrorists and World Order*. New York: Morrow, 1978.

Selwyn, Victor (ed.). *The Voice of War: Poems of the Second World War*. London: Michael Joeseph, 1995.

Shawcross, William. *Deliver Us from Evil: Peacekeepers, Warlords, and a World of Endless Conflict*. New York: Simon and Schuster, 2000.

Shearer, David. *Private Armies and Military Intervention*. Oxford: Oxford University Press, 1998.

Shue, Henry. *Basic Rights: Subsistence, Affluence, and U.S. Foreign Policy*, second edition. Princeton, NJ: Princeton University Press, 1996.

Shue, Henry. "Conditional Sovereignty." *Res Publica* 8, no. 1 (1999), pp. 1–7.

Shue, Henry. "Eroding Sovereignty: The Advance of Principle." In Robert McKim and Jeff McMahan (eds.), *The Morality of Nationalism*. New York: Oxford University Press, 1997, pp. 340–359.

Shue, Henry, and David Wippman. "Limiting Attacks on Dual Purpose Facilities Performing Indispensable Civilian Functions." *Cornell International Law Journal* 35, no. 3 (Winter 2002), pp. 559–580.

Sidgwick, Henry. *The Methods of Ethics*. London: Macmillan, 1962.

Sidgwick, Henry. "The Morality of Strife." In Henry Sidgwick, *Practical Ethics*. London: Swann Sonnenschein and Co., 1898, pp. 83–112.

Singer, Peter. *Practical Ethics*. Cambridge: Cambridge University Press, 1979.

Singer, Peter Warren. *Corporate Warriors: The Rise of the Privatized Military Industry*. Ithaca, NY: Cornell University Press, 2003.

Singer, Peter Warren. *Children at War*. New York: Pantheon Books, 2005.

Smith, Hugh. "Appendix A." In Charles C. Moskos and John Whiteclay (eds.), *The New Conscientious Objection: From Sacred to Secular Existence*. Oxford: Oxford University Press, 1993, pp. 209–211.

Spiller, Roger J. "S. L. A. Marshall and the Ratio of Fire." *RUSI Journal* 133 (1988), pp. 63–71.

Stremlau, John. *People in Peril: Human Rights, Humanitarian Action, and Preventing Deadly Conflict*. New York: Carnegie Corporation, 1998.

Suarez, Francisco. *Selections from Three Works of Francisco Suarez*, vol. 2. Oxford: Clarendon Press, 1944.

Taber, Robert. *The War of the Flea*. London: Paladin, 1972.

Taylor, A. J. P. "The Great War: the Triumph of E. D. Morel." In Peter Stansky (ed.), *The Left and War: The British Labour Party and World War I*. Oxford: Oxford University Press, 1969, pp. 118–130.

Teichman, Jenny. "On Pacifism." *Philosophical Investigations* 5 (1982), pp. 72–83.

Teichman, Jenny. *Pacifism and the Just War: A Study in Applied Philosophy*. Oxford: Basil Blackwell, 1986.

Thomson, Judith Jarvis. "A Defense of Abortion." *Philosophy and Public Affairs* 1, no. 1 (1971), pp. 47–66.

Thomson, Judith Jarvis. "Self-Defense." *Philosophy and Public Affairs* 20, no. 4 (1991), pp. 283–310.

Thomson, Kenneth W. *Moralism and Morality in Politics and Diplomacy: The Credibility of Institutions, Policies and Leadership*. Lanham, MD: University Press of America, 1985.

Townshend, Charles. *The British Campaign in Ireland 1919–1921*. Oxford: Oxford University Press, 1975.

Tzu, Hsun. *Basic Writings*, trans. Burton Watson. New York: Columbia University Press, 1966.

Tzu, Hsun, H. F. Tzu, and M. Tzu. *Basic Writings of Mo Tzu, Hsun Tzu, and Han Fei Tzu*, trans. B. Watson. New York: Columbia University Press, 1967.

Urmson, J. O. "Saints and Heroes." In A. I. Melden (ed.), *Essays in Moral Philosophy*. Seattle: University of Washington Press, 1958, pp. 198–216.

Vattel, Emmerich de. *The Law of Nations or The Principles of Natural Law*, trans. Charles Fenwick. Washington, DC: Carnegie Institution of Washington, 1916.

Villar, Roger. *Piracy Today: Robbery and Violence at Sea since 1980*. London: Conway Maritime Press, 1985.

Vitoria, Francisco de. *De Bello*. In James Brown Scott (ed.), *The Spanish Origin of International Law: Francisco De Vitoria and His Law of Nations*. Oxford: Clarendon Press, 1934, Appendix F, cvx–cxxxi.

Vitoria, Francisco de. *Indis at de Jure Belli Reflectiones*, ed. Ernest Nys. Washington, DC: Carnegie Institute of Washington, 1917.

Vitoria, Francisco de. *Political Writings*, ed. Anthony Pagden and Jeremy Lawrance. Cambridge: Cambridge University Press, 1991.

Waltz, Kenneth N. *The Spread of Nuclear Weapons: More May Be Better*. London: International Institute for Strategic Studies, 1981.

Walzer, Michael. *Arguing about War*. New Haven, CT and London: Yale University Press, 2004.

Walzer, Michael. *Just and Unjust Wars: A Moral Argument with Historical Illustrations*, third edition. New York: Basic Books, 2000 (fourth edition with new introduction, 2006).

Walzer, Michael. "No Strikes: Inspectors Yes, War No." *The New Republic*, September 30, 2002, pp. 19–22.

Walzer, Michael. *Obligations: Essays on Disobedience, War, and Citizenship*. New York: Simon and Schuster, 1970.

Walzer, Michael. "Political Action: The Problem of Dirty Hands." *Philosophy and Public Affairs* 2, no. 2 (Winter 1973), pp. 160–180.

Walzer, Michael. "Regime Change and Just War." *Dissent* 53 (2006), pp. 103–108. See also Walzer's *Just and Unjust Wars*, the new Introduction to the fourth edition, 2006.

Walzer, Michael. "Terrorism: A Critique of Excuses." In Steven Luper-Foy (ed.), *Problems of International Justice*. Boulder, CO: Westview Press, 1988, pp. 237–247.

Walzer, Michael. "The Moral Standing of States: A Reply to Four Critics." *Philosophy and Public Affairs* 9 (1980), pp. 209–229.

Walzer, Michael. "Universalism and Jewish Values" (the twentieth Morgenthau Memorial Lecture on Ethics and Foreign Policy). New York: Carnegie Council on Ethics and International Affairs, 2001.

Wasserstrom, Richard A. "Review of *Just and Unjust Wars.*" *Harvard Law Review* 92 (1978), pp. 536–545.

Weber, Max. "Politics as a Vocation." In Max Weber, *From Max Weber: Essays in Sociology*, ed. H. H. Gerth and C. Wright Mills. London: Routledge & Kegan Paul, 1948.

Wells, Donald A. *War Crimes and Laws of War.* Lanham, MD: University Press of America, 1984.

Wells, H. G. *A Short History of the World.* Harmondsworth: Penguin, 1922.

Wilkinson, Paul. *Political Terrorism.* London: Macmillan; New York: Halsted Press, 1974.

Williams, Bernard. "How to Think Sceptically about the Bomb." *New Society* 62 (November 18, 1982), pp. 288–290.

Williams, Rowan. "Chaos Dogs the End of War," text of lecture entitled. "The End of War? – Further Reflections After September 11." *Common Theology* 1, no. 2 (2002), pp. 7–12.

Wittgenstein, Ludwig. *On Certainty*, ed. G. E. M. Anscombe and G. H. Wright, trans. D. Paul and G. E. M Anscombe. Oxford: Basil Blackwell, 1969.

Woddis, Roger. "Ethics for Everyman." In Kingsley Amis (ed.), *The New Oxford Book of Light Verse.* Oxford: Oxford University Press, 1978, p. 223.

Wolff, Robert Paul. "On Violence." *Journal of Philosophy* 66 (1969), pp. 601–616.

Wylly, H. C. *History of the Manchester Regiment*, vol. 2. London: Forster Groom, 1925.

Yeager, General Chuck. *Yeager: An Autobiography*, ed. Leo Janos. London: Arrow Books, 1986.

Zahn, Gordon C. *In Solitary Witness: The Life and Death of Franz Jagerstatter.* New York: Holt, Rinehart and Winston, 1965.

Index

313